MO

MEXICO CITY

JULIE MEADE

CONTENTS

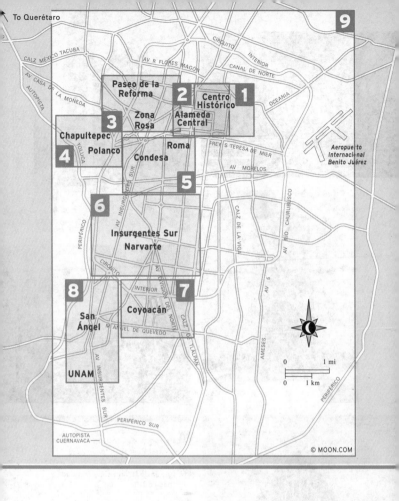

MAPS

DISCOVER
MEXICO CITY

Mexico City occupies a piece of land that seems destined to hold a grand place in history. Blanketing a broad alpine valley, it was once Tenochtitlan, an island city that was the most populous in the Americas—and by some estimates, the world—during the 15th century.

Razed following the Spanish conquest, Tenochtitlan's ruins lie beneath the modern metropolis, which covers 1,480 square kilometers and has a population of over 21 million.

Amid the urban sprawl, there are lovely residential enclaves, architectural landmarks, and a multitude of cultural treasures, from dazzling pre-Columbian artifacts to artist Frida Kahlo's childhood home. For those who love to eat, there is no better place to explore Mexico's varied palate. The city's famous food scene runs the gamut from relaxed street-side taco stands to elegant fine dining.

Mexico City defies expectations. Baroque palaces rise above streets noisy with traffic, generic convenience stores stand beside old-fashioned coffee shops filled with seniors sipping *café con leche*, and contemporary art galleries adjoin hole-in-the-wall bakeries and auto repair shops. Many of the descriptors most closely associated with the capital—crime, pollution, poverty—belie a city that is beguilingly low-key and friendly, rarely gruff, and invariably worth the effort it takes to explore. In this and every way, Mexico City is a place you must experience to understand. Come expecting one city and you'll likely find another. The contrasts, both jarring and delightful, define this mad metropolis, one of the most singular and marvelous places on earth.

10 TOP EXPERIENCES

1 **Visit Museo del Templo Mayor:** Mexico City's rich and tumultuous history is revealed at these ruins of a great temple-pyramid that was destroyed during the 16th-century Spanish siege on Tenochtitlan. The museum showcases artifacts recovered from the archaeological site (page 49).

2 Admire Palacio de Bellas Artes: With its grand marble facade and opulent art deco interior, the Palacio de Bellas Artes is one of Mexico's most striking buildings, as well as its keynote arts institution (page 84).

>>>

3 Tour Museo Nacional de Antropología: In this fascinating museum, the most impressive rooms are dedicated to the people who lived in Tenochtitlan, today Mexico City (page 144).

>>>

4 **Get to Know Frida Kahlo:** A superbly talented painter and a beloved icon throughout the world, Frida Kahlo is celebrated at the lovely, intimate museum in her childhood home (page 228).

5 **Enjoy Cantina Culture:** These relaxed neighborhood bars and gathering spots are an essential part of life in Mexico City. Spend a few hours enjoying the convivial atmosphere with a shot of tequila in hand (page 195).

6 **See Spectacular Teotihuacán:** Admire the views from the top of two spectacular temple-pyramids at Mexico's most visited archaeological site, a day trip just outside the city limits (page 299).

7 Stop by Contemporary Art Galleries: With the opening of new world-class museums and the continued excellence of many long-running galleries, the city's contemporary art scene continues to flourish (page 158).

>>>

8 Devour Tacos: Mexico City's tremendous food scene is reason alone to visit, and nothing is more emblematic of the capital than tacos, from inexpensive carnitas served at street stands to gourmet iterations (page 182).

<<<

9 Sip Pulque: This fizzy fermented beverage is made from the sap of the maguey cactus. Drinking pulque is a tradition in the capital and today the beverage is experiencing a deserved revival (page 96).

>>>

10 **Stroll through Traditional Markets:** If you only have time to visit one of the city's many colorful and atmospheric markets, make it Mercado de la Merced (page 104).

EXPLORE
MEXICO CITY

THE BEST OF MEXICO CITY

>DAY 1:
THE CENTRO HISTÓRICO

>> **Metro:** Zócalo

Mexico City's **Zócalo,** one of the largest public squares in the world, was once the center of the Mexica city of Tenochtitlan, the remains of which lie beneath the modern metropolis. After the conquest, the Zócalo became the heart of the new Spanish city, and was called the Plaza Mayora throughout the colonial era. Take a moment to feel the power and history of this grand plaza, then head north to visit the remains of Tenochtitlan's holiest site at the fascinating and recently expanded **Museo del Templo Mayor.** This twin temple-pyramid, which adjoined Tenochtitlan's central plaza, was destroyed by the Spanish and then buried for centuries beneath the colonial city. Its base was uncovered in the 1970s, along with hundreds of artifacts now held in the on-site museum. It's one of the Centro's most important sights.

Have lunch at **El Cardenal,** just

The Zócalo is the open plaza at the center of Mexico City.

BEST PEOPLE-WATCHING

MORNINGS AT CAFÉ JEKEMIR
There's a mix of seniors, students, and neighborhood locals sipping espressos at this long-running café in the Centro, which recently moved from its long-time location on the corner of Isabel la Católica to a storefront on the pedestrian street Regina (page 69).

SATURDAY MORNING AT THE TIANGUIS CULTURAL DEL CHOPO
You'll find a pierced-and-tattooed crowd at this unique Saturday morning punk-rock market, originally founded as an informal album exchange for music lovers (page 135).

SATURDAY NIGHT IN THE ROMA NORTE
Stroll along Álvaro Obregón, the Roma's central avenue, on a Saturday night, when crowds often spill from the barroom into the street (page 190).

SUNDAYS ON PASEO DE LA REFORMA
People from every age group, neighborhood, and walk of life come together on Sundays for the Paseo Dominical or the Ciclotón to pedal, skate, or stroll along the grand Paseo de la Reforma, which is closed to automobile traffic from 8am to 2pm (page 132).

ANY HOUR, ANY DAY AT THE BASÍLICA DE SANTA MARÍA DE GUADALUPE
At the shrine to the Virgen de Guadalupe, mass is held every hour from 6am to 8pm, drawing mobs of worshippers from across Mexico and Latin America, many arriving in traditional dress, as part of a bicycle tour, or on their knees (page 263).

On Sundays, the Paseo de la Reforma is closed to automobile traffic.

the Palacio de Bellas Artes

a block from the Zócalo, widely considered one of the best traditional Mexican restaurants in the city. After lunch, head east along the bustling pedestrian street Madero, stopping to see the current show in the **Palacio de Cultura Citibanamex,** if it's open, and taking note of two iconic buildings just before the Eje Central, the **Casa de los Azulejos** and the **Palacio Postal.** Next, cross the Eje Central to take a turn around the museum in the **Palacio de Bellas Artes,** one of the city's flagship cultural institutions, where the gorgeous art deco interiors are as opulent as its elaborate marble facade. It's worth the admission fee to ascend to the top floors of the building, where there are interesting murals by Diego Rivera, David Alfaro Siqueiros, and Rufino Tamayo, as well as contemporary art galleries.

Dusk is the perfect time to start a tour of the Centro's cantinas. Begin by sipping a tequila at the grandest old joint, **Bar La Ópera,** on Cinco de Mayo. Next, see the city in all its glittering glory for the top floors of the Torre Latinoamericana in the in-house bar and restaurant **Miralto.**

> DAY 2: CHAPULTEPEC AND THE CONDESA

>> **Metro:** Chapultepec, followed by Sevilla

Set aside the morning to tour the **Museo Nacional de Antropología,** a vast and absorbing museum dedicated to pre-Columbian and modern-day cultures in Mexico. You won't have time to see the whole museum, so streamline your visit by focusing on the spectacular rooms dedicated to the Mexica people of Tenochtitlan, as well as the Teotihuacán galleries. Back outside, take an hour or two to explore a bit of the surrounding **Bosque de Chapultepec** on foot, strolling past the multidisciplinary cultural center **Casa del Lago Juan José Arreola,** the pretty lake beside it, and the striking modern facade of the **Museo de Arte Moderno.** Stop into the museum if the show interests you, or continue your walk past the

base of the **Castillo de Chapultepec,** which sits on a rocky outcropping overlooking the park and the Paseo de la Reforma.

Just below the Castillo de Chapultepec are the main gates to the park. From here, take a taxi or jump on the Metro one stop from Chapultepec to Sevilla, then walk into the Roma Norte for a late lunch at **Contramar,** an ultra-popular, always-bustling seafood restaurant near the Glorieta de la Cibeles. There's often a wait around lunchtime, but the food and atmosphere are ideal.

After lunch, spend a few leisurely hours watching dogs romp and children play in **Parque México.** Stroll along Avenida Amsterdam, snapping photos of the Condesa's distinctive art deco architecture and enjoying the people-watching in the many neighborhood cafés. Wrap up the day with a leisurely beer at **Monstruo de Agua,** or at Roma favorite **Páramo.**

> DAY 3: COYOACÁN

>> **Metro:** Viveros

If you arrive in Coyoacán via the Metro stop Viveros, you can admire old country mansions and towering trees while walking into the heart of the neighborhood via Avenida Francisco Sosa. Peek into the rust-colored Moorish-inspired hacienda that is home to the **Fonoteca Nacional,** an interesting sound archive and gallery space. Down the road, take a breather in charming **Plaza Santa Catarina,** a quiet, cobbled square popular with locals and their dogs.

paddle boaters on the lake in the Primera Sección de Chapultepec

Museo Frida Kahlo

Once you arrive in the center of town, spend some time people-watching in **Jardín Hidalgo** and **Jardín Centenario,** the two old-fashioned public plazas at the center of the neighborhood.

Grab a mocha at Coyoacán classic **Café El Jarocho,** then wander through the **Mercado Coyoacán,** where you can snack on a tostada or two (the market is famous for them) to tide you over till lunch. From there, it's a few blocks to the **Museo Frida Kahlo,** a moving museum dedicated to the life and legacy of its namesake artist. Walk back to the Jardín Centenario for a late lunch on the patio at **Los Danzantes,** and accompany your meal with a shot of their eponymous mezcal. If you want to extend the evening, drop in for a craft beer (or another mezcal) at the convivial **Centenario 107,** just a few blocks away.

> DAY 4:
SAN ÁNGEL AND UNAM

>> Metrobús: La Bombilla, then CCU

Saturday is a popular time to visit the colonial-era neighborhood of San Ángel, where the weekly **Bazaar Sábado** attracts some

Museo Nacional de Antropología

Biblioteca Central at UNAM

excellent artisan vendors, as well as some modern designers. If you aren't visiting on a Saturday, check out the lovely **Museo de El Carmen,** housed in a colonial-era Carmelite monastery. From there, stroll through the neighborhood to the elegant **San Ángel Inn** for a late brunch, accompanied by one of their famous margaritas. Just across the street, Frida Kahlo and Diego Rivera fans should stop into the small but interesting **Museo Casa Estudio Diego Rivera,** the home where the couple lived and worked together in San Ángel.

From San Ángel, take the Metrobús along Insurgentes to the CCU stop, then spend the rest of the afternoon exploring the cultural center on the Universidad Nacional Autónoma de México

(UNAM) campus. Spend a few hours in the light-filled **Museo Universitario Arte Contemporáneo,** one of the finest contemporary art museums in Mexico City, opened in 2008. From there, wander into the northern section of the **Espacio Escultórico de la UNAM,** a massive outdoor sculpture garden built atop an expanse of volcanic rock in the 1960s.

Head south for an easy but classic pick for dinner: **tacos,** the city's signature dish. Eat them standing up at **Los Parados,** in the sidewalk at **Orinoco,** or vegan at **Gracias Madre Taqueria Vegana,** all in the Roma.

With More Time

DAY 5: TEOTIHUACÁN
- **Metro:** Line 6 to Terminal Autobuses del Norte, then a local **bus** to Teotihuacán

Have a hearty breakfast in or near your hotel, slather on some sunscreen, and pack a big bottle of water before making your way to the Terminal Autobuses del Norte, the first stop in your journey to the ruins at **Teotihuacán.** Mexico's most famous and most visited archaeological site is just 30 kilometers outside the city, and buses depart the terminal for the pyramids several times each hour.

Though little is known about its people, Teotihuacán was once the most powerful city-state in Mesoamerica, evidenced by its massive temples and visionary city planning. Today, you can get a glimpse into that mysterious past by walking along Teotihuacán's grand central avenue, the Calzada de los Muertos, to admire the twin pyramids that once stood at the city center, the Piramide del Sol (Pyramid of the Sun) and the Piramide de la Luna (Pyramid of the Moon).

MEXICO CITY WITH KIDS

Mexico City is large, loud, and relentlessly urban, yet it's a remarkably agreeable place to visit with family. Here, children are treated with respect and kindness, graciously welcomed at most restaurants and hotels, and usually granted free admission to museums and other cultural institutions. The capital's rich history and diverse local culture make it a truly magical and eye-opening place to visit—at any age.

A number of smaller boutique properties do not accept children, but many others, like the **Hotel Catedral** in the Centro or the **Hotel Stanza** in the Roma (which adjoins a large playground), don't charge extra for children under 12, making it an economical choice for families traveling together. The ultra-posh **St. Regis** has a children's center with arts and crafts, story time, and other kid-centric activities on-site.

>THURSDAY: CENTRO HISTÓRICO

The Centro Histórico is a magical neighborhood, filled with old palaces, bustling with visitors, and buzzing with years of history. Start with breakfast in the historic dining room at **Café de Tacuba,** then walk to the **Zócalo,** where you'll often find brightly dressed *concheros* (also called "Aztec dancers") performing a rhythmic dance to the beat of a drum.

For older children, Diego Rivera's extensive murals inside the **Secretaría de Educación Pública,**

traditional dancers in the Zócalo

trajineras at the dock in Xochimilco

or SEP, north of the Zócalo, provide an engaging look into Mexican history and popular culture—as well as Rivera's communist political views. There are often free English-speaking tour guides wandering through the plaza, who can help provide context and background for Rivera's work.

Have lunch at **Balcón del Zócalo,** a rooftop Mexican restaurant in the Zócalo Central hotel, which has gorgeous views of the cathedral and plaza. Next, walk down Cinco de Mayo to the **Dulcería de Celaya,** one of the oldest and most charming sweet shops in the city. It's particularly festive during Día de Muertos and Christmastime. From there, it's an easy stroll along the pedestrian avenue Madero to the **Torre Latinoamericana.** Take the elevator to the 44th-floor observation deck, which affords tremendous vistas of the city in every direction, including the

snowcapped volcanoes Popocatépetl and Iztaccíhuatl to the south.

Back on the ground, cross the Eje Central to the Alameda, peeking into the museum at the **Palacio de Bellas Artes.** Finally, let the kids stretch their legs along the paved paths in the **Alameda Central,** Mexico City's oldest urban

Torre Latinoamericana

park, which was remodeled and expanded in 2012.

>FRIDAY: XOCHIMILCO

Set aside the day to boat along the canals in **Xochimilco,** a small remnant of the vast system of waterways that once ribboned the Valley of Mexico. You can take the light-rail from Metro Tasqueña all the way to Xochimilco, and then a taxi to the docks, though if you wait till midmorning, lighter traffic can make a taxi or Uber an easier and faster option.

Enlist the kids to help pick out a *trajinera*, one of the colorful flat-bottomed boats typical to Xochimilco, and plan to spend a few hours exploring the canals. Departing from any of the docks, the main tourist corridors are often jammed with boaters (and mariachi musicians paddling by in canoes, waiting to be commissioned for a tune), creating a convivial atmosphere. If you'd also like to visit the traditional "floating gardens," or *chinampas*, where people still live and grow food, ask the boat's driver to take you farther into the canals for the *tour ecológico* (ecological tour), outside the main tourist zone.

Back on dry land, take a taxi (or take a taxi to the train station and the train to La Noria) to visit the former home of philanthropist and art collector Dolores Olmedo, now her namesake museum. Housed in an old hacienda, the **Museo Dolores Olmedo** contains a large collection of work by Frida Kahlo and Diego Rivera, among other modern artists, as well as Olmedo's collection of pre-Columbian artifacts. It's particularly delightful to wander the grounds, where peacocks and *xoloitzcuintle* (Mexican hairless dogs), Olmedo's favored pet, roam freely.

>SATURDAY: COYOACÁN

There is an old-fashioned feeling in central **Coyoacán,** a popular weekend destination for both visitors and Mexico City locals. Arrive in the morning, taking a lap around the famous coyote fountain in **Jardín Centenario,** then wandering through Jardín Hidalgo as it begins to fill up with vendors selling balloons, toys, and *raspados* (shaved ice). From the plaza, it's only a few blocks to the neighborhood's atmospheric market, **Mercado Coyoacán,** where there are artisan crafts, textiles, and baskets for sale, in addition to food and snacks. You can stop for a mocha and a doughnut at Coyoacán institution **Café El Jarocho** on the way.

Go early to buy your tickets for a midday performance at **La Titería** (there's a garden and small library where kids can play while you wait for the show to begin), a wonderful

the coyote fountain in Jardín Centenario

marionette theater in the center of historic Coyoacán. There are usually two performances on Saturday and Sunday, appropriate for kids of almost any age (though plays are in Spanish, they are both visually entertaining and include lots of music and dancing). After the show, get a low-key lunch at **La Barraca Valenciana,** where kids can have a ham-and-cheese *torta* (sandwich) while parents sip a glass of Spanish wine or a craft beer.

After lunch, visit the **Museo Nacional de Culturas Populares,** a small museum that showcases work by traditional Mexican artisans. The exhibits, which change frequently and are often dedicated to themes like corn or textiles, are educational, but also visually engaging and colorful. During holidays, like Día de Muertos, the museum hosts artisan markets or musical performances in their outdoor patio. Wrap up the day by wandering down Francisco Sosa, stopping for an artisanal ice cream at **Picnic.**

>SUNDAY: CHAPULTEPEC

Closed to automobile traffic every Sunday till 2pm, the **Paseo de la Reforma** fills with cyclists, in-line skaters, pedestrians, and dog walkers. Get an early start on the day to ride a bike (or simply stroll) along Reforma, checking out the many famous monuments, like the **Ángel de la Independencia,** as you make your way to the **Bosque de Chapultepec**'s main entrance.

Families flock to the Bosque de Chapultepec on Sunday, when museums are free and the footpaths are filled with vendors selling balloons, bubbles, rubber balls, tacos, and fresh fruit, among other treats. There may be a wait at the **Castillo de Chapultepec,** but it's an excellent family destination in the park, boasting marvelous views of the surrounding city and the Paseo de la Reforma, while the period rooms bring the opulence of 19th-century Mexico City to life.

motorized train in the Bosque de Chapultepec

Save Chapultepec's children's museum for a weekday (it's insanely crowded on the weekends); instead stop by the **Casa del Lago Juan José Arreola,** a wonderful cultural center that often has concerts and special workshops for kids. And even small children will enjoy the eye-catching interactive exhibits and video installations at the **Centro Cultural Digital,** just outside the main gates. From there, the family-style restaurant **El Pialadero de Guadalajara** is just around the corner.

MEXICO CITY'S PRE-COLUMBIAN PAST

Mexico City's streets tell the story of its past, with institutions, architecture, and landmarks that are testament to 600-plus years of culture and change.

>DAY 1:
CENTRO HISTÓRICO

After the Spanish conquest of Tenochtitlan, Spanish settlers destroyed the Mexica capital, building a European-style settlement atop the ruins—and, in many cases, using the stones from fallen Mexica temples to construct their own churches and palaces. Five hundred years later, Mexico's **pre-Columbian heritage** is embedded throughout the Centro Histórico—in its layout, in its place-names, and, quite literally, in its architecture.

In the 1970s, the ruins of the **Templo Mayor,** a twin temple-pyramid at the heart of Tenochtitlan, were unearthed after more than four centuries under the city. After an extensive excavation that demolished a number of colonial-era buildings beside the Catedral Metropolitana, the archaeological site was opened to the public, alongside the fascinating **Museo del Templo Mayor,** which contains dozens of pre-Columbian artifacts recovered from the site.

Though they haven't received permission to continue demolitions, archaeologists surmise that even more ruins lie beneath the

Templo Mayor is one of the most fascinating sights in Mexico.

BEST MURALS

CENTRO HISTÓRICO

The city's most famous mural is Diego Rivera's series *Epic of the Mexican People in Their Struggle for Freedom and Independence*, in the north patio of the **Palacio Nacional** (page 50), which is, unfortunately, closed indefinitely for renovation at press time. Fortunately, just a few blocks north, at the headquarters of the **Secretaría de Educación Pública** (page 56), there is a stunning series by the iconic Mexican artist. Here, Rivera covered the walls of two adjoining patios with elaborate depictions of Mexican history and culture.

At the **Antiguo Colegio de San Ildefonso** (page 53), find interesting murals by Rivera, David Alfaro Siqueiros, Fermín Revueltas Sánchez, and Jean Charlot, among others, in addition to extensive works by José Clemente Orozco in the main patio.

ALAMEDA CENTRAL

See monumental works by some of Mexico's modern art masters at the **Palacio de Bellas Artes** (page 84), including David Alfaro Siqueiros's *Nueva Democracia* (New Democracy), commemorating the Revolution of 1910. Cross the Alameda to see one of Rivera's most entertaining works in the **Museo Mural Diego Rivera** (page 100).

POLANCO

There are several murals by Siqueiros inside the **Sala de Arte Público David Alfaro Siqueiros** (page 161), a nonprofit gallery that occupies the artist's former home. Different artists periodically repaint the building's facade.

INSURGENTES SUR

The three-dimensional mural covering the arts space **Poliforum Siqueiros** (page 208) astonishes in its proportions, colors, and ambition. Inside, Siqueiros's *La Marcha de la Humanidad* covers the walls and ceiling of an entire room; it's currently being restored and is closed to the public.

DOCTORES

The wild and spectacular toy museum **Museo del Juguete Antiguo México** (page 269) in the Doctores neighborhood is covered in wonderful murals and graffiti art, and the owner is an expert in the many murals of the surrounding neighborhood.

CIUDAD UNIVERSITARIA

Juan O'Gorman designed the giant volcanic-stone mosaic that covers the facade of the **Biblioteca Central** (page 249). Next door, a famous work by Siqueiros adorns the Rectoría.

17th-century palaces on the street República de Guatemala, as evidenced recently at the **Centro Cultural de España,** a contemporary cultural center overseen by the Spanish government. In a planned expansion of the space, below-ground construction unearthed Mexica ruins, believed to have been part of a *calmécac*, a school for young Mexica nobles. The ruins are on display in the on-site **Museo del Sitio,** in the center's basement, a lovely complement to the center's avant-garde program of music and art events. After your visit, grab a coffee and a snack on the rooftop café, which overlooks the cathedral.

During the pre-Columbian era and throughout most of the last four centuries, canals linked central Mexico City to the farming communities in the southern Valley of Mexico, with a major waterway terminating in what is today the old Merced commercial district. Today's **Mercado de la Merced** remains one of the largest and most important markets in the city. You can walk to the Merced from the Zócalo (be aware that theft is not uncommon in this area), or take the Metro just one stop, from Pino Suárez to La Merced, on line 1. Before boarding, take note of the Templo Ehécatl-Quetzalcóatl inside the Metro station; this unusual round Mexica pyramid was uncovered by transit workers during construction of the subway line. Plans for the station were altered to accommodate the temple; today, in a delightful mix of old and new, the pyramid is on display in an open-air plaza within the station.

Take your time wandering through the towering stacks of fruits and vegetables, home supplies, and crafts for sale at the Mercado de la Merced, making your way down the circuitous aisles to neighboring **Mercado Sonora,** known for its herbal remedies, witchcraft supplies, and live animals. Finish up the day with a late lunch at the chile-pepper-centric, Merced-inspired restaurant **Roldán 37,** located on a surprisingly quiet pedestrian street in the old Merced commercial district.

▶DAY 2: CHAPULTEPEC

The **Museo Nacional de Antropología** is a must for any visitor to the city, but those with an interest in pre-Columbian cultures could easily spend a full day in this spectacular museum. Set aside time for the rooms dedicated to the cultures of the Valley of Mexico, which include, among other treasures, the famous Piedra del Sol, a basalt monolith carved with Mexica calendar glyphs (an adaptation of the calendar round used throughout Mesoamerica). It's also worth touring the recently remodeled second-floor ethnographic exhibits, which cover the dress, customs, language, and culture of Mexico's diverse cultures and ethnic groups.

stone statue of grasshopper in Chapultepec park

The museum's greater home, the **Bosque de Chapultepec,** is itself a site of great historic importance: Its springs provided freshwater to the city of Tenochtitlan and later the capital of New Spain, via an aqueduct that ran along what is today the Avenida Chapultepec. Though little is left, you can visit the site of the springs where the Mexica emperors came to bathe, today known as the **Baños de Moctezuma.** Just beside it, amateur anthropologists will enjoy spotting the pre-Columbian reliefs carved onto the walls of the Cerro de Chapultepec.

Although there are no ruins on the top of Cerro de Chapultepec, it is interesting to tour the Castillo de Chapultepec and look down on the greenery.

>DAY 3:
TLATELOLCO
AND SAN JUAN

During the 15th and 16th centuries, Tlatelolco was inhabited by Nahuatl-speaking people, allied with but separate from the people of Tenochtitlan. When the Spanish launched their final attack on the Mexica during the summer of 1521, the remaining residents of Tenochtitlan fled to Tlatelolco, where they were eventually overcome. Today, the ruins of Tlatelolco are located in the **Plaza de las Tres Culturas,** in the Tlatelolco neighborhood. The interesting site contains the foundations of what were once towering religious and ceremonial buildings, including the Tlatelolco's Templo Mayor, which is adjoined by Ex-Convento de Santiago Tlatelolco, originally constructed with the stones of the destroyed city in the early 16th century.

Take the Metrobús on the Paseo de la Reforma from Glorieta Cuitláhuac to Hidalgo or have an Uber or a radio taxi pick you up at the ruins site, as it's a bit too far (and a bit too rough) to walk from Tlatelolco back to the Centro. Now head to the one-of-a-kind **Mercado San Juan** for a plate of imported cheese and charcuterie from one of the market's remarkably fancy deli counters, or continue with the pre-Columbian theme by seeking out

the ruins of Tlatelolco in the neighborhood of the same name

Teotihuacán's main avenue, the Calzada de los Muertos

mole, maguey worms, iguana meat, *chapulines* (grasshoppers), and chocolate.

Next, set aside a few hours to learn more about Mexico's traditional cultures at the wonderful **Museo de Arte Popular,** just a few blocks from the market. The museum's exquisite collection of handicrafts from across the country includes some pre-Columbian art, which helps illuminate the aesthetic roots of today's artisan traditions.

> DAY 4: CIVILIZATIONS IN THE VALLEY OF MEXICO

One of the finest ruin sites in the country, the city of **Teotihuacán** is a must-see for anyone interested in anthropology and pre-Columbian civilizations. If you've visited Teotihuacán in the past, take a trip to the smaller and lesser-known settlement of **Cuicuilco,** located in the south of the city, near the Line 1 Metrobús stop at Villa Olímpica. Flourishing just before the rise Teotihuacán, the city of Cuicuilco was largely destroyed in a lava flow from a nearby volcano, but its remains include an interesting circular pyramid.

From Cuicuilco, it's a quick Metrobús ride to the main campus of the Universidad Nacional Autónoma de México (UNAM), where the many architectural and artistic treasures include the **Biblioteca Central,** adorned with a lava-stone mural by Juan O'Gorman. Alternatively, head just a bit farther south to **Tlalpan,** a more off-the-beaten-path neighborhood, which maintains a quiet, distinctly nontouristy feeling.

A DAY OF DESIGN

Mexico City is aesthetically vibrant and unique. The capital remains in the vanguard in art, design, and most especially architecture, making the city a top destination for many design-centric travelers.

>MORNING

Make a reservation for a morning tour at the **Casa Luis Barragán,** near Tacubaya. The former home of the famed architect—widely considered one of the most influential voices in modern Mexican design—was mostly left as it was when Barragán lived there, showcasing not only his talent as an architect but his pensive, minimalist personal style. Note the saturated colors and use of light, two of Barragán's signatures.

Just across the street, a large unmarked turquoise building is home to **Labor,** one of the more interesting contemporary galleries in the city. The gallery moved to its current location in 2011 and represents a range of international artists, including Mexican sensation Pedro Reyes.

>AFTERNOON

It's a short walk from the Casa Luis Barragán across Avenida Parque Lira and into the San Miguel Chapultepec neighborhood. This attractive residential community, wedged between the historic neighborhood of Tacubaya and the Bosque de Chapultepec, is the location of some of the city's most renowned contemporary art galleries, giving the otherwise sleepy area a hint of posh.

Order a glass of wine and a thin-crust pizza in the pretty garden at **Cancino,** where the neighborhood's gallerygoers often lunch. Cross the street to visit **Kurimanzutto,** one of the city's preeminent art spaces, co-owned by Mexico's best-known contemporary artist, Gabriel Orozco. Walk just a few blocks north to the long-running **Galería de Arte Mexicano,** which represents many important national artists, from Olga Costa to Francisco Toledo. Though the doors are usually closed at both of these galleries, ring the doorbell to see the current exhibits.

You can take the Metro from Constituyentes to Auditorio in Polanco (it's just one stop), though it's easier to hop in an Uber for the short ride across the park. Polanco's toniest avenue, Presidente Masaryk, is lined with designer shops from many of the world's

Cancino, a place for pizza and people-watching

the daytime kitchen at Ticuchi

celebrated labels (Dolce & Gabbana, Gucci), but it's much more fun to browse the Mexican-owned boutiques in the neighborhood, like famous silver shop **Tane** or wonderful boutique **Lago.**

›EVENING

If all that window-shopping works up an appetite, drop in for drinks and supper at **Ticuchi,** where famed chef Enrique Olvera highlights artisanal Mexican spirits along with beautifully plated handmade maize-based small plates. Top off the evening with a tour of the fantastic midcentury **Camino Real Polanco México,** staying for a drink in the hotel's swanky terrace bar at design-centric **Hotel Hábita.**

SATURDAY SHOPPING IN THE ROMA

Saturday is a good time to stroll around the Roma, visiting small shops, browsing markets, and soaking up the atmosphere in this popular neighborhood.

>MORNING

There's often a wait for Saturday brunch at star chef Eduardo Garcia's casual eatery **Lalo,** where diners tuck into avocado toast or *chilaquiles* on the sidewalk or at the long communal table inside. From there, walk a few blocks east to the **Mercado de Cuauhté-moc,** a weekly vintage market held in the Jardín Dr. Ignacio Chávez, on the border of the Roma and the Doctores neighborhood. Though not as well-known as the antiquities markets in La Lagunilla and the Plaza del Ángel, this weekly flea has some top-notch vendors and, often, excellent finds for sharp-eyed shoppers.

After the market, take your treasures out for a coffee at unpretentious, top-notch café **Cardinal,** on Córdoba. After that, walk along the Roma's main corridor, Álvaro Obregón, which is filled with creaky old bookshops, hip cocktail bars, and 19th-century mansions. Stop inside the art gallery and bookshop at multidisciplinary cultural center **Casa Lamm.**

Next, walk south along Orizaba, wandering past the shaded fountains in the **Plaza Luis Cabrera,** then turning east on Campeche on

Markets are the best place to buy fresh fruits and vegetables in Mexico City.

WHERE TO EAT

Mexico City's food culture spans classes, neighborhoods, and milieus. *Chilangos* are serious eaters, profoundly omnivorous, and discriminating even when snacking on the street. As a result, you will find good things to eat in every neighborhood and at every price point. From casual to elegant, here are the types of establishments you'll find in the capital.

PUESTOS AND TAQUERIAS

Quick bites at street stands and in neighborhood markets are ubiquitous and, by many accounts, among the best bites in the city. Tacos are a mainstay of the local diet, but you'll also see hundreds of other snacks for sale, including tamales, fresh fruit, seafood cocktails, smoked plantains, deep-fried quesadillas, corn on the cob, and cornflatbread-based snacks like *tlacoyos.* At some popular street stands, you can see a full pig being carved for *carnitas* as commuters rush past to the Metro. If you see a crowd around a *puesto,* it's a good bet that the food will be tasty.

A step up from balancing your plate in one hand and taco in the other, *taquerias* are simple sit-down eateries (sometimes with a bar and stools only) that serve tacos and other snacks, while a *tortería* is the same, but for *tortas.* The Roma, Condesa, and Narvarte neighborhoods are good places to try some of the best taquerias in the city, like Los Parados, Orinoco, El Vilsito, Tacos Los Condes, and, for veggies, Gracias Madre Taqueria Vegana.

FONDAS, COMEDORES, AND CANTINAS

You can have an inexpensive sit-down meal in the city's many *fondas* or *comedores,* small independent restaurants that usually serve breakfast, *almuerzo* (early lunch), and *comida* (the midday meal). At many of these places, the main offering is an inexpensive afternoon *comida corrida,* a three- or four-course meal that often includes a drink, soup, and entrée. A wait for a table around 2pm is often an indication that you've found a good *fonda.*

Also casual, *cantinas* are bars that serve food in addition to drinks, with some boasting remarkably good kitchens. Many offer free *botanas* (snacks) when you order drinks, which, in some places, can become a filling meal after a few beers or tequilas. Some cantinas have become so popular for eating that they are more like restaurants than bars. One worth noting is La Polar, in the San Rafael, where the *birria* (goat meat) stew is famous.

RESTAURANTES

Restaurantes are the most formal designation for an eatery with table service, though there's a very wide diversity of restaurants worth visiting in Mexico City, from an incredibly casual, old-timey spot, like Café El Popular, to a hot new neighborhood destination drawing hipsters and foodies, such as the superlative Máximo Bistrot Local, or an ultra-elegant fine-dining restaurant. Pujol in Polanco is the most famous spot in this category.

your way to **Huerto Roma Verde.** This lovely urban garden and active ecological organization hosts a weekend market, where lots of vegetarian and locally produced snacks are on sale. Often, these markets have special themes, like the annual edible-insect tasting or their flagship Festival de Maiz, el Frijol, y Amaranto (Corn, Bean, and Amaranth Festival), in addition to garden's frequent workshops, yoga classes, and speakers.

Alvaro Obregón Avenue in the Roma Norte neighborhood

>AFTERNOON

Do like the local crowd and set aside a few hours for lunch—though first you'll face the near-impossible task of deciding where to eat. If you don't have reservations for **Máximo Bistrot Local,** line up next door for a table at **Mi Compa Chava,** an über-popular, always-bustling Sinaloan-style seafood restaurant.

After lunch, wander along the shady streets Colima and Orizaba, stopping in at funky skate shops and boutiques, like **180° Shop** and **Happening Store,** or seeing what's on show at **Galería OMR** or gallery/design shop **Chic By Accident.** On the street Córdoba, visit indie boutique and shoemaker **Goodbye Folk,** contemporary gallery **Machete,** or art-and-architecture-themed bookshop **Casa Bosques.** Top off the afternoon at **Salon Rosetta,** a tiny yet gorgeous second-floor bar above the Italian restaurant Rosetta, or at the craft cocktail haven **Licorería Limantour.** Order some bar snacks and linger, or head south to have tacos, *tlacoyos,* and a craft beer at Roma hot spot **El Parnita.**

Happening Store

PLANNING YOUR TRIP

WHEN TO GO
There is no high season or low season for travel to Mexico City. At over 2,200 meters (over 7,000 feet) above sea level, the city's altitude tempers its tropical latitude, creating a temperate and sunny climate year-round. The short **summer rainy season** (June-Oct.) brings showers, but these are usually isolated to bursts in the afternoon and evening. If you're averse to crowds or traffic but still want to see the city, consider visiting during **Semana Santa** (the Easter holidays) or **Christmas,** when locals leave town and everything is noticeably quieter. Note that during these weeks, many restaurants, bars, and attractions also close.

ENTRY REQUIREMENTS
All foreign nationals visiting Mexico must have a valid **passport.** For citizens of most countries, a 180-day **travel permit,** known as the *forma migratoria multiple* (FMM), is issued automatically by immigration upon entry. The exact amount of time you are granted at entry can range from 30 to 90 days, at the immigration officer's discretion. (You can apply for an extension at an immigration office if necessary.) Hold on to your stamped FMM; you will need to return it

panoramic view of Chapultepec Castle

San Ángel's Bazaar Sábado

- **Monday:** Most public museums and cultural sights close, and Chapultepec park shuts its gates (though cyclists can pass through the Primera Sección). This makes Monday a good day to stroll the Roma and Condesa, shop markets like La Merced and the Mercado San Juan, take a day trip to the pyramids at Teotihuacán, or visit one of the few museums that are open, like the Museo del Juguete Antiguo México or Papalote Museo del Niño.
- **Wednesday:** The last Wednesday of every month, dozens of museums and cultural centers extend their hours as a part of the Noche de Museos event. Many offer free admission and special events like concerts or movie screenings.
- **Saturday:** San Ángel's popular Bazaar Sábado craft market takes place on Saturday, as does the Mercado de Cuauhtémoc, in the Roma, an excellent outdoor vintage market.
- **Sunday:** Many museums and cultural centers are free on Sunday, though, at some museums, free admission applies only to Mexican nationals or visa-holding foreign residents of Mexico. As a result, the most famous museums often fill to capacity. In the Centro, the excellent La Lagunilla art and antiquities market takes place, and in the Roma, the Mercado El 100, a local and organic food market, is held in the Plaza del Lanzador. On the first three Sundays of the month, the central stretch of the Paseo de la Reforma closes to car traffic from 8am to 2pm, making it a great day to stroll this historic avenue. On the last Sunday of the month, the Paseo de la Reforma and several other major avenues close to create bike paths throughout the city as part of the Ciclotón. Thousands of cyclists attend the event.

at the airport on your way home. When entering or leaving Mexico, children must be accompanied by their parents or, if unaccompanied or traveling with another adult, present an officially notarized

and translated letter from their parents authorizing the trip.

TRANSPORTATION

Most foreign visitors arrive in Mexico City via the **Aeropuerto Internacional Benito Juárez,** the city's main hub. The newly opened **Aeropuerto Internacional Felipe Ángeles (AIFA),** in the state of Mexico, is currently offering service to and from several destinations in Mexico, and international flights may be offered when ground transportation between the airport and the city center expands. Recently, both major airlines and low-cost carriers have begun offering service to smaller regional airports like **Toluca** and **Puebla,** which may add a bit of travel time but can be cheaper, particularly for travel within Mexico.

Getting around Mexico City on public transportation is cheap, easy, efficient, and generally safe. Easy-to-use transport options include buses, microbuses, Metro, Metrobús, and light-rail, though most visitors find the **Metro** and **Metrobús** systems are all they need to get everywhere they want to go. Secure radio taxis are an easy and inexpensive way to get around, as is ride-hailing service Uber. Within each neighborhood, walking is the best way to see everything. Given the accessibility of public transit, driving is not recommended for short trips to the city.

RESERVATIONS

It is generally not necessary (or even possible) to make reservations for cultural sights and museums in Mexico City. During regular weekday hours, most museums have no wait. Two important exceptions are the **Casa Luis Barragán,** which can only be visited via prebooked guided tour, and the **Museo Frida Kahlo,** which often sells out weeks in advance.

a line outside Museo Frida Kahlo

35

Reservations for the city's most famous **restaurants** are a must. For celebrated restaurants like **Pujol** or **Máximo Bistrot Local,** book as early as possible—at least a month before you plan to go. Newer restaurants generating a lot of buzz often require advance reservations as well, particularly on weekends. Call at least a few days ahead. Note that *comida,* or lunch, is considered the most important meal of the day in Mexico, so a 2pm reservation on Saturday or Sunday can be one of the toughest to get.

A number of popular **bars** accept reservations. Though not required, reservations are recommended at popular spots like **Ticuchi, Licorería Limantour,** and **Supra.** Increasingly, both bars and restaurants throughout the city accept reservations through WhatsApp.

If you are flexible about where you're staying (and especially if you are planning to stay in a budget hotel), it's fine to make **hotel reservations** a week or two before your arrival. However, if you want to stay in the Roma or the Condesa, and especially if you have your heart set on one of the popular small hotels in those areas (like **Condesa DF** or the **Red Tree House**), book your hotel reservation as soon as you plan your trip. It's also worth planning ahead if you will be visiting during a major holiday like Independence Day, popular vacation seasons like the winter holidays, or during a big event, like Pope Francis's 2016 visit to the capital, when hotels in the Centro Histórico were booked to capacity.

PASSES AND DISCOUNTS

With little exception, museums and cultural institutions in Mexico City have low admission prices. On top of that, museums often offer discounted or free admission on Sunday, and some have permanent discounts for children, seniors, educators, and people with disabilities. Increasingly, discounted admission, including free Sunday admission, applies only to Mexican nationals. There are no citywide passes for cultural centers, museums, or transportation.

GUIDED TOURS

Tour groups **Eat Mexico** (www. eatmexico.com) and **Club Tengo Hambre** (https://clubtengohambre.com) offer excellent tours of street food, markets, and taquerias. The Mexican government's **Instituto Nacional de Antropología e Historia** (INAH), or National Institute of Anthropology and History, offers guided tours of the city sights it oversees, including the **Museo Nacional de Antropología,** as well as cultural trips to destinations around central Mexico. The

Museo Nacional de Antropología

- **A new palace for the people:** In 2018, President Andrés Manuel López Obrador moved out of the presidential mansion known as Los Pinos and transformed it into a free art and cultural center, public garden, and exhibition space in the Primera Sección de Chapultepec.

- **Amazing art spaces:** There are several newcomers in Mexico City's contemporary art scene, particularly the gorgeous **LAGO/ALGO,** a gallery space overlooking the Lago Mayor in the Segunda Sección de Chapultepec.

- **New windows into history:** Archaeological discoveries continue to reveal the size and scope of the Mexica city of Tenochtitlan. In 2022, the **Zona Arqueológica and Museo del Templo Mayor** opened a new "subterranean museum" showcasing the Templo de Ehécatl and a part of a pre-Columbian ball court, currently opened at limited times.

- **New (free) collections:** In the Centro Histórico, a massive colonial-era palace has been restored and opened to the public as **Foro Valparaíso,** a spectacular museum that showcases Citibanamex's vast collection of historic Mexican art. In the Roma, the charming **Museo Soumaya–Casa Guillermo Tovar de Teresa** showcases the life and aesthetics of a preeminent early 20th-century Mexican intellectual.

- **More eats:** Outstanding places continue to open citywide, from twin restaurants **Caracol del Mar** and **Itacate del Mar** from chef Gabriela Cámara in the Centro Histórico to seafood hot spot **Mi Compa Chava** in the Roma.

- **More seats:** Many bars and restaurants expanded sidewalk seating, enlivening the city streets and making it possible for perennially popular places like **Panadería Rosetta** and **Lalo** in the Roma to accommodate far more diners than in the past (though you'll still have to wait for a table on the weekends!).

- **More vegan:** There is a multitude of wonderful vegan **fondas,** taquerias, and restaurants opening across the city, including **Gracias Madre Taqueria** in the Roma or **Mictlan Antojitos Veganos** in the Narvarte. You'll find vegan dishes at almost any restaurant these days (taquerias aside), and there's now a mainly plant-based menu at preeminent fine-dining restaurant **Pujol,** as well as at Enrique Olvera's new bar **Ticuchi.**

- **More views:** In the Centro Histórico, there are lovely views from the new terrace bar at hotel **Círculo Mexicano** and from the rooftop Mexican restaurant **Paxia,** as well as a bird's-eye view of the pedestrian street Madero from the **Museo del Estanquillo,** which expanded to include a top-floor café. Cocktail bar **Supra** in the Roma boasts panoramic views from the top of an office building.

- **More expats:** Remote workers from the United States and other foreign countries are flooding the city, changing the flavor (and affecting the prices) of neighborhoods like the Roma, the Condesa, and the Juárez.

- **More beer:** The craft beer scene is flourishing in Mexico City, with city-made brews like **Cosaco, Cru Cru, Monstruo de Agua, Falling Piano,** and **Flaco Cara de Perro,** among others, appearing on bar and restaurant menus throughout the city, along with new taprooms, including **Drunkendog** and **Patio Escondido,** both in the Roma.

- **New spirits:** Mezcal is now joined by lesser known Mexican spirits like *bacanora* and *sotol* at bars like **Tlecan** in the Roma.

- **Expanded green space:** The city's largest urban park, the Bosque de Chapultepec, has undergone an ambitious renovation project, which expanded its size considerably, revived its monuments and cultural institutions, and linked each of the park's distinct sections by footbridge and public transportation. The park's newly annexed Cuarta Sección (fourth section) includes new cultural institutions, like the Cineteca Nacional, a movie theater run by the Universidad Autónoma de México.

trips, operated under the name Turismo Cultural INAH, usually include transportation, a Spanish-speaking guide, and entrance fees (special trips can be arranged with English-speaking guides for groups). For more information, visit the INAH office in the Museo Nacional de Antropología (tel. 55/5553-2365 or 55/5215-1003, www.tci.inah.gob.mx).

CALENDAR OF EVENTS

FEBRUARY

For avid art fans, the best time to visit is during **Art Week Mexico,** when Mexico City's biggest contemporary art fair, **Zsona MACO** (México Arte Contemporáneo) (www.zsonamaco.com), is held over five days in the Centro Citibanamex in the Lomas de Sotelo, bringing a high-quality roster of exhibitors from the surrounding city and overseas. Newer Material Art Fair runs at the same time, and there are special exhibitions and events throughout the city.

MARCH AND APRIL

Semana Santa (Easter week or Holy Week) officially begins on Domingo de Ramos, or Palm Sunday, when handwoven palm crosses are sold outside the city's churches, and runs through Easter Sunday. The main reason to visit (or avoid) Mexico City during the Easter holidays is to experience a notably quieter metropolis. Traffic is subdued, museums are nearly empty, and you'll rarely need restaurant reservations—though a large number of shops, restaurants, and bars close for the week.

celebration of the Día de Nuestra Señora de Guadalupe in front of the Basílica de Santa María de Guadalupe

Independence Day parade on the Paseo de la Reforma

SEPTEMBER

Mexico commemorates its independence from Spain on September 16; however, the main **Día de la Independencia** festivities in Mexico City take place on the evening of September 15, when thousands of revelers crowd the Zócalo. At 11pm, the president of the republic appears on the balcony of the Palacio Nacional, reenacting Miguel Hidalgo's cry for independence, including "Viva México!"—also known as El Grito. Fireworks and parties follow. There is a military parade through the Centro and along the Paseo de la Reforma the next day.

DECEMBER

The Virgin of Guadalupe miraculously appeared to Saint Juan Diego on the hill of Tepeyac on December 12, 1531. Today, the **Día de Nuestra Señora de Guadalupe** is one of the most important religious holidays across Latin America. On the days leading up to the 12th, pilgrims walk through the city toward the Basílica de Santa María de Guadalupe in northern Mexico City, often setting off fireworks as they go, and thousands pack the area around the basilica.

Centro Histórico

Map 1

Mexico City's Centro Histórico is the heart and soul of the city, a fascinating mix of **grand colonial-era architecture,** quirky old-fashioned charm, and relentless urban energy. The oldest district in the capital, it was built in the 16th century atop the ruins of the island city of Tenochtitlan, following the Spanish defeat of the native Mexica people. Today, the blocks surrounding the **Zócalo** are dense with baroque palaces and churches, **fascinating museums,** and some of the best **traditional restaurants** in the city, as well as eye-opening pre-Columbian archaeological sites that were long buried beneath the modern city, including the Mexica's holiest site, the **Templo Mayor.**

TOP SIGHTS

- Most Astonishing Historical Site: **Zona Arqueológica and Museo del Templo Mayor** (page 49)
- Grandest Market: **Mercado de la Merced** (page 52)
- Amazing Murals: **Secretaría de Educación Pública** (page 56)

TOP RESTAURANTS

- Best New-School Spot in the Centro: **Azul Histórico** (page 63)
- Best Old-School Spot in the Centro: **El Cardenal** (page 64)
- Most Historic Atmosphere: **Bar La Ópera** (page 67)

TOP NIGHTLIFE

- Very Best View: **Miralto** (page 70)

TOP SHOPS

- Top Textiles: **Remigio** (page 78)
- Best Traditional Sweets: **Dulcería de Celaya** (page 78)

GETTING THERE AND AROUND

- Metro lines: 1, 2, and 8
- Metro stops: Zócalo, Allende, Pino Suárez, Isabel la Católica, Merced
- Metrobús lines: 4
- Metrobús stops: Eje Central, El Salvador, Isabel la Católica, Museo de la Ciudad, Circunvalación

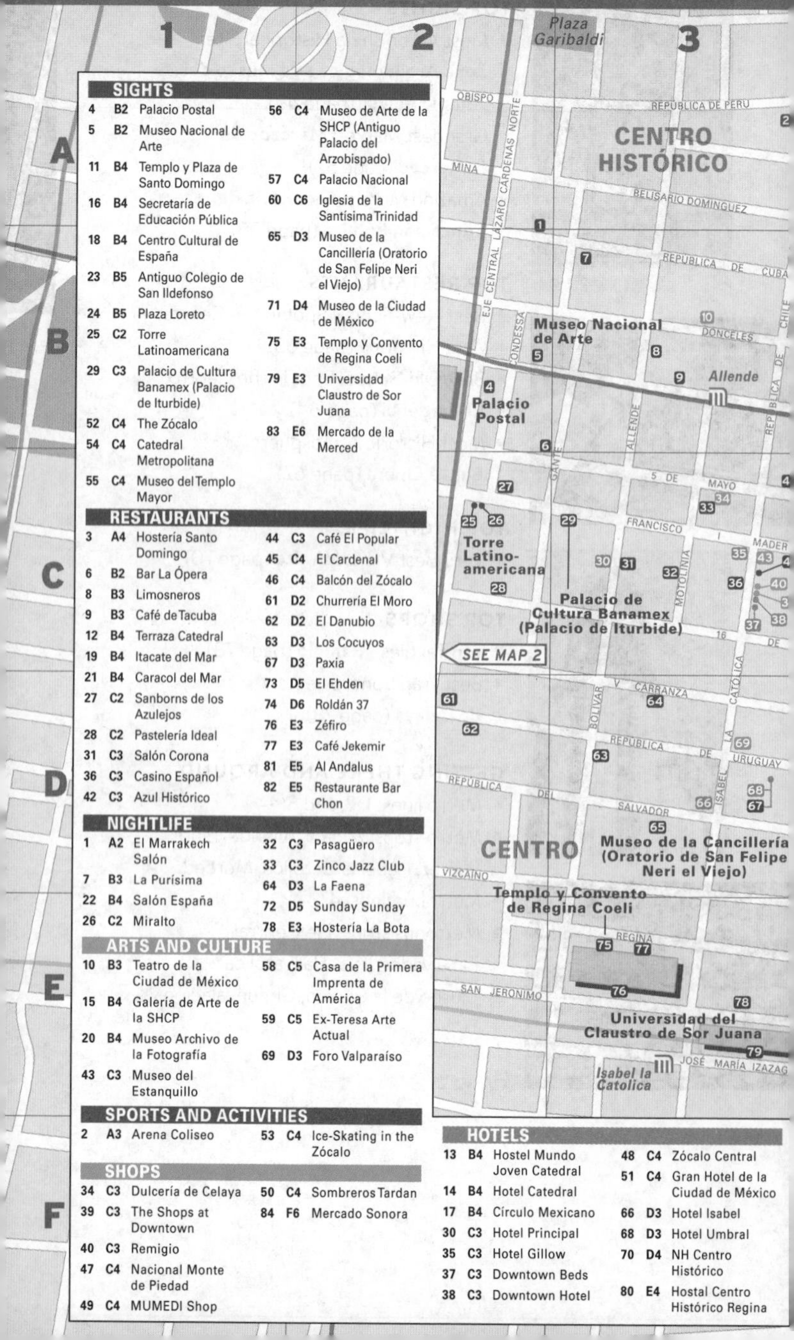
1
2
3
A
B
C
D
E
F
Plaza Garibaldi
CENTRO HISTÓRICO
OBISPO
REPÚBLICA DE PERÚ
MINA
EJE CENTRAL LÁZARO CÁRDENAS NORTE
BELISARIO DOMINGUEZ
REPÚBLICA DE CUBA
CHILE
DONCELES
CONDESA
Museo Nacional de Arte
Allende
Palacio Postal
REPÚBLICA DE
ALLENDE
GANTE
5 DE MAYO
FRANCISCO
MADERO
Torre Latinoamericana
Palacio de Cultura Banamex (Palacio de Iturbide)
MOTOLINIA
16 DE
SEE MAP 2
V. CARRANZA
BOLÍVAR
LA CATÓLICA
REPÚBLICA DE URUGUAY
REPÚBLICA DEL
SALVADOR
ISABEL
CENTRO
Museo de la Cancillería (Oratorio de San Felipe Neri el Viejo)
VIZCAÍNO
Templo y Convento de Regina Coeli
REGINA
SAN JERONIMO
Universidad del Claustro de Sor Juana
JOSÉ MARÍA IZAZAGA
Isabel la Católica

SIGHTS

- 4 B2 Palacio Postal
- 5 B2 Museo Nacional de Arte
- 11 B4 Templo y Plaza de Santo Domingo
- 16 B4 Secretaría de Educación Pública
- 18 B4 Centro Cultural de España
- 23 B5 Antiguo Colegio de San Ildefonso
- 24 B5 Plaza Loreto
- 25 C2 Torre Latinoamericana
- 29 C3 Palacio de Cultura Banamex (Palacio de Iturbide)
- 52 C4 The Zócalo
- 54 C4 Catedral Metropolitana
- 55 C4 Museo del Templo Mayor
- 56 C4 Museo de Arte de la SHCP (Antiguo Palacio del Arzobispado)
- 57 C4 Palacio Nacional
- 60 C6 Iglesia de la Santísima Trinidad
- 65 D3 Museo de la Cancillería (Oratorio de San Felipe Neri el Viejo)
- 71 D4 Museo de la Ciudad de México
- 75 E3 Templo y Convento de Regina Coeli
- 79 E3 Universidad Claustro de Sor Juana
- 83 E6 Mercado de la Merced

RESTAURANTS

- 3 A4 Hostería Santo Domingo
- 6 B2 Bar La Ópera
- 8 B3 Limosneros
- 9 B3 Café de Tacuba
- 12 B4 Terraza Catedral
- 19 B4 Itacate del Mar
- 21 B4 Caracol del Mar
- 27 C2 Sanborns de los Azulejos
- 28 C2 Pastelería Ideal
- 31 C3 Salón Corona
- 36 C3 Casino Español
- 42 C3 Azul Histórico
- 44 C3 Café El Popular
- 45 C4 El Cardenal
- 46 C4 Balcón del Zócalo
- 61 D2 Churrería El Moro
- 62 D2 El Danubio
- 63 D3 Los Cocuyos
- 67 D3 Paxia
- 73 D5 El Ehden
- 74 D6 Roldán 37
- 76 E3 Zéfiro
- 77 E3 Café Jekemir
- 81 E5 Al Andalus
- 82 E5 Restaurante Bar Chon

NIGHTLIFE

- 1 A2 El Marrakech Salón
- 7 B3 La Purísima
- 22 B4 Salón España
- 26 C2 Miralto
- 32 C3 Pasagüero
- 33 C3 Zinco Jazz Club
- 64 D3 La Faena
- 72 D5 Sunday Sunday
- 78 E3 Hostería La Bota

ARTS AND CULTURE

- 10 B3 Teatro de la Ciudad de México
- 15 B4 Galería de Arte de la SHCP
- 20 B4 Museo Archivo de la Fotografía
- 43 C3 Museo del Estanquillo
- 58 C5 Casa de la Primera Imprenta de América
- 59 C5 Ex-Teresa Arte Actual
- 69 D3 Foro Valparaíso

SPORTS AND ACTIVITIES

- 2 A3 Arena Coliseo
- 53 C4 Ice-Skating in the Zócalo

SHOPS

- 34 C3 Dulcería de Celaya
- 39 C3 The Shops at Downtown
- 40 C3 Remigio
- 47 C4 Nacional Monte de Piedad
- 49 C4 MUMEDI Shop
- 50 C4 Sombreros Tardan
- 84 F6 Mercado Sonora

HOTELS

- 13 B4 Hostel Mundo Joven Catedral
- 14 B4 Hotel Catedral
- 17 B4 Círculo Mexicano
- 30 C3 Hotel Principal
- 35 C3 Hotel Gillow
- 37 C3 Downtown Beds
- 38 C3 Downtown Hotel
- 48 C4 Zócalo Central
- 51 C4 Gran Hotel de la Ciudad de México
- 66 D3 Hotel Isabel
- 68 D3 Hotel Umbral
- 70 D4 NH Centro Histórico
- 80 E4 Hostal Centro Histórico Regina

4 **5** **6**

APARTADO

PENTA Y PENA

REPÚBLICA DE ARGENTINA

REPÚBLICA DE BOLIVIA

REPÚBLICA DE COLOMBIA

Templo y Plaza de Santo Domingo 11

Plaza Santo Domingo

Secretaría de Educación Pública 16

BELISARIO DOMÍNGUEZ

VICARIO

LEONA

Centro Cultural de España 22

Antiguo Colegio de San Ildefonso 23

SAN ILDEFONSO

Plaza Loreto 24

LORETO

14 19 21 17 12 13 15 18 20

JUSTO SIERRA

MIXCALCO

TACUBA

GUATEMALA

Zona Arqueológica and Museo del Templo Mayor

REPÚBLICA DE GUATEMALA

CORREO

59

Catedral Metropolitana 54 55 56 58

45 46 47 48

49

MONEDA

Zócalo

EMILIANO ZAPATA

Museo de Arte de la SHCP (Antiguo Palacio del Arzobispado) 57

Iglesia de la Santísima Trinidad 60

LA SOLEDAD

50

52 53

The Zócalo

Plaza de la Constitución

Palacio Nacional

Zócalo

ACADEMIA

SEPTIEMBRE

51

70

CORREGIDORA

72

73

V. CARRANZA

REPÚBLICA DE URUGUAY

ZAVALA

Museo de la Ciudad de México 71

REPÚBLICA DEL SALVADOR

DE FEBRERO

DE NOVIEMBRE

MESONES

REGINA

JOSÉ MARÍA PINO SUÁREZ

74

LAS CRUCES

JESÚS MARÍA

TALAVERA

ROLDÁN

AV. CIRCUNVALACIÓN

CABAÑA

80

81

82

MESONES

SAN JERÓNIMO

SAN PABLO

Pino Suárez

Mercado de la Merced 83

Merced

NEZAHUALCÓYOTL

CLAVIJERO

TOPACIO

SANTO TOMÁS

PTE. DE ST. TOMÁS

84

FRAY SERVANDO TERESA DE MIER

0 200 yds
0 200 m

DISTANCE ACROSS MAP
Approximate: 1.6 mi or 2.5 km

© MOON.COM

CENTRO HISTÓRICO WALK

TOTAL DISTANCE: 2 kilometers (1.2 miles)
TOTAL WALKING TIME: 2 hours

Walking is the best way to explore any neighborhood in Mexico City, but particularly the Centro Histórico. From the Zócalo, you can set out in any direction to find yourself surrounded by **colonial-era palaces, stone chapels, old public squares,** and **bustling pedestrian corridors.** The Centro's most spectacular streets run west from the Zócalo to the Alameda Central, amply demonstrating why Mexico City has been known for centuries as "the City of Palaces."

1 Start your tour in the **Zócalo,** appreciating the history and splendor of this expansive public square, often occupied by a temporary stage for concerts, political protests, and, every December, a massive ice-skating rink. On the west end of the Zócalo is the **Portal de Mercaderes.** Traders have sold goods here since the colonial era; today, the only notable establishment in this historic arcade is legacy hat shop Sombreros Tardan. Turn left (west) onto bustling pedestrian street Madero.

The historic street Madero is closed to automobile traffic and perfect for strolling.

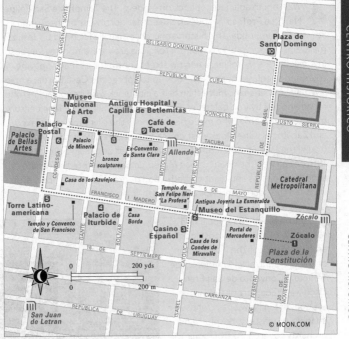

2 There are historic palaces all along Madero, many incongruously occupied by fast-fashion retailers and convenience stores. On the corner of Isabel la Católica, the marvelous **Antigua Joyería La Esmeralda** was originally built for an upscale jeweler. Designed in the French style popular in 19th-century Mexico, the first floor is now a retail shop, while the top floors are home to the lovely **Museo del Estanquillo.** Spend a little time at this free museum, where you can see the art and photography of Carlos Monsiváis, a political activist and journalist—and don't miss the rooftop terrace and café, with beautiful bird's-eye views of the streets below.

3 From here, take a half-block detour south on Isabel la Católica to the **Casino Español,** a neoclassical palace constructed by Emilio González del Campo in the early 20th century. Take the elevator to the second floor to admire the building's opulent interiors; better yet, come back later for a meal at the old Spanish restaurant of the same name. Across the street, the baroque **Casa de los Condes de Miravalle** is one of the oldest palaces in the Centro, built by a colonial-era mining magnate. Today, it is inhabited by the Downtown Hotel, the restaurant Azul Histórico, and a few Mexican design shops, including the excellent textile merchant **Remigio.**

4 Walk north again to get back on Madero. The **Templo de San Felipe Neri "La Profesa"** stands on the corner northwest of the Antigua Joyería La Esmeralda. This historic church, originally founded by Jesuits, maintains a reserve of colonial-era religious artwork, among the largest in Mexico. Pass Motolinia, a narrow street known for its many optometrists and eyeglass shops. Now, look up to appreciate **Casa Borda,** a massive palace that spans more than half a city block with its volcanic-stone facade ringed by iron balconies. The palace was built in the 18th century by José de la Borda, who made his fortune in the silver mines of Taxco and Zacatecas. One block west on Madero, the **Palacio de Iturbide** (today the Palacio de Cultura Citibanamex) was originally built in the late 18th century by the count of San Mateo Valparaíso. Note the ornate sandstone details and giant carved-wood doors—if they are open, stop in to see the soaring interior courtyard.

5 Just a block away, you'll find some of the city's most iconic architecture near the intersection of the Eje Central and Madero. The **Templo y Convento de San Francisco** was once part of the largest convent in New Spain, whose chapels, monastery, hospital, and orchards covered 30,000 square meters. Destroyed during the 19th-century Reformation, only this church remains. It's a curious juxtaposition between the old Franciscan church and the **Torre**

The Casa de los Azulejos is one of the most lavish colonial-era palaces in Mexico City.

Latinoamericana, which stands beside it. When the tower was built in the 1950s, it was the tallest in the city. Today, it's the only skyscraper downtown, affording unparalleled, unobstructed views from the 44th-floor observation deck—worth the time (and vertigo) to visit. Before heading north on the Eje Central, admire one of the most stunning buildings in the Centro: the blue-and-white-tiled **Casa de los Azulejos.** Though this palace has played many important roles throughout history, it has been a Sanborns restaurant since 1917—a wonderful place for breakfast.

6 Turn right (north) on the Eje Central. You'll see the gorgeous Palacio de Bellas Artes (earmark it for a future visit) on the opposite side of the street as you walk north toward the **Palacio Postal,** the city's main post office, two blocks north of the Torre Latinoamericana. This breathtaking landmark was heavily damaged in the 1985 earthquake, but it has been diligently restored.

Mexico City's main post office is housed in an opulent early-20th-century palace.

7 Turn right and walk east along Tacuba, the very first street in the capital of New Spain and once the home to Spanish aristocrats and governors. On the first block, you'll pass the **Palacio de Minería,** a mining school built between 1797 and 1813 by Spanish architect Manuel Tolsá. The grandeur of the building is testament to the importance of silver to the Spanish colonies. Today, it is home to UNAM's engineering college. Check out the gigantic meteorites in the building's foyer; each were recovered from somewhere inside the Mexican republic. Tolsá's statue of Spanish king Carlos IV, which once stood in the city's Zócalo, is now located in front of the **Museo Nacional de Arte,** an interesting museum and architectural masterpiece, just across the street from the Palacio de Minería.

a bronze statue of Itzcóatl, third emperor of the Mexica people

8 A few steps away, on the corner of Filomena Mata, Jesús Fructuoso Contreras's **bronze sculptures** of emperors Itzcóatl, Nezahualcóyotl, and Totoquihuatzin celebrate the alliance between the city-states of Tenochtitlan, Texcoco, and Tlacopan in 1430. This stretch of Tacuba is also home to several wonderful vintage perfume shops. To the right (south) on this block, the

Antiguo Hospital y Capilla de Betlemitas was, until 1820, a refuge for the poor and infirm, run by an order of nuns. Though much of the original building was damaged or destroyed over various centuries, the remains were beautifully restored in the 1990s and today house **MIDE, Museo Interactivo de Economía,** an interactive museum focused on economics.

9 The **Ex-Convento de Santa Clara,** on the next corner, was built in 1661 and adjoins the bustling Allende Metro stop. Like many of the Centro's churches, it was once part of a larger convent and religious complex that was destroyed during the 19th-century Reformation. Across the street, restaurant **Café de Tacuba** is a mainstay in the Centro, in business here for more than 100 years. Drop in for a hot chocolate and a *tamal*; the setting—with its old oil paintings, tiled walls, and soaring ceilings—is classic.

10 Continue on Tacuba. (Alternatively, walk east along Donceles, one block north of Tacuba. Here, you'll find a cluster of old-school used booksellers, who carry everything from encyclopedia sets and out-of-print paperbacks to dusty maps.) When you get to the street República de Brasil (about 3-4 blocks east), swing left (north) and go two blocks to finish your walk at the **Plaza de Santo Domingo,** an important colonial-era square and the site of the Inquisition in Mexico. It is still dominated by the old Dominican convent on the north end. At the east end of the plaza, beneath the archways, are kiosks operated by professional clerks and scribes who have been typing up letters and official documents for clients for decades.

Sights

TOP EXPERIENCE

⚙ Zona Arqueológica and Museo del Templo Mayor

A massive temple-pyramid in the heart of the city of Tenochtitlan, the Templo Mayor was the center of religious and political life for the Mexica people, who, until the 16th century, dominated Mesoamerica from their capital city in the Valley of Mexico. First built around 1325, the structure was enlarged by successive Mexica rulers, eventually reaching around 60 meters high. Dual staircases led up its face to two crowning temples, one dedicated to Huitzilopochtli, the god of war and sun, and the other to Tlaloc, the god of rain and agriculture.

After the Spanish conquest of Tenochtitlan, the Templo Mayor was razed and its stones were used to construct Spanish palaces and churches for a new European-style city, which would become the capital of New Spain and Mexico City today. The pyramid's location was eventually forgotten, though archaeologists long suspected it lay beneath or near the cathedral. On February 21, 1978, electric company workers digging near the cathedral uncovered an eight-ton monolith adorned with carvings of the moon goddess Coyolxauhqui. The discovery prompted a major excavation.

Templo Mayor

After demolishing four city blocks, archaeologists uncovered the base of the Templo Mayor, along with a multitude of artifacts.

Excavation at the site is ongoing. In 2017, the space was expanded to reveal the partial remains of a round temple dedicated to the god Ehécatl. In 2022, the viewing area was further expanded to include a "subterranean museum" with a larger view of the temple as well as a partial staircase from a ball court and remains from early colonial-era structures. The subterranean space is in development, but is open to visitors to the archaeological site on the weekends (2pm-5pm Sat., 9am-5pm Sun.).

The archaeological site is accompanied by a fascinating museum, which holds an extensive collection of pre-Columbian pieces, the majority recovered during the Templo Mayor's major excavation, including the Coyolxauhqui stone. Among other magnificent artifacts, the museum contains a four-meter-long carved monolith dedicated to the goddess Tlaltecuhtli, discovered in 2006.

MAP 1: Seminario 8, tel. 55/4040-5600, ext. 412930, www.templomayor.inah.gob.mx; 9am-5pm Tues.-Sun.; US$6, free on Sun.; Metro: Zócalo

The Zócalo

The Zócalo, also known as the Plaza de la Constitución, has been a public square since the founding of Tenochtitlan in 1325. Adjoining the city's holiest site, the Templo Mayor, the plaza was a place of ritual and celebration during the 14th and 15th centuries, in addition to being an important market. The Mexica

rulers' palaces lined the plaza, and causeways leading off the island radiated out from its four sides.

After the fall of Tenochtitlan, the Zócalo became the center of the Spanish city of Mexico, and it was known as the Plaza Mayor throughout the colonial era. It remained the center of government and religious activity: The cathedral borders the plaza to the north and the government palaces run along the east side. Today, the empty square serves as a concert venue, protest site, and performance art venue.

MAP 1: Plaza de la Constitución, bordered by Madero, Moneda, 16 de Septiembre, Corregidora, 5 de Febrero, República de Brasil, and Pino Suárez; free; Metro: Zócalo

Adjoining the Zócalo, Palacio Nacional was once the home of the colonial-era Spanish viceroys.

Palacio Nacional

The deep-red facade of the Palacio Nacional stretches grandly across the eastern edge of the Zócalo. After the destruction of Tenochtitlan, a palace was constructed on this site for Hernán Cortés. Reconstructed several times over history, it later became the official home for Spanish viceroys governing the colonies. After independence, the palace became the seat of government, and

the Cathedral Metropolitana

the bell from the church in Dolores Hidalgo, Guanajuato, was hung over the presidential balcony. It was this bell that war hero Miguel Hidalgo rang while issuing his famous battle cry, or *grito,* which heralded the start of the War of Independence from Spain. Today, it is the seat of the government and the home of the Mexican president.

For visitors, the highlight of the Palacio Nacional is the spectacular murals painted by Diego Rivera in the north plaza and stairwell. A masterwork of composition and color, Rivera executed this chronicle of the history of Mexico between 1929 and 1951. The panel entitled *The Great City of Tenochtitlan* provides a detailed rendering of the Mexica city, viewed from the market in Tlatelolco. Unfortunately, the Palacio Nacional closed to the public during the COVID-19 pandemic lockdown and work began on restoring the murals. At

press time, there was no date for reopening.

MAP 1: Plaza de la Constitución between Moneda and Corregidora, tel. 55/3688-1602; 10am-5pm Tues.-Sun.; free; Metro: Zócalo

Catedral Metropolitana

Dominating the Zócalo to the north, the Metropolitan Cathedral is a mortar-and-stone representation of the central role of the Catholic Church in Mexico's past and present. A modest church was built on this site in 1524 and named a cathedral in 1534. Shortly thereafter, New Spain's governors commissioned the construction of a bigger, grander church. The first stone was laid in 1553, but the cathedral wasn't completed for 240 years. Over the centuries, different architects left their mark on the cathedral, which mixes Renaissance, baroque, and neoclassical styles.

Within the cathedral's two

51

bell towers, 25 multiton bells are still rung by hand. During the September 19, 2017, earthquake, a cross known as La Esperanza, which topped the eastern tower, toppled and fell to the ground. Tours of the bell towers have since been suspended indefinitely, though they may be reopened once the site has been fully secured.

Inside the cathedral, you can see the impressive golden baroque altars and tour the interior of the choir with its two enormous pipe organs (US$1). If you'd like to hear these impressive instruments play, there are daily concerts at 9am (free).

MAP 1: Plaza de la Constitución between Monte de Piedad and Pino Suárez, tel. 55/41654052, www.arquidiocesismexico.org.mx; 8:30am-5pm daily; free; Metro: Zócalo

Museo de la Ciudad de México

Three blocks south of the Zócalo, a colonial-era mansion is today the city museum. Historians surmise that one of the conquistadores built a home on this site shortly after the conquest: The building's famous cornerstone is a large carved serpent head, likely taken from the Templo Mayor after the building's destruction and placed at the corner as a sign of Spanish domination.

The building's current baroque facade was constructed by the Conde de Calimaya in the late 18th century. Inside, there is a small chapel dedicated to the Virgen de Guadalupe with three colonial-era religious paintings, as well as galleries exhibiting the museum's permanent collections of paintings and sketches of the city and rotating exhibits of contemporary work.

MAP 1: Pino Suárez 30, tel. 55/5542-0487; 10am-6pm Tues.-Sun.; US$2, free on Wed.; Metro: Pino Suárez

☼ Mercado de la Merced

One of the largest retail markets in Mexico, the Mercado de la Merced is the centerpiece of a bustling commercial district known as the Antiguo Barrio de la Merced, which covers several city blocks on the eastern edge of the Centro. Trade has taken place here since the days of Tenochtitlan, when a canal transported goods from the agricultural communities of Xochimilco and Chalco to Moctezuma's palaces in what is now the Zócalo. A market was built on the former grounds of the Merced convent in the 1860s, though the current market building was constructed in 1957, several decades after the transport canal dried up.

chiles for sale at Mercado de la Merced

Wandering through the Merced is a feast for the senses and a bonanza for curious foodies. In the main market, you'll find stacks of banana leaves, baskets towering with dried chiles, bags of black *huitlacoche* (corn fungus), and bins of traditional Mexican herbs and spices. Farther inside, stalls sell kitchen supplies, woven baskets, piñatas, and handicrafts, while aromatic food stands offer everything from quick quesadillas to a full meal at rock-bottom prices. Adjoining the Merced is the interesting Mercado Sonora, which sells home goods, herbal medicines, live animals, and products for spells and witchcraft. Today's market is generally safe, but stay aware of your belongings and take care walking the streets nearby.

MAP 1: Circunvalación between General Anaya and Adolfo Gorrión, Col. Merced Balbuena, tel. 55/5522-7250; 6am-6pm daily; Metro: La Merced

Centro Cultural de España

Run by the Spanish government since 2002, this unique gallery, cultural center, and anthropology museum is housed in a 17th-century baroque palace behind the Metropolitan Cathedral. Throughout the year, the center presents exhibitions of contemporary work by Mexican and Spanish artists, often featuring experimental proposals and installations, in addition to hosting workshops, readings, and performances on-site. There's a design shop on the first floor, as well as a lovely terrace bar and café, with charming views of the back of the cathedral.

During an expansion of the space in 2006, construction workers encountered remains from the city of Tenochtitlan beneath the building's foundation. Archaeological study suggests these structures housed a *calmécac,* a Mexica school, from the 15th and 16th centuries. After the discovery, the CCE opened the Museo del Sitio, a small, interesting museum in the basement of the building, which showcases both the ruins and artifacts recovered from the site.

MAP 1: República de Guatemala 18, tel. 55/6592-9926, http://ccemx.org; 11am-9pm Tues.-Sat., 10am-4pm Sun.; free; Metro: Zócalo

Antiguo Colegio de San Ildefonso

The Antiguo Colegio de San Ildefonso was a Jesuit school from 1588 until 1767, when King Carlos expelled the Jesuits from New Spain. In the 19th century, under President Benito Juárez, it reopened as the Escuela Nacional Preparatoria, a prestigious secondary school.

In 1922, Secretary of Public Education José Vasconcelos hired a group of young Mexican artists to paint the walls of the school; it was the beginning of the mural project that would become emblematic of early 20th-century Mexican art. Diego Rivera, José Clemente Orozco, David Alfaro Siqueiros, Fermín Revueltas Sánchez, Ramón Alva de la Canal, Fernando Leal, and Jean Charlot all painted sections of the interior. Among the building's most important works, Orozco's murals cover three stories in the main patio.

In 1992, San Ildefonso became a museum and cultural center. In addition to the murals, it hosts rotating art exhibits, usually showcasing

THE CITY BENEATH THE CITY

This pre-Columbian temple is now part of a busy metro station.

In the year 1325, the Mexica people witnessed an eagle perched atop a cactus, holding a snake in its talons—today, the central image on the Mexican flag. A nomadic tribe, the Mexica had struggled for decades to settle in the already-populous Valley of Mexico, and the eagle came to them as a divine signal to found their city where it had landed, on an uninhabited island near the shore of Lake Texcoco. Over the next 200 years, the Mexica became enormously powerful, gaining control of city-states throughout Mesoamerica through aggressive warfare and forming a formidable alliance with fellow Nahuatl-speaking city-states Tlacopan and Texcoco. They named their city Tenochtitlan.

SPANISH CONQUEST

When Hernán Cortés and his army arrived in the Valley of Mexico in 1519, they were dazzled by what they found: an expansive, clean, and orderly city, larger than any in 16th-century Spain, surrounded by lakes and floating gardens. Causeways linked the island to the mainland while canals ribboned the city, bringing goods and produce to the large outdoor markets in the city center, which was replete with brightly painted temples, pyramids, and palaces.

Despite their initial admiration for the Mexica capital, the Spanish laid siege to and destroyed Tenochtitlan during the conquest. Directly on top of the vanquished city, they built an opulent European-style capital to rule New Spain, often using the stones from the fallen Mexica temples for their own churches and palaces. Though they destroyed the dams that protected the city from flooding, the Spanish continued to use the canals to transport goods, in addition to utilizing the causeways that linked the island to the mainland—today, the street Tacuba still runs along the ancient causeway.

INDEPENDENCE FROM SPAIN

By the time Mexico gained independence from Spain, there was little trace of the grand city of Tenochtitlan in the modern metropolis. The location of the Mexica's monuments and temples had been forgotten. The lakes were drained and slowly filled to build new neighborhoods outside the city center. The canals that brought goods to the island dried up and were paved over. The city beneath the city was buried in history.

SIGHTS

In the 20th century, a renewed interest in Mexico's pre-Columbian past sparked more extensive archaeological investigation of the Centro Histórico. Today, through accidental discovery and intentional excavation, the great city of Tenochtitlan continues to reveal itself. Here are some of the places that have emerged.

- In the late 1960s, the first line of Mexico City's Metro system was under construction when transport workers tunneled directly into the remains of a pre-Columbian pyramid, long buried beneath the city floor. Undeterred, the transport authority built a subway station around the pyramid, creating a small plaza with an open ceiling where the structure can be viewed by the millions of commuters who rush through the **Pino Suárez Metro Station** (Jose María Izazaga and Pino Suárez; 6am–midnight daily) in the Centro Histórico every year.

- The **Zona Arqueológica and Museo del Templo Mayor** (page 49) contain the remains of the biggest and most sacred temple in Tenochtitlan, which was remarkably preserved beneath the colonial-era buildings in the Centro Histórico for over 450 years. Archaeologists long believed the base of the temple was located under or near the cathedral, but when a massive stone sculpture of Coyolxauhqui was found behind the cathedral 1978, a full excavation of the site revealed the location of the Templo Mayor. Excavation of the site is ongoing, recently revealing the **Templo de Ehécatl** and remains of a pre-Columbian ball court.

- The former home to the viceroy who oversaw the Spanish colonies (and today the seat of the executive branch of the government), the **Palacio Nacional** (page 50) was built directly atop Mexica emperor Moctezuma's former residence. Modern-day excavation of the palace's ground floor has revealed the foundations of Moctezuma's home, which is now visible in various glass-topped windows in the palace floor. There is also a viewing station showing a former staircase within the Mexica ruler's palace, which is believed to have had over 100 bedrooms. Note that the Palacio Nacional was closed to visitors at press time.

- During an expansion of the colonial-era mansion in which its housed, the **Centro Cultural de España** (page 53) discovered the remains of a 15th-century calmécac, a Mexica school, which is now part of a small basement museum in this wonderful contemporary art and cultural space.

- The three-story palace known as the **Casa del Marqués del Apartado** (República de Argentina 10; hours vary), designed by architect Manuel Tolsá, was completed in 1805. During a remodel of the space in 1901, several massive stone sculptures were discovered beneath the building's ground floor, as well as the base and stairs of a Mexica temple, now visible in a ground-floor viewing area.

- The **Museo de la Secretaría de Hacienda y Crédito Público** (page 58) is today an art museum run by the country's tax authority, but it was once the palace of the archbishop of New Spain. The building suffered serious damage during the earthquake of 1985, and during renovation and retrofit of the space, construction workers discovered the foundations of the former Templo de Tezcatlipoca, along with artifacts and sculptures, which can be viewed in the museum's west wing.

contemporary work from Mexico and around the world, as well as special events and concerts.
MAP 1: Justo Sierra 16, tel. 55/3602-0034, www.sanildefonso.org.mx; 10am-5pm Wed.-Sun.; US$2.50 general admission; Metro: Zócalo

Templo y Plaza de Santo Domingo

Surrounded by churches and palaces, the Plaza de Santo Domingo was the second most important public square in colonial Mexico City, after the Zócalo. On the north end, the Templo de Santo Domingo was constructed in 1530 as part of a Dominican convent, which included a hospital, libraries, and a cloister, largely destroyed during the 19th-century Reformation. Opposite the square, the 1730-era Palacio de la Inquisición was home to the dreaded Inquisition in Mexico, an extension of its Spanish counterpart.

Look for the dozens of professional scribes beneath the plaza's western archways. They have been producing typed documents for paying clients since the mid-19th century and can help compose anything from a résumé to a love note at their small kiosks, in addition to producing official forms and contracts.
MAP 1: Brasil at Belisario Domínguez, tel. 55/5563-0479; Templo de Santo Domingo, hours vary; free; Metro: Zócalo

☼ Secretaría de Educación Pública

Former secretary of public education José Vasconcelos was the mastermind behind the public mural project in early 20th-century Mexico. During Vasconcelos's tenure, the offices of the Secretaría de Educación Pública (SEP) moved into two adjoining colonial-era buildings near the Plaza Santo Domingo, where the department is still headquartered today. Both buildings were extensively renovated, and Vasconcelos hired Diego Rivera to outfit them with some of the city's most elaborate murals, painted between 1923 and 1928. Covering two three-story patios, Rivera's paintings adorn every free surface, from the elevator vestibules to the space above the doorframes. There are many famous faces depicted in these works; on the top floor, the painting *El Arsenal* shows Rivera's wife, Frida Kahlo, holding a rifle.

On some days, there are English-speaking guides in the plaza; they can explain the history of the mural project and Rivera's artistic process, in addition to providing a primer on the personages and themes depicted in the paintings. Their services are provided by SEP, free of charge.
MAP 1: República de Argentina 28, tel. 55/3601-7599; 9am-6pm Mon.-Sun.; free; Metro: Zócalo

Diego Rivera painted an extensive series of murals in the courtyard of a colonial-era palace that today is headquarters of the Secretaría de Educación Pública.

HIGH-SPEED SIGHTSEEING

double-decker tour bus from Capitalbus

Despite a rather efficient (if overcrowded) public transportation system, getting from one place to another can be a challenge in Mexico City. An inexpensive, safe, and stress-free way to get the lay of the land, take lovely pics, and see a lot of sights in a short time is to take a bus tour of the city.

Turibus (www.turibus.com.mx) makes frequent circuits through the city's major neighborhoods on bright red double-decker buses. The company's most popular tour is the Circuito Centro Histórico, which runs from the Zócalo to the Auditorio Nacional via the Paseo de la Reforma, passing many of the city's important sites and museums, including the Monumento a la Revolución and the Museo Nacional de Antropología. The Circuito Sur Coyoacán departs from the Roma and travels south to the Museo Frida Kahlo and the center of Coyoacán. There are also routes to Polanco, which stop at the Museo Jumex, to the Basílica de Guadalupe, and to Teotihuacán. It takes over three hours to complete the city center tours nonstop; however, Turibus tickets are good all day, 7am-10pm, so you can get on and off as many times as you wish and transfer lines to visit other parts of the city. A one-day pass for the Turibus costs about US$8 Monday-Friday and about US$10 on the weekends. You can buy your ticket at a kiosk, online, or onboard the bus (just hop on at any official stop).

Also offering double-decker bus tours but taking different routes through the city, Capitalbus (http://capitalbus.mx) offers three sightseeing routes in its distinctive pink-and-white buses: Centro-Polanco, which runs from the Zócalo to Plaza Carso (site of Museo Jumex and Museo Soumaya); the weekends-only Reforma-Santa Fe, which stops at the Centro Cultural Los Pinos on the route to the southwest suburb of Santa Fe; Circuito Templos, which runs north to the Basílica de Santa María de Guadalupe; and the Centro-Sur, which runs to Coyoacán. Your ticket is good for 24 hours, during which time you can ride any of the three lines and get on and off the bus at official stops as often as you like. The bus schedules vary by line and day of the week, but generally run from 9am to 6pm daily. Tickets cost about US$12. There is also a ticket and information kiosk near the Zócalo, on Monte de Piedad, just west of the cathedral, and another at the Hemiciclo a Juarez and Bellas Artes in the Alameda Central. You can also buy tickets online.

Museo de Arte de la SHCP (Antiguo Palacio del Arzobispado)

Just east of the Zócalo, the former Palacio del Arzobispado (Archbishop's Palace) was built in the 1530s by Mexico's first archbishop, undergoing numerous lavish expansions until it reached its current size in the 18th century. Today, the building is an art museum run by the Finance Secretariat (Secretaría de Hacienda y Crédito Público, SHCP), with a sizable collection of Mexican art, much of which artists and collectors offered in lieu of tax payments (the program continues to operate for working artists across the country), including pieces by Diego Rivera and Rufino Tamayo, as well as contemporary artists.

The building suffered serious damage during the earthquake of 1985, and during renovation and retrofit of the space, a surprising discovery was made: Two meters beneath the palace's second courtyard, the foundations of the former Templo de Tezcatlipoca of Tenochtitlan were uncovered, including artifacts and painted murals. Today, the palace includes a viewing area for these ruins along the western wall.

MAP 1: Moneda 4, tel. 55/3688-1248 or 55/3688-1710, www.shcp.gob.mx; 10am-5pm Tues.-Sun.; free; Metro: Zócalo

Plaza Loreto

A few blocks from the Zócalo, this modest public square is centered around a circular fountain designed by Manuel Tolsá in the 18th century. It is flanked by two historic churches, the Iglesia de Nuestra Señora de Loreto (San Antonio Tomatlán and Jesús Maria Loreto, tel. 55/5702-7850; 10am-5pm daily) and the smaller Templo de Santa Teresa La Nueva (Loreto 15, tel. 55/5702-3204; 10am-5pm daily). Perhaps the most striking aspect of the former is the dramatic angle at which its heavy baroque facade is sinking into the soft topsoil, creating something of a funhouse effect as you enter.

Facing the plaza to the south, the Sinagoga Histórica Justo Sierra (Justo Sierra 71, tel. 55/5522-4828, http://sinagogajustosierra.com; 11am-5pm Sun.-Fri.; free) was the first synagogue in Mexico City, and today it is open to the public as a cultural center and museum. Visitors will notice the building doesn't resemble a typical synagogue: The founders, many of whom came from anti-Semitic environments in Europe, built their temple behind a colonial-era facade, intentionally keeping their religious activities out of the public eye.

MAP 1: Bounded by Calle Loreto, Justo Sierra, and San Ildefonso; free; Metro: Zócalo

Iglesia de la Santísima Trinidad

A baroque masterpiece tucked away on a scruffy pedestrian backstreet a couple of blocks east of the Zócalo, La Santísima has an elaborate churrigueresque facade that depicts saints, angels, and apostles in stunning relief. Though a smaller hermitage was built here in the 16th century, the current building dates from the 18th century. Since then, the church has sunk almost three meters into the spongy soil below (it was built atop a former lakebed) and has undergone various restoration projects as a result.

MAP 1: Emiliano Zapata 60, at Santísima; hours vary; free; Metro: Zócalo

Museo de la Cancillería (Oratorio de San Felipe Neri el Viejo)

The congregation of San Felipe Neri built its first church in Mexico City in 1684. In the 18th century, the church and adjoining chapels were embellished with churrigueresque-style details, which were fortunate to survive to the present day: In 1768, an earthquake toppled the rest of building. After years of disuse, the entire complex was renovated and is now the site of a small museum overseen by the Secretaría de Relaciones Exteriores (Secretariat of Foreign Affairs), opened in 2011, which exhibits portraits, books, and other artifacts, as well as contemporary artwork and cultural pieces from across the world.

Just to the east, another beautiful 18th-century chapel that was part of the Oratorio de San Felipe Neri is now home to the Biblioteca Miguel Lerdo de Tejada (República de El Salvador 49, tel. 55/9158-9837; 9am-5pm Mon.-Fri.), a library with holdings in social sciences and humanities and a collection of rare books from the 16th through 19th centuries.

MAP 1: República de El Salvador 47, tel. 55/3686-5100, ext. 8327, www.gob.mx/sre; 11am-5pm Mon.-Fri.; free; Metro: San Juan de Letrán or Isabel la Católica

the Templo de Regina Coeli

Templo y Convento de Regina Coeli

Once part of a larger Conceptionist convent founded in 1573, the massive Templo de Regina Coeli dominates the eastern end of the pedestrian street Regina. It was remodeled along with many of the convent's buildings in the mid-17th century, including several of its baroque altars, though most of the original pieces are missing or have been destroyed. It is still a Catholic parish, holding regular mass, and is often open to the public in the mornings. It's worth stopping in when the doors are open to see the soaring nave and altar.

MAP 1: Regina 3, tel. 55/5709-2640; hours vary, but generally 10am-1:30pm and 4pm-6pm Tues.-Fri., 10am-4pm Sat.; free; Metro: Isabel la Católica

Universidad del Claustro de Sor Juana

During the late 17th century, beloved Mexican poet Sor Juana Inés de la Cruz wrote much of her remarkable, passionate verse from within the confines of her small room in the Convento de San Jerónimo in central Mexico City, a

The baroque Palacio de Iturbide was built in the late 18th century.

nunnery that was originally founded in 1585. By the middle of the 19th century, when it was closed by the Reform Laws, the convent had at least 200 permanent residents.

Today, the remains of the convent are beautifully restored and occupied by a small private university with an arts and cultural focus, called the Universidad del Claustro de Sor Juana. Register at the front desk to visit the ex-convent's main courtyard, around which the nuns' former cells are arranged. There is also a small contemporary art gallery open to the public, in what was once a bathing area for the nuns, as well as occasional evening concerts in the college's auditorium, which contains a collection of antique instruments.
MAP 1: Izazaga 92, tel. 55/5709-4066 or 55/5709-4126, www.ucsj.edu. mx; 10am-5pm Mon.-Fri., 10am-3pm Mon.-Sat..; free; Metro: Isabel la Católica

Palacio de Cultura Citibanamex (Palacio de Iturbide)

A massive baroque mansion with elaborate sandstone carvings around the windows and doorframes, the Antiguo Palacio de Iturbide was constructed between 1779 and 1785 for the family of the count of San Mateo de Valparaíso. However, the palace is best known as the home of Emperor Agustín de Iturbide, who lived there briefly during his short reign during the tumultuous post-Independence era.

Banamex purchased the palace in 1964, and after a long renovation project, it became the home of the Fomento Cultural Banamex, a foundation dedicated to the promotion and exhibition of Mexican art and handcrafts; it was officially inaugurated as the Palacio de Cultura Banamex in 2004 (changed to Citibanamex after the bank's merger with Citibank). Today, the foundation hosts high-quality

exhibitions of painting, folk art, and crafts in the palace's impressive courtyard; recent shows have included a review of silver design throughout Mexico's history, colonial painting, and a selection from the grand masters of popular art in Iberoamerica.
MAP 1: Madero 17, tel. 55/1226-0247, www.fomentoculturalbanamex.org; 11am-7pm daily during exhibitions; free; Metro: Allende

Museo Nacional de Arte

The Mexican National Art Museum holds the most extensive collection of Mexican artwork in the country, with thousands of pieces from the very early colonial era to the mid-20th century. A tour of the museum chronicles the changing attitudes toward religion, government, and education over the course of many centuries, providing an engaging look at Mexican social history through works of art. Particularly interesting are the 19th-century rooms, which show the emergence of a Mexican national character in the wake of the country's independence, a marked transition from the European-style religious paintings that dominate the colonial-era galleries.

Completed in 1910, the building itself is a masterpiece of modernist architecture, designed by Italian architect Silvio Contri. The lavish interior unites architectural styles from classical to Gothic and is replete with curved marble staircases, gilded moldings, and elaborate iron lamps. In front, there is a bronze statue of King Carlos IV, one of the best-known works by Spanish architect Manuel Tolsá.
MAP 1: Tacuba 8, tel. 55/8647-5430, ext. 5050 and 5066, www.munal.com.mx; 11am-5:30pm Tues.-Sun.; US$4 adults, free students, teachers, seniors, people with disabilities; free Sun.; Metro: Bellas Artes or Allende

Palacio Postal

On the site of what was once the Franciscan hospital, Mexico City's central post office is one of the most distinctive architectural landmarks in the city, designed by Italian architect Adamo Boari (who also oversaw the Palacio de Bellas Artes across the street) and Mexican engineer Gonzalo Gorita. Constructed in 1902, the palace was built with a

The Museo Nacional de Arte is a fascinating museum and an architectural jewel.

Palacio Postal

mix of sandstone and *chiluca,* a very light, almost translucent stone, and it is covered with fine detail, including iron dragon light fixtures and elaborate stone carving around the windows and the top-floor arches. The spacious interior is filled with lavish detail, including gleaming cashier counters and old brass elevators. It's hard to believe this gorgeous palace was built for public use—but even today, it is a fully functioning post office, where you can buy stamps or mail a postcard home.

MAP 1: Tacuba 1, tel. 55/5510-2999, www.palaciopostal.gob.mx; 8am-7:30pm Mon.-Fri., 8am-4pm Sat., 10am-2pm Sun.; free; Metro: Bellas Artes

The Torre Latinoamericana, a city landmark, was built in the 1950s.

Torre Latinoamericana

The iconic Torre Latinoamericana was the capital's tallest building at its inauguration in 1956. Though it long ago lost that distinction, the Latinoamericana is still one of the few skyscrapers downtown, giving its top floors one of the most privileged vantage points in the city. On the 44th floor of the building, an open-air observation deck affords stunning, panoramic views of the city from north to south and east to west. On clear days, the volcanoes Iztaccíhuatl and Popocatépetl may even be visible to the southeast. If you're feeling a little vertigo, take heart: The tower was specially designed to withstand Mexico City's seismic instability and soft topsoil, with a foundation reaching deep into the earth and a flexible structure that sways with ground movement. Indeed, the Torre Latinoamericana survived the 1957, 1985, and 2017 earthquakes.

MAP 1: Eje Central Lázaro Cárdenas 2, tel. 55/5518-7423, www.miradorlatino. com; 10am-9pm Mon.-Fri., 9am-10pm Sat.-Sun.; unlimited same-day reentry US$8 adults, US$6 kids; Metro: Bellas Artes

Restaurants

PRICE KEY

$	Entrées less than $10
$ $	Entrées $10-20
$ $ $	Entrées more than $20

MEXICAN

✪ Azul Histórico $$

Chef Ricardo Muñoz Zurita's Azul Histórico is set in the tree-shaded courtyard of a colonial-era palace, which it shares with the Downtown Hotel and the Shops at Downtown. Its charming yet relaxed atmosphere is well suited to both a leisurely Sunday lunch and a fancy Saturday dinner, and also goes perfectly with the restaurant's appealing menu of creatively rendered Mexican dishes. With heavy influence from Veracruz, Campeche, and other southern states, the menu includes dishes like *ceviche verde* and hibiscus-stuffed tacos, in addition to monthly specials that showcase more unusual dishes from across the republic.

MAP 1: Isabel la Católica 30, tel. 55/5510-1316, www.azul.rest; 9am-11pm daily; Metro: Zócalo

Azul Histórico

Balcón del Zócalo $$

For many first-time visitors to Mexico City, lunching at one of the many restaurants overlooking the Zócalo is a must. While most of these touristy establishments offer lackadaisical service and overpriced steak, Balcón del Zócalo, on the top floor of the Zócalo Central hotel, offers a surprisingly nice menu of well-prepared Mexican food, a lovely plant-filled dining room, and, most importantly, a gorgeous view, overlooking the eastern wing of the cathedral.

MAP 1: Av. Cinco de Mayo 61, tel. 55/5130-5130, www.balcondelzocalo.com; 10am-10pm daily; Metro: Zócalo

Café de Tacuba $

Occupying two floors of a 17th-century mansion, this old-fashioned family restaurant has long been a keynote establishment in the Centro Histórico. The fun of eating here is enjoying the Old Mexico atmosphere in the dining room, with its tall wood-beamed ceilings, pretty frescoes, and old oil paintings. Fittingly, the kitchen serves a range of homey, traditional dishes, like chicken in *pipián* (a sauce of ground pumpkin seeds and spices), enchiladas, and *sopes* (round corn cakes topped with beans and cheese). It's also a fine spot for a *pan de dulce* and hot chocolate in the evenings.

MAP 1: Tacuba 28, tel. 55/5521-2048, www.cafedetacuba.com.mx; 8am-11pm daily; Metro: Allende

SANBORNS: A SHOPPING AND DINING INSTITUTION

One of the most opulent dining rooms in Mexico City is home to a Sanborns restaurant.

Billionaire Carlos Slim's department-store-and-restaurant chain **Sanborns** (www.sanborns.com.mx) is an institution in Mexico City, notable for its ubiquity. The restaurants all have a similar diner-like atmosphere, which is appropriate to their reasonably priced, pleasantly familiar, yet somewhat characterless menu of Mexican standards. In addition to the dining room, all locations have a separate bar, many of which feature live music in the evenings and drinks accompanied by the chain's signature salted peanuts. The atmosphere at a Sanborns bar can vary wildly; at some, a guitarist and singer might draw a large crowd for a kitschy-fun Friday night, while others may be close to empty. The most famous location, and the one most worth visiting, is located in the courtyard of the gorgeous 16th-century palace Casa de los Azulejos on the Madero in the centro histórico.

At all of the department store's locations, you'll find a good selection of electronics, cameras and camera equipment, home goods, bath and beauty products, candy, and books, as well as a well-stocked newsstand. There are also pharmacies in every location, with over-the-counter and prescription medications. In addition, there are Inbursa ATMs inside all Sanborns branches, which charge a low commission and good exchange rates (and are often a safe and private place to take out cash).

Don Toribio $

Located in an old-fashioned third-floor dining room with balconies opening onto the bustling streets below, this popular breakfast-and-lunch spot has a classic Mexico City ambience. The well-priced lunch menu, which includes soup of the day, an entrée, and a drink, is a big draw for the local crowd—come 2pm, the restaurants' tables are reliably filled with diners. You'll find a branch of the restaurant on the ground floor of the building, but it's worth huffing up three flights of stairs (or hopping in the elevator) to eat in the main dining room.

MAP 1: Simón Bolívar 31, tel. 55/5510-9198; 8:30am-6pm daily; Metro: Allende

✪ El Cardenal $$

This classic spot serves traditional Mexican dishes from across the

Café de Tacuba is an old-fashioned Mexican restaurant.

republic, in addition to seasonal specials, like chinicuiles, red maguey worms, in August, September, and October, and Valencia-style salt cod, a traditional Christmas dish, in December. With baskets of fresh breads and pitchers of hot chocolate, breakfast is a popular meal here, though you'll find many interesting options, from *moles* to Oaxacan-style chiles rellenos, on the lovely lunch and dinner menu. The original location on Palma occupies a multistory French-style mansion, but there are several other branches, including in the Hilton Mexico City Reforma (Juárez 70, Centro, tel. 55/5518-6632) and in San Ángel (Av. de la Paz 32, San Ángel, tel. 55/5616-5187).

MAP 1: Palma 23, tel. 55/5521-8815, www.elcardenal.com.mx; 8am-6:30pm Mon.-Sat., 9am-6:30pm Sun.; Metro: Zócalo

Limosneros $$

The low-lit, stone-walled dining room at Limosneros provides an elegant accompaniment to the restaurant's menu of beautifully prepared Mexican food. You'll find some unusual ingredients and preparations in dishes like rabbit *"carnitas"* or soup with *quelites* (traditional Mexican greens). It's all nicely complemented by a small-batch mezcal or glass of Mexican wine from the restaurant's well-chosen list.

MAP 1: Ignacio Allende 3, tel. 55/5521-5576, http://limosneros.com. mx; 1:30pm-10pm Mon., 1:30pm-11pm Tues.-Sat., 1pm-6pm Sun.; Metro: Allende

Paxia $$

Located on the plant-filled rooftop of the Umbral Hotel, this restaurant by well-known Mexico City restaurateur Daniel Ovadía brings creativity, care, and a touch of playfulness to every meal, from the beautifully plated dishes, like octopus with nopal, to the order of fresh salsa prepared with mortar and pestle at your table. Striking views, delicious cocktails, and gracious service make dining here a memorable experience—a good choice for a date night in the Centro Histórico.

MAP 1: Venustiano Carranza 69, tel. 55/2289-6295, https://bullandtank.com; 1pm-11:30pm Tues.-Sat., 1pm-7pm Sun.; Metro: Zócalo

Restaurante Bar Chon $

A down-to-earth eatery in the bustling Merced district, Restaurante Bar Chon has a unique menu based largely on unusual and pre-Hispanic ingredients and recipes. Come here to try crocodile meat, *venado con huitlacoche* (venison with corn fungus), and *chinicuiles* (caterpillars) among other exotic dishes. (Note that based on seasonal availability, not all the dishes on the menu may be offered.) Despite its rather scruffy location, Chon's dining room is clean and relaxed, drawing tourists and locals alike.

MAP 1: Regina 160, tel. 55/5542-0873; 11am-6pm Mon.-Sat.; Metro: Merced or Pino Suárez

Roldán 37 $$

Deep within the Merced commercial district, a pedestrian street leads to an old two-story home where chef Rómulo Mendoza's family once stored green chile peppers that were sold at city markets. Today, that home has been transformed into a lovely traditional restaurant, where Mendoza and his team serve food "from the Merced." The specialty is chiles rellenos, served in a variety of styles, including Mexico's national dish, *chiles en nogada*, during the summer and fall season.

MAP 1: Roldán 37, tel. 55/5542-1951; noon-7pm Mon.-Thurs., noon-9pm Fri.-Sat.; Metro: Pino Suárez or Merced

Sanborns de los Azulejos $

Owned by billionaire Carlos Slim, Sanborns has hundreds of locations across the city, all serving the same menu of traditional Mexican dishes. It's not uncommon to see one Sanborns directly across the street from the one you're sitting in. The restaurant's ubiquity has made it an institution in the capital, and if there's one Sanborns you should visit, it's the **Casa de los Azulejos.** Occupying the patio of a gorgeous 16th-century palace adorned with hand-painted tiles, the dining room

is perpetually packed with locals lingering over coffee.

MAP 1: Av. Madero 4, tel. 55/5512-1331, www.sanborns.com.mx; Mon.-Sat. 7am-1am, 7am-midnight Sun.; Metro: Bellas Artes or Allende

Zéfiro $$

The culinary school at the Universidad del Claustro de Sor Juana operates one of the best-known chef-training programs in the country, with a course of instruction that focuses entirely on Mexican ingredients and preparations. At Zéfiro, the school's elegant student-run restaurant, you can taste the work of the Claustro's burgeoning chefs, who design the menu and helm the kitchen. Most diners come for the weekday four-course lunch, which changes monthly and often mixes traditional and contemporary flavors.

MAP 1: San Jerónimo 24, tel. 55/5130-3385, www.ucsj.edu.mx/zefiro; 1pm-5pm Tues.-Fri., 1pm-6pm Sat.; Metro: Isabel la Católica

Café El Popular $

Chinese-owned bakeries were ubiquitous in Mexico City during the early 20th century. Owned by immigrants, these cafés originally served Chinese food and breads, but their menus gradually became more Mexican than international. Among the few survivors in this unique genre, old-fashioned Café El Popular has two locations on Cinco de Mayo—the more charming of which is the smaller spot to the east. It's a perfect place for a traditional Mexican breakfast accompanied by a *café con leche,* served in a glass tumbler at your table.

MAP 1: Cinco de Mayo 50 and 52, tel. 55/5518-6081; 24 hours daily; Metro: Allende

CANTINAS

✪ Bar La Ópera $$

This historic cantina has been in operation since 1895, and the old-fashioned interior is filled with French-inspired carved-wood panels, glittering mirrors, and globe lamps. Waiters in vests and bow ties attend to the evening crowd of locals and tourists, who come hoping to locate the bullet hole that Pancho Villa allegedly shot into the cantina's tin ceiling. Atmosphere trumps the food here, but Mexican snacks, like chorizo, guacamole, and *queso fundido* (a pot of melted cheese), are nicely done.

MAP 1: Av. Cinco de Mayo 10, tel. 55/5512-8959, www.barlaopera.com; 1pm-11:20pm Mon.-Sat., 1pm-6pm Sun.; Metro: Bellas Artes or Allende

Salón Corona $

This convivial family-owned cantina opened in 1928 and has since expanded to several locations beyond the original spot on Bolívar. It's a friendly, bustling place with good eats and cold drinks, perfect for watching a Sunday afternoon soccer game or passing an evening with beer and bar snacks, like beef tacos in *mole verde* (green *mole*) and *tortas al pastor* (chile-rubbed pork sandwiches). If the tables at the original location on Bolívar are full, there are two branches nearby, at Filomena Mata 18 and on the pedestrian street Gante.

MAP 1: Bolívar 24, tel. 55/5512-9007, www.saloncorona.com.mx; 10am-11pm Sun.-Thurs., 10am-2am Fri.-Sat.; Metro: Allende

TACOS, *TORTAS*, AND SNACKS

Los Cocuyos $

When celebrity chef and adventurous eater Anthony Bourdain came to Mexico City for his television show *No Reservations,* his hosts quickly escorted him to this long-running street stand, where the specialty is beef tacos with a "nose to tail" approach. Despite its Hollywood connections, don't expect any glamour at this sidewalk joint. Call out your order over the vats of sizzling meats, then prepare to dine standing on the sidewalk.

MAP 1: Bolívar 56, no phone; 10am-5am daily; Metro: San Juan de Letrán

SEAFOOD

Caracol del Mar $$

Located in an open-air patio dining room on the ground floor of Círculo Mexicano, this charming seafood restaurant is overseen by Gabriela Cámara, the chef and entrepreneur behind the classic Roma restaurant Contramar. Dishes like *aguachile* with Pacific shrimp or grilled octopus in a spicy salsa macha are beautifully plated and superbly delicious—and go nicely with one of the restaurant's signature cocktails. The scene is very relaxed during the week, but make a reservation for a table on the weekends.

MAP 1: República de Guatemala 20, tel. 55/5949-8304; 9am-9pm Mon.-Wed., 9am-10:30pm Thurs.-Sat., 9am-7pm Sun.; Metro: Zócalo

El Danubio $$

El Danubio is long heralded as the top seafood restaurant in the Centro, and the pride of that moniker emanates throughout the dining room, which is decorated with autographs of the famous people who have eaten here. In business since 1936, El Danubio is old-fashioned yet delicious, with a strong Spanish influence in the cuisine. House specialties, like the *sopa verde* (green seafood soup) and *langostinos* (grilled crawfish) go equally well with a glass of Rioja or a shot of tequila.

MAP 1: Uruguay 3, tel. 55/5512-0912, www.danubio.com; 1pm-7pm Mon.-Fri., 1pm-7:30pm Sat.-Sun.; Metro: San Juan de Letrán

Itacate del Mar $

The more casual sister of Caracol del Mar, Itacate del Mar has an appealing and well-priced breakfast, lunch, and dinner menu, with an emphasis on Mexican-style seafood dishes—though vegetarians and vegans will also find some good choices on offer. An excellent torta de camarón (fried shrimp sandwich), sope (round corn flatbread) topped with achiote-rubbed fish, and eggplant-and-green-*mole* tostadas are among the many delicious offerings. There are shared tables inside the relaxed high-ceilinged space, as well as sidewalk seating on the remarkably tranquil street, just behind the cathedral.

MAP 1: República de Guatemala 20, tel. 55/1920-4041, https://itacatedelmar.com; 10am-6pm daily; Metro: Zócalo

MIDDLE EASTERN
Al Andalus $

There was a large influx of Lebanese immigrants to Mexico in the early 20th century, and as a result, you'll find some fine Middle Eastern cuisine in the capital. Among the best, Al Andalus, tucked into the heart of what was once a predominantly immigrant district, is in a renovated two-story colonial house, with professional, efficient service and a menu of excellent Middle Eastern specialties, like shawarma, hummus, and *kepa bola* (a mix of wheat, ground lamb, and onion).

MAP 1: Mesones 171, tel. 55/5522-2528; 10am-6pm daily; Metro: Pino Suárez

El Ehden $

On the second floor of a large mansion, tucked between the many textile merchants of Venustiano Carranza, this off-the-beaten-track Lebanese restaurant is a clean and simple spot popular with locals for its quality and price. Stacks of warm pita accompany dishes like grilled lamb, *jocoque* (Middle Eastern-style strained yogurt), stuffed grape leaves, and other regional specialties.

MAP 1: Venustiano Carranza 148, 2nd fl., tel. 55/5542-2320; noon-6pm daily; Metro: Zócalo or Pino Suárez

SPANISH
Casino Español $$

Worth a visit for the old-world ambience alone, the Casino Español is an old-fashioned Spanish restaurant housed in a gorgeous early 20th-century mansion, with soaring ceilings, massive chandeliers, and stained-glass windows creating an opulent backdrop to the menu of

Casino Español is an old-fashioned Spanish restaurant.

delicious, traditional dishes like paella and *lechón* (suckling pig). There is a less formal café downstairs, popular for lunch with locals, but if you want the full experience, head to the more serious dining room upstairs, order a glass of Rioja, and make an afternoon of it.

MAP 1: Isabel la Católica 31, tel. 55/5521-8894, www.cassatt.mx; 8am-6pm daily; Metro: Allende

COFFEE AND SWEETS

Café Jekemir $

This popular long-running coffeehouse, which traces its roots back to the 1930s, occupies a spacious spot beside the Templo Regina Coeli, on the pedestrian street Regina. It attracts a loyal clientele of neighborhood locals, students, and newspaper-reading intellectuals. Amid the merry bustle, baristas churn out a steady stream of coffee and espresso drinks, all made from 100 percent Mexican beans, as well as a concentrated Turkish coffee.

MAP 1: Regina 7, tel. 55/5709-7086, http://cafejekemir.com; 8am-9pm Mon.-Sat.; Metro: Isabel la Católica

Churrería El Moro $

Hidden within the chaos of the Eje Central, this old-time café specializes in a classic sugar fix: churros and hot chocolate, a match-made-in-heaven combination for a rainy afternoon. Peer into the kitchen to see how churros are swirled by hand into crunchy rounds. The simple 1935-vintage atmosphere makes the experience all the sweeter: blue-and-white tiles on the walls, wood-beamed ceilings, and Formica tables provide a quintessentially Mexican backdrop for a favorite Mexican treat. In recent years, the *churrería* has expanded to several other locations, including a lovely branch in front of Parque México (Av. Michoacán 27) in the Condesa and another on the corner of Frontera and Álvaro Obregón in the Roma (Frontera 122).

MAP 1: Eje Central 42, tel. 55/5512-0896, http://elmoro. mx; 7am-11pm Mon.-Thurs., Sun., 7am-midnight Fri.-Sat.; Metro: San Juan de Letrán

Pastelería Ideal $

Opened in 1927, Pastelería Ideal is a traditional Mexican bakery specializing in *pan de dulce:* lightly sweetened rolls, pastries, buns, and empanadas that are meant to be accompanied by coffee or hot chocolate. Here, as in most old-fashioned bakeries in Mexico, you grab a tray and a set of tongs, select the bread and pastries you want from the shelves, then bring it all to the register, where they'll tally up the cost and bag it.

MAP 1: 16 de Septiembre 18, tel. 55/5130-2970, http://pasteleriaideal. com.mx; 6am-8pm daily; Metro: San Juan de Letrán

Nightlife

BARS AND LOUNGES

✪ Miralto

The famous observation deck at the top of the Torre Latinoamericana is on the building's 44th floor, but you can linger over the same breathtaking view (and a martini) at Miralto, a restaurant and bar on the 41st floor of the tower. After a recent remodel, Miralto is more stylish and bit pricier than in the past—but there's no time of day when the view is anything short of million-dollar. If you are going to the restaurant, reservations are necessary; the bar is first-come, first-served.

MAP 1: Eje Central 2, 41st fl., tel. 55/5518-1710, www.miralto.com.mx; 9am-9pm Mon.-Fri., Sun., 9am-10pm Sat.; no cover; Metro: Bellas Artes

Terraza Catedral

In the blocks around the Zócalo, there are no shortage of rooftop bars eager to sell you an overpriced margarita. This invariably low-key spot distinguishes itself with well-priced drinks and an unfussy attitude, despite boasting some truly beautiful vistas. Located on the top floor of a colonial-era building long occupied by backpacker haven Mundo Joven, it's a destination for the many young travelers staying at the hostel, though you'll also find locals and tourists from other hotels in the mix. There are often DJs at night and live jazz ensembles on Thursdays.

MAP 1: República de Guatemala 4, tel. 55/5518-1726; 1pm-11pm Mon.-Thurs., 2pm-midnight Fri.-Sat.

CANTINAS

La Faena

Set in a lovely, crumbling colonial-era building, this rather unusual bar pays homage to bullfighting: Here, ornate old matador costumes fill glass display cases around the barroom, while the old tile floors and dusty chandeliers make an oddly elegant contrast to the decidedly unpretentious plastic chairs and cantina tables that fill the space. Clientele is a varied local crowd, but don't be surprised to see a hipster or two in the mix. Cash only.

MAP 1: Venustiano Carranza 49B, tel. 55/5510-4417; noon-6pm Mon., noon-8pm Tues.-Thurs., noon-11:30pm Sat., noon-6pm Sun.; no cover; Metro: San Juan de Letrán

Salón España

This old-fashioned cantina is well-known for its extensive selection of tequila; you can order a shot from more than 150 bottles, from well-known to rare, making it one of the best bars for tequila in the city. Don't be deterred by the less-than-impressive entryway; the interior is clean, relaxed, and friendly. *Botanas* (snacks), like tacos or quesadillas, are served free with drinks, as is traditional to cantinas.

MAP 1: Luis González Obregón 25, tel. 55/5704-0014; 11am-midnight Mon.-Sat., 11am-7pm Sun.; no cover; Metro: Zócalo

NIGHTLIFE LISTINGS

It's hard to keep up with everything there is to see and do in Mexico City, but a few websites and periodicals can help you navigate the onslaught of movies, art openings, museum shows, concerts, and sporting events taking place across the city. There are a plethora of blogs and crowd-sourced websites covering food and culture in the city, but the following well-established publications are a reliable resource to stay up-to-date on the city's cultural life.

TIME OUT MEXICO

The international magazine *Time Out* (www.timeoutmexico.mx) brings its signature service journalism to the capital, covering nightlife, dining, film, art and culture, and shopping throughout the metropolis. Witty and perceptive, the print version of *Time Out Mexico* is free to readers (pick it up wherever you see a copy), though you can also download the entire edition on the website.

CHILANGO

The Mexico City-centric lifestyle magazine *Chilango* (www.chilango.com) covers upcoming events in the arts, nightlife, and dining. Its robust website also maintains extensive listings for restaurants, bars, shops, museums, and more, in every neighborhood in the city.

NEWSPAPERS

The print and online versions of Mexico City's long-running newspapers, including *El Universal* (www.eluniversal.com.mx) and *Milenio* (www.milenio.com), are good places to find news in food, art, culture, music, and literature in the capital and across Mexico, as well as sports coverage. *La Jornada* (www.jornada.com.mx) publishes news about literature, art, and anthropology in Mexico, as well as reviewing current theater, music, and film events in the city.

LIVE MUSIC

Hostería La Bota

A lively, student-friendly watering hole, Hostería La Bota is a mainstay among the small crop of bars and *mezcalerías* on the pedestrian streets Regina and San Jerónimo. Come here for poetry readings, live music and dance, and book presentations, or just to enjoy a very cold beer in a low-key environment. With its worn wooden tables covered in notes and scribbles and a barroom filled floor-to-ceiling with posters, the atmosphere is college-town cool. **MAP 1:** San Jerónimo 40, tel. 55/5709-9016; 1pm-11pm daily; no cover; Metro: Isabel la Católica

Zinco Jazz Club

This cosmopolitan jazz club is known for bringing some of the best performers to the capital, from international jazz trios to home-grown brass bands. The cozy venue has a classic cabaret atmosphere, with black walls, flickering candles, and a red curtain swaying behind the stage. If you're headed to Zinco, look for the basement door in the art deco Edificio Banco de México, on the corner of Motolinia and Cinco de Mayo. **MAP 1:** Motolinia 20, tel. 55/1131-7760, http://zincojazz.com; 9pm-2am Wed.-Sat.; showtimes vary; tickets US$10-30; Metro: Bellas Artes

NIGHTCLUBS

Sunday Sunday

This ultra-popular Sunday-night dance party is held on a top-floor terrace of a high-rise just off the Zócalo. Expect big crowds and

live music and a youthful crowd at Hosteria La Bota

high-quality DJs who keep the weekend vibes rolling into Monday morning. Come early if you want to enjoy the views from the rooftop in daylight, though crowds get bigger and bigger as the night progresses.
MAP 1: Tabaqueros 16, no tel.; generally 3pm-2am Sun.; tickets at Eventbrite, $20; Metro: Zócalo

LGBTQ+

El Marrakech Salón

This upbeat, ultra-fun, straight-friendly bar is hopping in the evenings, when an eclectic crowd convenes for DJs, people-watching, and kitschy entertainment. Things heat up here on the weekends, when strippers and drag shows get started around 11pm and the dance floor rocks till closing. The friendly attitude and youthful crowd have made this gay bar one of the most popular spots on the lively strip of dance halls and cantinas on República de Cuba.
MAP 1: República de Cuba 18, no phone; 6pm-2am Thurs.-Sat.; no cover; Metro: Bellas Artes

La Purísima

If you're having a ball at El Marrakech Salón and want to take the party up a notch, cross the street to La Purísima, a clubbier spot that nonetheless retains the same friendly atmosphere as its neighbor. Disco balls and strip shows lean a bit kitschy, but the upbeat crowd makes for a great night out. After years in business, Marrakech and La Purísima remain staples in the LGBTQ+ club scene.
MAP 1: República de Cuba 17, tel. 55/5704-1995; 6pm-3am Thurs.-Sat.; no cover; Metro: Bellas Artes

NOCHE DE MUSEOS

The last Wednesday of every month, museums throughout the city stay open late, generally providing free or reduced-price admission to visitors after official closing time. Many museums go far beyond simply opening their doors to the public, planning concerts, speakers, or guided tours of the galleries after hours. Some wonderful institutions participate in the event throughout the city, but you'll cover the most ground in the area around the Alameda Central and the Centro Histórico, where a great number of museums participate, and many are within close walking distance of each other.

In recent years, there has been a Celtic music concert at the Casa de la Primera Imprenta de América, a screening of *Nosferatu* with live music at the Museo Franz Mayer, free guided tours of the Palacio de Bellas Artes, an open mike at the Colegio de San Idlefonso, a flamenco concert at the Palacio Postal, and a mime show at the Museo de El Carmen. During the pandemic lockdown, many museums began offering free cultural programs online, including film screenings and cultural talks, and many continue to do so. Follow Noche de Museos on Facebook to see some of the in-person and online offerings each month.

Arts and Culture

GALLERIES
Galería de Arte de la SHCP

The Mexican government allows working visual artists to pay a portion of their annual taxes with works of art. As a result, the Secretariat of Finance and Public Credit has amassed a rather diverse collection of work from across the republic. You can see a selection of that massive reserve at the free SHCP gallery, which is on the ground floor of a neoclassical 19th-century mansion, just behind the cathedral. Exhibits change frequently and include varied but generally high-quality painting and sculpture.

MAP 1: Guatemala 8, tel. 55/3688-1718; 10am-5pm daily; free; Metro: Zócalo

MUSEUMS
Casa de la Primera Imprenta de América

Nestled amid the grand palaces of Moneda, this little building was likely constructed in the early colonial era and gained national importance when it became the home of New Spain's first printing press. Today, it is a cultural center, operated by the Universidad Autónoma Metropolitana, showcasing ongoing exhibits related to books, typography, and art. It also holds a replica of the original printing press, which was brought to Mexico from Italy in 1539.

MAP 1: Licenciado Primo de Verdad 10, tel. 55/55221535; 10am-6pm Mon.-Fri., 10am-3pm Sat.-Sun.; free; Metro: Zócalo

Ex-Teresa Arte Actual

On the small side street Licenciado Verdad, a towering 17th-century baroque church has been transformed into a wholly unique gallery space dedicated to contemporary performance, video, installation, and sound art, such as a 2022 show by artist Bill Viola. Shows often have a

73

very experimental focus, which contrasts sharply with the atmosphere in the old church, originally constructed from 1678 to 1884. What was once the nave—with its wobbly, sinking floors—has been cleared to create the exhibition space. The gallery sometimes doubles as a cinema in the evening.
MAP 1: Licenciado Verdad 8, tel. 55/4122-8020 or 55/5522-2721, www.exteresa.bellasartes.gob.mx; 10am-6pm Tues.-Sun.; free; Metro: Zócalo

Ex-Teresa Arte Actual is a beautiful free museum with reliably engaging avant garde exhibits.

Foro Valparaíso

Owned and overseen by Citibanamex's cultural foundation, the massive colonial-era Palacio de los Condes de San Mateo de Valparaíso has been beautifully restored and opened to the public as a spectacular 22-room museum that showcases the bank's collection of Mexican artwork. Most rooms are dedicated to colonial-era painting—with some fascinating large-scale works depicting Mexico City in the early colonial era—though the collection includes Rufino Tamayo, Frida Kahlo, and other famous modern artists. Admission is free.

MAP 1: Venustiano Carranza 60, tel. 55/1226-4290 or 55/2262-6367, www.banamex.com/valparaiso; 10am-6pm Wed.-Sun.; free; Metro: Zócalo

Museo Archivo de la Fotografía

A fascinating stop for photography and history buffs, this small museum features rotating exhibits from its massive permanent collection of photographs of 19th- and 20th-century Mexico City. These images showcase the rapid and often miraculous transformations that took place in the capital during the previous decades. The galleries are located in the 16th-century Casa de las Ajaracas, the final structure on the street República de Guatemala. The buildings beside it were demolished in 1994 to continue excavation of the Templo Mayor archaeological site.
MAP 1: República de Guatemala 34, tel. 55/2616-7057, www.cultura.df.gob.mx/recintos/maf; 10am-6pm Tues.-Sun.; free; Metro: Zócalo

dual spiral staircases inside the opulent palace of the Foro Valparaiso

There are creative cultural exhibits and a cool roof deck at the Museo del Estanquillo.

Museo del Estanquillo

This thought-provoking museum features the artwork and photography collected by Carlos Monsiváis, a political activist, journalist, and prolific chronicler of life in Mexico City, who remains influential even after his 2010 death. The museum organizes rotating thematic shows dedicated to Mexican art and culture. There are also permanent exhibits showcasing the writer's personal collection of sketches, photos, advertisements, comics, and photos.
MAP 1: Isabel la Católica 26, tel. 55/5521-3052, ext. 101, www. museodelestanquillo.cdmx.gob.mx; 10am-6pm Wed.-Mon.; free; Metro: Allende

THEATER, CLASSICAL MUSIC, AND DANCE
Teatro de la Ciudad de México, Esperanza Iris

Designed to resemble La Scala in Milan, the Teatro de la Ciudad was constructed in the early 20th century by actress Esperanza Iris. After its inauguration, it was the top performance venue in the city, though its audience declined after the opening of the Palacio de Bellas Artes in the 1930s. Today, it hosts performances from a range of disciplines, from flamenco to circus acts.
MAP 1: Donceles 36, tel. 55/5510-2197; US$10-50, depending on seats; Metro: Allende

Festivals and Events

SEPTEMBER
Día de la Independencia

Mexico celebrates its 1810 independence from Spanish rule on September 16. In Mexico City, the president of the republic appears on the balcony in the Palacio Nacional at 11pm on September 15, reenacting independence hero Miguel Hidalgo's cry for independence, "Viva México!"—also known as El Grito—to a crowd of thousands in the Zócalo below. There is a massive military parade through the Centro and along the Paseo de la Reforma the following day. In 2017, the parade featured the military's troupe of trained search-and-rescue dogs, who would become world famous just a few days later, in the aftermath of the earthquake on September 19, 2017, when they helped assist rescue efforts.

Centro Histórico: Plaza de la Constitución; Sept. 15-16

DECEMBER
Ice-Skating in the Zócalo

In what has now become a holiday tradition, the municipal government installs a giant ice-skating rink (over 600 square meters!) and a sledding hill in the Zócalo every December. Skate rentals and skating are free with a valid identification. Not surprisingly, there can be a wait of several hours on busy days. If you do get out on the ice, you'll

ice-skating in the Zócalo

glide below the famous facades of the Palacio Nacional and the Metropolitan Cathedral. Whether you brave the lines or not, it's a quirky celebratory event right in the heart of the city.

MAP 1: The Zócalo, Plaza de la Constitución, bordered by Madero, Moneda, 16 de Septiembre, Corregidora, 5 de Febrero, República de Brasil, and Pino Suárez; 10am-10pm daily early Dec.-mid Jan; free; Metro: Zócalo

Recreation

SPECTATOR SPORTS
LUCHA LIBRE
Arena Coliseo

This popular wrestling arena is more rough-and-tumble than the larger and more well-known Arena México, and a trip here is definitely an adventure. The audience is a bit rowdy, but foreign visitors will feel safe, as long as they sit well back from the ring to avoid flying bodies and chairs. Use precaution coming and going from the stadium, especially after dark.

MAP 1: República de Perú 77, tel. 55/5588-0266, www.cmll.com; matches usually Tues. and Fri. evenings, Sun. afternoon; US$18; Metro: Garibaldi

Shops

ANTIQUES AND COLLECTIBLES
Nacional Monte de Piedad

Housed in a colonial-era building right on the Zócalo, this massive nonprofit pawnshop offers fixed low-interest loans to the needy in exchange for pawned household items. In times of economic crisis, people line the surrounding blocks waiting to put their personal possessions, from watches to blenders, in hock for a loan. You'll mostly find jewelry, gemstones, watches, and smartphones for sale in the second-floor shop, including some antique pieces.

Right on the Zócalo, Montes de Piedad is a government-run pawn shop located in a beautiful colonial-era palace.

77

MAP 1: Monte de Piedad 7,
tel. 55/5278-1700 or 55/5278-1800,
www.montepiedad.com.mx;
8:30am-5:45pm Mon.- Sat.;
Metro: Zócalo

CLOTHING, SHOES, AND ACCESSORIES
✪ Remigio

Owned by one of Mexico's most well-known textile merchants, this wonderful shop sells fine handmade clothing and fabrics from the southern state of Oaxaca. Here, old painted chests and wooden shelves are piled with gorgeous handloomed textiles, meticulously embroidered blouses, colorful cotton *huipiles* (a traditional tunic from Oaxaca), and elegantly simple plant-dyed fabrics. The work here is high quality and original, with upscale prices to match.

MAP 1: Isabel la Católica 30-7, 2nd fl.,
tel. 55/4552-9471; 11am-7pm Mon.-Sat.,
2pm-7pm (sometimes closed) Sun.;
Metro: Zócalo

Sombreros Tardan

This quality hat shop has been in business right on the Zócalo since 1847. Though it originally began as an import shop, it was later bought by the Tardan family, who developed their own line of felt and wool hats during the early 20th century. Even today, Tardan remains among the best hatmakers in Mexico. Come here to browse the nice selection of men's sombreros, which run from beanies to cotton caps to Panama hats.

MAP 1: Plaza de la Constitución 7, tel.
55/5512-3902, www.tardan.com.mx;
10am-7pm Mon.-Sat.; Metro: Zócalo

DESIGN AND GIFT SHOPS
MUMEDI Shop

The shop inside the Museo Mexicano de Diseño (MUMEDI) was not added as an afterthought; rather it is a principal element in the museum's mission to promote Mexican design and contains even more of the interesting work as in the adjoining gallery space. A great place to pick up a unique gift or souvenir, MUMEDI stocks graphic tees, jewelry, toys, ceramics, wallets, handbags, and other curiosities, of which about 80 percent were designed by Mexican artists.

MAP 1: Madero 74, tel. 55/5510-8609,
www.mumedi.mx; 9am-8pm daily;
Metro: Zócalo

GOURMET FOOD AND IMPORTS
✪ Dulcería de Celaya

This old-fashioned sweet shop is a feast for the eyes as well as the taste buds: Its 19th-century interior is

Dulcería de Celaya

filled with gilded moldings, mirrored walls, and glimmering display cases packed with handmade candies. If you aren't familiar with Mexican sweets, this old shop is a great place to start, though it sets the bar high—it's been in business since 1874, so the recipes have been perfected. Try the excellent coconut-stuffed limes; crystallized fruit, like figs, sweet potatoes, and *acitrón* (cactus); or lightly sweetened, fluffy meringues.

MAP 1: Cinco de Mayo 39, tel. 55/5521-1787; 10:30am-7:30pm daily; Metro: Allende

PUBLIC MARKETS
Mercado Sonora

Just south of the Mercado de la Merced, the interesting Mercado Sonora sells traditional goods for home and kitchen and, most famously, supplies for healing and witchcraft. Some stands are dedicated to herbs and traditional remedies, while others sell esoteric items, like amulets, candles, and colored stones. As is common in many markets in Mexico, animals are on sale in back, including dogs, cats, hamsters, snakes, and rabbits, as well as, unfortunately, exotic species, like rare birds and parrots.

MAP 1: Av. Fray Servando Teresa de Mier 419, tel. 55/1931-1931, www.mercadosonora.com.mx; 8am-5pm daily; Metro: Merced

SHOPPING CENTERS
The Shops at Downtown

Located within the same colonial-era palace as the stylish Downtown Hotel, this small yet elegant shopping center is dedicated to Mexican-made products and Mexican-owned retail. With shops selling everything from chic clothing and specialty chocolate to high-end artisanal crafts to mezcal, this shopping center is a great place to browse for a gift—and its historic breezeways are wonderful for wandering on a warm afternoon.

MAP 1: Isabel la Católica 30, tel. 55/5521-2098, http://theshops.mx; 11am-9pm daily, individual shop hours vary; Metro: Zócalo

Alameda Central   Map 2

On the western edge of the Centro Histórico, the Alameda Central is the oldest park in Mexico City. Always bustling with activity, it is home to one of the most important arts institutions in the capital, the **Palacio de Bellas Artes,** and in the surrounding blocks, there are many fine **colonial-era churches** and excellent museums, including the **Laboratorio de Arte Alameda** and the **Museo de Arte Popular.** The **San Juan** neighborhood, to the south, is known for its top-notch **street food** and excellent **traditional market.** To the north, the fascinating archaeological site in **Tlatelolco** is adjoined by a contemporary cultural center run by the **Universidad Nacional Autónoma de México.**

TOP SIGHTS

- Cultural Heart of the Capital: **Palacio de Bellas Artes** (page 84)

TOP NIGHTLIFE

- Quintessential Cantina: **Tío Pepe** (page 95)
- Best Hidden *Mezcalería:* **Bósforo** (page 95)
- Freshest Pulque: **Pulquería Las Duelistas** (page 95)

TOP ARTS AND CULTURE

- Top Stop for Photography Buffs: **Centro de la Imagen** (page 97)
- Best Celebration of Craft: **Museo de Arte Popular** (page 99)
- Most Memorable Evening: **Ballet Folklórico at the Palacio de Bellas Artes** (page 101)

TOP RECREATION

- Campiest Good Time: **Lucha Libre at the Arena México** (page 101)

TOP SHOPS

- Varied Vintage Market: **La Lagunilla** (page 103)
- Most Exotic Produce: **Mercado San Juan** (page 105)

GETTING THERE AND AROUND

- Metro lines: 1, 2, 3
- Metro stops: Bellas Artes, Hidalgo, Balderas, San Juan de Letrán, Garibaldi, Tlatelolco
- Metrobús lines: 3, 4
- Metrobús stops: Hidalgo, Balderas, Plaza San Juan, Eje Central

INSET (Ins)

Plaza de las Tres Culturas 2

Zona Arqueológica Tlatelolco 3

Iglesia de Santiago Tlatelolco 5

1

4

Centro Cultural Universitario Tlatelolco

GUERRERO

Guerrero

Garibaldi

Templo San Hipólito 10

Hidalgo

TABACALERA

PUENTE DE ALVARADO

13

Plaza Santa Veracruz

14

16

17

Bellas Artes

Alameda Central 15

Palacio de Bellas Artes

18 19

ALAMEDA CENTRAL

PENSADOR MEXICANO

SEE MAP 3

11

9

12

24

25 26

27

AV JUÁREZ

29

INDEPENDENCIA

30

31

DONATO GUERRA

21

22

Juárez

Ministerio Público

23

ARTÍCULO 123

VICTORIA

San Juan de Letran

AV MORELOS

20

28

AYUNTAMIENTO

35

36

42

41

43

Plaza José María Morelos

Mercado San Juan

37 38

40

Plaza de San Juan

SAN JUAN

33

CENTRO

32

Plaza de la Ciudadela

34

39

Salto del Agua

Balderas

ARCOS DE BELÉN

44

DR RÍO DE LA LOZA

SEE MAP 5

SIGHTS

2	Ins	Plaza de las Tres Culturas	8	B4	Plaza Garibaldi	
3	Ins	Zona Arqueológica Tlatelolco	10	C2	Templo San Hipólito	
4	Ins	Centro Cultural Universitario Tlatelolco	15	C3	Alameda Central	
			18	C3	Palacio de Bellas Artes	
5	Ins	Iglesia de Santiago Tlatelolco	30	D3	Barrio Chino	
			40	E3	Plaza de San Juan	

RESTAURANTS

20	D1	Café La Habana	37	E3	Mercado San Juan
21	D2	Café 123	39	E3	Fonda Mi Lupita Mole Nupcial
25	D2	La Cervecería de Barrio	42	E3	El Huequito
28	D2	El Cuadrilátero	43	E3	El Caguamo
32	E1	Farmacía Internacional			

NIGHTLIFE

1	Ins	Salón Los Angeles	31	D3	Tío Pepe
26	D2	Bósforo	41	E3	Pulquería Las Duelistas

ARTS AND CULTURE

7	B4	Museo del Tequila y El Mezcal	16	C3	Museo Franz Mayer
9	C2	Museo Mural Diego Rivera	17	C3	Museo Nacional de la Estampa
11	C2	Laboratorio de Arte Alameda	19	C3	Palacio de Bellas Artes
13	C2	Museo Kaluz	22	D2	Teatro Metropolitán
14	C3	La Nana, Laboratorio Urbano de Arte Comprometido	27	D2	Museo de Arte Popular
			29	D3	Museo Memoria y Tolerancia
			34	E1	Centro de la Imagen

SPORTS AND ACTIVITIES

44	F1	Arena México

SHOPS

6	A4	La Lagunilla	36	E2	La Ciudadela Centro Artesanal
12	C2	Barrio Alameda	38	E3	Mercado San Juan
33	E1	Not a Gallery			
35	E1	Blue Demon Jr. Galería			

HOTELS

23	D2	Hotel Fleming	24	D2	Hilton Mexico City Reforma

0   200 yds

0   200 m

DISTANCE ACROSS MAP
Approximate: 2.1 mi or 3.3 km

© MOON.COM

Sights

✪ Palacio de Bellas Artes

The majestic Palacio de Bellas Artes (Palace of Fine Arts) is one of the city's finest buildings and a highly respected cultural institution that hosts live performances and art exhibitions overseen by the Instituto Nacional de Bellas Artes (National Institute of Fine Arts). Overseen by Italian architect Adamo Boari, construction on the palace began in 1904 but halted when the Mexican Revolution began in 1910. Twenty years later, architect Federico Mariscal took over the project, completing the rooftop cupola and the building's interiors in art deco style. In the opulent main auditorium, a stunning Tiffany glass curtain was designed by Mexican artist Dr. Atl.

During the pandemic lockdown of 2020, the famous art deco lobby of Bellas Artes closed to visitors. At press time, it was accessible via guided tour only, at 1pm and 1:30pm, Tuesday to Friday (arrive by 12:30pm to secure a spot), though it will likely reopen to general admission as pandemic restrictions ease. Until then, the two on-site museums are the best way to see the building's interior.

On the second and third floors, the Museo del Palacio de Bellas Artes (tel. 55/10004622, ext. 2132

the Palacio de Bellas Artes Museum

a sunny day on the Alameda Central

or 2112, http://museopalaciodebellasartes.gob.mx, 10am-6pm Tues.-Sun., $4) has hosted some of the most important art shows of the past decade, including a 2007 Frida Kahlo retrospective. Admission includes access to the Palacio's many murals, which include David Alfaro Siqueiros's *Nueva Democracia* (New Democracy) on the second level. On another wall, Diego Rivera's 1934 *El Hombre Contralor del Universo* (known as *Man at the Crossroads* in English) was originally commissioned by Nelson Rockefeller, though, famously, the American business magnate canceled the project when Rivera included a likeness of Lenin in the piece. On the top floor, the Museo Nacional de Arquitectura exhibits building floor plans, photos, and other archived memorabilia related to Mexico City's historic buildings.

MAP 2: Corner of Av. Juárez and Eje Central, tel. 55/5512-2593, www.palacio.bellasartes.gob.mx; 10am-9pm Tues.-Sun.; free to enter the lobby, US$4 admission to museum and mezzanine level; Metro: Bellas Artes

Alameda Central

Just west of Bellas Artes, the Alameda Central is the largest green space in the center of the city and the oldest public park in the Americas. Today, it is a tree-filled respite from the bustle of the Centro Histórico—despite being flanked by major avenues on all sides and serviced by two Metro stations and two Metrobús stops.

Inaugurated in the 16th century, the original Alameda was filled with poplars, or *alamos*—hence, the park's name. Throughout the centuries, it evolved from an exclusive strolling park to a bustling family-oriented destination. The Alameda's popular spirit was celebrated by

85

Diego Rivera in his famous work *Dream of a Sunday Afternoon on the Alameda Central,* located in the **Museo Mural Diego Rivera** on the west end of the park. The most prominent of the Alameda's many fountains and neoclassical statues is the **Hemiciclo de Benito Juárez,** a semicircle of eight marble columns facing Avenida Juárez on the south. Due to the monument's continual defacement by political protestors, it is often blocked off from public access.

MAP 2: Bordered by Juárez, Hidalgo, Eje Central, and Paseo de la Reforma; Metro: Bellas Artes or Hidalgo

Barrio Chino

Established in the 1960s, Mexico City's tiny two-block Chinatown doesn't reflect the full influence of Chinese immigration to the city, which surged in the late 19th and early 20th centuries. Even so, it is a fun and atmospheric street to stroll along, checking out the bevy of economical Chinese restaurants serving chop suey and street vendors selling Mexican-Chinese hybrid snacks, like steamed buns filled with Nutella or passion fruit.

Mexico City's small but atmospheric Chinatown

MAP 2: Dolores street between Juárez and Victoria; 24 hours; free; Metro: Bellas Artes or San Juan de Letrán, Metrobús: Juárez

Plaza de San Juan

In the bustling neighborhood four blocks south of the Alameda, this small plaza is closely associated with the El Buen Tono cigarette company, which once adjoined it. Founded by Frenchman Ernesto Pugibet in the late 19th century, El Buen Tono grew rapidly—eventually manufacturing 3.5 billion cigarettes per year—and the plant, employee housing, and warehouses overtook the neighborhood. Though much of the industrial complex has since been razed, there are vestiges of its presence: The adjoining artisan market, for example, was once part of the tobacco factory warehouses.

On the west side of the plaza, the pretty but often overlooked church of **Nuestra Señora de Guadalupe del Buen Tono** (once the site of the chapel of the old San Juan convent, which was established in the early colonial era) was constructed by Pugibet for factory workers, and it was designed by well-known Mexican architect Miguel Ángel de Quevedo.

MAP 2: Buen Tono and Ayuntamiento; 24 hours daily; free; Metro: Salto de Agua or San Juan de Letrán

Templo San Hipólito

This church, on the corner of Hidalgo and Zarco, is said to have been founded by Hernán Cortés in remembrance of the Noche Triste, on June 30, 1520, when Cortés's forces fled the city of Tenochtitlan, resulting in major Spanish

Plaza Pugibet in the San Juan neighborhood

casualties. In 1559, the Spanish constructed a church on this site, right at the beginning of the causeway leaving the island and, for the following centuries, the outer limits of the city. The church was repeatedly rebuilt over the centuries, with much of the building dating to the 1730s. Today, the church is dedicated to Jude the Apostle, and on the 28th of every month, a special mass is celebrated in the saint's honor.

MAP 2: Zarco 12, tel. 55/5510-4796; 8am-9pm daily; free; Metro: Hidalgo

Plaza Garibaldi

In early 20th-century Mexico City, Plaza Garibaldi was a fashionable nightlife destination, filled with cabarets and nightclubs. It has since lost much of its madcap splendor, but it remains a vibrant part of the city, coming to life on the weekends as dozens of mariachi bands roam the square, playing tunes to the crowds of revelers. (If you'd like to commission a song, ask the price and pick a tune. Expect to pay $10-20 per song.)

Many tourists and locals come to Garibaldi after a few tequilas to visit the many bars and *pulquerías* that ring the square, the most notable of which is Salon Tenampa (Plaza Garibaldi 12, tel. 55/5526-6176, www.salontenampa.com; 2pm-2am daily), the legendary mariachi bar that first opened in Garibaldi in 1925.

Though a 2012 renovation made Garibaldi safer, there is a history of crime in the area, and some bars along the plaza make a business of cheating tourists. Stick to the Tenampa or other recommended establishments, and never wander on the backstreets around Garibaldi after dark.

MAP 2: Eje Central at República de Honduras; Metro: Garibaldi

Plaza de las Tres Culturas

Several blocks north of the Plaza Garibaldi, the Plaza de las Tres Culturas (Plaza of the Three Cultures) in Tlatelolco is surrounded by symbols of three distinct periods of Mexican history: the remains of the pre-Columbian city of Tlatelolco, the 16th-century Iglesia de Santiago Tlatelolco, and several modern buildings, including the tower housing the Secretaría de Relaciones Exteriores and a 1960s-era apartment complex designed by famous Mexican architect Mario Pani.

Tlatelolco was a Mexica city-state, sister to the great Tenochtitlan. Here, after months of battle, Cortés and his men finally conquered the Mexica and their leader Cuauhtémoc. The event is commemorated with a plaque in the middle of the Plaza de las

Tres Culturas, with a famous inscription: "Heroically defended by Cuauhtémoc, Tlatelolco fell to the power of Hernán Cortés. It was neither a triumph nor a defeat. It was the painful birth of the mestizo nation that is the Mexico of today."
MAP 2: Eje Central Lázaro Cárdenas and Ricardo Flores Magón; 24 hours; free; Metro: Tlatelolco

Zona Arqueológica Tlatelolco
A sister city-state to the Mexica capital of Tenochtitlan, Tlatelolco was founded in 1337 and became a major settlement in the Valley of Mexico, home to the largest and most important market in Mesoamerica. It was here that the Mexica leaders fled after withstanding months of siege by the Spanish forces in Tenochtitlan. On August 13, 1521,

the Mexica people were at last defeated by Cortés and his forces on this site.

The Spanish forces destroyed most of the city of Tlatelolco and constructed a church atop the remains of the city—as in the Zócalo, the first church was likely built using rubble from the destroyed pyramids. The site was excavated in 1944 and again from 1960 to 1968, uncovering both pre-Columbian and colonial-era artifacts. Today, the surprisingly extensive and nicely maintained site reveals the foundations of religious and ceremonial buildings from the former city, including the Templo Mayor of Tlatelolco. The temple to Ehécatl-Quetzalcóatl is an interesting half-round, half-rectangular structure, where a late

the remains of the pre-Columbian city of Tlatelolco, in the modern neighborhood of the same name

1980s excavation recovered the remains of 41 people and more than 50 offerings. The smaller Templo Calendárico displays 13 glyphs from the Mesoamerican calendar carved into each of its four facades.

As part of your visit to the archaeological site, stop into the free and fascinating Museo de Sitio Caja de Agua (55/5583-0295, 8:30am-2pm Mon.-Fri., weekends by appointment; free), the remains of an early colonial-era water basin that was painted with murals that unite pre-Columbian and Spanish visual elements, including eagles, jaguars, and a cross with the monogram INRI.

MAP 2: Corner of Eje Central Lázaro Cárdenas and Ricardo Flores Magón, tel. 55/5583-0295, www.tlatelolco. inah.gob.mx; 8am-3pm daily; free; Metro: Tlatelolco, Metrobús: Glorieta Cuitláhuac

Centro Cultural Universitario Tlatelolco

Centro Cultural Universitario Tlatelolco

Next to the Tlatelolco archaeological site in the Plaza de las Tres Culturas, this expansive cultural center is run by the Universidad Nacional Aútonoma de México (UNAM). The centerpiece of the museum is the Memorial de 68, which is dedicated to the legacy of October 2, 1968, the day on which several hundred student protesters were massacred in the Plaza de Tres Culturas by Mexican military (*guardias presidenciales*) just before the start of the Mexico City Olympics. The museum also hosts a range of interesting temporary exhibits and art shows, many thematically related to Tlatelolco and its history, as well as a wide range of workshops and cultural events.

MAP 2: Ricardo Flores Magón 1, tel. 55/5117-2818, http://ccutlatelolco.com; 11am-7pm Wed.-Sun.; US$2; Metro: Garibaldi or Tlatelolco

Iglesia de Santiago Tlatelolco

Immediately following the Spanish conquest of Mexico, Cortés ordered the building of a church in Tlatelolco, the site of the last stand and fall of the Mexica people. Likely constructed using the stones of the Templo Mayor of Tlatelolco, which the Spanish razed, the church was rebuilt several times during the early years of the colonies. The current structure, made largely of the tezontle volcanic stone that was also used in the pyramids, dates from 1610. The adjoining convent and its pretty central garden are now overseen by the Secretaría de Relaciones Exteriores (SRE) and also open to the public.

MAP 2: Plaza de las Tres Culturas, Eje Central Lázaro Cárdenas and Ricardo Flores Magón; free; Metro: Tlatelolco, Metrobús: Glorieta Cuitláhuac

Restaurants

PRICE KEY

$	Entrées less than $10
$ $	Entrées $10-20
$ $ $	Entrées more than $20

MEXICAN

Café La Habana $

This spacious old coffeehouse has long been frequented by journalists working at the periodicals headquartered nearby. It's a wonderful spot to enjoy a traditional breakfast amid the rustling of newspapers and the whirl of ceiling fans, accompanied by one of the café's signature dark-roast drinks, which are prepared on an impressive old-fashioned, hand-pulled espresso machine. Adding to the café's legend, it is rumored Che Guevara and Fidel Castro planned the Cuban Revolution here.

MAP 2: Morelos 62, tel. 55/5535-2620; 7am-midnight Mon.-Sat., 8am-midnight Sun.; Metro: Juárez, Metrobús: Juárez

Fonda Mi Lupita Mole Nupcial $

Nestled between chicken vendors and pancita joints in the San Juan neighborhood, this tiny eatery specializes in a richly spiced *mole* that is native to the state of Mexico. You can pick the cut of chicken—pechuga (breast), alon (wing), cabeza (head), etc.—that will be served with the *mole,* or order it in enchiladas or *tortas* with chicken or cheese. They also have daily *mole* specials, such as an unusual pistachio *mole,* which, like the namesake *mole nupcial,* make for a filling and economical meal.

MAP 2: Buen Tono 22 (entrance on Delicias), tel. 55/5521-1962; 1pm-6pm daily; Metro: Balderas, Metrobús: Balderas

Fonda Mi Lupita Mole Nupcial is a simple spot that specializes in mole.

TACOS, *TORTAS,* AND SNACKS

El Caguamo $

A small street stand rarely gets as much press as El Caguamo, but once you sit down at this little seafood-only *puesto,* it becomes clear why it's been the subject of so much food-blog chatter. Though it's a small operation, the food here is deliciously prepared and incredibly fresh, drawing locals for ceviche-topped tostadas, deep-fried seafood quesadillas, and shrimp cocktails. Grab a bar-stool and order from the friendly cooks; they'll pass you a cup of shrimp-broth soup, gratis.

MAP 2: Ayuntamiento and López, no phone; 11am-6pm daily; Metro: San Juan de Letrán

El Cuadrilátero $

This popular neighborhood *tortería* is owned by former pro wrestler Super Astro, and the shop is decorated with *lucha libre* masks, posters, and other memorabilia from his career. The signature dish is La Gladiador, a 1.3-kilo *torta* stacked with egg, six kinds of meats, and cheese. Those who finish it in 15 minutes get the whole sandwich for free. Fortunately, any *torta* here will satisfy your appetite; try the *pierna adobado* (chile-rubbed pork), which is prepared in-house.

MAP 2: Luis Moya 73, tel. 55/5510-2856; 8am-7pm Mon.-Fri., 8am-8pm Sat.; Metro: San Juan de Letrán

El Huequito $

Tacos al pastor are emblematic of the capital, and every taqueria has its own secret recipe (and every local a favorite spot to get them). At El Huequito, which opened in 1959, you won't find the typical chile-rubbed *pastor,* but rather spit-roasted pork tacos that are doused in salsa and rolled into small tortillas. You can order a plate of tacos on the street, where the original stand is still in operation, or head to the larger branch on Bolívar (Bolívar 58, tel. 55/5510-4199), where *pastor* is served alongside rib, pork, chicken, and beef tacos.

MAP 2: Ayuntamiento 21, tel. 55/5518-3313, www.elhuequito.com.mx; 8am-10pm daily; Metro: San Juan de Letrán

CAFÉS
Café 123 $

Though just a few blocks from many prime tourist attractions, the western blocks of the street Articulo 123 feel rather rough and abandoned. It's a surprising setting for this quirky café and furniture shop, with its appealing menu, much of it Asian-inspired soups, noodles, and rice dishes, along with pastries and espresso drinks. In pleasant complement to its urban surroundings, the atmosphere is eclectic industrial-chic, principally attracting a young coffeehouse crowd.

MAP 2: Articulo 123, tel. 55/5512-1772, articulo123.com; noon-6:30pm Mon.-Thurs., noon-7:30pm Fri.-Sun.; Metro: Hidalgo or Juárez

Farmacía Internacional $

On the ground floor of a soaring multifamily apartment complex on the busy thoroughfare Bucareli, this all-day café has a cozy-cool

The quirky-cool atmosphere at Farmacía Internacional is ideal for weekend brunch.

STREET SNACKS

Mexico City has a fondness for tacos, *tortas,* and other *garnachas* (simple snacks). These quick bites are one of the most distinctive aspects of the capital's food scene.

TLACOYOS

What: Handmade torpedo-shaped corn cakes are stuffed with beans, cheese, garbanzo paste, or *chicharrón* (pork rind), grilled until crunchy, then topped with nopal, cheese, onions, and salsa.
When: Morning to midafternoon.
Where: On street corners throughout the Centro Histórico and San Juan; outside the **Mercado de Medellín** (page 203); at **El Parnita** (page 177) in the Roma.

a black-bean-stuffed tlacoyo topped with nopales and cheese

TORTAS

What: These sandwiches are made on a *telera* (flat white roll with a thin crust) and served with *chiles en vinagre* (pickled jalapeños). The *telera* is brushed with refried beans and piled with meat, lettuce, tomato, and avocado. Popular fillings include *milanesa* (pounded, breaded beef) and eggs with chorizo. Vegetarians can order *tortas* filled with avocado, cheese, eggs, or beans.
When: Breakfast, lunch, and dinner.
Where: Outside Metro stops; on street corners throughout the city; **El Cuadrilátero** (page 91); **La Barraca Valenciana** (page 234); **Tortas Don Polo** (page 215).

TORTA DE CHILAQUIL

What: A *telera* or *bolillo* (a soft white roll) is stuffed with *chilaquiles* (fried tortillas doused in red or green salsa), then accompanied with chicken, pork, or beef.
When: Breakfast.
Where: At **La Esquina del Chilaquil** (page 181).

PAMBAZOS

What: These popular sandwiches are made from a white roll (also called a *pambazo*) dipped in a mild guajillo chile sauce, stuffed with cooked potatoes and chorizo, and garnished with sour cream and lettuce.
When: All hours.
Where: At street stalls in *tianguis* (open-air markets) throughout the city; as an appetizer at **Café de Tacuba** (page 63); meat-free at **Mictlan Antojitos Veganos** (page 212); made with Yucatec-style pulled pork at **Fonda 99.99** (page 210).

PLÁTANOS MACHOS

What: *Plátanos machos* (plantains) and *camotes* (sweet potatoes) are baked over mesquite coals, imparting a smoky flavor to these sweet, starchy treats. They are served with sweetened condensed milk and cinnamon.

When: Early evening.

Where: Vendors roam central neighborhoods at dusk; listen for their distinctive low-pitched whistle.

TAMALES AND *ATOLE*

What: Tamales in *hoja de maiz* (corn husk) or *hoja de plátano* (banana leaf) are prepared as a breakfast food, often accompanied by *atole*, a warm, sweetened corn-based drink flavored with chocolate, rice, strawberry, amaranth, or guava, or served natural and lightly sweetened.

When: Early mornings and dinnertime.

Where: **La Ventanita de Ticuchi** (page 150) in Polanco; **Tamales Madre** (page 120) in the Juárez; **Tamales Doña Emi** (page 181) in the Roma; at corner stands in the mornings; from bicycles and outside traditional Mexican bakeries at night; outside churches on Sunday mornings.

TORTA DE TAMAL

What: A stick-to-your-ribs variation on the typical *tamal* for breakfast, this is a *tamal* in a corn husk, stuffed between a sliced *bolillo* (white-bread roll).

When: Early morning.

Where: Morning street-corner tamale vendors are the only place you'll find them.

ELOTES AND *ESQUITES*

What: *Elotes* are boiled ears of corn served on a stick, slathered in mayonnaise and sprinkled with chile powder, salt, and cheese. *Esquites* are loose corn kernels, sometimes cooked with the herb *epazote*, served in a small cup then topped with mayonnaise, cheese, chile powder, and lime juice.

When: Nighttime.

Where: Public squares, parks, outside churches and convenience stores; **Peltre Lonchería** (page 212); **Eno** (page 149); **Molino El Pujol** (page 180).

Elotes and esquites are sold on streets throughout the city.

QUESADILLAS

What: Hand-pressed corn tortillas are stuffed with cheese and fillings, cooked on a griddle, or deep-fried in oil or lard. *Flor de calabaza* (squash flower), hongos (mushrooms), and *huitlacoche* (corn fungus) are a few of the popular guisados (fillings) for quesadillas. Note that in Mexico City quesadillas may only be filled with a *guisado* unless you specify that you'd like it *con queso* (with cheese).

When: Afternoon and evening.

Where: Parks and street corners; almost any restaurant.

Mercado San Juan

ambience, with exposed brick walls and vintage tile floors. The appealing breakfast menu is short but hits all the right notes, with well-made dishes like avocado toast, vegetarian quiche, and soft-boiled eggs with asparagus, and the coffee bar is excellent. Expect a hip local crowd and a wait on weekends.

MAP 2: Bucareli 128-F, https://f-i.com. mx; 8:30am-8:30pm Mon.-Fri., 9am-5pm Sat.-Sun.; Metro: Cuauhtémoc or Balderas, Metrobús: Balderas

MARKETS
Mercado San Juan $

The San Juan Market is best known for its high-quality and unusual fish,

meats, produce, and cheeses, but it is also a great place to nosh. Head to the market's famous cheesemongers, where you can order Spanish-style tapas, baguette sandwiches, or charcuterie and cheese plates; they'll even pour you a small glass of Spanish wine on the house. The most famous is La Jersey (Local 147), but most cheese shops offer the same lunch specials.

MAP 2: Ernesto Pugibet 21, between Luis Moya and Buen Tono, no phone; 7am-5pm daily; Metro: San Juan de Letrán

Nightlife

CANTINAS
⊕ Tío Pepe

Located in the Centro's small and quirky Barrio Chino (Chinatown), Tío Pepe is a wonderful old cantina that maintains a worn but grand early 20th-century atmosphere with its polished dark-wood bar, turquoise walls, and gold molding along the ceilings. Come early in the evening to sip tequila at one of the cozy booths with red-Formica-topped tables, as a friendly, relaxed crowd fills up the space. Sometimes roving musicians will arrive, enlivening the atmosphere.

MAP 2: Independencia 26, tel. 55/5521-9136; noon-10pm Mon.-Fri., noon-11pm Sat.; no cover; Metro: Bellas Artes

TEQUILA AND MEZCAL
⊕ Bósforo

An unmarked bar a few blocks south of the Alameda Central, Bósforo's specialty is small-batch mezcal from Oaxaca and the greater republic. Bartenders can recommend a drink from the often-changing list, and shots are served with orange wedges and salt, as is traditional. Hidden behind metal doors but often crowded on the weekends, the bar has a great soundtrack and a pleasingly clandestine, locals-in-the-know atmosphere.

MAP 2: Luis Moya 31, tel. 55/5512-1991; 4pm-1:30am Wed., 4pm-2:30am Thurs.-Sat.; no cover; Metro: Bellas Artes

PULQUERÍAS
⊕ Pulquería Las Duelistas

Las Duelistas is one of the oldest traditional *pulquerías* in Mexico City, but you'd never guess it from the predominantly young clientele, who bring a bit of punk-rock vibe to the joint. It's a friendly, convivial place, and the *curados* are delicious, made fresh daily and served ice-cold, in flavors like celery or guava. Like most traditional *pulquerías*, it opens early—and sometimes runs out of drinks before the 9pm closing.

MAP 2: Aranda 28, tel. 55/13940-958; 10am-9pm Mon.-Sat.; no cover; Metro: San Juan de Letrán

LIVE MUSIC AND DANCING
Salón Los Angeles

This old-fashioned dance hall's proud motto is *"Quién no conoce Los Angeles, no conoce México"* (Who doesn't know Los Angeles, doesn't know Mexico). Celebrating 85 years in operation in 2022, the ballroom is a mainstay in the capital's dance scene. Here, top-quality live bands play *son cubano, danzón,* rumba, swing, and *cumbia,* among other tropical sounds, while well-dressed couples dance with purpose. The neighborhood is rough, so come and go by taxi or Uber. It is only open Tuesdays and Saturdays.

MAP 2: Lerdo 206, Col. Guerrero, tel. 55/5597-5181 or 55/5597-8847, http://salonlosangeles.mx; 5pm-10pm Tues., 5pm-11pm Sat.; cover US$5-10; Metro: Garibaldi

PULQUE: ANCIENT DRINK WITH A NEW LIFE

A fizzy, lightly alcoholic, and highly nutritious drink called pulque, made from the sap of the maguey, was produced by the native people of Mesoamerica. The drink was considered sacred by the Mexica, who had strict rules regarding its consumption. After the Spanish conquest, the drink became more widely available, and by the 19th century, there were *pulquerías* in every neighborhood of Mexico City. As beer became more popular, pulque began to lose its popularity, and, over time, only a few of the old pulquerías remained open.

Pulquería Las Duelistas is one of the oldest and best pulquerías in the city.

Pulque must be kept cold and consumed within a few days—and the fresher it is, the better it tastes. There is no commercial production. Most traditional *pulquerías* open midmorning and close by late afternoon (or whenever the pulque runs out). With its viscous and fizzy texture, milky color, and notably sweet yet fermented flavor, pulque is an acquired taste for some. It can be drunk in its natural state, though it is more popular in *curados*, flavored with fruit pulp or nuts and sweetened with honey or cane sugar.

Today, pulque is experiencing a revival as new generations recognize this unique and delicious drink. Some of the oldest surviving *pulquerías* have begun to attract new clientele, while nouveau *pulquerías* have opened in the Roma and Condesa neighborhoods.

Following are some of the *pulquerías*, bars, and restaurants, both new and historic, that serve pulque in Mexico City.

- **Pulquería Las Duelistas** (page 95) is an excellent old-school *pulquería*, popular with a young crowd. In the Santa María la Ribera, **La Joya** (page 126) is one of the longest-running *pulquerías* in the city and an ultra-low-key spot. In these traditional spots, pulque is usually served in large mugs and very inexpensive, costing as little as $3-4 per liter.

- **El Hidalguense** (page 177), a wonderful family-style restaurant, serves *aguamiel (a nonalcoholic drink made from fresh maguey sap)*, ultra-fresh pulque, and a range of *curados* made with fresh fruit.

- While traditional *pulquerías* open during the day, you can drink pulque at night at **La Nuclear Pulquería** (page 194) in the Colonia Roma.

- Pick up a sweet *pan de pulque* (a bread made with pulque) at **Panadería Rosetta** (page 190).

Arts and Culture

CONCERT VENUES

Teatro Metropólitan

Originally built as a cinema in the 1940s, this famous old theater was revamped as a concert venue in the 1980s. You may recognize the building from a scene in director Alfonso Cuarón's movie Roma. Despite its cool art deco facade, its interior is neoclassical, including giant classical sculptures in the orchestra pit. Located just a few blocks from the Alameda, it generally puts on rock en español and Latin music, along with some international groups. You can purchase tickets through Ticketmaster.

MAP 2: Av. Independencia 90, tel. 55/5510-2197 or 55/5130-5741; showtimes generally between 6pm and 9pm; US$5-15 depending on performer and seats; Metro: Hidalgo

MUSEUMS

✪ Centro de la Imagen

After a three-year-long renovation, this breathtaking public photography gallery reopened in October 2015 with expanded exhibition spaces, projection rooms, and a changing outdoor "photo mural." The center offers frequent workshops and special events, while ongoing exhibits focus on both contemporary work and the history of photography. It's worth visiting the space just to see the architectural creativity of the galleries, built inside a renovated 18th-century cigarette factory, and the exhibits are reliably high quality.

MAP 2: Plaza de la Ciudadela 2, tel. 55/4155-0850, centrodelaimagen. cultura.gob.mx; 11am-6pm Wed.-Sun.; free; Metro: Balderas, Metrobús: Juárez

Laboratorio de Arte Alameda

Mexico City's penchant for combining avant-garde ideas and old-fashioned spaces is beautifully manifested in the Laboratorio de Arte Alameda. Housed in the former convent of San Diego, right on the Alameda Central, this contemporary art museum's usually excellent exhibitions explore the relationship between art and technology. As such, there is often a heavy emphasis on video and electronic art, with many works conceived specifically for the space.

MAP 2: Dr. Mora 7, tel. 55/8647-5660, https://inba.gob.mx/recinto/32; 11am-5pm Tues.-Sun.; US$2; students, teachers, and seniors free; general admission free Sun.; Metro: Hidalgo, Metrobús: Hidalgo

La Nana, Laboratorio Urbano de Arte Comprometido

An art school and cultural center behind the Museo Franz Mayer, La Nana offers a wide range of classes for adults and children, from watercolor painting and comic illustration to sign language and circus arts—most free of charge. They also host thematic art exhibits, such as one in 2022 featuring printmaking by local artists made with experimental nontoxic ingredients. The best time to visit the space is when a new show opens. The building itself is historic, once an electricity plant and later home to the famous 20th-century dance hall Salón México.

MAP 2: Segundo Callejón San Juan de Dios 25, Col. Guerrero, tel. 55/5518-5424; 9am-7pm Mon.-Fri., 9am-1pm Sat.; free; Metro: Hidalgo, Metrobús: Hidalgo

Museo Kaluz

It's worth visiting this small museum to see the interior of the historic Hospedería de Santo Tómas de Villanueva, more recently known as the Hotel Cortés, which was constructed in the 17th century and long served as a hotel for visitors to the city. Note the beautiful baroque niche above the door, which dates from 1780. The museum, which opened in 2021, has a collection of Mexican art, historic and

There are art exhibits, community classes, and unique special events at cultural center La Nana.

contemporary; some of the most interesting pieces depict Mexico City through history. The top-floor terrace has a quiet café and nice views of the Alameda Central.

MAP 2: Hidalgo 85, tel. 55/2345-3168, https://museokaluz.org; 10am-6pm Wed.-Mon.; $5 general admission, $2 students, teachers, seniors, free Wed.; Metro: Hidalgo, Metrobús: Hidalgo

The roof deck at Museo Kaluz overlooks the Alameda Central.

✪ Museo de Arte Popular

The Museo de Arte Popular (MAP), in a five-story art deco building, is dedicated to the preservation and exhibition of Mexican folk art and craft. Unlike most craft museums, MAP isn't organized by region or chronology, but by theme, like "religion," "parties," and "daily life," with antique and contemporary pieces from a range of traditions exhibited together. Many of the pieces on display are highly original and rare, though the museum also makes space for beautiful everyday objects and more simple handicrafts. In the fifth-floor galleries, there is a wonderful 1947 mural by Mexican artist Miguel Covarrubias that was rescued from a nearby building and installed at the museum. On the second floor, the museum hosts temporary exhibitions.

MAP 2: Revillagigedo 11, entrance on Independencia, tel. 55/5510-2201, www.map.cdmx.gob.mx; 10am-6pm Tues.-Sun., until 9pm Wed.; US$3; Metro: Juárez, Metrobús: Hidalgo

Museo del Tequila y El Mezcal

This small museum chronicling the history and culture of agave distillation in Mexico opened as a part of the Plaza Garibaldi's 2010 renovation. In addition to the permanent exhibit, which includes a site-appropriate display dedicated to mariachi music, the museum hosts special events and rotating exhibits related to spirits. Your tour of the museum ends on the roof deck, where guests can enjoy a view of Plaza Garibaldi over a small complimentary shot of tequila and mezcal.

You can stay for another drink if you're enjoying the view of the plaza.

MAP 2: Plaza Garibaldi, tel. 55/5529-1238, www.mutemgaribaldi.mx; museum 2pm-9pm daily; terrace and cantina 1pm-10pm Sun.-Wed., 1pm-2am Thurs.-Sat.; US$4; Metro: Garibaldi

Museo Franz Mayer

Explore the roots of Mexican artisan and aesthetic traditions at this interesting design museum, which displays the impressive collection of German-born financier Franz Mayer, including furniture, religious artifacts, tapestries, and books dating from the 16th through the 19th centuries. In addition to Mayer's collection, the museum continues to make new acquisitions and hold ongoing shows dedicated to contemporary decorative arts. Located in the former San Juan de Dios monastery, the space itself is both historic and beautiful.

MAP 2: Av. Hidalgo 45, tel. 55/5518-2266, www.franzmayer.org.mx; 10am-5pm Tues.-Fri., 10am-6pm Sat.-Sun.; US$4, US$2 students, teachers, and seniors, general admission free on Tues.; Metro: Hidalgo, Metrobús: Hidalgo

Museo Franz Mayer

There are often moving exhibits at the educational Museo Memoria y Tolerancia.

Museo Memoria y Tolerancia

This striking modern museum, designed to promote tolerance, non-violence, and human rights, has a permanent exhibition divided into two parts: Memory, which explores 20th-century genocides, starting with the Holocaust, and Tolerance, which explores diversity, dialogue, human rights, and related themes, both in Mexico and internationally. There is a kid-centric exhibit, designed to teach unity and tolerance to school-children. Most interesting, however, are the museum's thematic exhibits, such as the artist-driven LGBT+ allá del Arcoíris in 2021 or the 2016 Yoko Ono show *Land of Hope*.

MAP 2: Plaza Juárez s/n, tel. 55/5130-5555, www.myt.org.mx; 9am-6pm Tues.-Fri., 10am-7pm Sat.-Sun.; US$4 permanent collection, US$3.25 students, teachers, and seniors, $2 temporary exhibits; Metro: Bellas Artes or Hidalgo, Metrobús: Bellas Artes or Hidalgo

Museo Mural Diego Rivera

On a corner of the Alameda Central, this petite museum is dedicated to Diego Rivera's mural *Sueño de una Tarde Dominical en la Alameda Central* (Dream of a Sunday Afternoon in the Alameda Central), which he originally created in the 1940s for architect Carlos Obregón Santacilia's Hotel del Prado on this side, which collapsed in the 1985 earthquake. The marvelously composed park scene portrays many famous Mexican personalities, including Hernán Cortés, former presidents Porfirio Díaz and Antonio López de Santa Anna, printmaker José Guadalupe Posada, and artist Frida Kahlo.

MAP 2: Corner of Balderas and Colón, tel. 55/1555-1900, ext. 5417, https://inba.gob.mx/recinto/46/museo-mural-diego-rivera; 10am-5pm Tues.-Sun.; US$2; Metro: Hidalgo, Metrobús: Hidalgo

Museo Nacional de la Estampa

Printmaking has an important place in Mexican art and popular culture, and the Museo Nacional de la Estampa, or MUNAE, celebrates that tradition with ongoing exhibitions of woodcut, lithography, engraving, and other printed works by Mexican artists. The museum's collection of more than 12,000 prints includes works by David Alfaro Siqueiros and Rufino Tamayo, as well as an extensive collection of work by celebrated Mexican satirist and printmaker José Guadalupe Posada.

MAP 2: Hidalgo 39, Plaza de la Santa Veracuz, tel. 55/8647-5220, www.museonacionaldelaestampa.bellasartes.gob.mx; 10am-6pm Tues.-Sun.; US$3, free on Sun., students and teachers free daily; Metro: Bellas Artes, Metrobús: Hidalgo

THEATER, CLASSICAL MUSIC, AND DANCE
✪ Palacio de Bellas Artes

The theater inside the Palacio de Bellas Artes is the building's opulent keystone, with box seats rising along the stage, murals on the walls, and a Tiffany glass curtain onstage. The performance schedule features international music and dance, but particularly noteworthy is the **Ballet Folklórico de México de Amalia Hernández,** which performs in the theater every Tuesday and Sunday and showcases traditional dances and music from across Mexico, performed in colorful costume.

MAP 2: Eje Central and Av. Juárez, tel. 55/8647-6500, ext. 2152, 2153, or 2154, www.palacio.bellasartes.gob.mx or www.balletfolkloricodemexico.com.mx; showtimes vary; US$15-150, depending on seats and event; Metro: Bellas Artes

The Palacio de Bellas Artes is one of the city's flagship cultural institutions.

Recreation

SPECTATOR SPORTS
LUCHA LIBRE
✪ Arena México

The best place to see one of Mexico City's celebrated *lucha libre* matches is in the rowdy, upbeat Arena México. This "Catedral de la Lucha" has been in business for more than 50 years and is still going strong. It draws a mixed crowd and is a generally convivial environment, though things can get rough near the ring.

LUCHA LIBRE

Lucha libre, a campy, upbeat, and athletic style of wrestling, has been one of Mexico's most popular spectator sports since the early 20th century. *Lucha libre* resembles the massive arena shows put on by professional wrestling organizations in the United States, with dramatic choreographed performances, long-standing and contentious rivalries between wrestlers, and story lines driven by the divide between the "good guys" and the "bad guys."

masks worn by *lucha libre* wrestlers

However, *lucha libre* matches are stylistically different than what you'd find in the WWE ring, incorporating more fighters from lighter weight classes as well as a strong emphasis on acrobatics and aerial moves. The best wrestlers are excellent athletes and charismatic showmen, drawing diverse fans of every age and riling up the crowd with their performances.

HEROES OF *LUCHA*

Though the sport emerged in Mexico at the beginning of the 20th century, its popularity reached an apex during the 1950s, when *luchadores* (wrestlers) became tremendously famous outside the ring. The most notable name from that era, silver-masked El Santo (the Saint) remains the most well-known Mexican wrestler to this day. El Santo and other big stars—like Blue Demon, Mil Máscaras, and, later, Blue Demon Jr. and El Santo's son (appropriately known as El Hijo de Santo)—are also beloved for their starring roles in a slew of hammy, borderline surrealist films from the 1950s and '60s, wherein famous wrestlers duke it out with mummies, vampires, and other improbable villains.

THE MASK

In the ring, the wrestlers have flamboyant alter egos, and they typically dress in flashy tights and capes. Most notably, many don a signature face-covering mask, which conceals their true identity from the public. In important matches, opponents will often bet their masks in the duel; the loser must remove his mask at the end, the ultimate sacrifice for a *luchador.* Today, wrestling masks are a popular souvenir, on sale at hip boutiques and design shops, such as the Blue Demon Jr. Galería (page 103) or at La Ciudadela Centro Artesanal (page 103).

REAL-LIFE INSPIRATION

With its populist appeal and memorable characters, *lucha libre* has even been the inspiration for a real-life activist, known as Superbarrio, who organizes protests in support of labor unions and the poor. In the capital, you can see Superbarrio's signature "SB" symbol painted onto the walls of buildings that are inhabited by squatters, indicating that Superbarrio and his allies are protecting the inhabitants from eviction.

LUCHA TODAY

Like many of Mexico's inimitable traditions, *lucha libre* is experiencing a surge in popularity today, as new stars like the wrestler Místico draw huge crowds, and a growing range of people attend arena matches. In the United States, a popular children's cartoon, *Mucha Lucha,* stars Mexican wrestlers as protagonists; some well-known Mexican wrestlers have signed with WWE; and *lucha libre* promoters are organizing events and expanding their reach within the American audience. Mexican-style *lucha libre* is also very popular in Japan, and several Japanese *luchadores* have gained widespread popularity in Mexico.

Sundays are family day and the best choice for attending a match with kids, who also get a discount on ticket prices.

MAP 2: Dr. La Vista 189, Col. Doctores, tel. 55/5588-0508, www.cmll.com; matches usually evenings Tues. and Fri., afternoon Sun.; US$10-25; Metro: Cuauhtémoc

Shops

ART, ANTIQUES, AND COLLECTIBLES

Blue Demon Jr. Galería

Lucha libre superstar Blue Demon Jr., son of the legendary wrestler Blue Demon, opened this gallery and souvenir shop just across the street from the Plaza de la Ciudadela in 2022. Wrestling masks, plush toys, T-shirts, action figures, paintings, mugs, and myriad other souvenirs created in homage to Blue Demon Jr. are on sale, as well as Blue Demon Jr.'s own artwork. Blue Demon Jr. is often in house on days when he doesn't have a fight, and he'll happily sign any merchandise you pick up—and even pose for a photo.

MAP 2: Emilio Dondé 7, tel. 55/5444-1813; 10:30am-6:30pm Mon.-Sun.; Metro: Balderas, Metrobús: Balderas

✪ La Lagunilla

The popular La Lagunilla flea market sets up along the Paseo de la Reforma every Sunday, just outside the La Lagunilla covered market, spilling onto a few side streets heading east into Tepito. It's an interesting place to wander for an hour or two, browsing the piles of old books, silverware, luggage, curios, movie posters, vinyls, antique furniture, art, tin toys, old photographs, vintage jewelry, and other unique items for sale. Get there early for the best selection.

MAP 2: Several blocks along and east of Paseo de la Reforma at the corner of Eje 1 Norte; 9am-5pm Sun.; Metro: Garibaldi

Not a Gallery

A roster of talented tattoo artists work out of this spacious multidisciplinary space on Bucareli. You can make an appointment to get inked, or drop by to see the art they are showing in this clean white-walled, high-ceilinged space. The focus is on contemporary work by local artists and often includes interesting pieces at accessible price points. They also host popular music events.

MAP 2: Bucareli 120, tel. 56/2440-3056; 11am-6pm Tues.-Sun., tattoos by appointment; Metro: Balderas, Metrobús: Balderas

ARTS AND CRAFTS

La Ciudadela Centro Artesanal

La Ciudadela is a sprawling open-air craft market where over 300 vendors sell handmade products from across the country. Prices here are incredibly reasonable, and the selection is extensive, covering many of Mexico's major craft traditions, from Tlaquepaque's colorful ceramics and Pueblan blue-and-white Talavera to wooden utensils, woven

PUBLIC MARKETS

Often atmospheric and interesting, neighborhood markets are among the best places to shop for fruits and vegetables, dairy, meat, and tortillas. Many have a well-known specialty, like delicious seafood stands or a large selection of flowers and piñatas.

- If you only have time to visit one market, there is none more emblematic of the city than the immense and atmospheric **Mercado de la Merced** (page 52) on the edge of the Centro Histórico. Right next to the Merced, the **Mercado Sonora** (page 79) is best known for its offbeat, esoteric offerings, like medicinal herbs, healing candles, witchcraft products, and live animals.

Mercado San Juan

- Much smaller than the Merced but equally authentic, the **Mercado San Juan** (page 105) in the old San Juan neighborhood is known throughout the city for its unusual selection of meats and produce, like quail eggs, tropical fruits, alligator steaks, toasted grasshoppers, and other delicacies. It's also a great place for snack.

- For traditional fruits, vegetables, tortillas, Mexican crafts, souvenirs, and lots of eateries serving seafood and tostadas, **Mercado Coyoacán** (page 237) in central Coyoacán is an atmospheric popular destination for both tourists and locals.

- For an on-the-ground perspective on Mexico City's food economy, head to the **Central de Abasto de la Ciudad de México** (page 272), a wholesale market that supplies 80 percent of the capital's edibles. There is nothing you won't find here, from potatoes to crabmeat, and the sheer size is astonishing.

Mercado San Juan

an array of colorful hand-embroidered textiles for sale at the Mercado de Artesanías La Ciudadela

baskets, shawls, and musical instruments. Take your time browsing the selection, as quality varies tremendously by vendor.

MAP 2: Plaza de la Ciudadela 1 and 5, tel. 55/5510-1828, http://laciudadela.com.mx; 10am-8pm Tues.-Sat., 10am-4pm Sun.; Metro: Balderas; Metrobús: Balderas

PUBLIC MARKETS
✪ Mercado San Juan

The San Juan market is known for its exotic produce, unusual meats (from crocodile to iguana), fresh fish, and abundance of gourmet and imported products. It's a great place to shop for food to take home, like *mole* sauce and vanilla beans, or to pick up something unusual, like starfruit or razor clams. It's small but densely packed, so wander around to see what's on offer; many vendors will offer you a taste of what they're selling.

MAP 2: Ernesto Pugibet, between Luis Moya and Plaza de San Juan; 7am-5pm daily, individual vendor hours vary; Metro: San Juan de Letrán

SHOPPING CENTERS
Barrio Alameda

A 1920 art deco building right on the Alameda Central has been beautifully restored and reopened as Barrio Alameda, a shopping and culinary center. The vendors have changed frequently since the plaza opened, but you'll always find an interesting mix of art, design, music, and clothing shops, as well as coffee, pizzas, and ice creams, on three separate floors surrounding a central atrium. Note that there is no elevator in the building.

MAP 2: Dr. Mora 9, tel. 55/5512-3810, www.barrioalameda.com; 11am-1am daily, individual shop hours vary; Metro: Hidalgo, Metrobús: Hidalgo

Paseo de la Reforma   Map 3

The Paseo de la Reforma is a monument-studded avenue lined with banks, high-rise office buildings, and **luxury hotels.** In the 19th century, as the *centro histórico* became more crowded, wealthy families began building European-style houses in the uninhabited land on either side of this grand avenue. Among these were the **San Rafael** and **Santa María la Ribera** neighborhoods to the north of Reforma and the **Juárez** to the south. Today, all three are interesting urban areas with an engaging mix of old and new: auto shops, taco stands, and old coffee joints continue to operate alongside boutiques, contemporary art galleries, and museums, including the avant-garde

Museo Universitario del Chopo in the Santa María. Crossing Insurgentes to the west, the Cuauhtémoc neighborhood is a pretty residential area that has long been inhabited by foreigners, especially those coming to work or do business at the **U.S. Embassy.**

TOP SIGHTS
- Marvelous Art Deco Memorial: **Monumento a la Revolución Mexicana** (page 116)

TOP RESTAURANTS
- Best Bread and Coffee: **Café Nin** (page 123)
- Sweetest Spot: **La Especial de Paris** (page 125)

TOP NIGHTLIFE
- Best Nouveau Cantina: **Salón Ríos** (page 126)

TOP ARTS AND CULTURE
- Interesting Alt Museum: **Museo Universitario del Chopo** (page 129)

TOP RECREATION
- Super Sunday Morning: **Paseo Dominical** (page 132)

TOP SHOPS
- Best Browsing: **Juárez Shopping District** (page 133)

GETTING THERE AND AROUND
- Metro lines: 1, 2
- Metro stops: Insurgentes, Cuauhtémoc, Revolución, San Cosme
- Metrobús lines: 1
- Metrobús stops: Insurgentes, Hamburgo, Reforma, Revolución, Buenavista

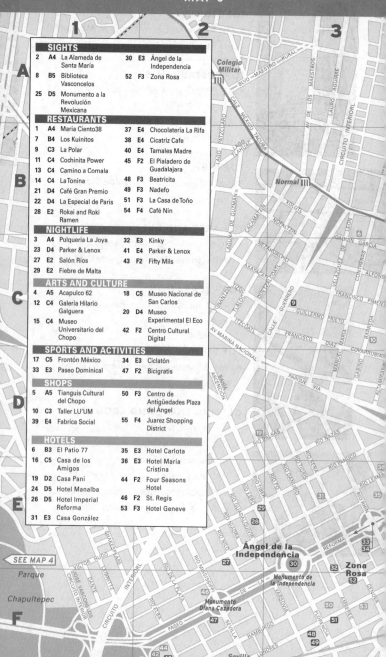

SIGHTS

2	A4	La Alameda de Santa María
8	B5	Biblioteca Vasconcelos
25	D5	Monumento a la Revolución Mexicana
30	E3	Ángel de la Independencia
52	F3	Zona Rosa

RESTAURANTS

1	A4	Maria Ciento38
7	B4	Los Kuinitos
9	C3	La Polar
11	C4	Cochinita Power
13	C4	Camino a Comala
14	C4	La Tonina
21	D4	Café Gran Premio
22	D4	La Especial de Paris
28	E2	Rokai and Roki Ramen
37	E4	Chocolatería La Rifa
38	E4	Cicatriz Cafe
40	E4	Tamales Madre
45	F2	El Pialadero de Guadalajara
48	F3	Beatricita
49	F3	Nadefo
51	F3	La Casa de Toño
54	F4	Café Nin

NIGHTLIFE

3	A4	Pulqueria La Joya
23	D4	Parker & Lenox
27	E2	Salón Ríos
29	E2	Fiebre de Malta
32	E3	Kinky
41	E4	Parker & Lenox
43	F2	Fifty Mils

ARTS AND CULTURE

4	A5	Acapulco 62
12	C4	Galería Hilario Galguera
15	C4	Museo Universitario del Chopo
18	C5	Museo Nacional de San Carlos
20	D4	Museo Experimental El Eco
42	F2	Centro Cultural Digital

SPORTS AND ACTIVITIES

17	C5	Frontón México
33	E3	Paseo Dominical
34	E3	Ciclatón
47	F2	Bicigratis

SHOPS

5	A5	Tianguis Cultural del Chopo
10	C3	Taller LU'UM
39	E4	Fabrica Social
50	F3	Centro de Antigüedades Plaza del Ángel
55	F4	Juarez Shopping District

HOTELS

6	B3	El Patio 77
16	C5	Casa de los Amigos
19	D2	Casa Pani
24	D5	Hotel Manalba
26	D5	Hotel Imperial Reforma
31	E3	Casa González
35	E3	Hotel Carlota
36	E3	Hotel María Cristina
44	F2	Four Seasons Hotel
46	F2	St. Regís
53	F3	Hotel Geneve

SEE MAP 4

4

5

6

Alameda de
Santa María

2 La Alameda
de Santa María

SANTA MARÍA
LA RIBERA

1

SALVADOR DIAZ MIRON

JOSE ANTONIO ALZATE EJE 1 NORTE

BODET

FRESNO
SABINO
NARANJO
TORRES
DR. ATL

SOR JUANA INES DE LA CRUZ

7

DR. ENRIQUE GONZALEZ MARTINEZ

DR. MARIANO AZUELA

AV. JESUS GARCIA

MARTINEZ DE LA TORRE EJE 1 NORTE

Buenavista

**Biblioteca
Vasconcelos** **8**

SATUMO

ESTRELLA

GUERRERO
LUNA

SOL

EJE 1 PTE.

ZARAGOZA
CAMELIA

HEROES

DEGOLLADO

Guerrero

MOCTEZUMA

CARLOS J. MENESES

PEDRO MORENO

MAGNOLIA

San Cosme

11

AZBALCETA

13

RIBERA DE

SANTA MARIA
LA RIBERA

DR ATL

AMADO NERVO

VIOLETA

ALDAMA

HEROES FERROCARRILEROS

MINA

14

SAN COSME

ERRERA

12

Revolución

PUENTE DE ALVARADO

18

Hidalgo

SEE MAP 2

SAN RAFAEL

AV. INSURGENTES

16

EDDISON

AV. DE LA

17

**Monumento a la
Revolución Mexicana** **25**

Plaza de la
República

REPUBLICA

REFORMA

DR MORA

Alameda
Central

AV. JUAREZ

TABACALERA

ROSAS MORENO
MIGUEL SCHULTZ
SERAPIO RENDON

21

20

22

SADI CARNOT

MAESTRO ANTONIO CASO

24

PARIS

ARQUE VIA

Jardin
del Arte

PASEO DE LA

DONATO GUERRA

Juárez

INDEPENDENCIA

AV. MORELOS

Monumento
á Colon

26

ARTICULO 123

VICTORIA

23

ATENAS

BUCARELI

AYUNTAMIENTO

Monumento
Cuauhtémoc

41

GRAL PRIM

GONZALEZ

MARTINEZ

EMILIO DONDE

PUGIBET
ERNESTO

Plaza José
María Morelos

LUCERNA
MILAN
ROMA

GINEBRA

HAMBURGO
LONDRES

37 **38**

40

VERSALLES
BERLIN

BARCELONA

ABRAHAM

DR. TOLSA

EMBIO

REVILLAGIGEDO
LUIS

ARCOS DE BELÉN

Plaza de la
Ciudadela

Balderas

AV. INSURGENTES
NAPOLES

39

LIVERPOOL
DINAMARCA

55

MARSELLA

54

Cuauhtémoc

AV. CHAPULTEPEC

DR. RAFAEL LUCIO

DR. RIO DE LA LOZA

Insurgentes

SEE MAP 5

AV. CUAUHTEMOC
EJE 1 PONIENTE

DR. CLAUDIO BERNARD

PUEBLA

DURANGO

DR. LICEAGA

0   300 yds

0   300 m

DISTANCE ACROSS MAP
Approximate: 2.7 mi or 4.3 km

© MOON.COM

PASEO DE LA REFORMA WALK

TOTAL DISTANCE: 3 kilometers (1.8 miles)
TOTAL WALKING TIME: 45 minutes

The central stretch of the Paseo de la Reforma, which runs from the Centro Histórico through the Bosque de Chapultepec, is one of the city's main thoroughfares. A **wide, old-fashioned avenue** designed to resemble the grand boulevards of Europe, it was first commissioned by Hapsburg emperor Maximilian and completed by President Porfirio Díaz at the end of the 19th century. **Fashionable neighborhoods** cropped up quickly along Reforma, and the avenue remains one of the city's most exclusive addresses.

On **Sundays,** the avenue is **closed to automobile traffic** from 8am to 2pm, so it's a wonderful time to take a stroll or rent a bike for a leisurely exploration of Reforma's many **monuments** and **public sculptures,** from the Alameda Central to the main entrance of the **Bosque de Chapultepec.**

1 Occupying the enviable address Paseo de la Reforma 1, the art deco **Edificio El Moro**—better known to many as La Lotería, the home of the national lottery—was inaugurated in 1945. This elegant skyscraper,

a fountain decorated with a statue of Diana Cazadora on the Paseo de la Reforma

with its strip of windows running up the front facade, was once the highest building in Mexico City. It suffered damage in the September 2017 earthquake, evident from the cracks in its facade, though the building remains in operation. Beside it, a statue of King Carlos of Spain originally marked the start of Reforma; it has been replaced by a giant yellow modernist interpretation of a king on horseback by sculptor Sebastián.

2 About a half-kilometer west of La Lotería, the statue of Christopher Columbus atop the **Monumento a Colón,** was finally removed in 2020 by head of government Claudia Sheinbaum following decades of protest from political activists and the sculpture's frequent defacement. Going forward, the traffic circle will honor Indigenous women, with plans to install a replica of a pre-Columbian sculpture known as **La Joven de Amajac** in the place where Colón formerly presided.

3 Walk another 500 meters west to the **Monumento a Cuauhtémoc,** which stands at the intersection of Paseo de la Reforma and Insurgentes. Cuauhtémoc was the last leader of the city of Tenochtitlan, who led the Mexica people in their final stand against the Spanish invaders in 1521 in Tlatelolco, just a few kilometers from this spot.

4 The palm tree at the center of the next traffic circle, just west of Insurgentes, grew sick and was removed, with great fanfare, in 2022, after over 100 years on the spot. (There are photographs of the palm on Reforma in 1920.) It was replaced by an *ahuehuete,* a type of cypress native to Mexico and the country's national tree. Northwest of the tree, you'll see the mirrored **Bolsa Mexicana de Valores,** the home of the Mexican stock exchange, designed by architect Juan José Díaz

Infante Núñez. This futuristic building is notable for its glassy, spherical entryway, joined by an unusual three-section skyscraper entirely covered in mirrors.

5 Halfway up the block, the **U.S. Embassy** (blocked off by giant fences since 2001) is always thronged by visa applicants waiting for appointments. At the following intersection, one of the city's most iconic landmarks, the **Ángel de la Independencia,** was erected by President Porfirio Díaz as a tribute to Mexico's independence from Spain.

6 At the westernmost *glorieta* (traffic circle) before Chapultepec, the circular fountain is topped by a **statue of the Roman goddess Diana Cazadora** (Diana the Huntress), constructed in 1942. Diana's nudity created such a scandal that the sculptor, Juan Francisco Olaguíbel, was forced to add bronze undergarments. The bronze clothing was removed in 1967, in anticipation of the Mexico City Olympics in 1968.

7 Just east of the main entrance to the Bosque de Chapultepec are four the city's five tallest skyscrapers—the **Torre Reforma,** the **Torre BBVA Bancomer,** the **Torre Mayor,** and **Chapultepec Uno,** which was completed in 2019 and is home to a new Ritz-Carlton hotel. Just outside the park's main entrance, the **Estela de la Luz** (Pillar of Light), is a 104-meter, quartz-covered tower commemorating Mexico's 2010 bicentennial of independence from Spain and the concurrent centennial of the Revolution of 1910. Its construc-

the Estela de la Luz and the Torre Mayor

tion was mired in controversy, first by going massively over budget and later for overshooting its September 2010 construction deadline by 15 months and missing the anniversary celebrations altogether. If you aren't worn out, continue your tour through the **Bosque de Chapultepec** (page 140).

SANTA MARÍA LA RIBERA WALK

TOTAL DISTANCE: 3.5 kilometers (2.2 miles)
TOTAL WALKING TIME: 1 hour

The San Rafael and the Santa María la Ribera show a different side of Mexico City. These **vibrant, working-class neighborhoods** are a bit rough around the edges, but their historic streets are emblematic of the capital's appeal, filled with **crumbling mansions, cheap eats,** and **lovely museums.** No longer off the beaten track, both neighborhoods are also home to contemporary art galleries, stylish restaurants, and cool shops.

1 Take the Metro to the San Cosme station, located on the Ribera de San Cosme, a central artery that divides the San Rafael from the Santa María. Head east along the avenue, and note the **Casa de los Mascarones** (Ribera de San Cosme 71) across Calle Naranjo from the Metro station. This gorgeous, 18th-century baroque palace now houses the national university's foreign-language institute.

2 Next, explore a bit of the San Rafael neighborhood. Walk east for two blocks on the Ribera de San Cosme, then turn right (south) onto Serapio Rendón. Emblematic of the district's faded grandeur, the **Cine Ópera** (Serapio Rendón 9) is a dilapidated art deco movie house with an impressive facade, adorned by two towering stone statues.

the abandoned beauty of the Cine Ópera

3 From the Cine Ópera, return to the Ribera de San Cosme, then walk two blocks east and turn left (north) onto Dr. Enrique González Martínez to reach the **Museo Universitario del Chopo,** one of the city's finest and most architecturally unique museums. The Gothic-inspired iron-and-glass building, constructed in Germany, originally held the city's natural history museum. Since 1975, it has been a contemporary art space operated by the Universidad Nacional Autónoma de México.

4 From El Chopo, go north one block to Calle Amado Nervo, then west one block to reach the street Dr. Atl. After going north for several blocks, you will reach **La Alameda de Santa María,** a tranquil

the stunning Moorish pavilion in La Alameda de Santa María

public square at the heart of the neighborhood. Particularly impressive is the soaring, multicolor **Moorish pavilion** at the park's center. It had several homes, including a place in the Alameda Central, before being moved to the Santa María in 1910. On the southwest corner of the plaza, **Salón Paris** (Jaime Torres Bodet 152) is an old cantina where celebrated Mexican songwriter José Alfredo Jiménez composed his first songs.

the Museo de Geología

5 Adjoining the plaza to the west, the historic **Museo de Geología** contains a woolly mammoth skeleton among other geological wonders and is housed in a 19th-century mansion commissioned by Porfirio Díaz.

6 Go one block south to Salvador Díaz Mirón, then walk a few blocks east to Insurgentes, where you can hop the Metrobús south at Buenavista. Before departing, take a turn around the **Biblioteca Vasconcelos,** just beside the Buenavista train station. The library is a breathtaking public space, with unique floating bookshelves surrounding a central atrium.

Biblioteca Vasconcelos

Sights

✪ Monumento a la Revolución Mexicana

Mexico City's monument to the Revolution of 1910 wasn't originally designed as a war memorial: the towering dome was built during the first phase of construction on a luxurious, neoclassical congressional building, commissioned by President Porfirio Díaz in the early 20th century. When the Revolution of 1910 broke out, the project was abandoned.

In 1933, Carlos Obregón Santacilia took over the project. He completed the volcanic-stone facade and added art deco finishes to each of the four corners, working with sculptor Oliverio Martínez. Crypts in the monument's feet hold the remains of Revolution heroes Venustiano Carranza, Francisco I. Madero, Francisco "Pancho" Villa, Plutarco Elias Calles, and Lázaro Cárdenas.

Leading up to the centennial of the Revolution, in 2010, the monument and surrounding plaza received a full renovation, which included the addition of a glass elevator that ascends from the ground floor to the monument's dome, where visitors can stroll beneath the vaulted roof, with a view of the city below.

The basement-level Museo

The Monumento a la Revolución was built in commemoration of the Mexican Revolution of 1910.

Nacional de la Revolución (9am-5pm Mon.-Fri., 9am-7pm Sat.-Sun., tel. 55/5566-1902) opened as a part of the renovation project. The permanent exhibit chronicles the major events and philosophies that drove different factions to action during the Revolution of 1910, as well as a few period artifacts, like Pancho Villa's riding saddle and vintage guns.

MAP 3: Plaza de la República s/n, between Vallarta and Gomez Farías, tel. 55/5592-2038 or 55/5591-1894, www.mrm.mx; noon-8pm Mon.-Thurs., noon-10pm Fri.-Sat., 10am-8pm Sun.; complete access US$4, elevator/dome only US$3; Metro: Revolución

Biblioteca Vasconcelos

This huge, architecturally stunning public library, designed by Mexican architects Alberto Kalach and Juan Palomar, opened next to the Buenavista train station in 2006. Its unique layout features "floating" bookshelves that surround a towering central atrium, which is filled with comfortable chairs and desks for reading. Hanging from the roof in the middle of the space is the famous "whale" sculpture, *Matrix Móvil*, by artist Gabriel Orozco.

Despite the overall beauty of the project, the library was mired in controversy for both its cost and unexpected construction issues after its opening. Even so, critics cannot diminish the original design of the building, which also serves as an informal public space where locals and families roam through the stacks, take advantage of the free Internet-connected computers, or attend free concerts in the library's

interior of Biblioteca Vasconselos

auditorium. An on-site bookstore is run by Conaculta, the National Council for Culture and Arts.

MAP 3: Eje 1 Norte (Mosqueta), corner of Aldama, tel. 55/9157-2800, www.bibliotecavasconcelos.gob.mx; 9:30am-4:30pm daily; free; Metro: Buenavista, Metrobús: Buenavista

La Alameda de Santa María

The main attraction of this tranquil, tree-filled park at the center of the Santa María la Ribera neighborhood is the gorgeous, brightly colored Moorish-style kiosk in the middle of the square, made entirely of iron, which was originally constructed for Mexico's pavilion at the World's Fair in 1886. It was moved to several locations around Mexico City before

moorish kiosk in the Alameda in the Santa Maria

settling in its current location in the Santa María.

On the west side of the Alameda is UNAM's **Museo de Geología** (Jaime Torres Bodet 176, tel. 55/5547-3948 or 55/5547-3900, www.geologia.unam.mx, 10am-5pm Tues.-Sun.; US$2; closed at press time following COVID), which is housed in a beautiful old mansion. The main gallery holds a reconstructed woolly mammoth skeleton, and glass cases display the museum's collection of fossils, stones, minerals, and meteorites. The opulent building was originally commissioned by Porfirio Díaz, and some visitors are more interested in the space itself than its contents: The sweeping art nouveau wrought-iron staircase in the entryway is a highlight.

MAP 3: Between Dr. Atl and Salvador Díaz Mirón; 24 hours daily; free; Metro: Buenavista, Metrobús: Buenavista

Ángel de la Independencia

In the center of a busy traffic circle on the Paseo de la Reforma, the Ángel de la Independencia is a striking 36-meter-high column topped with a gold-plated bronze angel. It was inaugurated by President Porfirio Díaz on September 16, 1910, to commemorate the country's centennial of independence from Spain. One of the city's most recognizable landmarks, it is the site of frequent political rallies and spontaneous street celebrations whenever Mexico's national soccer team pulls off a victory. And, like many Mexican monuments, it's had its share of drama: In 1957, the bronze

The Zona Rosa was once the city's poshest district.

angel toppled from its perch during a major earthquake.

When crossing Reforma to the monument, use caution—there are no official crosswalks, and traffic flows from all four directions. Within the column's base, a small passageway contains three niches, which store the remains of 12 heroes from the independence struggle.

MAP 3: Paseo de la Reforma and Florencia; free; Metro: Insurgentes

Zona Rosa

Though its beautiful Porfiriato-era mansions were built in the 19th century, the Zona Rosa became a famous bohemian enclave in the mid-20th century, eventually becoming the most fashionable arts and nightlife district in the city. Once a must-see for any visitor to the city, today it's less appealing, filled with fast-food restaurants, loud nightclubs, and currency exchange houses. That said, there are still some nice hotels and good eats in the area, and it is famous for its LGBTQ+-friendly attitude, with gay nightlife concentrated on the street Amberes.

MAP 3: Bordered by the Paseo de la Reforma to the north, Av. Chapultepec to the south, Insurgentes to the east, and Florencia to the west

Restaurants

PRICE KEY

$	Entrées less than $10
$ $	Entrées $10-20
$ $ $	Entrées more than $20

MEXICAN

Beatricita $

At the turn of the 20th century, a taco shop owned by Beatriz Muciño Reyes—nicknamed "La Beatricita"—was all the rage in the capital. The taqueria proliferated throughout the city, and though most branches have since closed, the Beatricita in the Zona Rosa maintains the legacy. Now a small *fonda*, Beatricita offers tasty, inexpensive breakfast and lunch, served with a basket of handmade tortillas, which come to the table so hot you can barely hold them.

MAP 3: Londres 190D, tel. 55/5511-4213; 10am-5pm daily; Metro: Insurgentes

La Casa de Toño $

Inexpensive and centrally located, La Casa de Toño is a mainstay in the Zona Rosa and throughout the city, best known for its generously served pozole, a Mexican hominy soup garnished with onion, oregano, radishes, and lettuce—though you can also get a plate of enchiladas, flautas, tostadas, or guacamole at this super-casual spot. The restaurant is frequently packed, even in the off-hours, but a wait is guaranteed at weekend brunch.

MAP 3: Londres 144, tel. 55/5386-1125, http://lacasadetono.com.mx; 8am-11pm daily; Metro: Insurgentes, Metrobús: Insurgentes

GOODBYE, COLUMBUS

the traffic circle that was dedicated to Columbus will now honor Indigenous women

Commissioned in the 19th century by short-lived Mexican monarch Emperor Maximiliano de Hapsburg, the Paseo de la Reforma is a wide tree-filled boulevard, originally designed to resemble the grand avenues of Europe. Today, it is a well-known landmark and an important cross-city artery, running from the Lomas to Chapultepec to the shrine of the Virgen de Guadalupe at La Villa. Along its central section, the avenue is a bit of an open-air museum, dotted with tributes and statues to historic figures and events. Highly symbolic, these monuments are often sites of protest and gathering, particularly at the **Ángel de la Independencia,** where crowds gather to celebrate a victory in a soccer game or protest the rise in oil prices.

For many years, the **Monumento a Colón** was among the most prominent statues on the Paseo de la Reforma. Conservative president Antonio Escandón commissioned the statue, which showed Christopher Columbus surrounded by the figures of three

El Pialadero de Guadalajara $

On the western edge of the Juárez neighborhood near Chapultepec, this always-bustling family-style restaurant serves food from the state of Jalisco, including an outstanding *carne en su jugo* (a beef stew typical to Guadalajara), *birria* (goat stew), and pozole, a hominy soup with spiced broth, served with oregano, diced onion, radishes, and cabbage. The service is lickety-split and the atmosphere is thoroughly Mexican, with framed portraits of horses on the walls, drinks served in big clay jugs, and traditional wood-and-leather furniture.

MAP 3: Hamburgo 332,
tel. 55/5211-7708, www.
elpialaderodeguadalajara.mx;
10am-9pm Mon.-Fri., 9am-9pm
Sat.-Sun.; Metro: Chapultepec

Tamales Madre $

Tamales, a staple of Mexican cuisine, are given star treatment at this tiny Juárez eatery. Made with heirloom corn and filled with locally

Spanish friars who helped evangelize the Western Hemisphere. It stood at a prominent traffic circle near the hotel Fiesta Americana for close to 150 years.

For decades, activist groups protested the statue's placement and the legacy it glorifies. The monument was frequently defaced, and on several occasions protestors tried to topple the statue from its pedestal, though they were stopped by city police. Calls for the statue's removal intensified in the summer of 2020, when monuments, statues, and buildings in the United States and across the world were being renamed or removed as part of a massive social justice movement.

On October 10, 2020, just two days before the October 12 holiday that commemorates Columbus's landing in the Americas (celebrated in Mexico as Día de la Raza), the city government removed the statue of Colón. It was initially announced that the figure had been removed for routine restoration; many months later, chief of government Claudia Sheinbaum revealed that the statue would not be returned to the Paseo de la Reforma. In its place, the city would install a monument to honor Indigenous women, selecting the sculpture Tlali by well-known Mexican artist Pedro Reyes to top the pedestal.

In the days following the announcement, there was a public outcry regarding the selection of Reyes, a male artist who does not identify as Indigenous, for a project intended to celebrate Indigenous women. For many, the selection exemplified the historic silencing and marginalization of women and Indigenous people. In response, Sheinbaum shifted the selection process to a Comité de Monumentos y Obras Artísticas en el Espacio Público de la Ciudad de México (the Committee for Monuments and Artistic Works in the Public Spaces of Mexico City), who later announced that the circle would display a replica of the La Joven de Amajac, a pre-Columbian sculpture from the huasteca region in Veracruz. (The original is part of the collection at the Museo de Antropología in Chapultepec.)

Not long after the announcement, a group of activists took control of the traffic circle and installed a metal silhouette of a women holding up her fist at the top of the pedestal. In memory of the many women who have disappeared or been killed in Mexico, the group unofficially christened the traffic circle "La Glorieta de las Mujeres Que Luchan" (Roundabout of the Women Who Fight). Activist groups continue to pressure the government to make the monument a memorial to the victims of femicide and violence, though, at press time, the city government is going forward with the committee's plans to install La Joven de Amajac.

sourced ingredients like cacao or plantain, they are delicate and delicious—and unlike most tamales, which are made with manteca de cerdo (pig fat), they are predominantly vegetarian. In addition to the namesake dish, there are coffee drinks, hot chocolate, delicious atole (a sweet and lightly flavored corn-based drink), and beer.

MAP 3: Calle Liverpool 44a, tel. 55/5705-3491, https://tamalesmadre. com; 10am-6pm Tues.-Sun.; Metro: Cuauhtémoc, Metrobús: Hamburgo

a view from the plant-filled sidewalk seating at Tamales Madre

The always-bustling El Pialadero de Guadalajara is a good spot for families.

La Tonina $

Opened by *lucha libre* (wrestling) star La Tonina Jackson back in 1951, this simple weekday-only eatery specializes in Sonoran-style food. You can order tacos filled with northern Mexican dishes like *machaca con huevo* (eggs scrambled with dried meat) or *frijoles maneados* (refried beans with cheese, lard, and chorizo), but the star of the show is the perfectly spiced *chilorio* (slow-cooked shredded pork), folded into freshly made flour tortillas. Finish up with a *gordita de nata*, a soft, lightly sweetened flour flatbread.

MAP 3: Serapio Rendón 13, tel. 55/5912-0366; 9am-7pm Mon.-Fri.; Metro: San Cosme

CANTINAS
La Polar $

An old-style cantina in the San Rafael neighborhood, La Polar serves what is widely considered to be Mexico City's best *birria*, a stew of shredded lamb in a spicy broth, served with tortillas, onion, salsa, and avocado. A no-frills place with a loyal clientele, the cantina is often packed with crowds of locals enjoying the music by roving *norteño* and mariachi bands, accompanied by a mug of beer on tap.

MAP 3: Guillermo Prieto 129, tel. 55/5546-5066, www.lapolar.com.mx; 7am-2am daily; Metro: San Cosme

TACOS, *TORTAS*, AND SNACKS
Cochinita Power $

Cochinita pibil, slow-cooked pulled pork seasoned with achiote and other spices, is one of the most popular dishes from Mexico's Yucatán peninsula. At this small and hip taco shop, *cochinita* gets the star treatment: It's served in tacos, in *tortas*, on top of *chilaquiles*, and as *panuchos* (round corn cakes topped with *cochinita pibil* and pickled red onion, also a specialty of the

Yucatán). As is standard, all dishes are accompanied by ultra-spicy salsa made with habanero chile.

MAP 3: Altamirano 19, tel. 55/2121-7222; noon-10pm Mon.-Fri., 10am-10pm Sat.-Sun.; Metro: San Cosme

Los Kuinitos $

At this long-running taqueria in the Santa María la Ribera, tender *carnitas* (braised pork) are chopped on a wood block right before your eyes, scooped generously into warm tortillas, topped with cilantro and diced onion, and plated with a piece of fresh *chicharrón* (deep-fried pork skin). Los Kuinitos is also famous for its savory *gorditas* (round corn cakes) stuffed with *chicharron prensado* (spiced deep-fried pork skin).

MAP 3: Sor Juana Inés de la Cruz 91-B, tel. 55/5547-6326; 10am-6pm daily; Metro: Buenavista, Metrobús: Buenavista

ASIAN
Rokai and Rokai Ramen $$$

On a quiet street in the Cuauhtémoc neighborhood, the tiny bistro Rokai has earned a reputation for serving some of the best Japanese food in the city, including sushi that is superlatively fresh and delicious. Rokai Ramen, next door to the original izakaya, offers the same excellent sushi, but the focus is on the steaming bowls of ramen, filled with tender handmade noodles. Both restaurants, equally small, have an appealing Japanese-inspired minimalist design—and both are very popular. Reserve in advance or expect a wait on weekends.

MAP 3: Río Ebro 87 and 89, tel. 55/5207-7543, WhatsApp reservations 56/3035-4220, www.edokobayashi.com; Rokai 1pm-11pm Mon.-Sat., 1pm-7pm Sun.; Ramen 1pm-11pm Mon.-Sat., 1pm-6pm Sun.; Metro: Insurgentes

Nadefo $

Once you walk through the doors of this spacious Korean spot, it's hard to believe you're still in Mexico City. Here, a predominantly Korean crowd gathers around big tables, each with a central grill, lingering late into the evening over boisterous conversation and bottles of *soju*. The thing to order here is cuts of raw meat (tongue, shrimp, and rib are all excellent), which you cook tableside and top with one of the many condiments brought out to you.

MAP 3: Liverpool 183, tel. 55/5525-0351; 12:30pm-10:30pm daily; Metro: Sevilla

INTERNATIONAL
Cicatriz Cafe $$

The menu is short and sweet at this Juárez bistro and cocktail bar, and the industrial-chic vibe inside goes well with the cool American-style fare on offer. Have ricotta toast or a chia bowl for breakfast, get a kale salad or tuna salad in the afternoon, or just drop in for a coffee or a cocktail. At night, it's as much a bar as restaurant, and worth visiting for the interesting creative crowd.

MAP 3: Dinamarca 44, tel. 55/4041-7931, www.cicatrizcafe.com; 9am-11pm daily; Metro: Insurgentes or Cuauhtémoc, Metrobús: Hamburgo

☻ Café Nin $

The perfectly made pastries, breads, and cakes from Panadería

Cafe Cicatriz is a popular place to gather for good food and drinks.

Rosetta deserve to be eaten on a pretty plate, in a gorgeous old home, and accompanied by a top-notch espresso drink. Achieving this particular breakfast-time nirvana is reason alone to visit Café Nin, the Juárez café run by Rosetta chef-owner Elena Reygadas. In addition to the breads, you can order from the full breakfast menu, which includes dishes like *chilaquiles* with *burrata* and a tomato-and-goat-cheese quiche; come in the afternoon for a sandwich or fresh-made gnocchi.

MAP 3: Havre 73, tel. 55/9155-4805, www.cafenin.com.mx; 7am-9pm daily; Metro: Insurgentes, Metrobús: Hamburgo

ITALIAN
Maria Ciento38 $

The surprisingly spacious and tranquil courtyard dining room at this Sicilian-style restaurant provides the perfect respite from the urban energy of the Santa María la Ribera neighborhood. There are traditional antipasti and homemade pastas on the menu, but the thin-crust pizza is the restaurant's best offering, served crisp and with a variety of toppings, like house-made Sicilian sausage. It's a popular weekend destination for both breakfast and lunch.

MAP 3: Santa María la Ribera 138, tel. 55/7159-2039, https://mariaciento38. com; 1pm-10pm Mon.-Wed., 10am-10pm Thurs.-Sat., 10am-8pm Sun.; Metro: Buenavista, Metrobús: Buenavista

COFFEE AND SWEETS
Café Gran Premio $

This old-timey neighborhood coffee shop is a true throwback, populated by sundry locals and seniors dressed in ties and caps. During the daytime, many patrons seem to know

Maria Ciento38 is a relaxing spot in the Santa María La Ribera.

each other (and the waitstaff) well, greeting each other as they come in and chatting casually between tables. The menu is limited to espresso drinks (made on a vintage machine), a few sweets, and tamales, but the people-watching is the most delectable part of the experience.
MAP 3: Antonio Caso 72, tel. 55/5535-0934; 8am-10pm Mon.-Sat., 9am-9pm Sun.; Metro: Revolución

Camino a Comala $

The baristas at this small San Rafael café prepare drinks with remarkable perfectionism. It's a nice spot to order a flat white or a pour-over after walking around the San Rafael or Santa María la Ribera neighborhoods. With its rustic wood tables and a couch in back, it's a low-key and relaxed atmosphere, just a block from the bustling Ribera de San Cosme.

MAP 3: Miguel E. Schultz 7, tel. 55/5592-0313; 8am-10pm Mon.-Sat., 9am-9pm Sun.; Metro: San Cosme, Metrobús: Revolución

Chocolatería La Rifa $

At this small storefront and café, native Mexican chocolate, sourced from the states of Tabasco, Chiapas, and Oaxaca, is made into candies, bars, and, most notably, beverages, both hot and cold. When ordering, you can choose between a drink prepared sweet, bittersweet, or bitter, made with hot water (as is traditional in Mexico) or milk. La Rifa also serves coffee (some spiked with chocolate, naturally) and snacks, like tamales and sweet breads, to accompany your beverage.
MAP 3: Dinamarca 47, tel. 55/9155-8551; 8:30am-9pm daily; Metro: Insurgentes

✪ La Especial de Paris

In operation since 1921, this tiny ice-cream shop is easy to overlook along traffic-choked Insurgentes, but it is the surprising home of the best old-fashioned *nieves* in Mexico City. Every flavor here is crafted by hand using natural ingredients, and options run from old-fashioned choices like Veracruz vanilla bean to more unique choices like ginger, cardamom, and cacao. Sit at the bar, order a cone, and listen to the friendly ice-cream scooper discuss the making of artisan sweets.
MAP 3: Insurgentes 117, tel. 55/9131-5937; noon-8:30pm daily; Metro: Revolución, Metrobús: Reforma

Nightlife

BARS AND LOUNGES
Fifty Mils

The upscale cocktail bar in the Four Seasons, widely reputed as serving some of the best drinks in the city, doesn't only attract the well-heeled travelers staying at this long-running luxury hotel. Amid the businesspeople and tourists, CDMX locals come to sip on chile-spiked mezcal cocktails or the bar's take on the margarita, with tequila, Aperol, and cardamom. The atmosphere matches the Four Seasons' luxe reputation, with plush couches and huge draped windows, though there is also more casual seating on the plant-filled outdoor patio.

MAP 3: Four Seasons Hotel, Paseo de la Reforma 500, tel. 55/5230-1818 or 55/5230-1616, www.fiftymils. com; noon-midnight Tues.-Sat., 6pm-midnight Sun.; Metro: Chapultepec, Metrobús: Chapultepec

Fiebre de Malta

The expansion of pandemic-era sidewalk seating gave a needed improvement to the ambience at this small taproom, and the big selection of Mexican craft beer is the reason to put it on your list. Here, you'll find more than a dozen Mexican brews on tap—often including Mexico City breweries Falling Piano, Cyprez, and Morenos—and dozens more in bottles. Beer trumps food and cocktails, so this is a good place to come before or after dinner.

MAP 3: Río Lerma 156, Cuauhtémoc, tel. 55/7589-8731, www.fiebredemalta. com; 1pm-midnight Mon.-Wed., 1pm-1am Thurs.-Sat., 1pm-11pm Sun.; Metro: Insurgentes

CANTINAS
✪ Salón Ríos

This lively bar in the Cuauhtémoc neighborhood is contemporary in feeling, yet inspired by classic cantinas. The relaxed atmosphere, attentive service, boisterous crowd, and classic bar snacks (ceviche, duck tacos) make it a lovely Friday-evening destination—as the perpetual crowds attest. The centerpiece of the bustling salon is the handsome, huge, and well-stocked wood-and-mirror bar, where tattooed bartenders serve up an endless stream of drinks, all swiftly shuttled to waiting tables.

MAP 3: Río Lerma 220, Cuauhtémoc, tel. 55/5207-5272, http://salonrios.mx; noon-2am Tues.-Sat., noon-midnight Sun.-Mon.; Metro: Chapultepec, Metrobús: El Ángel

PULQUERÍAS
Pulquería La Joya

When historic pulquería La Xochitl closed its doors in 2020, a pair of neighborhood locals continued its legacy by reopening the space as La Joya, changing the name but very little else about this genial old spot. As is traditional, pulque is the only thing on the menu, served in a range of delicious curados (pulque that is sweetened and flavored

Salón Ríos is a modern cantina with an old-fashioned charm.

with fruit or nuts). With the wonderfully laid-back vibe typical to traditional pulquerías, it remains popular with locals in the Santa María la Ribera.

MAP 3: Eligio Ancona 122, Santa María la Ribera, tel. 55/1186-9706; 11am-6pm Sun.-Mon., 11am-10pm Thurs.-Sat., Metro: Buenavista, Metrobús: Buenavista

LIVE MUSIC
Parker & Lenox

"Hidden" behind Parker—a stylish American-diner-style restaurant serving burgers and fries, among other classics—Lenox is a speakeasy jazz club with a cool old-timey design inspired by 1930s aesthetics. The period feel is furthered by nightly jazz performances, usually by high-quality local acts—and it all goes splendidly with a Negroni or an old-fashioned from the bar menu. If you're going on the weekend, it's best to reserve a table in advance.

MAP 3: Milan 14, tel. 55/5546-6979; 6pm-midnight Tues.-Sun.; $0-10; Metro: Cuauhtémoc, Metrobús: Reforma

LGBTQ+
Kinky

The reincarnation of old-time favorite Lipstick, Kinky is a place you go for a straight-up good time, with numerous DJ-directed dance floors, a karaoke stage, and an open terrace with striking views of the Paseo de la Reforma. The low cover and accessible drink prices—including beer sold by the liter—ensure a nightly crowd.

MAP 3: Amberes 1, tel. 55/5514-4920, www.kinkybar.com.mx; 9pm-3am Thurs., noon-4am Fri.-Sat.; cover US$3-4; Metro: Insurgentes

Sungay Brunch

Held once a month on Sundays, these huge daytime parties, which take place in different locations across the city, are a celebration of

127

queer culture in CDMX. You can count on excellent live DJs and a friendly, upbeat crowd. Follow @ sungaybrunch on Instagram to see upcoming events and venues, as well as a link for tickets. Parties sell out, so it's worth it to reserve in advance.

MAP 3: Locations vary; usually 1pm-midnight; $10-15

Arts and Culture

CULTURAL CENTERS
Centro Cultural Digital

Just outside the main gates to the Bosque de Chapultepec, the Centro Cultural Digital is a two-story subterranean cultural center dedicated to the intersection of technology, art, Internet, video games, and new-media disciplines. Stop in and you might find a massive sound-and-light installation in the downstairs gallery, a workshop on curating online art exhibitions, or local teenagers participating in a weekend-long video game-programming competition.

MAP 3: Paseo de la Reforma s/n, esq. Lieja, tel. 55/1000-2637, www.centroculturadigital.mx; 11am-6pm Tues.-Sun.; free; Metro: Chapultepec

GALLERIES
Acapulco 62

This contemporary art gallery occupies a gorgeous old mansion on the northeast corner of the Alameda of the Santa María la Ribera, with a street-level gallery and a second-floor space with a balcony overlooking the street. A reliable place to see interesting work, the gallery represents a range of contemporary artists, most living and working in Mexico City.

MAP 3: Dr. Atl 217, tel. 55/7822-0132, http://acapulco62.com; noon-8pm Tues.-Sun.; Metro: Buenavista, Metrobús: Buenavista

Galería Hilario Galguera

Located in a restored mansion on a quiet street in the San Rafael neighborhood, this contemporary gallery garnered international press after hosting a major show by world-famous British artist Damien Hirst in 2006. In addition to this splashy exhibition, the gallery's excellence continues, with ongoing exhibitions of both Mexican and international artists, including Jannis Kounellis, James HD Brown, and Mauricio Limón. The gallery's front door is always closed, but they are welcoming to visitors; ring the doorbell to enter.

On the ground floor of the Estela de la Luz, on the Paseo de la Reforma, is an interesting digital-arts museum.

MAP 3: Francisco Pimentel 3, Col. San Rafael, tel. 55/5546-6703, www.galeriahilariogalguera.com; 10:30am-5:30pm Mon.-Thurs., 10am-2pm Fri., by appointment Sat.; free; Metro: San Cosme, Metrobús: Plaza de República

MUSEUMS

Museo Experimental El Eco

Another of the many valuable cultural institutions overseen by the Universidad Nacional Autónoma de México, this small avant-garde museum was originally founded by German-born Mexican artist Mathias Goeritz in the mid-20th century. The space aims to be both experimental and interdisciplinary, with several large galleries with towering ceilings, a "bar area" (which doesn't function as a bar, though it looks like one), and a patio, which includes a sculptural installation by Goeritz. The ongoing temporary exhibitions include installation, video, and sound art, many of which are specifically commissioned for the space.

MAP 3: Sullivan 43, Col. San Rafael, tel. 55/5535-5186, www.eleco.unam. mx; 11am-6pm Wed.-Sun.; free; Metro: Revolución, Metrobús: Reforma

Museo Nacional de San Carlos

Housed in the opulent former palace of the Marqués de Buenavista, the Museo Nacional de San Carlos holds an impressive collection of European artwork, ranging from the 14th to the early 20th century. The collection was originally established in the 18th century at the Academia San Carlos art school and later augmented with a sizable donation from the Mexican government. The design of the palace is attributed to celebrated 18th-century Valencian architect Manuel Tolsá.

MAP 3: Av. Puente de Alvarado 50, Col. Tabacalera, tel. 55/8647-5800, www.mnsancarlos.com; 11am-5pm Wed.-Mon.; US$3; Metro: Revolución or Hidalgo, Metrobús: Plaza de la República

Museo Universitario del Chopo

✪ Museo Universitario del Chopo

The Museo Universitario del Chopo is housed in an impressive art nouveau structure, which was built in Düsseldorf and shipped to Mexico in the early 20th century. Later abandoned, the building was eventually declared a landmark, reopening as the Museo Universitario del Chopo in 1975. Featuring work by avant-garde artists, with themes addressing technology, gender identity, and other contemporary topics, the museum has a long connection to music and alternative subcultures. It helped to start the weekly album exchange that is today the famous Saturday music market **Tianguis Cultural del Chopo.**

MAP 3: Dr. Enrique González Martínez 10, Col. Santa María la Ribera, tel. 55/55352288, ext.100, or 55/5546-3471, www.chopo.unam.mx; 11am-6pm Tues.-Sun.; US$2, US$1 students, free on Wed.; Metro: San Cosme, Metrobús: El Chopo

Festivals and Events

JUNE
Marcha del Orgullo LGBTI CDMX (LGBTI Pride March)

The massively attended Marcha del Orgullo LGBTI CDMX, also known as the March del Orgullo Lésbico, Gay, Bisexual, Travesti, Transexual, Transgénero e Intersexual (LGBTTTI), takes places along the Paseo de la Reforma, usually on the same weekend as New York City's pride festivities, in remembrance of the events at Stonewall Inn. The crowd, which usually numbers over 300,000, gets as glammed up as the marchers, and the party continues late in the evening and into the next day.

MAP 3: Paseo de la Reforma, the Ángel de la Independencia to the Zócalo; end of June

OCTOBER
Desfil de Alebrijes Monumentales

Alebrijes, fantastical animal sculptures that are painted bright colors, are a handcraft typical to the state of Oaxaca. Every year, the Museo de Arte Popular near the Alameda Central hosts a parade of giant "alebrijes"—made with papier-mâché rather than the traditional carved wood—which process from the Zócalo to the Ángel de la Independencia, generally in the month of October. They remain on show along the Paseo de la Reforma for a month thereafter and make a visit to the famous avenue even more fun, especially with kids.

MAP 3: Paseo de la Reforma; fall, usually October

Recreation

PARKS

Equal Bicigratis

Nonprofit Equal Bicigratis offers free bike loans for those who'd like to pedal around the city. All you need is a valid ID (like a passport) and the bike is yours for three hours. Many visitors take advantage of the service to join the thousands of cyclists on the Paseo de la Reforma on Sundays, but there are dozens of Bicigratis kiosks in the city, operating every day but Monday, including one in the Glorieta de la Cibeles in the Roma, another in Plaza Hidalgo in central Coyoacán, and several more along the Paseo de la Reforma, at the statue of Diana Cazadora, the Estela de la Luz, and the Ángel de la Independencia.

MAP 3: Paseo de la Reforma near the Diana Cazadora, tel. 55/5574-6798; 10:30am-5:30pm Tues.-Sat., 9am-3pm Sun.; free; Metro: Auditorio, Metrobús: Auditorio

CYCLING

Ciclotón

On certain Sundays, the city closes several of its major thoroughfares to automobile traffic (in addition to the Paseo de la Reforma, as on other Sundays), allowing tens of thousands of cyclists to pedal uninhibited through the city's central districts. Hydration, medical, and bike-repair stations are set up

Sundays on the Paseo de la Reforma

BIKE MEXICO CITY

Not long ago, riding a bicycle in central Mexico City was a death-defying proposition, braved by only a few die-hard cyclists and those who had no more efficient means of getting around. Today, the city has cordoned off a network of new bike lanes throughout the central neighborhoods and, most impressive, rolled out a massive (and still growing) urban bike-share program called **Ecobici.** Now it's common to see riders of every stripe pedaling bright red Ecobici five-speeds along the Paseo de la Reforma or through the Roma on their way to work, restaurants, or the movies.

Ecobici kiosk on the Paseo de la Reforma

Annual subscriptions to Ecobici cost less than US$30, though visitors can register for a temporary membership with a valid ID (passport or resident visa) and a credit card, for about US$20 for a week or US$10 for three days. You can register online at www.ecobici.cdmx.gob.mx. Several kiosks in the center of the city also accept paperwork and issue Ecobici memberships, including a kiosk in front of the shopping center **Reforma 222**, on the Paseo de la Reforma between Havre and Nápoles.

Ecobici members can ride bicycles between stations for up to 45 minutes for no charge; if you keep your bike longer, there is about a US$2.50 charge per hour. There are Ecobici stations throughout the Roma, Condesa, Centro Histórico, Juárez, Polanco, San Rafael, Del Valle, Nápoles, and Mixcoac neighborhoods, as well as along the Paseo de la Reforma. You can find a full list of registration offices, a map of current Ecobici stations, and a map of municipal bike lanes at the official website (www.ecobici.cdmx.gob.mx).

throughout the designated route, which can run anywhere from 19 to 45 km. Check the Ciclotón's official website for the most recent news and route updates.

MAP 3: Ángel de la Independencia (Station 1), http://indeporte.cdmx.gob.mx; 8am-2pm final Sun. of each month; Metro: Sevilla

✪ Paseo Dominical Muévete en Bici

Through the city-sponsored environmental program Muévete en Bici, the first three Sundays of every month, from 8am to 2pm,

the iconic Paseo de la Reforma is closed to automobile traffic between the main entrance of the Bosque de Chapultepec and the Centro Histórico. (The street is also closed the fourth Sunday of the month, for Ciclotón.) Thousands of people come to ride along this wide and beautiful avenue, or to take advantage of the space to jog, roller-skate, walk their dog, or even hula hoop. There are often free Zumba classes at the Ángel de la Independencia, free bicycle lessons for children and adults near the statue of Diana Cazadora, and free bike-repair stations along the route. Check the program's Facebook page for information on road closures and events.

MAP 3: Paseo de la Reforma between Bosque de Chapultepec and the Alameda Central, and Avenida Juárez along the Alameda, www.semovi.cdmx. gob.mx; 8am-2pm first three Sun. of each month; Metro: Chapultepec

Frontón México

SPECTATOR SPORTS
JAI ALAI
Frontón México

Frontón México, Mexico City's jai alai stadium, reopened in 2017 after almost 20 years of abandonment. The event heralds a significant comeback for the sport (similar to the Basque game pelota), which had almost disappeared from Mexico following its glamorous heyday in the mid-20th century, when politicians and celebrities were often among the spectators. A league of top international *pelotaris* (jai alai players) have been recruited for a new generation of fans. Matches are fast-paced and fun to watch, and it's traditional to bet on the games.

MAP 3: De la República 17, tel. 55/5128-3400, http://frontonmexico. com.mx; box office 10am-6pm Mon.-Sat., 10am-4pm Sun., matches held evenings Fri.-Sun.; $5, half price on Sun.; Metro: Hidalgo, Metrobús: Plaza de la República

Shops

SHOPPING DISTRICTS
✪ Juárez Shopping District

As real estate becomes scarcer and more expensive in the adjacent Roma neighborhood, the Juárez has become a hot spot for new restaurants, bars, and boutiques. Today, the district's 19th- and 20th-century mansions are filled with new concepts and flavors, making it a lovely place for a relaxed stroll, stopping into shops and cafés as you go. There are a number of independent boutiques in the neighborhood, mostly concentrated along the streets Marsella and Havre, with some notable shops including Carla Fernández, Fábrica Social, Utilitario Mexicano, Simple by Trista, and Cihuah.

MAP 3: Havre between Liverpool and Marsella, Marsella between Niza and Berlin; Metro: Cuauhtémoc, Metrobús: Hamburgo

ANTIQUES AND COLLECTIBLES
Centro de Antigüedades Plaza del Ángel

This open-air plaza in the Zona Rosa is filled with atmospheric antiques shops. Here, you'll find furniture, paintings, art objects, silver, and decorative pieces from the 19th and mid-20th centuries, as well as a smattering of European and Asian pieces. On Saturday and Sunday, additional vendors sell jewelry, sculpture, old photographs, postcards, and other sundries in an outdoor market, where you can find everything from nicely preserved vintage to high-end antiques, laid out on rugs or on folding tables in the plaza.

MAP 3: Londres 161 and Hamburgo 150, no tel., www. antiguedadesplazadelangel.com.mx; 11am-7pm Mon.-Fri., 10am-4pm Sat., noon-5pm Sun.; market 9am-4pm Sat.-Sun.; Metro: Insurgentes

ARTS AND CRAFTS
FONART

The Fondo Nacional para el Fomento de las Artesanías (FONART) is a government trust dedicated to strengthening and promoting arts and crafts traditions throughout Mexico. As part of its mission, the organization operates several excellent craft shops, where you can buy beautiful and high-quality ceramics, textiles, furnishings, baskets, and other unique items from native communities across Mexico. The work here is excellent and well-priced, and artisans directly benefit from your purchase.

MAP 3: Paseo de la Reforma 116, tel. 55/5546-7163, www.fonart.gob. mx; 10am-7pm Mon.-Fri., 10am-4pm Sat.-Sun.; Metro: Juárez; Metrobús: Hamburgo

CLOTHING, SHOES, AND ACCESSORIES
Carla Fernández

Carla Fernández's eponymous line of men's and women's clothing is largely inspired by Mexico's traditional aesthetics. Working with artisan communities, Fernández produces elegant, contemporary dresses, blouses, pants, ponchos, and shawls that incorporate traditional details, like elaborate embroidery and handmade textiles. There is another branch in the Roma Norte (Álvaro Obregón 200, tel. 55/5264-2226; 11am-7pm daily).

MAP 3: Marsella 72, tel. 55/5511-0001, www.carlafernandez.com; 11am-7pm daily; Metro: Insurgentes, Metrobús: Hamburgo

Fábrica Social

The brightly colored clothing that swings on the racks at this small boutique unites social conscience and creativity. To create its unique apparel, this nonprofit group brings together contemporary designers and Indigenous artisans, who work together on the design and development of seasonal lines of womenswear that pair traditional techniques with a modern aesthetic. Though pricier than most traditional Mexican clothing, the styles are contemporary enough to suit more urban clients. In addition to their small Juárez storefront, there is a branch in the Condesa (Amsterdam 159; 11am-7pm daily).

MAP 3: Dinamarca 66, tel. 55/5535-3431, www.fabricasocial.org; 11am-7:30pm Mon.-Sat., 11am-7pm Sun.; Metro: Cuauhtémoc, Metrobús: Hamburgo

MAP 3: Gabino Barreda 104, tel. 55/6388-1078, www.tallerluum. com.mx; 10:30am-6pm Mon.-Fri., by appointment Sat.-Sun.; Metro: San Cosme

DESIGN
Taller LU'UM

Design collective Taller LU'UM works with traditional artisan communities to produce an original line of contemporary home goods and accessories. At this small showroom in the San Rafael neighborhood, you can see samples of their work, like hanging lamps, mobiles, bedspreads, and furnishings. In a unique twist on the traditional display, accessories are often suspended from the ceiling, rather than laid out on tables or shelves.

MUSIC
Tianguis Cultural del Chopo

Just north of the Buena Vista train station, this open-air street market was initially founded as a site of exchange for rare record collectors and music fans. Today, over 200 stands sell vinyl and CDs, band T-shirts, posters, and other punk- and music-related goods, with booths that specialize in thrash metal, rare or out-of-print titles, and bootlegs. Held on Saturday, it's always packed with a young crowd decked out in tattoos, piercings, and head-to-toe black.

MAP 3: Along Aldama, at Eje 1 Norte, in Col. Buena Vista; 10am-4pm Sat.; Metro: Buenavista; Metrobús: El Chopo

Chapultepec and Polanco Map 4

The **Bosque de Chapultepec,** a vast **urban forest,** is filled with monuments, lakes, jogging paths, and wooded glens for picnicking. It is also the site of many of the capital's most important cultural institutions, including the spectacular **Museo Nacional de Antropología,** with its enormous collection of art and artifacts from Mexico's diverse pre-Columbian cultures. To the north of the park, across the Paseo de la Reforma, posh Polanco is a destination for **fine dining, upscale hotels,** and **quality shopping,** while the **San Miguel Chapultepec,** to the park's south, is an up-and-coming **gallery district.**

TOP SIGHTS

- The Jewel of Mexico: **Museo Nacional de Antropología** (page 144)
- Most Moving Architecture: **Casa Luis Barragán** (page 147)

TOP RESTAURANTS

- Special Splurge: **Pujol** (page 148)
- Best Regional Bites: **Guzina Oaxaca** (page 149)

TOP NIGHTLIFE

- Matchless *Mezcalería*: **Ticuchi** (page 153)

TOP ARTS AND CULTURE

- Radical Reinvention: **Centro Cultural Los Pinos** (page 154)
- Most Interesting Contemporary Art: **Museo Jumex** (page 160)
- Best Ambience for Art: **Museo Tamayo** (page 161)

TOP RECREATION

- Best Saturday Stroll: **Bosque de Chapultepec** (page 162)

TOP SHOPS

- Best Local Boutique: **Lago** (page 165)
- Most Elegant Silver: **Tane** (page 167)

GETTING THERE AND AROUND

- Metro lines: 1, 7
- Metro stops: Chapultepec, Juanacatlán, Constituyentes, Polanco, Auditorio

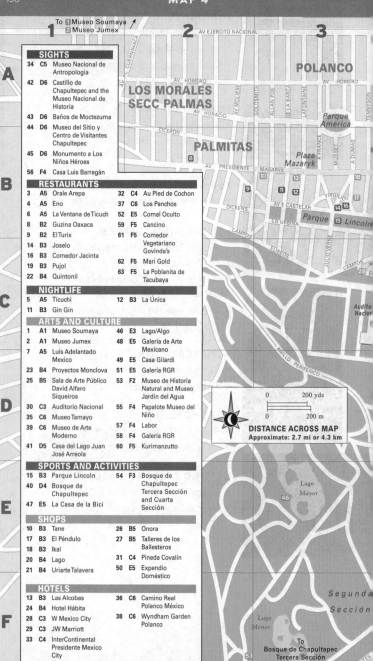

To 1 Museo Soumaya
2 Museo Jumex

AV EJERCITO NACIONAL

POLANCO

LOS MORALES
SECC PALMAS

PALMITAS

Parque
América

Plaza
Mazaryk

Parque Lincoln

Audito
Nacior

Lago
Mayor

Segunda
Sección

Lago
Menor

To
Bosque de Chapultepec
Tercera Sección
and Cuarta Sección

SIGHTS

34	C5	Museo Nacional de Antropología
42	D6	Castillo de Chapultepec and the Museo Nacional de Historia
43	D6	Baños de Moctezuma
44	D6	Museo del Sitio y Centro de Visitantes Chapultepec
45	D6	Monumento a Los Niños Héroes
56	F4	Casa Luis Barragán

RESTAURANTS

3	A5	Orale Arepa	32	C4	Au Pied de Cochon
4	A5	Eno	37	C6	Los Panchos
6	A5	La Ventana de Ticuch	52	E5	Comal Oculto
8	B2	Guzina Oaxaca	59	F5	Cancino
9	B2	El Turix	61	F5	Comedor Vegetariano Govinda's
14	B3	Joselo			
16	B3	Comedor Jacinta	62	F5	Mari Gold
19	B3	Pujol	63	F5	La Poblanita de Tacubaya
22	B4	Quintonil			

NIGHTLIFE

| 5 | A5 | Ticuchi | 12 | B3 | La Única |
| 11 | B3 | Gin Gin | | | |

ARTS AND CULTURE

1	A1	Museo Soumaya	46	E3	Lago/Algo
2	A1	Museo Jumex	48	E5	Galería de Arte Mexicano
7	A5	Luís Adelantado Mexico	49	E5	Casa Gilardi
23	B4	Proyectos Monclova	51	E5	Galería RGR
25	B5	Sala de Arte Público David Alfaro Siqueiros	53	F2	Museo de Historia Natural and Museo Jardín del Agua
30	C3	Auditorio Nacional	55	F4	Papalote Museo del Niño
35	C6	Museo Tamayo	57	F4	Labor
39	C6	Museo de Arte Moderno	58	F4	Galería RGR
41	D5	Casa del Lago Juan José Arreola	60	F5	Kurimanzutto

SPORTS AND ACTIVITIES

15	B3	Parque Lincoln	54	F3	Bosque de Chapultepec Tercera Sección and Cuarta Sección
40	D4	Bosque de Chapultepec			
47	E5	La Casa de la Bici			

SHOPS

10	B3	Tane	26	B5	Onora
17	B3	El Péndulo	27	B5	Talleres de los Ballesteros
18	B3	Ikal			
20	B4	Lago	31	C4	Pineda Covalín
21	B4	Uriarte Talavera	50	E5	Expendio Doméstico

HOTELS

13	B3	Las Alcobas	36	C6	Camino Real Polanco México
24	B4	Hotel Hábita	38	C6	Wyndham Garden Polanco
28	C3	W Mexico City			
29	C3	JW Marriott			
33	C4	InterContinental Presidente Mexico City			

| 0 | 200 yds |
| 0 | 200 m |

DISTANCE ACROSS MAP
Approximate: 2.7 mi or 4.3 km

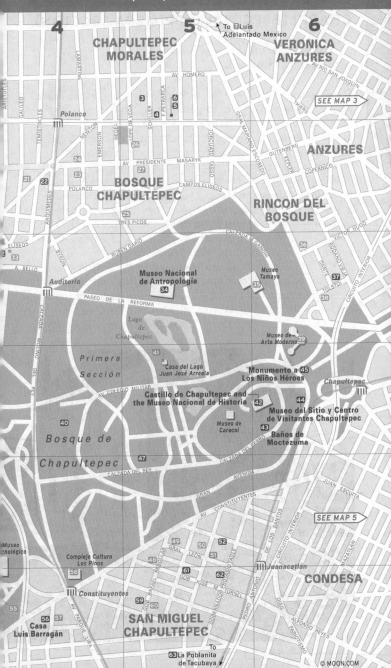

4 5 6

To **7** Luis
Adelantado Mexico

CHAPULTEPEC
MORALES

VERONICA
ANZURES

AV RÍO SAN JOAQUIN

AV HOMERO

THIERS

SEE MAP 3

3

SCHILLER

F PETRARCA

6
5

LAMARTINE

GALILEO

ARISTOTELES

TEMISTOCLES

NEWTON

EMERSON

HEGEL

LOPE DE VEGA

26

GRAL. MARIANO ESCOBEDO

GUTENBERG

KEPLER

ANZURES

Polanco

AV PRESIDENTE
MASARYK

TORCUATO TASSO

COPERNICO

27

24

23

BOSQUE
CHAPULTEPEC

CAMPOS ELISEOS

RINCON DEL
BOSQUE

21

22

ARQUIMEDES

POLANCO

25

TRES PICOS

ELISEOS

BYRON

RUBEN DARÍO

CALZADA M. GANDHI

VICTOR HUGO

33

A. BELLO

36

BODANY VELA

DANTE

CIRCUITO INTERIOR

Auditorio

Museo Nacional
de Antropología

Museo
Tamayo

37

TOLSTOI

34

35

38

CALZADA MILITAR DEL REY

PASEO DE LA REFORMA

Lago
de
Chapultepec

Museo de
Arte Moderno **39**

Primera

41

Sección

Casa del Lago
Juan José Arreola

Monumento a **45**
Los Niños Héroes

Chapultepec

AV. COLEGIO MILITAR

Castillo de Chapultepec and
the Museo Nacional de Historia

42

44

Museo del Sitio y Centro
de Visitantes Chapultepec

40

Museo de
Caracol

43

Baños de
Moctezuma

Bosque de

CALZADA DEL CERRO

47

Chapultepec

CALZADA DEL REY

AVENIDA

GRAN

JUAN ESCUTIA

AV. CONSTITUYENTES

SEE MAP 5

Museo
cnológico

49

50

52

CIRCUITO INTERIOR

MAZATLAN

Complejo Cultura
Los Pinos

GRAL. LEON

51

48

Juanacatlán

CONDESA

61

62

GOB. JOSE M. TORNEL

58

GOB. RAFAEL REBOLLAR

PEDRO ANTONIO

DIAG.

ALFONSO REYES

PANOTORNO

Constituyentes

59

60

GOBERNADOR PROTASIO TAGLE

55

56 **57**

Casa
Luis Barragán

AV PARQUE LIRA

SAN MIGUEL
CHAPULTEPEC

To
63 La Poblanita
de Tacubaya

© MOON.COM

CHAPULTEPEC WALK (PRIMERA SECCIÓN)

TOTAL DISTANCE: 3.75 kilometers (2.3 miles)
TOTAL WALKING TIME: 1.5 hours

The Bosque de Chapultepec is a beloved and expansive **urban park,** as well as a place of great history and culture. On weekdays, it's the perfect place to escape the city's chaos; the park is surprisingly quiet and relaxing. On weekends, by contrast, it's a joyous jumble of humanity, as families from across the city come to relax, party, and play soccer amid the park's many meadows and wooded groves.

Chapultepec's remarkable landscape design includes dozens of **fountains, gardens,** and **winding, wooded footpaths,** which make it a delight to explore. If you are inspired by what you find in the Primera Sección—the most accessible and most visited section of the park—consider a trip to the Segunda Sección, a large swath of parkland, filled with monuments and offbeat museums. Highlights are the unusual mural by **Diego Rivera** at the natural history museum, the colossal children's museum, and **ALGO,** a stunning art and cultural space that adjoins the long-running restaurant Lago, just beside the park's largest lake. While the remoter third section of Chapultepec is currently more difficult to access, the city is

Castillo de Chapultepec

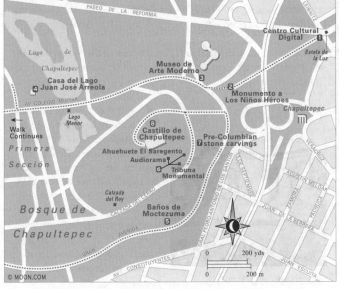

undertaking a massive renovation and expansion of Chapultepec, which will enlarge its size considerably and link the sections by footbridge and transportation.

Tip: If you want to cover more ground, consider renting a bicycle to tour the park (see Recreation for details). With wheels, you can easily visit every corner of the Primera Sección, including the carousel and the impressive Fuente a Nezahualcóyotl.

1 Chapultepec's main entrance is appropriately regal, marked by green wrought-iron gates and flanked by bronze lions, right on the Paseo de la Reforma. Before you go inside, take a moment to visit the interesting **Centro Cultural Digital,** located just below the **Estela de la Luz,** a contemporary monument commemorating Mexico's 200 years of independence. Admission is free, and the center often hosts fun, eye-catching exhibits in the two-story belowground space.

2 Once you've entered the park, the first thing you'll see is the massive six-pillar **Monumento a Los Niños Héroes,** which commemorates the six young army cadets who jumped to their death rather than surrender to the

Monumento a Los Niños Héroes

U.S. military during the 1847 American invasion of Chapultepec during the Mexican-American War.

3 Continue along the footpath past the back of the **Museo de Arte Moderno** and its pretty sculpture garden onto the pedestrian street Colegio Militar.

Casa del Lago Juan José Arreola

4 Just ahead, one of the park's artificial lakes, the **Lago de Chapultepec,** is filled with ducks and paddleboaters. On a grassy meadow beside the lake, the **Casa del Lago Juan José Arreola** is one of the city's oldest cultural centers, with workshops, artist residencies, movie screenings, and dozens of other ongoing art and cultural events—including many workshops designed for children and families.

5 As Colegio Militar loops back toward the entrance to the park (about 500 meters), look for the turnoff to the smaller footpath known as the **Calzada del Rey,** and head east. Walking about a kilometer along this wooded route, you'll pass the remains of one of the many spring-fed pools constructed by Mexica emperor Moctezuma. After years of abuse, the **Baños de Moctezuma** have been reduced to little more than a sad, sunken pool encased in concrete—but the historic value is phenomenal.

Ahuehuete El Saregento

6 About 200 meters farther ahead, you'll pass the **Tribuna Monumental,** a giant outdoor amphitheater. The **Audiorama,** in a quiet wooded grove just behind the amphitheater, is a quirky little corner of the park built in the 1970s. Here, speakers play a tasteful program of music, meant to be enjoyed on one of the many benches scattered throughout the space. Genres vary from new age to classical to traditional Mexican, depending on the day of the week. There's also a small on-site lending library, if you want to relax with

Visitors can rent paddle boats at Lago Menor.

a book. Just beside the amphitheater is one of the oldest cypress trees in the park, known as **Ahuehuete El Saregento.** Though the tree is no longer living, its trunk shows it has stood here for more than 550 years, suggesting that it may have been among the many cypresses planted by the emperor of Texcoco, Nezahualcóyotl, in the 15th century.

7 In the 15th century, Chapultepec's springs provided freshwater for the island community of Tenochtitlan via aqueduct, and it was a favorite retreat for Mexica emperor Moctezuma, who came to bathe in its pools. In 1966, excavations revealed **pre-Columbian embellishments** carved into the stones, just below the castle on the Cerro de Chapultepec. Though only fragments of these works remain intact, it's fascinating to spot these historic pieces amid the natural landscape.

8 Head up the Cerro de Chapultepec to end your walking tour at the **Castillo de Chapultepec,** a fascinating museum that offers lovely views of the greenery below.

Sights

✪ Museo Nacional de Antropología

The National Anthropology Museum is an expansive, educational, and thought-provoking museum that provides an unparalleled look into the diverse cultures of pre-Columbian and modern-day Mexico. The massive two-story space is divided into 23 exhibition rooms and filled with an astounding array of artifacts from pre-Columbian cultures in Mexico, including the Olmecs of the Gulf Coast, Teotihuacán, the post-Teotihuacán Toltecs, the Zapotecs and people of Oaxaca, the Mexica, and the Maya. Some key pieces among the collection include the colossal Olmec heads carved from giant monoliths, the carved lintel from Yaxchilan in the Maya room, and the Toltecs' towering stone warriors.

The galleries dedicated to the Valley of Mexico are the centerpiece of the museum. Here, some of the collection's most stunning artifacts are on display, including a stone sculpture of the goddess Coatlicue (originally found in Mexico City's Zócalo), a richly carved sacrificial urn called the Piedra de Tizoc, and, the museum's most famous piece, the Piedra del Sol (also called the "Aztec calendar"), which illustrates the

Museo Nacional de Antropología

20 signs and 13 numerals of the Mesoamerican calendar round.

If time allows, it's worth touring the less-visited second floor, where ethnography exhibits are dedicated to the native cultures of Mexico today, including the Huichol, Cora, Purépecha, and Otomí. There are dioramas of typical dwellings, an excellent collection of textiles and crafts, and extensive wall text in Spanish and English gives depth to the exhibits.

MAP 4: Paseo de la Reforma and Calzada Gandhi, tel. 55/4040-5300, www.mna.inah.gob.mx; 9am-5pm Tues.-Sun.; US$5, free for children under 13, teachers, seniors, people with disabilities; Metro: Chapultepec or Auditorio, Metrobús: Antropología

Baños de Moctezuma

At the southern base of the Cerro de Chapultepec, behind the Niños Héroes monument, there are remains of one of the many spring-fed pools where Mexica emperors came to bathe, later used by the Spanish as a retreat during the colonial era. Today, the baths are just an empty, sunken pool, but the history of this patch of land is phenomenal. Nearby, there are pre-Columbian carvings on the rocks around the base of the Cerro de Chapultepec, just below the castle.

MAP 4: Primera Sección, Bosque de Chapultepec, south of the castle; Metro: Chapultepec or Constituyentes, Metrobús: Chapultepec or Gandhi

Castillo de Chapultepec and the Museo Nacional de Historia

Overlooking the Paseo de la Reforma from the Cerro de Chapultepec, this opulent castle and Mexican history museum was originally built as a country house for Spanish royalty under Viceroy Bernardo de Gálvez in the late 18th century. Later, the castle was taken over by the government, serving as a military college for several decades after the War for Independence. During the 1847 U.S. Army invasion of Mexico City during the Mexican-American War, the *castillo* was the last bastion of defense. In an infamous moment in Mexican history, U.S. forces overtook the castle, raising an American flag on its roof.

During the brief rule of Maximilian I in the 1860s, the emperor made the Castillo de Chapultepec his official residence, refurbishing it with grand salons, flowered terraces, and a rooftop garden. After Maximilian and Carlota were overthrown by Benito Juárez, the castle was converted to the Mexican presidential residence. Under President Porfirio Díaz, the castle's interior reached new heights of luxury. Progressive president Lázaro Cárdenas finally dedicated the castle to becoming a public museum in 1939; it opened in 1944.

Today, the castle is home to the Museo Nacional de Historia, with a permanent collection of paintings, documents, and artifacts documenting the changing eras in Mexican national history. Equally interesting are the many rooms preserved in period furnishings. The gardens are well-tended, and the views of the Paseo de la Reforma from the terraces are postcard-worthy.

the Castillo de Chapultepec

MAP 4: Primera Sección, Bosque de Chapultepec, tel. 55/5241-3100, www.mnh.inah.gob.mx; 10am-3pm Tues.-Sat.; US$5, free for children under 13, seniors, teachers, people with disabilities; Metro: Chapultepec, Metrobús: Chapultepec

Monumento a Los Niños Héroes
At the foot of the Cerro de Chapultepec, this six-column monument commemorates the heroic defense of the Castillo de Chapultepec by six young soldiers against invading U.S. troops during the Mexican-American War. On September 13, 1847, when it was clear the Americans would take the castle, six military cadets—Juan de la Barrera, Juan Escutia, Fernando Montes de Oca, Vicente Suárez, Francisco Marquéz, and Agustín Melgar—wrapped themselves in Mexican flags and jumped to their deaths from the castle ramparts rather than surrender. Their deaths are honored by six tall columns, each topped with a black eagle. The Americans ultimately prevailed and flew their flag over Mexico City.

MAP 4: Primera Sección, Bosque de Chapultepec, east of the castle; free; Metro: Chapultepec

Museo del Sitio y Centro de Visitantes Chapultepec
The small but interesting visitor's center in the Bosque de Chapultepec chronicles the history of the park through illustrated texts and interactive exhibits that chronicle its more than 5,000 years of history and culture. You'll also find a small gift shop and public bathrooms inside the space. Just behind the Monumento a Los Niños Héroes at the main entrance to the park, this is a good place to get oriented before starting a bicycle or walking tour of Chapultepec.

MAP 4: Calzada Mahatma Gandhi s/n, tel. 55/5925-4372, www.chapultepec. org.mx; Metro: Chapultepec, Metrobús: Chapultepec

The visitor's center in Chapultepec chronicles the long history of the park and its inhabitants.

✪ Casa Luis Barragán

Luis Barragán is one of Mexico's greatest modern architects and interior designers, known for integrating a clean modernist style with an innovative use of light, bright primary colors, local building materials, and subtle Mexican vernacular elements. Born in Guadalajara in 1902, he built several residences in his hometown before relocating to Mexico City, where his most famous work was completed.

Today, Barragán's former home and studio near Tacubaya, built between 1947 and 1948, is preserved as a museum. With its interesting use of natural light and intimate, beautiful spaces, the building is representative of Barragán's work but also provides a rather touching look into the architect's life and personal aesthetics. Throughout the living quarters, Barragán's personal belongings, furniture, and art collection—which includes work by Miguel Covarrubias, Diego Rivera, and Henry Moore—are on display; you can even peek into the bathroom of the architect's monastic bedroom. In 1988, the home was named a national monument by the Mexican government, and in 2004, it was recognized as a UNESCO World Heritage Site.

Visitors must preregister for a guided tour, in English or Spanish, of the three-story space, which takes you through the entire home, including the garden, and ends in the small gallery space, which was once Barragán's studio. You can make reservations via the website, and note that you must buy a photo permit for about US$30 if you want to take photos, even on a phone. On your way out, the small bookshop at the entrance has a lovely selection of books on design and architecture.
MAP 4: Av. General Francisco Ramírez 12-14, Tacubaya, tel. 55/5515-4908 or 55/5272-4945, www.casaluisbarragan. org; open via guided tours by appointment only, 11am-5pm Mon.-Fri., 11am-2pm Sat.-Sun., US$25, students US$10; Metro: Constituyentes

Restaurants

PRICE KEY

$	Entrées less than $10
$ $	Entrées $10-25
$ $ $	Entrées more than $25

MEXICAN

✪ Pujol $$$

No restaurant has had more influence on 21st-century Mexico City cuisine than the modernist Mexican fine-dining restaurant Pujol. Here, chef Enrique Olvera made his name serving refined and innovative Mexican food, using traditional ingredients in contemporary presentations. The restaurant is located in a gorgeously designed modern building, surrounded by lush gardens. Many dishes come from the wood-fired oven, and there is an omakase-style tasting menu offered at the bar.
MAP 4: Francisco Petrarca 254, tel. 55/5545-4111, www.pujol.com.mx; 1:30pm-10:30pm daily; Metro: Polanco

Quintonil $$$

Quintonil's focus is on modern food with native Mexican ingredients (its name comes from the Nahuatl word for a type of *quelites*, wild greens consumed since the pre-Columbian era). There is a seasonal tasting menu, but you can also order appetizers and main courses à la carte, like a *tamal* with Jerusalem artichokes, *chilacayotes* (yellow squash) in *mole* sauce, or a green rice flavored with poblano chiles, avocado, cilantro, and cheese from Chiapas.
MAP 4: Newton 55, tel. 55/5280-2680, www.quintonil.com; 1pm-4:30pm and 6:30pm-11pm Mon.-Sat.; Metro: Polanco

Comal Oculto $

This tiny spot in the San Miguel Chapultepec is centered around the comal, the round Mexican griddle used to make tortillas and other corn flatbreads. The menu includes lots of antojitos (traditional Mexican snacks), like sopes (round corn flatbreads) and gorditas. A house specialty are the tacos with slow-cooked pork shoulder, though there are ample vegetarian options too. As casual as they come, this street-side spot serves food at just three sidewalk tables.
MAP 4: Gral. Gómez Pedraza 37, no tel.; 9am-6pm Mon.-Fri., 9am-5pm Sat.; Metro: Constituyentes

Comedor Jacinta $$

A refreshingly low-key option in Polanco's bustling restaurant and shopping district, this lovely spot is helmed by well-known fine-dining chef Edgar Núñez Magaña. The appealing menu caters to any mood, with options like fava bean soup, beef in a sauce of *chile pasilla* (a

There is an appealing menu of diverse Mexican dishes at Comedor Jacinta.

mild dried chile pepper), and bone-marrow-topped *sopes* (round corn flatbreads). The setting, with potted cacti, handblown Mexican glassware, and a bar well-stocked with tequila and mezcal, complements the thoroughly Mexican menu.

MAP 4: Virgilio 40, tel. 55/5086-6965, http://comedorjacinta.com; 1pm-11pm Mon.-Tues., 1pm-midnight Thurs.-Sat., 1:30-7pm Sun.; Metro: Polanco

Eno $$

Owned by famed Pujol chef Enrique Olvera, this casual bistro is a good pick for a big breakfast or a light lunch, either at the original Polanco branch or in the Roma (Chihuahua 139, tel. 55/7576-0918). Get a plate of the delicious four-cheese *molletes* (a soft roll topped with refried beans and melted cheese) or a super-size bowl of *chilaquiles verdes* with a fried egg in the morning; drop in for a *torta* stuffed with panela cheese, roasted chiles, and guacamole at lunch. There can be a wait for weekend brunch.

MAP 4: Francisco Petrarca 258, tel. 55/5531-8535, www.eno.com.mx; 7am-10pm Mon.-Fri., 9am-10pm Sat., 9am-5pm Sun.; Metro: Polanco

☻ Guzina Oaxaca $$

Alejandro Ruíz, the chef behind the elegant restaurant Casa Oaxaca in the city of Oaxaca, brings his creative approach to cuisine to this lovely restaurant in Polanco. Try excellent renditions of typical Oaxacan plates, like tacos, stuffed duck, and *mole coloradito* (a complex sauce made with chiles, spices, and chocolate, native to Oaxaca), or the chef's signature *mole negro*, served with turkey, as is traditional,

and accompanied by rice and plantains. Casual but attractive, the restaurant subtly recalls Oaxacan aesthetics with details like embroidered throw pillows on the dining room's benches.

MAP 4: Presidente Masaryk 513, tel. 55/5282-1820, www.guzinaoaxaca.com; 9am-11pm Mon.-Sat., 9am-6pm Sun.; Metro: Auditorio or Polanco, Metrobús: Auditorio

Mari Gold $$$

Mexican and Indian flavors can be surprisingly complementary, as chefs Norma Listman and Saqib Keval showcased at their first collaboration, Masala y Maíz, in the Colonia Condesa. Here, the chefs take up this concept again, with dishes like a delicate dosa topped with hoja santa. Natural wines are the highlight of the drink menu—including a delicious house wine. The slender dining room, with tables lined up end to end, has an avant-garde feeling, which works well for the neighborhood's gallery crowd, who often show up at lunch hour.

MAP 4: Protasio Tagle 66A, tel. 55/9021-1046; 10am-5pm Wed.-Sun.; Metro: Juanacatlán

La Poblanita de Tacubaya $

A totally traditional Mexican restaurant with a surprisingly extensive menu, this family-style spot serves delicious renditions of the classics, from a simple but delicious *tacos de guisado* filled with guacamole and *chicharrón* (pork rind) to elaborate *mole poblano* ladled over chicken breast. The *poblanita* in the name refers to the state of Puebla, and *poblano*-style food is the house specialty—though don't let that limit your order.

MAP 4: Luis G. Vieyra 12, tel. 55/2614-3314, www.lapoblanita.com.mx; 9am-7pm daily; Metro: Juanacatlán

TACOS, *TORTAS*, AND SNACKS
El Turix $

El Turix does one thing, and it does it well: *cochinita pibil,* achiote-spiced pulled pork prepared in the Yucatec style. You can order it in soft tacos, in a *torta* (sandwich style), or on *panuchos* (thick, circular corn cakes from the Yucatán). This singularly focused spot has garnered a loyal following, and at the hour of the afternoon *comida,* there is often a long line of expectant diners snaking out the door and around the block.

MAP 4: Emilio Castelar 212, tel. 55/5280-6449; noon-10pm daily; Metro: Auditorio

La Ventanita de Ticuchi $

This all-vegetarian Oaxacan-style kitchen serves Enrique Olvera's mezcal bar Ticuchi in the evenings. During the day, its window (*ventanita*) is open to the street, serving small plates of beautiful antojitos (Mexican snacks) like tamales, *gorditas,* and tetelas (triangle-shaped corn cakes stuffed with cheese, hoja santa, and beans). Seating is limited: you can grab a stool at the bar overlooking the kitchen or at one of the tables set up atop palm mats on the street.

MAP 4: Petrarca 254, tel. 55/2589-4363; 1pm-6pm Mon.-Sat.; Metro: Polanco, Metrobús: Antropología

Los Panchos $

In business since 1945, Los Panchos has been catering to a loyal local clientele for generations. The atmosphere here is a bit more upscale than what you'd find at most taquerias, with a full bar and table service. The food, however, is traditional, homey, and generously served. Best known for the *carnitas* (braised pork), the extensive menu includes plenty of other options, from a fresh guacamole to huge *sopes* (thick corn cakes) topped with beans and cheese.

MAP 4: Tolstoi 9, tel. 55/5254-5430 or 55/5254-2082, www.lospanchos.mx; 9am-10pm Mon.-Sat., 9am-8pm Sun.; Metro: Chapultepec

FRENCH
Au Pied de Cochon $$$

Considered one of the best French restaurants in the capital, this high-end venue in the InterContinental Presidente has an extensive menu of classics, from foie gras to cassoulet. While the food is good, the most amazing thing about this long-running establishment is its operating hours: Au Pied de Cochon is open 24 hours a day. Come late and

the daytime kitchen at Ticuchi

PRE-COLUMBIAN FOODS

Many popular Mexican dishes have roots in pre-Columbian cuisine. Today, Mexican chefs are using more indigenous Mesoamerican ingredients in their cooking, and foods that once seemed more adventurous, like insects and worms, have become almost commonplace in the city's top restaurants. Here are a few you'll find on menus in the capital.

CHAPULINES

Grasshoppers, collected in the wild then fried until crispy, are an excellent source of protein and deliciously salty. They add an acidic bite to guacamole and quesadillas. In 2013, Mexican artist Pedro Reyes developed a grasshopper hamburger (or "grasswhopper") as a part of his work *Entomofagia,* through which Reyes hoped to promote the environmental and health benefits of eating insects.

Find them: In tacos at **Guzina Oaxaca** (page 149); mixed into melted cheese at **Corazón de Maguey** (page 232); in guacamole at **Las Tlayudas** (page 210) in the Narvarte neighborhood.

QUELITES

Quelites refers to any wild, indigenous greens—some more common in Mexican cooking, like *huauzontles* (a bitter broccoli-esque vegetable), and others less common, like *pápalo* (a perfumed, citrusy herb that is used in Puebla). In modern farming, many of these "weeds," which often grow naturally in the milpa, are eradicated by farmers, but as appreciation of the milpa and its many products grows, *quelites* have experienced a renewed popularity.

Find them: In soup at **Limosneros** (page 65); in tamales at **Guzina Oaxaca** (page 149); with fish at fine-dining restaurant **Quintonil** (page 148), which is named after a type of *quelite* in the Amaranthus genus; at outdoor quesadilla stands throughout the city.

HUITLACOCHE

The soft black fungus that grows naturally on corn is not only edible, it's delicious. With a mild mushroom-like flavor, huitlacoche is generally in season during the summer rains, from July to September. *Huitlacoche* has more nutritional properties—including essential amino acids—than the corn it grows on.

Find it: At produce stands in the **Mercado San Juan** (page 105); in ravioli at **Los Danzantes** (page 232); in tamales at **Tamales Doña Emi** (page 181).

ESCAMOLES

Ant larvae, which have been consumed since the pre-Columbian era, are served fried in butter and seasoned with the herb *epazote*. Frying them in butter enhances the mild nutty flavor of the larvae. A dish popular in Mexico City, *escamoles* are generally a pricey delicacy, as they are difficult to harvest and have a very short season (they are harvested annually in the spring).

Find them: When they are in season, **El Cardenal** (page 64); in the **Mercado San Juan** (page 105).

CHINICUILES

A caterpillar commonly found in maguey and agave, chinicuiles are often served baked or fried, then folded into a taco. Frying before serving gives the shells a crisp texture, complementing the caterpillars' pungent, savory flavor. These little caterpillars were often added to bottles of mezcal to prove that the drink was made from maguey. Usually, they are available during the fall.

Find them: **Restaurante Bar Chon** (page 65), **El Cardenal** (page 64), and **La Casa de los Tacos** (page 234).

Venezuelan restaurant Orale Arepa in Polanco

you'll likely see a posh crowd enjoying a post-party nosh.

MAP 4: InterContinental Presidente Mexico City, Campos Eliseos 218, el. 55/5327-7756; 24 hours daily; Metro: Auditorio

ITALIAN
Cancino $

Right across the street from contemporary gallery Kurimanzutto, Cancino often draws an artsy crowd. There are panini and salads on the menu here, in addition to the restaurant's signature thin-crust oven-baked pizzas—which lean experimental, with toppings like gorgonzola and pear. If you just want to rest your legs, there's a small coffee bar, La Ventanita, also inside the space, where you can get an espresso and a snack, to enjoy at the sun-dappled garden tables.

MAP 4: Gobernador Rafael Rebollar 95, tel. 55/4333-0770, http://archipielagocorp.com/cancino.html; 8am-11:30pm daily; Metro: Juanacatlán

VEGETARIAN AND VEGAN
Comedor Vegetariano Govinda's $

There is always a big crowd of local lunchers at the small, inexpensive, and quirky-fun cafeteria at the Hare Krishna temple, which occupies a huge corner building in the San Miguel Chapultepec neighborhood. Served by the temple's devotees, the daily fixed-priced three-course vegetarian menu, which only runs a couple of dollars and often has an Indian influence, includes samosas or other appetizers, a veggie entrée with a small salad, a fruit drink, and dessert.

MAP 4: Tiburcio Montiel 45, tel. 55/5276-9879; 11am-7pm daily; Metro: Juanacatlán

VENEZUELAN
Orale Arepa $

Generously served Venezuelan arepas, cachapas (sweet corn pancakes), and patacones (plantain cakes) are made with quality ingredients and a lot of love at this casual Polanco eatery. While Venezuelan food uses many of the same building blocks (corn, beans, cheese) as Mexican cuisine, the flavors are very different, making for a satisfying contrast to Mexico City's predominant styles. There's a café-like feeling inside the casual blond-wood restaurant and plenty of sidewalk tables outside.

MAP 4: Schiller 330, tel. 55/9155-6133; 8am-9pm Mon.-Sat., 8am-7pm Sun.; Metro: Polanco, Metrobús: Auditorio

COFFEE AND SWEETS
Joselo $

Overlooking Parque Lincoln, this small café is a good place to relax after strolling through Polanco's busy shopping district. The espresso drinks are strong and expertly made. Grab a sidewalk table for the best people-watching, or head to the terrace upstairs to sit among the treetops.

MAP 4: Emilio Castelar 107, tel. 55/5281-0849; 7am-8:45pm Mon.-Fri., 8am-8:45pm Sun.; Metro: Polanco or Auditorio, Metrobús: Auditorio

Nightlife

BARS AND LOUNGES
Gin Gin

After opening one successful location in the Roma, this pre-Prohibition-style cocktail lounge found a second and more upscale home near Parque Lincoln in Polanco. As the name implies, the beautifully made cocktails are focused on gin, with the bar's signature drink featuring ginkgo, ginger, and other elixir-like ingredients. Come here for a pretty crowd and a pretty bar. It's best to reserve a table ahead (which you can do on the website).

MAP 4: Pedro Calderón de la Barca 72, tel. 55/5214-8302, www.gingin.mx; 4pm-2am daily; Metro: Auditorio, Metrobús: Auditorio

✪ Ticuchi

All the details are attended to at this candlelit Polanco bar, owned by famed chef Enrique Olvera. The list of small-batch mezcal is among the most interesting in the city. The cocktails are unusual and delicious, incorporating artisan spirits and local flavors. The service is elegant. The music is spot-on. And the kitchen is (as you'd expect) excellent, serving vegetable-forward, maize-centric small plates, perfect for a light dinner. There are occasionally live DJs, but on most nights, it's a relaxed, romantic place for a drink. Reserve in advance.

MAP 4: Petrarca 254, tel.55/2589-4363, https://ticuchi.mx, 6:30-11pm Mon.-Sat.; Metro: Polanco, Metrobús: Auditorio

CANTINAS
La Única

A reimagined cantina with a swanky Polanco vibe, La Única is a good place to gather with a group over dinner and drinks on a Friday night. The formal service and luxe atmosphere make it a chic but fun destination for a night out—especially in the upstairs dining room, where there is a party-like atmosphere and often live DJs in the evening. The extensive menu of traditional Mexican dishes, which leans heavily on meats and seafood, has the upscale prices to match the neighborhood and ambience.

MAP 4: Anatole France 98, tel. 55/4333-2103, www.launica.mx; 1pm-midnight Sun.-Mon., 1pm-1am Tues.-Sat.; Metro: Auditorio or Polanco, Metrobús: Auditorio

Arts and Culture

CONCERT VENUES
Auditorio Nacional

One of the city's preeminent concert halls, with a capacity of 10,000, the Auditorio Nacional has a varied lineup that runs from internationally famous singers like Marc Anthony and Elton John to popular *cumbia* groups and Mexican *banda* to classical music concerts by international orchestras. Next door, the smaller Lunario (tel. 55/9138-1350, www.lunario.com.mx) is a 1,000-seat venue that hosts ongoing shows by lesser-known performers, with programming running from jazz groups to funk. Tickets are available via Ticketmaster.

MAP 4: Paseo de la Reforma 50, tel. 55/9138-1350, www.auditorio.com.mx; US$25-200, depending on seats and event; Metro: Auditorio, Metrobús: Auditorio

CULTURAL CENTERS
Casa del Lago Juan José Arreola

Overseen by the Universidad Nacional Autónoma de México (UNAM), this multimedia cultural and educational center operates an ongoing program of cinema, visual arts exhibitions, concerts, theater, and poetry readings, in addition to offering workshops in disciplines as diverse as yoga, classical guitar, and chess. Housed in several turn-of-the-20th-century buildings next to the lake in Chapultepec park, the center was opened by writer Juan José Arreola in 1959, with a focus on promoting experimental artwork in a high-profile setting.

MAP 4: Bosque de Chapultepec, Primera Sección s/n, tel. 55/5211-6086, www.casadellago.unam.mx; 11am-5pm Wed.-Sun.; free; Metro: Auditorio, Metrobús: Antropología

✪ Centro Cultural Los Pinos

When Andrés Manuel López Obrador took office in 2018, one of his first acts as president was to convert the opulent presidential mansion known as Los Pinos into a free art and cultural center. AMLO moved into the old presidential residence in the Palacio Nacional, and Los Pinos was transformed into a beautiful public garden, exhibition space, and cultural hub, which continues to grow in size and scope.

Visitors to Los Pinos can stroll through the former presidential residences and gardens, view the art collection amassed by the presidency over the years, or attend one of the many special events, like plays, film screenings, and artisan markets, which take place on the weekends. A highlight of the complex is Cencalli La Casa del Maíz y la Cultura Alimentaria, a museum that chronicles and celebrates the importance of maize in Mexican culture, from the pre-Columbian era through the present.

MAP 4: Puerta 1, Primera Sección Chapultepec, tel. 55/4155-0200 ext. 2412, https://lospinos.cultura.gob. mx; 11am-6pm Tues.-Sat.; free; Metro: Constituyentes, Metrobús: Parque Lira

The former presidential mansion at Los Pinos is now a public arts and cultural center.

LAGO/ALGO

Among the most impressive art spaces in the city is ALGO, which shares a building with long-running restaurant Lago, in the Segunda Sección of Chapultepec. The striking modernist building was originally designed in the 1960s by architect Alfonso Ramírez Ponce and was carefully renovated in 2020-2021. Established Roma neighborhood gallery OMR oversees the cultural end of the project, mounting varied contemporary shows in building's many beautiful spaces. While the city is working on a large-scale renovation project that will make this section of the park more accessible to pedestrians, it's easiest to arrive via taxi until that project is complete. Reservations are required and can be made online.

MAP 4: Bosque de Chapultepec, Pista El Sope s/n, 2a Seccion, https://algo. lago.com.mx; 10am-7pm Wed.-Sun., 10am-6pm Sun.; free; Metro: Constituyentes

GALLERIES
Proyectos Monclova

After establishing a strong reputation in contemporary art at its Colonia Roma gallery, Proyectos Monclova relocated to an airy multistory building in the heart of Polanco. Representing both Mexican and international artists, the gallery shows contemporary photography, sculpture, installation, and mixed-media pieces, and there are usually several reliably interesting exhibitions running in the gallery simultaneously.

MAP 4: Lamartine 415, tel. 55/5525-9715, http:// proyectosmonclova.com; 10am-6pm Mon.-Fri., 10am-4pm Sat.; free; Metro: Insurgentes, Metrobús: Álvaro Obregón or Parque Pushkin

RGR

Originally founded in Venezuela, this contemporary gallery has been based in Mexico City since 2018. Representing the work of famed

Lago/Algo, in the Segunda Sección of Chapultepec, is one of the most impressive art spaces in the city.

Venezuelan artists Carlos Cruz-Diez and Jesús Rafael Soto, both of whom worked within the kinetic art and op-art movements, the gallery represents a range of contemporary abstract artists, many also focused on optical illusion, the interplay of color, and movement, making shows here dependably delightful.

MAP 4: Gral. Antonio León 48, tel. 55/8434-7759, www.rgrart.com; 10:30am-6:30pm Mon.-Thurs., 10:30am-4:30pm Fri., 11am-4:30pm Sat.; Metro: Juanacatlán

Galería de Arte Mexicano

Founded in 1935, the Galería de Arte Mexicano has a grand legacy, having once hosted shows by the 20th century's most famous names, including Rivera, Kahlo, Orozco, Covarrubias, and Tamayo. In the residential San Miguel Chapultepec neighborhood, the gallery continues to focus on Mexico-based artists, representing well-known contemporary names, including Francisco Castro Leñero and Jan Hendrix. It's a beautiful space, and the exhibitions are high quality; ring the doorbell to visit.

MAP 4: Gob. Rafael Rebollar 43, Col. San Miguel Chapultepec, tel. 52/5272-5696, www.galeriadeartemexicano.com; 11am-5:30pm Mon.-Thurs., 11am-2:30pm Fri.; free; Metro: Juanacatlán or Constituyentes

Kurimanzutto

Partners José Kuri, Mónica Manzutto, and Gabriel Orozco opened this spacious contemporary gallery in 2008. Orozco shows his work here, as have numerous other high-profile international and Mexican artists, including Allora y Calzadilla, Rirkrit Tiravanija, Abraham Cruzvillegas, and Akram Zaatari. Opening parties are well-attended by a chic crowd, but the true attraction here is the excellent art. Drop by during the week and you're likely to have the gallery all to yourself.

MAP 4: Gob. Rafael Rebollar 94, tel. 55/5256-2408, www.kurimanzutto.com; 11am-6pm Tues.-Thurs., 11am-4pm Fri.-Sat.; free; Metro: Constituyentes or Juanacatlán

Labor

Located in an unmarked turquoise home just across the street from the Casa Luis Barragán, this tucked-away contemporary gallery represents an interesting roster of artists, including the excellent Mexican artists Pedro Reyes and Hector Zamora. Originally opened in 2010, it relocated to this quiet home in 2012, where a shaded garden adjoins the clean, white gallery space. Ring the doorbell during business hours and you'll be buzzed in.

MAP 4: Francisco Ramírez 5 , Col. Daniel Garza, tel. 55/6304-8755, www.labor.org.mx; 11am-6pm Mon.-Thurs., 11am-3pm Fri.-Sat.; free; Metro: Constituyentes

Luis Adelantado Mexico

Valencia, Spain-based gallerist Luis Adelantado's Mexico City gallery is located in a massive warehouse north of Polanco, in a burgeoning arts district. With its concrete floors and towering white walls, the space is minimal and urban-chic, well suited to the avant-garde exhibitions of large-scale work that the gallery often hosts. Check out the smaller galleries in the back of the space, and don't miss the off-the-wall bathrooms.

MAP 4: Laguna de Términos 260, Col. Anahuac, tel. 55/5545-6645, www.luisadelantado.com; 10am-6pm Mon.-Fri., by appointment Sat.; Metro: San Joaquín

MUSEUMS

Casa Gilardi

Luis Barragán's very last project was this private home in the San Miguel Chapultepec neighborhood. Though it is still a home today (inhabited by one of the original owners!), the first two floors are open to private tours (US$20) by appointment. If you've already visited Barragán's house and studio nearby, Casa Gilardi will show an evolution in the artist's late stage and the full development of his point of view. The mirrorlike indoor pool, which stretches beside the dining room and almost seems to glow, is a highlight of the space.

MAP 4: Antonio León 82, tel. 55/5271-3575, casagilardi@gmail.com; tours by appointment only; Metro: Constituyentes

Museo de Arte Moderno

Inaugurated in 1964, Mexico City's largest modern art museum is housed in an industrial concrete building, with a central atrium surrounded by the four main exhibition halls, three of which are dedicated to changing exhibits, while the fourth displays work from the permanent collection. The quality of the exhibits varies; however, the museum's permanent collection contains work by Diego Rivera, Leonora Carrington, and Remedios Varo, as well as Frida Kahlo's largest work, *Las Dos Fridas,* a twin self-portrait by the artist.

CONTEMPORARY ART IN MEXICO CITY

The contemporary art scene in Mexico City has been growing rapidly in recent years. Today there is a perceptible energy within the local art scene, with many distinctive institutions, gallerists, and artists at work here today. To see the most art in a short period time, visit during **Art Week Mexico,** held annually in February, when the well-established **Zsona MACO México** art fair and newer **Material Art Fair** are both running. For a week-plus, CDMX is all about art, with galleries and pop-up exhibits citywide. Here's what to see during the rest of the year.

Museo Jumex

THE INSTITUTIONS

For anyone with an interest in contemporary art, the following three museums are city's leading institutions.

MUSEO JUMEX

Location: Plaza Carso, Polanco

Type: Private; owned and overseen by the Fundación Jumex Arte Contemporáneo, the largest Latin American art collection in the world, owned by Eugenio López Alonso, heir to the Jumex company.

Architect: David Chipperfield

Representative exhibitions: Major retrospectives by artists like Urs Fischer, Ulises Carrión, and Andy Warhol—in 2017, Jumex exhibited the largest collection of Warhol's work in Mexico; "Memories of Underdevelopment: Art and the Decolonial Turn in Latin America, 1960-1985"

Tip: Admission to this premier arts institution is free to the public, so get there early to beat the inevitable daily crowds.

MUSEO TAMAYO

Location: On the Paseo de la Reforma in the Bosque de Chapultepec

Type: Public; overseen by the Instituto Nacional de Bellas Artes (National Institute of Fine Arts), though it was originally founded by Oaxacan artist Rufino Tamayo and his wife, Olga, who donated their personal collection of contemporary art to the project. The Tamayo foundation remains active in governance.

Architects: Teodoro González de León and Abraham Zabludovsky

Representative exhibitions: Retrospectives for Ed Ruscha, Yayoi Kusama, Isamu Noguchi; solo and group shows by local and international contemporary artists like "AYRTON. Four Exhibitions by Armando Andrade Tudela, Nina Canell, FOS and Tania Pérez Córdova" and "Ceremonía: Claudia Fernández."

Tip: Don't be misled by the name. Though 20th-century modern artist

Rufino Tamayo helped found this contemporary art project, his work is very rarely on show here.

MUSEO UNIVERSITARIO ARTE CONTEMPORÁNEO (MUAC)
Location: Centro Cultural Universitario (University Cultural Center) on the main campus of the Universidad Nacional Autónoma de México (UNAM)
Type: Academic; overseen and operated by UNAM.
Architect: Teodoro González de León
Representative exhibitions: Retrospectives of big-name contemporary artists like Anish Kapoor and Yves Klein; collective and solo exhibits featuring artists like Melquiades Herrera and Jill Magid; "Images and Revolt: Prints from 68"
Tip: MUAC is a must for art lovers, but check the schedule before making the long trek south to the university; sometimes the museum is closed to visitors when new shows are being installed.

ALSO EXCELLENT
These smaller venues are also places worth putting on your list.

EX-TERESA ARTE ACTUAL (CENTRO HISTÓRICO)
Overseen by: UNAM
Representative exhibitions: Experimental sound and video art, such as 2022 exhibition by American artist Bill Viola.

LABORATORIO DE ARTE ALAMEDA (ALAMEDA CENTRAL)
Overseen by: Instituto Nacional de Bellas Artes (National Institute of Fine Arts)
Representative exhibitions: Artwork that invites interaction and incorporates science by emerging and established artists, such as the movable sculptures by kinetic artist Theo Jansen.

MUSEO CARRILLO GIL (SAN ÁNGEL)
Overseen by: The foundation of Mexican art collectors Alvar Carrillo Gil and Carmen Tejero de Carrillo Gil
Representative exhibitions: Selections from the Carrillo Gil collection of Diego Rivera, David Alfaro Siqueiros, and José Clemente Orozco are permanently on view, alongside contemporary and experimental work by emerging Mexican artists.

MUSEO DEL CHOPO
Overseen by: UNAM
Representative exhibitions: Contemporary and experimental exhibitions, often focused on subcultures, protest, and politics.
There are dozens more venues that exhibit contemporary artwork in Mexico City, with excellent shows held at other CDMX institutions like the Museo de Arte Moderno, the Centro Cultural de España (Centro Histórico), LAGO/ALGO, Centro Cultural de Tlatelolco, Casa del Lago, Museo del Estanquillo, and Museo Experimental El Eco, among others.

GALLERY DISTRICTS
There are some excellent contemporary art galleries in Mexico City. You'll likely find the highest concentration of contemporary art spaces in the San Miguel Chapultepec neighborhood, where excellent institutions like Kurimanzutto, Galería de Arte Mexicano, and RGR are based. There are also noteworthy galleries in the San Rafael, the Santa María la Ribera, the Juárez, Polanco, Tacubaya, Anahuac, and the Roma.

OUTSTANDING MUSEUM GIFT SHOPS

Mexico City's museums have excellent gift shops, many of which feature rare books, unique works by local designers, and high-quality pieces by traditional artisans. Here are five museum gift shops worth visiting:

In complement to the stunning variety of craft showcased in the **Museo Nacional de Culturas Populares** (page 241), the museum's pleasantly overstuffed gift shop has an extensive collection of traditional Mexican *artesanías*, including elaborate *árboles de la vida*, metalwork and jewelry, lacquered wood trays and boxes, and an array of textiles. If you don't make it to the museum, there is another branch of the gift shop in Polanco (Aristóteles 8, tel. 55/7090-3589, 9am-6pm daily) and in the international wing of the airport (tel. 55/4313-0282, 6am-10pm daily).

Get art books, graphic mugs and water bottles, unusual toys, colorful textiles, designer jewelry and housewares, and other unique gifts at the large and well-selected gift shop at the **Museo Tamayo** (page 161) in Chapultepec. With an emphasis on contemporary design, the shop considers itself an extension of the museum's collection, often showcasing the work of local designers.

Though you'll find work from a number of international designers, Mexican-produced products are the focus at the museum store at the **Museo Universitario Arte Contemporáneo (MUAC)** (page 255), on the UNAM campus. Plus, there are (literally) thousands of art and design books on sale, including some rare titles and editions published by the museum.

Though it's a small shop, the varied selection of well-priced books at the **Museo Jumex** (page 160) makes this museum bookshop worth visiting. Books printed by the Jumex foundation, which highlight recent exhibitions at the museum, are often excellent.

MAP 4: Paseo de la Reforma and Gandhi, tel. 55/8647-5530, https://mam.inba.gob.mx; 11am-7pm daily; US$3, free to students, teachers, seniors, free general admission on Sun.; Metro: Chapultepec, Metrobús: Gandhi

Museo de Historia Natural and Museo Jardín del Agua

Mexico City's old-timey natural history museum first opened in 1790, though it changed locations several times before moving to its current space in Chapultepec in 1964. Today, it's filled with vintage wildlife dioramas, taxidermy animals, and fossils. In 2012, the museum inaugurated a new ecological and art project, Museo Jardín del Agua, through which it restored 16 hectares in surrounding Chapultepec park, including the Diego Rivera fountain-mural *El Agua, Origen*

de la Vida en la Tierra (*Water, the Origin of Life on Earth*).

MAP 4: Segunda Sección, Bosque de Chapultepec, tel. 55/5515-0739, ext. 112 and 113, http://data.sedema.cdmx.gob.mx/museodehistorianatural; 10am-5pm Tues.-Sun.; US$2 includes admission to Rivera mural, children and teachers $1, seniors free; Metro: Chapultepec

✪ Museo Jumex

Over the past two decades, the Fundación Jumex, owned by juice company heir Eugenio López Alonso, has assembled what is widely regarded as the most important collection of art in Latin America. In 2013, the foundation opened a contemporary art museum, designed by David Chipperfield, next to Carlos Slim's eye-catching Museo Soumaya, in Plaza Carso. One of the most interesting contemporary art venues in the city, the museum distinguishes itself with a robust program of contemporary exhibits, including shows by internationally renowned artists, from John Baldessari in 2017 to Urs Fischer in 2022. Free to visit, it's often crowded.

MAP 4: Miguel de Cervantes Saavedra 303, Col. Ampliación Granada, tel. 55/5395-2615, http://fundacionjumex. org; 10am-5pm Tues.-Fri. and Sun., 10am-7pm Sat.; free; Metro: San Joaquín or Polanco

Museo Soumaya

In the 1990s, Mexican multibillionaire Carlos Slim opened the Museo Soumaya as a place to house and exhibit his extensive art collection. Today the collection resides in a striking space designed by Slim's son-in-law Fernando Romero. The building's distinctive exterior, a glittery swoosh of asymmetrical metal, covers five stories of galleries exhibiting European and Mexican art from the Renaissance to the present day.

Museo Soumaya

MAP 4: Plaza Carso, Blvd. Miguel de Cervantes Saavedra 303, Col. Ampliación Granada, tel. 55/1103-9800, www.soumaya.com.mx; 10:30am-6:30pm daily; free; Metro: Polanco or San Joaquín

✪ Museo Tamayo

Originally founded by Oaxacan artist Rufino Tamayo, this excellent contemporary art museum opened in 1981 and continues to host high-quality temporary exhibitions by both Mexican and international artists. (Contrary to what some visitors expect, Tamayo's work is shown only infrequently, as part of special exhibits.) It's worth visiting for the beautiful modern space alone, designed by architects Abraham Zabludovsky and Teodoro González de León. After an extensive 2012 remodel, there are now expanded gallery spaces in the eastern wing, as well as a very attractive (and delicious) café and a design-centric gift shop on the premises.

MAP 4: Paseo de la Reforma 51, tel. 55/4122-8200, www.museotamayo.org; 10am-6pm Tues.-Sun.; US$3.50, children under 12, students, and teachers free, general admission free on Sun.; Metro: Chapultepec

Sala de Arte Público David Alfaro Siqueiros

Celebrated 20th-century muralist David Alfaro Siqueiros dedicated his life to creating public art, and this small but wonderful museum honors his legacy by displaying works by Siqueiros himself, in addition to hosting fine exhibitions of contemporary art. In keeping with the theme, the museum's facade is constantly repainted via the museum's *Proyecto Fachada* (Facade Project), exploring themes in politics and social justice that were close to Siqueiros's heart.

MAP 4: Tres Picos 29, Polanco, tel. 55/8647-5340, www.saps-latallera.org; 10am-6pm Tues.-Sun.; US$2, free for students, teachers, seniors, and children under 12, free on Sun.; Metro: Auditorio

Papalote Museo del Niño

Mexico City's wonderful children's museum's playful exhibits range in themes from science and the human body to the natural world, engaging children with hands-on activities, like blowing soap bubbles, shopping at a miniature supermarket, or climbing into a giant replica of a rainforest canopy. Note that audiovisual materials throughout the museum, including movies, are in Spanish. The museum has limited

a top spot for tots: the Museo del Niño in Chapultepec

capacity (there can be a wait to get in), though it is still hugely crowded on the weekends.

MAP 4: Av. Constituyentes 268, Segunda Sección, Bosque de Chapultepec, tel. 55/5237-1781, www.papalote.org.mx; hours vary, generally 9am-6pm Mon.-Thurs., 10am-7pm Fri.-Sun.; US$10, free for children under 2; Metro: Constituyentes

Recreation

PARKS

✪ Bosque de Chapultepec: Primera Sección and Segunda Sección

Covering nearly 700 hectares of forested land, the Bosque de Chapultepec not only provides respite for weekenders but also helps control the climate and air quality in the water-starved, pavement-covered Valley of Mexico. With its natural springs and verdant vegetation, the area around the Cerro de Chapultepec was once a retreat for Mexica emperors and, later, colonial-era aristocrats;

there are ruins of numerous pre-Columbian baths in the park. Today, the tree-lined pathways of the Primera Sección (First Section) of Chapultepec are popular for jogging, dog-walking, and in-line skating, and they're thronged with strolling families (and food vendors and toy sellers) on Sundays. If time allows, it's interesting to explore the Segunda Sección (Second Section), a bit remoter from major thoroughfares but filled with shaded forests, unusual fountains, and quiet plazas. Currently, the Segunda Sección is tricky to access from the Primera

Sección, but as part of their large-scale expansion and improvement of the park, the city government has developed a plan to expand pedestrian crossings between each area of the park, in addition to building a trolley that will run the full length of the park.

MAP 4: Between Paseo de la Reforma, Pedro A. de los Santos, Calzada de las Lomas, and Av. Constituyentes; Primera Sección 5am-4:30pm Tues.-Sun., other sections daily 24 hours; free; Metro: Chapultepec, Auditorio, Constituyentes

Bosque de Chapultepec: Tercera Sección and Cuarta Sección

The more rugged and lesser known Tercera Sección of Chapultepec is located to the west of the Segunda Sección and is filled with denser forest, hilly terrain, and walking paths. There are fewer monuments, attractions, and facilities in this section of the park, and it is far less visited than the first and second sections—though that is likely to change. In 2019, the government announced a plan to restore all three existing sections of Chapultepec, including new lighting, restored fountains, and expanded pedestrian paths, as well as to add new attractions and easier access to the third section.

As part of the restoration project, the city government has also announced plans to expand the park with the addition of a fourth area. The Cuarta Sección, which was officially annexed in 2019, will be developed on land that was previously occupied by the Secretary of National Defense, all 88 hectares of which, along with the historic buildings, have been donated to the city

Jacaranda trees in bloom in the Primera Sección of Chapultepec park

government. Among the most anticipated additions to the Cuarta Sección is a branch of the Cineteca Nacional, an art house movie theater run by the Universidad Autónoma de México, which is slated to open in a former gunpowder factory in late 2022.

MAP 4: Bordered to the south by Avenida Constituyentes; 24 hours daily; free; Metro: Constituyentes

La Casa de la Bici Chapultepec

Incredibly, this tiny bicycle rental kiosk has been in operation since 1921. If you are coming from the western entrances to the park near the San Miguel Chapultepec neighborhood, it's the closest place to rent a bike—and, unlike Igual Bicigratis, they have children's bikes as well. The limited fleet of bikes is squeaky and battered, but they're all you need to cruise through the park.

MAP 4: Av. Parque Lira S/N, no tel.; 10am-7pm Tues.-Sun.; $4/hour; Metro: Chapultepec or Constituyentes

Parque Lincoln

In the heart of Polanco, this pretty, family-friendly park is a nice place for a stroll on a Sunday afternoon. There is a huge playground on the park's eastern edge (that's invariably packed on the weekends), as well as a small aviary (US$0.50 entrance fee) filled with noisy parrots, cockatiels, parakeets, and one splendid peacock. On the weekends, there are motorized toy boats for rent on the park's mirrorlike ponds (US$4 for 15 minutes). In addition to the permanent sculpture collection in the park, it is also a venue for art and design projects, notably a large shipping-container showroom set up during the annual Design Week Mexico.

MAP 4: Between Edgar Allan Poe, Luis G. Urbana, Emilio Castelar, and Aristóteles; 24 hours daily; free; Metro: Auditorio

Shops

POLANCO SHOPPING DISTRICT

Polanco's tony main avenue, Presidente Masaryk, is lined with upscale European and American fashion houses like Fendi, Louis Vuitton, and DKNY; newer design and jewelry shops; and posh sidewalk cafés and restaurants. Come here to pick up some designer clothes and luxury items or to enjoy a bit of high-end window-shopping.

MAP 4: Presidente Masaryk between Newton and Moliere; Metro: Polanco

ARTS AND CRAFTS
Expendio Doméstico

It's surprising how many covetable items are stocked into this tiny storefront in the San Miguel Chapultepec, a branch of a home goods and kitchen store that first opened in the upscale Lomas de Chapultepec neighborhood. Specializing in traditional Mexican products, the shop stocks many beautiful and duly useful everyday items, from metal lime juicers to hand-painted tequila glasses to burnished clay pitchers.

MAP 4: General Cano 42, tel. 55/1857-6607, https:// expendiodomestico.mx; 11am-2:30pm and 3:30pm-7pm Mon.-Fri., 11am-4pm Sat.-Sun.; Metro: Juanacatlán

Ikal

Ikal's urban-chic Polanco boutique represents a diverse array of independent Mexican designers, with clothes, jewelry, shoes, footwear, and beauty and home goods in a range of prices and aesthetics, from punk rock to rustic. Spend some time here and you're certain to find something that interests you, whether it's leather booties by Mexican shoe designer Caarmela, a structured raincoat by Camino, or a woven clutch by Tulum-based brand Gaela.

MAP 4: President Masaryk 340, tel. 55/7922-9928 (Whatsapp), https:// ikalstore.com; 10am-8pm daily; Metro: Polanco, Metrobús: Auditorio

✪ Lago

This beautifully curated independent boutique stands out among the spate of international designers and luxury car shops that line Polanco's snazzy central avenue Presidente Masaryk. Showcasing clothes, jewelry, accessories, and home goods by emerging and established Latin American designers, you'll find labels like Juun, Belisa Pulido, and Carla Fernández among the racks. From embroidered blouses to contemporary silver jewelry, the pieces here are high quality and unique.

Polanco boutique Lago has an excellent selection from Latin American designers.

MAP 4: Presidente Masaryk 310, tel. 55/7261-9343, https://lagolatam.com; 11am-8pm daily; Metro: Polanco, Metrobús: Auditorio

Onora

Everything at Onora is handmade in Mexico by skilled traditional artisans working in tandem with a contemporary designer. The distinctive Mexican aesthetic and techniques are easily recognizable to anyone familiar with Mexican handcraft—you'll find everything from lacquered trays to tequila glasses—yet the pieces are also original, with designs unlike those found in most artisan markets. It's a lovely place to pick up a set of mezcal glasses or a handwoven tablecloth to take home.

MAP 4: Lope de Vega 330, tel. 55/5203-0938, http://onoracasa.com; 11am-7pm Mon.-Fri., 11am-3pm Sat.; Metro: Polanco

Traditional Mexican design gets a contemporary twist at Onora.

Uriarte Talavera

In the early colonies, Spanish settlers introduced Talavera-style tin-enameled glazing to Mexico's skilled Indigenous potters. The technique flourished, with artisans incorporating dazzling pigments and expressive painting styles to the process. Blue-and-white hand-painted Talavera ceramics became a hallmark of the state of Puebla, and Uriarte—established in 1824—is the country's oldest and most revered producer. Come to the Polanco store to browse the handmade and hand-painted flatware, mugs, tea sets, vases, and more.

MAP 4: Galileo 67A, tel. 55/5280-0635, www.uriartetalavera.com.mx; 11am-7pm Wed.-Fri., 10am-7pm Sat.-Sun.; Metro: Polanco

BOOKS

El Péndulo

This high-quality bookstore opened its first branch in the Condesa (Nuevo León 115, tel. 55/5286/9493; 8am-11pm Mon.-Fri., 9am-11pm Sat.-Sun.), but it has since expanded across the city, with shops in the Zona Rosa (Hamburgo 126, tel. 55/5208-2327; 8am-11pm Mon.-Fri., 9am-11pm Sat.-Sun.) and the Roma (Álvaro Obregón 86, tel. 55/5574-7034; 8am-11pm Mon.-Wed., 8am-midnight Thurs.-Fri., 9am-midnight Sat., 9am-11pm Sun.) as well as this one in Polanco. Branches share a cozy decor with an earthy color scheme, as well as an in-house coffee shop called the Cafebrería. Though predominantly stocking Spanish titles, the Polanco branch has a nice English fiction selection, mixing both classics and contemporary novels.

MAP 4: Alejandro Dumas, tel. 55/5280-4111, www.pendulo.com; 8am-11pm Mon.-Fri., 9am-11pm Sat., 9am-10pm Sun.; Metro: Polanco

CLOTHING, SHOES, AND ACCESSORIES

Pineda Covalín

Founded by two Mexican designers, Cristina Pineda and Ricardo Covalín, this high-end clothing and accessories company sells purses, ponchos, scarves, neckties, and other wearables, most of which are made of silk and printed with colorful Mexican-inspired designs. For those who'd like a touch of something Mexican in their wardrobe but don't plan to buy traditional clothes, it's an elegant option. There are numerous branches, including in The Shops at Downtown (Isabel la Católica 30, tel. 55/5510-4421) and inside the Sheraton (Paseo de la Reforma 325, tel. 55/5533-5562).
MAP 4: Campos Eliseos 215, tel. 55/5282-2720, www.pinedacovalin.com; 9am-8pm daily; Metro: Polanco

JEWELRY

Talleres de los Ballesteros

This upscale silver shop was originally founded in Taxco, Guerrero, a city known for its silver mines as well as its important contribution to the development of a uniquely Mexican aesthetic in jewelry design, which combines pre-Columbian elements with modern sensibilities. At this high-end Polanco boutique, both sterling jewelry and tableware from Ballesteros's Taxco workshop are for sale in a wide variety of styles, with some very nice traditionally Mexican work along with contemporary pieces.
MAP 4: Av. Presidente Masaryk 126, tel. 55/5545-4109, www.ballesteros.net; 10am-7pm Mon.-Sat.; Metro: Polanco

☆ Tane

Tane is one of the oldest and finest silver shops in Mexico, producing both jewelry and silver accessories for the home. Designs are generally elegant and highly contemporary, and the collections include some one-of-a-kind pieces and artist-designed series. Prices are high-end, but the workmanship is beautiful. There are additional locations in San Ángel (Altavista 147, #7, San Ángel Inn, tel. 55/5550-5632) and in the Four Seasons Hotel (Paseo de la Reforma 500, tel. 55/5203-2624).
MAP 4: Presidente Mazaryk 430, tel. 55/5282-6200, www.tane.com.mx; 10am-7pm Mon.-Fri., 11am-7pm Sat.; Metro: Polanco

Tane, Mexico's most famous silversmith

Roma and Condesa   Map 5

Through most of the 20th century, these adjacent **residential neighborhoods** were home to writers, intellectuals, journalists, and artists, as well as middle-class families. Filled with schools, parks, taquerias, and small businesses, the Roma and Condesa became increasingly popular with the city's expatriate community during the early 2000s, and today, they are ground zero for Mexico City's celebrated **dining and nightlife scene.** The oval-shaped and tree-shaded Avenida Amsterdam is emblematic of the Condesa, as is the lush **Parque México,** and the multitude of art deco and modern buildings make a pleasant backdrop for the **boutique hotels** and **stylish eater-**

ies scattered throughout the neighborhood. In the youth-oriented Roma, there are many **late 19th-century mansions,** many notable for their **eclectic architecture,** now home to **galleries, fine restaurants,** and **popular cocktail bars.**

TOP SIGHTS

- Nicest Neighborhood Park: **Parque México** (page 176)

TOP RESTAURANTS

- Best Ranch-to-Table: **El Hidalguense** (page 177)
- Most Creative Vegan: **Los Loosers** (page 180)
- Superlative Seafood: **Mi Compa Chava** (page 185)
- Favorite Neighborhood Chef: **Máximo Bistrot Local** (page 187)

TOP NIGHTLIFE

- World-Famous Craft Cocktails: **Licorería Limantour** (page 190)
- Coolest Crowd: **Café de Nadie** (page 190)
- Most Convivial Atmosphere: **Páramo** (page 191)

TOP RECREATION

- Greenest Garden: **Huerto Roma Verde** (page 199)

TOP SHOPS

- Best Bookshop for Browsing: **Librería Rosario Castellanos** (page 200)
- Unique Boutique: **Chic By Accident** (page 201)

GETTING THERE AND AROUND

- Metro lines: 1, 3, 9
- Metro stops: Insurgentes, Sevilla, Hospital General, Niños Héroes, Chilpancingo, Patriotismo
- Metrobús lines: 1
- Metrobús stops: Insurgentes, Álvaro Obregón, Sonora, Campeche

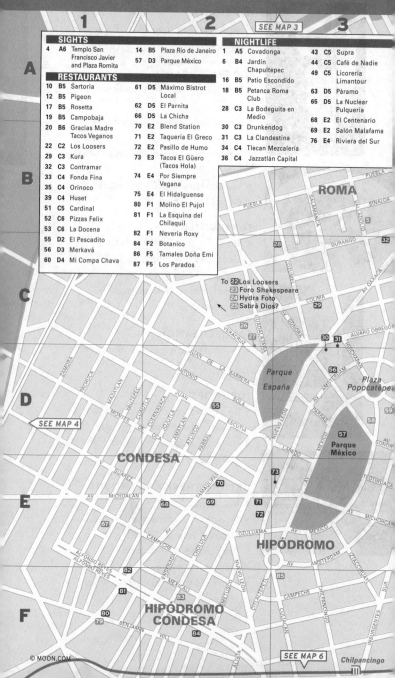

SEE MAP 3

SIGHTS

4	A6	Templo San Francisco Javier and Plaza Romita
57	D3	Parque México

RESTAURANTS

10	B5	Sartoria
12	B5	Pigeon
17	B5	Rosetta
19	B5	Campobaja
20	B6	Gracias Madre Tacos Veganos
22	C2	Los Loosers
29	C3	Kura
32	C3	Contramar
33	C4	Fonda Fina
35	C4	Orinoco
39	C4	Huset
51	C5	Cardinal
52	C6	Pizzas Felix
53	C6	La Docena
55	D2	El Pescadito
56	D3	Merkavá
60	D4	Mi Compa Chava
61	D5	Máximo Bistrot Local
62	D5	El Parnita
66	D5	La Chicha
70	E2	Blend Station
71	E2	Taquería El Greco
72	E2	Pasillo de Humo
73	E3	Tacos El Güero (Tacos Hola)
74	E4	Por Siempre Vegana
75	E4	El Hidalguense
80	F1	Molino El Pujol
81	F1	La Esquina del Chilaquil
82	F1	Neveria Roxy
84	F2	Botanico
86	F5	Tamales Doña Emi
87	F5	Los Parados

14	B5	Plaza Río de Janeiro

NIGHTLIFE

1	A5	Covadonga
6	B4	Jardín Chapultepec
16	B5	Patio Escondido
18	B5	Petanca Roma Club
28	C3	La Bodeguita en Medio
30	C3	Drunkendog
31	C3	La Clandestina
34	C4	Tlecan Mezcalería
36	C4	Jazzatlán Capital
43	C5	Supra
44	C5	Café de Nadie
49	C5	Licorería Limantour
63	D5	Páramo
65	D5	La Nuclear Pulquería
68	E2	El Centenario
69	E2	Salón Malafama
76	E4	Riviera del Sur

PUEBLA

ROMA

SINALOA

PUEBLA

SALAMANCA

DURANGO

COZUMEL

32

AV OAXACA

To 22 Los Loosers
23 Foro Shakespeare
24 Hydra Foto
25 Sabrá Dios?

COLIMA

ALVARO OBREGÓN

VERACRUZ

GUADALAJARA

AV SONORA

26

27

29

30 31

HUICHAPAN

56

JUAN DE LA BARRERA

ANTONIO

JUAN

SOLA

Parque España

AV AMSTERDAM

Plaza Popocatépe

SEE MAP 4

ZAMORA

PACHUCA

MAZATLÁN

MONTES

TLAXCALA

CUERNAVACA

DE OCA

ATLIXCO

TEPOTZOTLÁN

AMATLÁN

PARRAS

ESCUTIA

55

AV NUEVO LEÓN

PARRAS

LAREDO

AV MÉXICO

57
Parque México

AV SONOR

58

59

CONDESA

SUÁREZ

TAMAULIPAS

70

AV MICHOACÁN

68

69

71

72

TEOTIHUACA

MICHOACÁN

67

CAMPECHE

CUXULTA

OZULUAMA

AV MÉXICO

HIPÓDROMO

AMSTERDAM

IZTACCIHUATL

ALFONSO REYES
ALFONSO REYES

82

83

MEXICALI

ENSENADA

NUEVO LEÓN

TEOTIHUACAN

CITLALTEPETL

85

CAMPECHE

CHILPANCINGO

SUR

81

HIPÓDROMO CONDESA

80

79

BENJAMIN

84

HILL

POPOCATEPETL

CUICUILCO

ALTATA

INSURGENTES

SEE MAP 6

Chilpancingo

© MOON.COM

4   **5**   SEE MAP 2   **6**

ARTS AND CULTURE

15	**B5**	Museo del Objeto del Objeto (MODO)	**39**	**C5**	Casa Lamm
17	**B6**	Proyectos Monclova	**40**	**C5**	La Teatrería
21	**C2**	Foro Shakespeare	**44**	**C5**	Galería OMR
35	**C4**	Museo Universitario de Ciencias y Artes Roma (MUCA Roma)			

SPORTS AND ACTIVITIES

78	**E5**	Huerto Roma Verde

ROMA NORTE

Plaza Morelia

Templo San Francisco Javier and Plaza Romita

Jardin Dr Ignacio Chavez

To ⑥ Jardin Chapultepec

Plaza Río de Janeiro

Jardin Alexander Pushkin

Plaza de los Cibeles

Plaza Luis Cabrera

0   200 yds
0   200 m

DISTANCE ACROSS MAP
Approximate: 1.7 mi or 2.7 km

ROMA SUR

Mercado Medellín

To ⑦ Huerto Roma Verde

To ⑧ Tamales Doña Emi

SHOPS

2	**A5**	Casa Bosques	**38**	**C4**	Delirio
8	**B5**	Chic by Accident	**41**	**C4**	Happening
11	**B5**	Goodbye Folk	**45**	**C5**	Retroactivo Records
13	**B5**	180° Shop			
15	**B5**	La Canasta	**59**	**D3**	Under the Volcano Books
21	**B6**	Mercado de Cuauhtémoc	**77**	**E4**	Mercado de Medellín
24	**C2**	Hydra Foto	**79**	**F1**	Librería Rosario Castellanos
25	**C2**	Sabrá Dios?			
37	**C4**	Carla Fernández			

HOTELS

9	**B4**	La Valise	**58**	**D3**	Hippodrome Hotel
26	**C2**	Villa Condesa	**64**	**D5**	Ignacia Guest House
27	**C2**	Condesa DF	**67**	**E1**	Condesa Haus
42	**C5**	Casa Nima	**83**	**F2**	Distrito Condesa
48	**C5**	Hotel Milan	**85**	**F3**	Red Tree House
54	**C6**	Hotel Stanza			

ROMA AND CONDESA WALK

TOTAL DISTANCE: 2.2 kilometers (1.3 miles)
TOTAL WALKING TIME: 1.5 hours

In a stroll through the attractive, walkable Roma and Condesa neighborhoods, you'll pass many eye-catching **old mansions,** pretty green **parks,** and popular **public plazas.** Though many people come here to eat or go out, these neighborhoods are also known for their **early 20th-century architecture.** If you want to see some of the keynote spots, here's where to start.

THE ROMA

Largely constructed during the opulent Porfiriato era at the end of the 19th century, the northern blocks of the Colonia Roma are filled with impressive mansions, some beautifully preserved, others abandoned since the 1985 earthquake. The greatest concentration of historic architecture is along Avenida Álvaro Obregón and Calle Colima, as well as around the Plaza Río de Janeiro. Some of the neighborhood's wildly original buildings are good examples of

a grand traffic circle in the Roma

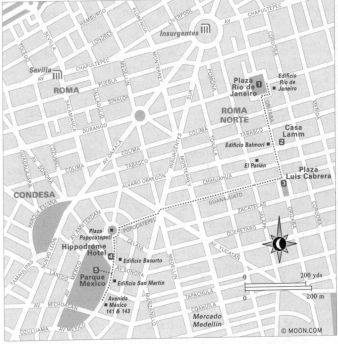

19th-century eclecticism, which incorporates elements from different eras, including art nouveau, art deco, and neocolonial styles.

1 Start your day in the pleasant **Plaza Río de Janeiro,** a favored gathering spot for dog walkers and Roma families. With an unusual peaked roof, the **Edificio Río de Janeiro** apartment building—known locally as La Casa de las Brujas (Witches' House)—is on the east side of the park. It was constructed by British architect Regis A. Pigeon in 1908, and it was among the first buildings erected in the plaza, then called the Parque Roma. Architect Francisco Serrano added its deco facade in the 1930s.

2 Walk south along Orizaba to Álvaro Obregón, the Roma's central avenue and the hub of its happening dining and nightlife scene. On the northeast corner of Orizaba and Álvaro Obregón, **Casa Lamm** is a beautifully restored mansion, originally built by

Casa Lamm is one of the Roma's most opulent early 20th-century mansions.

architect Lewis Lamm in 1922. Since the 1990s, Casa Lamm has been home to a cultural center, restaurant, and gallery, with restored interiors and gardens open to the public (the entrance is half a block east on Álvaro Obregón). Just across the street, on another corner of Álvaro Obregón and Orizaba, **Edificio Balmori** (Orizaba 101) is a palace-like building with a sandstone facade and elegant French windows, originally constructed as residence apartments. The slightly sunken first floor is now filled with street-level boutiques. Take a short detour west to **El Parián** (Álvaro Obregón 130) on the south side of the street. This unusual building opened as a market in 1833 but was severely damaged in the 1985 earthquake; it was eventually restored and reopened as a dining and shopping center, which now includes several popular restaurants and the excellent bar **Café de Nadie.** Notice the beautiful carved stone details surrounding the doorways and windows.

3 Return east to the bustling corner of Orizaba and Álvaro Obregón, then continue south to arrive at **Plaza Luis Cabrera,** at Guanajuato and Orizaba. Stroll around the large fountain at the center of the plaza, which is ringed by restaurants and beautiful old buildings. From the plaza, head west along Guanajuato, toward the Condesa. You'll have to cross a few large and noisy avenues—first Avenida Insurgentes, then Avenida Yucatán—to reach the tree-lined street Popocatépetl, to the southwest, which will take you into the quiet heart of the Condesa.

THE CONDESA

The Condesa was mainly built in the 1920s, on land that was part of a hacienda owned by the Condesa de Miravalle, the neighbor-

There are two private residences designed by architect Luis Barragán on Avenida México in the Condesa.

hood's eponymous *condesa,* or countess. In an unusual move, the Condesa's developers incorporated a former horseracing track into their street plan, creating the oval-shaped Avenida Amsterdam, which runs in a circle around likewise oval-shaped Parque México. Today, Amsterdam is one of the most beautiful streets in the city, ringed with deco and modern architecture, filled with trees, and popular with joggers and dog walkers.

4 Walk west on Popocatépetl; one block later you'll be standing at the intersection of Avenida Amsterdam. Continue southwest on Popocatépetl to arrive at shady **Plaza Popocatépetl,** just a block south of Avenida Amsterdam. At the center of this attractive plaza is an unusual art deco fountain constructed around 1927. From the plaza, walk south along Avenida México, passing one of the most famous buildings in the neighborhood: the **Edificio Basurto** (Avenida México 187). Designed by Francisco Serrano and built between 1942 and 1945, the Basurto was once the tallest building in the city. It is a gem of art deco design, with a unique horseshoe-shaped lobby. It was badly damaged in the September 2017 earthquake, but remained standing after extensive renovation. Just across the street from the Basurto, the **Edificio Tehuacan** is another jewel of Mexican art deco. Today it's the **Hippodrome Hotel.**

5 Cross Avenida Sonora to enter **Parque México,** a jewel of landscape architecture filled with cypresses and palm trees. Wander the footpaths past art deco fountains, the large duck pond, and the unique outdoor theater, Foro Lindbergh, known locally El Redondel. On weekdays, an unofficial attraction of Parque México is watching the many talented dog trainers who work there. Parque México's big dog park, just south of El Redondel is also a good spot for canine lovers to do some quality people- and dog-watching. Much of the architecture around Parque México was built in the early 20th century, when art deco was in style.

Parque México is a popular spot with local families.

On the east side of the park, one notable structure is the **Edificio San Martín** (Avenida México 167), built in 1931. Celebrated architect Luis Barragán constructed two family homes on the Avenida México in 1936. Walk south along the eastern border of the park to see them, at **Avenida México 141** and **143.** Both are private homes and not open to the public, but their exteriors display some of Barragán's trademark style.

Finish up your afternoon with a hot chocolate and a churro at the Condesa branch of the CDMX classic Churrería El Moro (Michoacán 27), overlooking Parque México. If you'd like to explore more of the neighborhood, it's an easy walk to the Condesa's many restaurants and nightspots, much of them concentrated just west of the park, near the intersection of Michoacán and Tamaulipas.

Sights

✪ Parque México

One of the prettiest urban respites in Mexico City, the Parque México is a big reason why the Condesa has become one of the nicest neighborhoods in the city. Much beloved by locals, the large oval-shaped park, encircled by the tree-lined Avenida México, was built in the center of what was once a horse track. Officially named Parque San Martín (though no one ever calls it that), Parque México provides a wonderful, surprisingly peaceful respite from the noise and traffic of the city, filled with footpaths, towering trees, and lush gardens. In addition to being a relaxing neighborhood spot, Parque México is known for its art deco landscape architecture. Wander past its ponds and unusual fountains, and stop to admire the graffiti-covered outdoor auditorium Foro Lindbergh, where kids often ride bikes or kick soccer balls after school. During the week, Condesa locals come here to jog, walk their dogs, host Scout meetings, or read; on the weekends, families come to stroll and play.

From Parque México, walk one block in any direction to Avenida Amsterdam, an oval-shaped avenue with a tree-filled pedestrian median, lined by many architecturally interesting buildings. From Amsterdam, follow Michoacán four blocks west, across Nuevo León and Tamaulipas; you'll find yourself in the middle of the Condesa restaurant and café zone. Or, swing north on Nuevo León to visit Parque España, a smaller but equally pretty park just a few blocks from Parque México.
MAP 5: Av. México, between Av. Sonora and Av. Michoacán; Metro: Chilpancingo, Metrobús: Sonora

Plaza Río de Janeiro

A nice place to start a stroll around the Roma neighborhood is the Plaza Río de Janeiro. Surrounded by old mansions and apartment buildings, this low-key park rings a central fountain, with a rather incongruous replica of Michelangelo's *David* statue in the center. On the east side of the square, La Casa de las Brujas (Witches' House), as the Edificio Río de Janeiro is popularly known, is a red-brick castle, built in 1908, with notable art deco accents.
MAP 5: Durango and Orizaba; Metro: Insurgentes

Rectoría San Francisco Javier and Plaza Romita

Long before the 19th-century development of the Roma neighborhood,

Parque México is a lush, beautifully landscaped park.

the land was a part of the small pre-Columbian settlement of Aztacalco. There, in 1530, Spanish settlers built a small chapel named Santa María de la Natividad to serve the community. Many centuries later, as the area began to develop, that chapel was the center of a subdistrict of the Roma neighborhood known as La Romita. Though the greater Roma was wealthy, La Romita became famous for its crime, thieves, and poverty. Luis Buñuel filmed part of his famous movie *Los Olvidados,* about destitute children in Mexico, in La Romita. Today, it is a pretty tree-filled plaza, adjoined by the Rectoría San Francisco Javier, which is believed to stand in the original 16th century chapel's place.

MAP 5: Plaza Romita between Morelia and Guayamas, tel. 55/5207-7700; Templo San Francisco Javier: 9am-8pm daily; Plaza Romita: 24 hours daily; free; Metro: Niños Héroes

Restaurants

PRICE KEY
$	Entrées less than $10
$ $	Entrées $10-20
$ $ $	Entrées more than $20

MEXICAN
✪ El Hidalguense $
All the food at this wonderful weekend-only restaurant comes directly from the owner's ranch in the state of Hidalgo. It is best-known for the *barbacoa* (slow-cooked lamb), which is prepared to melt-in-your-mouth perfection, but everything on the menu is fresh and delicious, from the simple nopal (prickly pear) salad to the *frijoles aztecas* (refried beans mixed with spices and scrambled egg), the wild-mushroom *mixiotes* (roasted in a maguey leaf), to the fresh pulque.

MAP 5: Campeche 157, tel. 55/5564-0538; 7am-6pm Fri.-Sun.; Metro: Centro Médico, Metrobús: Campeche

El Parnita $
Whether you come at lunch for a relaxed meal with friends and family, or join the lively crowds late in the evening for drinks and snacks, El Parnita is a solidly delicious, reliably fun, and pleasantly low-key place to eat. With a menu dedicated to *antojitos,* or little snack, you can mix and match to create a meal from the selection of items like shrimp tacos, ceviche-topped tostados, or *tlacoyos* (corn cakes) filled with cheese. Top everything with the restaurant's excellent trio of fresh salsas.

MAP 5: Yucatán 84, tel. 55/5264-7551, http://elparnita.com; 9am-10pm Tues.-Sun.; Metro: Insurgentes or Chilpancingo, Metrobús: Sonora

Fonda Fina $$
A genuine love for traditional Mexican food is what drives the menu at this lovely Roma spot, a chef-driven homage to the city's

MODERN ARCHITECTURAL MASTERS

Mexico City's unique cityscape has been shaped by a long tradition of creative architecture, from the baroque masterpieces of the colonial era to the showy design of its
newest museums. During the first half of the 20th century, as the city grew, a number
of important architects left their mark on the city, creating some of its most iconic
sights. Here are just a few of the biggest names.

FRANCISCO J. SERRANO (1900-1982)

- **Principal style:** Art deco
- **Iconic work:** The towering **Edificio Basurto** (Avenida México 187), built from
  1942 to 1945. At 14 floors, it was one of the city's tallest buildings at the time of its
  construction.
- **Legacy:** Though Serrano is best known for the Basurto, he designed numerous art
  deco buildings in the Condesa, such as the **Edificio México** (Avenida México 123)
  and the **Edificio Jardines** (Amsterdam 285), creating a distinctive ambience in
  those neighborhoods.

LUIS BARRAGÁN (1902-1988)

- **Iconic work:** The architect's home, **Casa Luis Barragán** (page 147), is now a museum and UNESCO World Heritage Site; **Casa de los Amigos** (page 282), a guesthouse and social justice organization in the Tabacalera neighborhood, formerly the
  home of muralist José Clemente Orozco; **Casa Gilardi** (Antonion León 82), in the
  San Miguel Chapultepec; **Capilla de las Capuchinas** (page 265) in Tlalpan.
- **Creative influences:** European modernism, Le Corbusier, artist Chucho Reyes,
  artist-architect Mathias Goeritz, Saint Francis of Assisi
- **Legacy:** A pioneer in Mexican modernism and "emotional architecture," Barragán
  was the first recipient of the Pritzker Prize, in 1980. His acceptance speech discussed
  the importance of contemplation and solitude.

JUAN O'GORMAN (1905-1982)

- **Iconic work:** Frida Kahlo and Diego Rivera's former residences in San Ángel, today
  the **Museo Casa Estudio Diego Rivera** (page 254); the massive lava-rock mosaics
  on the UNAM's iconic **Biblioteca Central** (page 249) and at **Centro SCOP** (page
  208) in the Narvarte neighborhood.
- **Creative influences:** Functionalism, Le Corbusier, Mathias Goeritz, Diego Rivera,
  muralism, Frank Lloyd Wright
- **Legacy:** O'Gorman had a wide-ranging creative career. Though he was an architect
  and professor of architecture at the National Polytechnic Institute, he is well-known
  as a painter and muralist.

many *fondas*. Here, flavorful dishes like tamales, braised ribs, or *chamorro* (pork leg) are presented with thoughtfulness and creativity, and go well with one of the delicious Mexican craft beers or mezcal cocktails on offer. Finish up with a typical Mexican dessert, like *buñuelos*. Reservations are recommended.

MAP 5: Medellín 79, tel. 55/5208-3925; 1pm-11pm Mon.-Wed., 1pm-midnight Thurs.-Sat., 1pm-7pm Sun.; Metro: Insurgentes

La Chicha $

La Chicha has the youthful energy and kitschy-cool look of many Roma hangouts, but the menu of

MARIO PANI (1911-1983)

- **Iconic work: Conjunto Urbano Nonoalco Tlatelolco** (Av. Ricardo Flores Magón and Insurgentes Norte), a 101-tower housing project in the Tlatelolco neighborhood that included schools, shops, and hospitals; **Centro Urbano Presidente Alemán** (see **Tortas Don Polo** on page 215), in the Colonia del Valle
- **Principal style:** Functionalism. Pani was a pioneer in designing and constructing many low-cost *multifamiliares* (multifamily apartment buildings) throughout the city.
- **Legacy:** Pani is celebrated for his contribution to urban life in Mexico City. Disastrously, the Conjunto Urbano Nonoalco buildings were badly damaged in the 1985 earthquake; one collapsed entirely, and several others were condemned and demolished.

PEDRO RAMÍREZ VÁZQUEZ (1919-2013)

- **Iconic work: Museo Nacional de Antropología** (page 144), with its soaring central canopy and fountain; the **Basílica de Santa María de Guadalupe** (page 263), the shrine that contains the cloak bearing the Virgin of Guadalupe's image; the **Museo de Arte Moderno** (page 157), with its circular atrium, in Chapultepec; and the **Estadio Azteca** (page 271) sports stadium.
- **Principal style:** Modernism. A tour of Ramírez Vázquez's modernist architectural work is, in many ways, a tour of Mexico City's most famous sites, as he designed an incredible number of the city's iconic arts and cultural institutions.
- **Legacy:** In addition to his work as an architect, Ramírez Vázquez was the president of the organizing committee for the 1968 Mexico City Olympics and the 1970 World Cup, both iconic events in Mexico City's history.

TEODORO GONZÁLEZ DE LEÓN (1926-2016)

- **Iconic work: Museo Tamayo** (page 161), together with his frequent collaborator Abraham Zabludovsky; **Centro Cultural Bella Época** (page 200), now a bookstore and cultural center, in the Condesa; **Museo Universitario Arte Contemporáneo** (page 255), the contemporary art museum on UNAM's central campus.
- **Creative influences:** Le Corbusier (he worked as a draftsman in the famed Swiss architect's studio), modernism, traditional Mesoamerican architecture.

RICARDO LEGORRETA (1930-2011)

- **Iconic work:** Legorreta designed more than 100 buildings over his career, including the unique and imaginative **Camino Real Polanco México** (page 285) in Polanco; **Plaza Juárez** and the adjoining **Museo Memoria y Tolerancia** (page 100), across the street from the Alameda Central; the hotel **Casareyna** (page 313) in Puebla.
- **Creative influences:** Luis Barragán, modernism, pre-Columbian design
- **Known for:** His use of vibrant colors

bar snacks and sandwiches—like *patatas bravas* (Spanish-style fried potatoes topped with paprika), pickled-eggplant-and-goat-cheese tostadas, and intensely savory wild-mushroom tacos—stands out. On weekdays, La Chicha serves an inexpensive three-course *comida corrida* (fixed-price lunch), which is generous and surprisingly inventive. Plus, they have Cosaco beer on tap.
MAP 5: Orizaba 171, tel. 55/5574-6625; 11am-2am Mon.-Sat., 11am-11pm Sun.; Metro: Insurgentes, Metrobús: Álvaro Obregón

☸ Los Loosers

Los Loosers began as a delivery service (with meals pedaled to your door on one-speed bicycles) and built a loyal following with the famous mushroom burger. The non-mobile version, on a shady street in the Condesa, retains a bit of the original project's rebellious spirit—and you can still order the burgers, though the menu includes both Mexican and Asian-inspired dishes. Creative flavors and technique stand out in dishes like *tacos al pastor* made with grilled mushrooms and the bean-stuffed tetela (triangle-shaped corn flatbread) wrapped in hoja santa and topped with almond-milk cheese.

MAP 5: Sinaloa 236, no tel., www. losloosers.mx; 1pm-9pm Tues.-Fri., 11am-9pm Sat., 11am-6pm Sun.; Metro: Chapultepec, Metrobús: Chapultepec

Molino El Pujol $

Famed chef Enrique Olvera has dedicated his career to traditional Mexican cooking, and this simple but superlative *tortilleria* is an outgrowth of that work. The cornerstone of the project are tortillas, made in house with heirloom corn and sold by the dozen, along with other kitchen items, like honey and salsas. There is also a lovely menu of traditional Mexican breakfasts and snacks, served at the small indoor bar and sidewalk tables. Try the seasonal tamales, esquites (heirloom corn kernels topped with mayonnaise, chile, and cheese), or conchas (sugar-topped sweet rolls).

MAP 5: Benjamín Hill 146, tel. 55/5271-3515; 9am-7pm daily; Metro: Chilpancingo or Patriotismo, Metrobús: Campeche

Pasillo de Humo $$

In a lovely, light-filled space on the second floor of the food market Parian Condesa, this casual Oaxacan-inspired restaurant is one of the best spots in the Condesa neighborhood. Try inspired versions of classic dishes, like the *pollo con mole almendrado* (chicken in almond *mole* sauce), dried chiles stuffed with beans and cheese, or a *tlayuda* (a large toasted tortilla filled with beans) accompanied with *tasajo*, Oaxacan salt-cured beef.

MAP 5: Nuevo León 117, tel. 55/5211-7263; 9am-10pm Mon.-Wed., 9am-11pm Thurs.-Sat., 9am-7pm Sun.; Metro: Patriotismo, Metrobús: Campeche

TACOS, *TORTAS*, AND SNACKS
Gracias Madre Taqueria Vegana $

The plant-based tacos at this super-popular nighttime taco stand taste remarkably similar to their traditional counterparts. The pastor is

There are always crowds for top-notch vegan tacos at Gracias Madre.

crisp and earthy; the arrachera has a nice beef-like chew; and the taco de chicharrón en salsa verde has a texture that is a dead ringer for the real thing—and perhaps even more delicious than many versions that include real pig skin.

MAP 5: Jalapa, between Tabasco and Colima, www. graciasmadretaqueriavegana.com; 4pm-11pm Mon.-Sat.; Metro: Insurgentes, Metrobús: Álvaro Obregón or Jardín Pushkin

Orinoco $

Tacos, tacos, tacos shouts the neon sign flashing in the window of Orinoco, a new-school taquería that has accrued an avid loyal following for its delicious renditions of the capital's favorite dish, including a beloved chicharrón taco. At the Roma location, you can sit inside the ultra-casual white-tiled dining room to watch the tacos being made or grab a sidewalk table along Avenida Insurgentes. It's always bustling and open late.

MAP 5: Insurgentes Sur 253, https:// taqueriaorinoco.com; 1pm-3:30am Sun.-Mon. and Wed.-Thurs., 1pm-11pm Tues., 1pm-5am Fri.-Sat.; Metro: Insurgentes, Metrobús: Durango

the late-night taco crowd at Orinoco

Tamales Doña Emi $$

Tamales at this Roma institution often run out within hours of their opening, and for good reason: They are among the best you'll find in the city, served steaming hot, rich in flavor, and filled with top-notch ingredients, from classics, like pork with salsa verde, to more unusual combinations, like *huitlacoche* with goat cheese. Though most customers take their tamales to go, there are a few outdoor tables and some barstools for eating.

MAP 5: Jalapa 278, tel. 55/5564-5316; 8am-noon (or until sold out) Mon.-Fri., 8:30am-noon Sat.-Sun.; Metro: Centro Médico

La Esquina del Chilaquil $

There are often dozens of hungry patrons waiting in line at this friendly Condesa food stand, where the specialty is a stick-to-your-ribs concoction: A *bolillo* (white roll) is stuffed with *chilaquiles* (fried tortillas, bathed in red or green salsa— your choice), and then stuffed some more with breaded chicken breast or pulled pork. Take your heavy-duty sandwich to a nearby park bench for an efficient, cheap, and delicious meal.

MAP 5: Alfonso Reyes and Tamaulipas, no phone; 8am-1pm daily; Metro: Chilpancingo, Metrobús: Chilpancingo

Los Parados $

The name of this famous taquería means, roughly "the stand-ups," and indeed you must be prepared to eat while standing, perhaps jostled within a crowd of people, when visiting this well-known late-night joint. There are a wide variety of delicious tacos here (and top-notch salsas to

TACOS: MEXICO CITY'S MAIN DISH

From ultra-cheap to gourmet, simple to elaborate, vegan to viscera-stuffed, tacos are a surprisingly wide-ranging dish. Here are just a few of the many types of tacos you can find in the capital.

AL PASTOR

- **What it is:** Spit-roasted pork, usually marinated in a bright red chile-and-achiote rub, topped with a slice of pineapple. *Tacos al pastor* are a specialty of the capital and one of its most ubiquitous dishes.
- **Top it with:** Pineapple, cilantro, white onion, and red or green salsa.
- **When to eat it:** Late at night. Most taquerias specializing in *pastor* don't open till evening and are busiest after 10 or 11pm.
- **Where to get it:** El Vilsito (page 213), Orinoco (page 181), Los Parados (page 181), El Huequito (page 91), Tacos Los Condes (page 214), or Hostal de los Quesos (page 213), among many others.

BARBACOA

- **What it is:** Lamb wrapped in maguey leaves and slow-cooked in a pit.
- **Top it with:** Diced white onion, cilantro, lime juice, spicy salsa. It's often accompanied by *consomé de barbacoa*, a rich lamb-broth soup with garbanzo beans, believed to be a hangover cure.
- **When to eat it:** Early to midmorning.
- **Where to get it:** El Hidalguense (page 177); Arroyo (page 267); on the corner of Durango and Cozumel in the Roma Norte (Sat.-Sun. mornings only).

CARNITAS

- **What it is:** Slow-cooked braised pork, traditionally prepared in a huge copper or stainless-steel pot. *Carnitas* are also popular stuffed into *gorditas*, round corn flatbreads toasted on a griddle.
- **How to order it:** Most or all of the pig is used in *carnitas*: Maciza is the shoulder. Costilla (rib), panza (belly), and chamorro (leg) are popular choices. Adventurous eaters can try buche (stomach), trompa (snout), tripa (tripe), or more unusual parts like nana (uterus). Or get them surtida, a mix of meats.
- **When to eat it:** Morning to early afternoon.
- **Where to get it:** Rincón Tarasco (page 267) or Los Kuinitos (page 123); street stands across the city.

FISH TACOS

- **What it is:** Tacos stuffed with fish of any kind, ranging from Baja-style deep-fried white-fish tacos to the shredded marlin popular along the Pacific coast.
- **Where to get it:** For excellent marlin and shrimp tacos, try Mi Gusto Es (page 215). Get battered and fried fish tacos at El Pescadito (page 185) or the *pescado al pastor* at Contramar (page 185).

TACOS ÁRABES

- **What it is:** Spit-roasted pork served in a soft pita-like flour tortilla.
- **Top it with:** Chipotle salsa and *jocoque (lebne)*.
- **When to eat it:** Afternoon and evening. They're a popular post-bar snack.
- **Where to get it:** Taquería El Greco (page 184), Tacos Manolo (page 214), and Tacos Beyrut (page 311) in the city of Puebla, where tacos árabes were invented.

TACOS DE GUISADO

- **What it is:** Tacos stuffed with *guisos* (stews), like roasted *chile poblano, picadillo* (seasoned ground beef), and *papa con chorizo* (potato with sausage). These are often good for vegans and vegetarians, as *rajas* (strips of chile), Swiss chard, and *chile poblano* are classic *guisos*.
- **Top it with:** Some taquerias offer guacamole, rice, black beans, or hard-boiled egg in your taco, in addition to the *guiso*.
- **When to eat it:** Early and midmorning. At popular spots, they will start to run out by early afternoon.
- **Where to get it:** Tacos El Güero (page 184) or La Poblanita de Tacubaya (page 149); at street stands near the corner of Álvaro Obregón and Insurgentes.

TACOS DORADOS

- **What it is:** Also called flautas, these are deep-fried tacos, traditionally stuffed with potato, cheese, beans, shredded chicken, among other fillings.
- **When to eat it:** Any time of day.
- **Where to get it:** Don Toribio (page 64) in the centro histórico has flautas on their lunch menu; El Rey de las Ahogadas (page 213) in the Colonia del Valle.

CHORIZO, LONGANIZA, MORONGA, AND CECINA

- **What it is:** A wide range of Mexican sausages, from red to green, sweet to spicy, and usually made of pork. *Longaniza* is a long red sausage. *Moronga* (or *morcilla*) is blood sausage. *Cecina* is salt-cured beef, also called *tasajo* when prepared in the Oaxacan style.
- **Where to get it:** Try *longaniza* at Los Cocuyos (page 67) or Tacos Los Condes (page 214). Get *cecina* or chorizo at Super Tacos Chupacabras (page 236).

COCHINITA PIBIL

- **What it is:** Achiote-seasoned shredded pork, typical to the state of Yucatán.
- **Top it with:** Habanero salsa and pickled red onions.
- **Where to get it:** Cochinita Power (page 122) in the San Rafael and El Turix (page 150) in Polanco both specialize in cochinita pibil. Yucatec restaurant Fonda 99.99 (page 210) also serves cochinita in tacos and tortas.

TACOS DE CANASTA

- **What it is:** Also called tacos al vapor (steamed tacos), these small tacos are stuffed with simple fillings—*chicharrón*, beans, and potato are typical options—and warmed in oil, then stored and served in giant baskets, where the steam keeps them warm.
- **Where to get it:** Tacos Joven (page 214) in the Narvarte makes a traditional (but super-size) version of these typical CDMX snack.

VEGAN

- **What it is:** Tacos with no meat or cheese, either made to resemble a typical taco with seitan or textured vegetable protein or just with vegetables. Vegan tacos are rapidly growing in popularity, with offerings that even the most meat-centric eater will appreciate.
- **Where to get it:** Por Siempre Vegana (page 184) and Gracias Madre (page 180), both in the Roma, look (and taste!) like traditional tacos stands, but everything is free of animal products. Mictlan (page 212) in the Narvarte and Los Loosers (page 180) in the Condesa make unique and delicious vegan tacos with a creative twist.

top them), from nopal (prickly pear) with cheese to chorizo, as well as Mexico City staple *pastor*.

MAP 5: Monterrey 333,
tel. 55/8596-0191; 12:30pm-3am
Mon.-Thurs., 12:30pm-5am Fri.,
12:30pm-1am Sun.; Metro: Chilpancingo
or Centro Médico, Metrobús:
Chilpancingo

Por Siempre Vegana $

At first glance, this busy taco stand seems like any other, pulsing with energy as the busy cooks serve up hot-off-the-griddle tacos to the gathered crowd. Here, though, the food is 100 percent vegan, with some tacos made to resemble traditional dishes (they make a very convincing and delicious *pastor*, for example), in addition to tacos stuffed with mushrooms and other veggies. If you're vegan but want to live the full-on taco experience, this is the place to go.

MAP 5: Corner of Manzanillo and Chiapas, tel. 55/3923-7976; 1am-11pm Mon.-Sat., 1pm-9pm Sun.; Metro: Patriotismo, Metrobús: Campeche

Tacos El Güero (Tacos Hola) $

This hole-in-the-wall spot is a neighborhood institution, known for its tasty *tacos de guisado*. You choose your fillings from the daily offerings—like potato with chorizo, shredded chicken, or spinach—which are stuffed into a double tortilla and topped with beans, rice, or guacamole on request. If you come during the lunch rush, don't be deterred—just join the crowd and be patient. The efficient *taqueros* will make sure everyone gets served.

MAP 5: Amsterdam 135,
tel. 56/1866-8923; 10:30am-around 4pm
Mon.-Sat.; Metro: Chilpancingo

Taquería El Greco $

The *taco árabe* with pita bread is a popular culinary fusion of Middle Eastern shawarma-style wraps and Mexican *tacos al pastor*. It's the specialty of the house at this small taquería, a mainstay in the Condesa. Here, lean pork is cooked on a spit, then sliced off and crisped further on the grill before going into the various tacos and *tortas*, including the *árabe*. The same *taquero* has been slicing tacos here for decades.

MAP 5: Michoacán 54,
tel. 55/5553-5742; 2pm-10:30pm
Mon.-Sat.; Metro: Chilpancingo,
Metrobús: Chilpancingo

SEAFOOD
Campobaja $$

With its big wooden tables and views of the treetops, the charming open-air dining room at this second-floor restaurant is an inviting place to spend a few hours with some delicious food and drinks. At this seafood-centric spot, chefs build the constantly changing menu around the freshest catch of the day, with lots of raw plates like oysters, tuna-topped tostadas, *aguachiles*, and ceviches highlighting the quality fish, in addition to Baja-inspired dishes like shrimp burritos and machaca de pescado. A nice list of wines from Baja California complement the food.

MAP 5: Colima 124-E, tel.
55/7091-5660, https://campobaja.com;
1pm-10pm Tues.-Sat., 1pm-6pm Sun.;
Metro: Insurgentes, Metrobús: Jardín Pushkin

Contramar $$

An ultra-popular lunch spot in the Roma Norte, Contramar is widely cited as the city's top spot for seafood, as the constant crowds attest. Ceviches, *tacos de camarón*, fried fish, and the beloved *tostadas de atún* (tuna tostadas) are reliably fresh and deliciously prepared, and go as well with a glass of white wine as a cold *cerveza*. The bright, airy dining room is always bustling with loud, happy, well-heeled diners. Service is attentive and on point. MAP 5: Durango 200, tel. 55/5514-9217 or 55/5514-3169, www.contramar.com. mx; noon-8pm daily; Metro: Sevilla, Metrobús: Durango

El Pescadito $

At lunchtime, there's often a long line running out the door of this friendly taqueria, which serves delicious Sonoran-style fish tacos at bargain prices. The classic taco is stuffed with deep-fried fish and served in a double tortilla, but the gooey chile relleno taco, topped with fried shrimp, is just as good. Order directly from the guys cooking the fish, then dress up your tacos with coleslaw, cabbage, tomatoes, and a spoonful of green or red salsa at the communal bar. MAP 5: Atlixco 38, tel. 55/6268-3045, www.elpescadito.com.mx; 11am-6pm Mon.-Fri., 10am-6pm Sat.-Sun.; Metro: Patriotismo or Juanacatlán

La Docena $$

The original La Docena was a hit in its hometown of Guadalajara, and in 2015, the owners opened a second branch in the Roma to much local enthusiasm. Oysters, the house specialty, are served on the half shell, but also in po'boys (and in beer with Clamato, if you're feeling adventurous). The atmosphere is reliably festive, especially on the weekends, when the sidewalk tables and bar seats fill with diners. MAP 5: Álvaro Obregón 31, tel. 55/5208-0748, http://ladocena.com. mx; noon-midnight daily; Metro: Niños Héroes or Insurgentes, Metrobús: Jardín Pushkin or Álvaro Obregón

✪ Mi Compa Chava $$

There's always a joyous bustle in the dining room at this superlative Mexican-style seafood spot. As waitstaff rush trays of iced oysters to waiting tables, diners tuck into seafood cocktails or snap Instagram-worthy pictures of the beautifully plated tuna-topped tostadas. Micheladas, craft beer, mezcal, and surprisingly excellent coffee and desserts complete the experience. On weekends, the wait for a table can be two hours or more, but once you're seated, order a bucket full of iced beer and make your way through the menu. MAP 5: Zacatecas 172, reservations (available on weekdays only) via WhatsApp 55/7838-5054; noon-8pm Tues.-Sun.; Metro: Insurgentes, Metrobús: Álvaro Obregón

ASIAN
Kura $$

This spacious Japanese restaurant has been a Roma hot spot since its opening in 2016. Most diners come for the high-quality sushi and sashimi, but the extensive menu includes ramen, tempura, noodles, dumplings, wagyu, yakitori, and plenty of shareable small plates—some authentically Japanese, others more untraditional. The light-filled space in an old Roma mansion, along with the constant crowds and impressive bar (sake alone fills eight pages of the menu!), make Kura a reliably enjoyable place for a meal.

MAP 5: Colima 378, WhatsApp 55/7989-3102; 11:30am-midnight Sun.-Mon., 11:30am-11:30pm daily; Metro: Insurgentes, Metrobús: Álvaro Obregón

ITALIAN
Pizzas Félix $

Chewy Neapolitan-style pizzas, served hot from the oven and topped with ingredients like house-made ricotta and shiitake mushrooms, are the main attraction of a meal at Félix, but the menu is rounded with top-notch starters like and kale Caesar and cucumber-chile salad, as well as a bar menu that includes craft cocktails, local beer, mezcal, and wine. It's an upbeat spot at any time of day and open late enough for a post-bar nosh before bedtime.

MAP 5: Álvaro Obregón 64, http://pizzafelix.mx; 1pm-11:45pm Sun.-Wed., 1:30pm-1:30am Thurs.-Fri., noon-1:30am Sat.; Metro: Insurgentes, Metrobús: Álvaro Obregón or Jardín Pushkin

Rosetta $$$

Chef Elena Reygadas serves consistently creative, fresh, and lovingly prepared Italian food in an elegantly restored Roma mansion. Start the meal with an appetizer, like roasted bone marrow, then follow up with one of the delicious pastas or entrées, which always include interesting options, like beet risotto or house-made pappardelle with wild mushrooms. Even if you aren't eating at the restaurant, it's worth dropping into

Salon Rosetta right above the restaurant; here you'll find an intimate atmosphere and with interesting craft cocktails and bar snacks.

MAP 5: Colima 166, tel. 55/5533-7804, http://rosetta.com.mx; 1pm-5:45pm and 6:30pm-11:30pm Mon.-Thurs., 1pm-5:30pm and 6:30pm-11:30pm Fri., Sat., and holidays; Metro: Insurgentes, Metrobús: Álvaro Obregón

Sartoria $$

Everything is handmade, from the pasta to the limoncello, at Sartoria, an Italian restaurant from chef Marco Carboni. The use of fresh, locally sourced ingredients is showcased in colorful salads, tender house-made pastas, and seasonal risottos, which are prepared with care and plated with panache. While food is Italian, native Mexican ingredients make an appearance in dishes like *quelite*-stuffed raviolis. The dining room, with its arched roof and wood tables, has a subdued elegance, lovely for a date night.

MAP 5: Orizaba 42, tel. 55/7265-3616, https://sartoria.mx; 1pm-midnight Mon.-Sat., 1pm-11pm Sun.; Metro: Insurgentes, Metrobús: Insurgentes

INTERNATIONAL
Botancio $$$

A lush tree-filled patio is the oasis-like setting for this upscale Condesa restaurant, which draws a mix of well-heeled locals and visitors for the unique ambience and delicious kitchen. The palate here is distinctive and draws heavily on the use of fresh herbs and produce, from a deeply scented kale salad with sage dressing to pork belly with orange and *pico de gallo*—though you'll also find classic choices, like a grilled

EATING IN THE OFF-HOURS

New York has claimed the reputation as "the city that never sleeps," but Mexico's capital has its own round-the-clock culture. For many capital residents, late nights aren't an anomaly, but a way of life, and there's never an hour of the day when you won't find great eats and a good time here. Here's where to go.

IF YOUR ONE-YEAR-OLD GOT YOU UP AT 5AM
Take advantage of the early rising to have breakfast at traditional **Fonda Margarita** (page 210), a super-casual and beloved breakfast-only restaurant where a line starts to form before the 5:30am opening.

IF YOUR FAMILY WANTS A TREAT AFTER THE SHOW AT BELLAS ARTES
Go out for a creamy hot chocolate and a sugar-topped churro at **Churrería El Moro** (page 69), a lovely old-fashioned sandwich and churro shop that's till 1am on the weekends.

IF YOU NEED A 3AM PICK-ME-UP
Old-time **Café El Popular** (page 66) in the Centro Histórico will set you up with spicy enchiladas, tamales, and a glass tumbler filled with their signature café con leche, at any hour of the day or night.

IF YOU CAN'T DECIDE BETWEEN SLEEP AND TACOS
In the Roma, you can hit **Los Parados** (page 181) till 5am on the weekends. In the Centro, **Los Cocuyos** (page 67) is open all night.

IF THE COCKTAIL BARS HAVE ALL CLOSED IN THE ROMA
Join other revelers for a late-night taco run at the corner of **Insurgentes and Álvaro Obregón,** where popular tacos stands are open all night long.

IF YOU'RE MASSIVELY JET-LAGGED AND ALREADY MISS PARIS
Join other stylish jet-setters for a 3am meal at **Au Pied de Cochon** (page 150), a fancy French restaurant in the InterContinental Presidente Mexico City. It is, remarkably, open 24 hours a day.

---

rib-eye burger, on the constantly changing menu. If you'd just like to enjoy the atmosphere, make a reservation of the beautiful in-house bar, which stays open past the restaurant's closing.

MAP 5: Alfonso Reyes 217, tel. 55/5271-2152; restaurant 1pm-11pm Tues.-Sun., bar 6pm-1:30am Tues.-Sun.; Metro: Chilpancingo, Metrobús: Álvaro Obregón

✪ Máximo Bistrot Local $$$
The market-to-table ethos is fundamental to the menu at Máximo Bistrot Local, where chef Eduardo Garcia brings his kitchen experience and culinary creativity to the restaurant's constantly changing

menu. Depending on what's in season, lunch offerings could include anything from mussels in coconut broth to organic rib eye to chocolate crème brûlée. If you didn't get a reservation, try the chef's more casual breakfast-and-lunch spot Lalo (Zacatecas 173,

Lalo is a popular spot for weekend brunch.

tel. 55/5564-3388, http://eat-lalo.com; 8am-noon and 1pm-6pm Tues.-Sat.), just across the street.

MAP 5: Tonalá 133, tel. 55/5264-4291, maximobistrot.com.mx; 1pm-11pm Tues.-Sat.; 1pm-6pm Sun.; Metro: Insurgentes, Metrobús: Álvaro Obregón

Huset $$

Set in the shaded outdoor patio of a Colonia Roma mansion, this country-inspired restaurant focuses on farm-fresh ingredients. The menu changes frequently but tends to favor simple but sophisticated plates, like roast chicken (made in the in-house wood-fired oven) or lemon gnocchi with mushrooms. Cocktails are delicious, and the atmosphere is ultra-relaxing, far from the bustle of the city.

MAP 5: Colima 256, tel. 55/5511-6767, http://husetroma. com; 1:30pm-midnight Tues.-Wed., 1:30pm-2am Thurs.-Fri., 10am-2am Sat., 10am-midnight Sun.; Metro: Insurgentes, Metrobús: Álvaro Obregón

Merkavá $$

Inventive, flavorful, and vegetable-forward, this small restaurant describes itself as a "Jerusalem kitchen," serving dishes like lamb-stuffed dolmas, roasted cauliflower with za'atar, and several types of hummus, as well as Middle Eastern-inspired desserts, tea, and Turkish coffee. If you go with a group, order the sampler of 14 appetizers—all of which are delicious and include olives, falafel, *lebne* (strained yogurt), beet salad, lentil salad, and other savories.

MAP 5: Amsterdam 53, tel. 55/5086-8065, http://bullandtank.com/merkava; 1pm-midnight Tues.-Sat., 1pm-7pm Sun.; Metro: Sevilla, Metrobús: Álvaro Obregón

Pigeon $$

The famous art nouveau Edificio Río de Janeiro, also known as La Casa de las Brujas, has found a stylish match in bar and restaurant Pigeon, which occupies the ground

atmosphere at Pigeon, just overlooking the Plaza Río de Janeiro

floor of the building. Dishes like roasted sweet potato, house-made gnocchi with ricotta, or grilled chicken are great for sharing or eating solo, and the cocktails are delicious. Amiable service, an upbeat crowd, and views of the tree-filled plaza across the street make it a perfect spot for a late dinner.

MAP 5: Río de Janeiro 56; 1:30pm-midnight Tues.-Wed., 1:30pm-2am Thurs.-Sat., 1:30pm-8pm Sun.; Metro: Insurgentes, Metrobús: Durango

the atmospheric Blend Station

COFFEE AND SWEETS

Blend Station $

The atmosphere is ace at this Condesa coffee shop, with its high ceilings and natural light, whimsical murals on the walls, and coffee drinks served in big glazed ceramic mugs. It's a perfect place to spend a few hours with a book or a friend—though on weekday mornings, the ambience is a bit like an open office (laptops abound). Accompany your coffee with a plate of fancy toast (like avocado and egg) or a breakfast bowl (acai with fruit and yogurt).

MAP 5: Tamaulipas 60, tel. 55/5086-6590, http://blendstation.com.mx; 8am-8pm daily; Metro: Patriotismo, Metrobús: Campeche

Cardinal $

It's easy to develop a caffeine habit at this stellar coffee shop: Inside the small space, there are comfortable tables and chairs, atmospheric Edison bulbs hanging over the bar, free Wi-Fi, glass water bottles on every table, and, most important, ridiculously good coffee. Here, beans (all grown and roasted in Mexico) are carefully selected then matched

with one of the café's many brewing methods, among them Aeropress, siphon, drip, Chemex, and, of course, espresso. The staff can tell you about the flavor and provenance of the beans they are currently brewing.

MAP 5: Córdoba 132, tel. 55/6721-8874; 8am-9pm Mon.-Sat., 9am-8pm Sun.; Metro: Niños Héroes or Insurgentes, Metrobús: Parque Pushkin

Neveria Roxy $

This wonderful vintage ice-cream parlor has been in business since the 1940s, serving generations of Condesa families who keep the place in business with their enthusiastic patronage. Order a cone with two scoops of traditional Mexican *nieve* (similar to sorbet or sherbet, generally with a lower dairy content than most ice creams). Everything is made in-house, with flavors ranging from familiar, like pistachio and lemon, to more unusual, like *maracuyá* (passion fruit) and tamarind. There's a second equally charming branch (Ave. Fernando Montes de Oca 89, tel. 55/5286-1258).

MAP 5: Tamaulipas 161, tel. 55/5256-1854, http://neveriaroxy.com.mx; 11am-8pm daily; Metro: Patriotismo

Panadería Rosetta $

There are near-constant crowds at this superlative bakery, which has earned its reputation for excellence with a daily assortment breads, pastries, cookies, and sweets, ranging from cacao-and-ricotta danishes to loaves of chestnut bread to the lightly sweet pan de pulque. Since its early days as a little hole-in-the-wall shop, the bakery has expanded into a larger space, including many more sidewalk tables for those who want to eat breakfast here—though you should still expect a considerable wait for weekend brunch, when you can accompany your bread with perfectly made espresso drinks or a slice of quiche.

MAP 5: Colima 179, tel. 55/5207-2976; 7am-10pm Mon.-Sat., 7:30am-9:30pm Sun.; Metro: Insurgentes, Metrobús: Insurgentes; smaller location Puebla 242, 7am-8pm Mon.-Sat., 7:30am-6pm Sun.

Nightlife

BARS AND LOUNGES

❂ Café de Nadie

An invariably stylish crowd, expertly made cocktails by invariably stylish bartenders, and live DJs spinning vinyl make this small bar a destination for locals and visitors to the capital. Located at the southern entrance to El Parián market, it manages to be both ultra-cool and laid-back, like the city surrounding it. It's an ace spot to spend the evening—if you can get a table. There's usually a wait and no reservations are accepted.

MAP 5: Chihuahua 135, no tel., www.cafedenadie.mx; 4pm-11pm Mon., 2pm-2am Tues.-Thurs., noon-2am Fri., 10am-2am Sat., 10am-11pm Sun., Metro: Insurgentes, Metrobús: Álvaro Obregón

Jardín Chapultepec

Set in a plant-filled patio with gravel floors and picnic tables, this ultra-casual patio bar often feels like a friend's cool backyard party—but with Mexican craft beer on tap. If you want to make an afternoon of it, there's a menu of pizza and other bar snacks, and for major sporting events, they set up a big screen outside. On a warm afternoon, it's often crowded with locals and their dogs—it's pet-friendly.

MAP 5: Av. Chapultepec 398, tel. 55/7097-1302; 1pm-midnight Tues.-Fri., 9am-midnight Fri.-Sat., 9am-9pm Sun.; no cover; Metro: Insurgentes, Metrobús: Insurgentes

❂ Licorería Limantour

Right on Álvaro Obregón, the Roma's main drag, this buzzing two-story bar has been a mainstay in the CDMX nightlife scene since its opening in 2011. In addition to the lively atmosphere, the bar distinguishes itself with a lineup of ultra-creative cocktails, carefully made with local herbs, fresh produce, and interesting mixers. Grab a seat at the bar before it fills up—which it

Licorería Limantour is one of the Roma's most popular cocktail bars.

always does on the weekends—to chat with the friendly bartenders. Despite the top-shelf drinks and constant crowds, it's an unpretentious and welcoming spot.

MAP 5: Álvaro Obregón 106, tel. 55/5264-4122, https://limantour.tv; 6pm-midnight Sun.-Tues., 6pm-1am Wed., 6pm-2am Thurs.-Sat., 6pm-2:30am Sun.; no cover; Metro: Insurgentes, Metrobús: Álvaro Obregón

✪ Páramo

There's a convivial house-party-like ambience at this perpetually packed second-floor bar and eatery, located just above restaurant El Parnita and owned by the same family. The top-notch food and drinks are a big part of the appeal: snacks like fried fish tacos and guacamole go perfectly with the selection of craft beer, Mexican wine, and mezcal on offer. But it's the fun crowd and ace atmosphere that's the real draw here, whether you're seated in the plant-filled barroom or one of the cozy smaller salons. Things get going early here and don't wrap till closing.

MAP 5: Yucatán 84, tel. 55/5941-5125, reservations via WhatsApp 55/7349-0436; 3pm-1:30am daily; no cover; Metro: Insurgentes, Metrobús: Álvaro Obregón

Supra

On the top floor of one of the tallest buildings in the Colonia Roma, Supra draws nightly crowds for its stellar 360-degree views of one of the biggest cities on earth. With vistas like this, food and drinks are better than they have to be, and the bar offerings are incredibly extensive, including signature cocktails, spritzes, craft beer, wine, mezcal, and more. Reservations are recommended at all times but are absolutely necessary in the evenings, when the city surrounds you in a sea of lights.

MAP 5: Álvaro Obregón 151, 14th fl., tel. 55/3270-4367, supraroma. wpcomstaging.com; no cover; 1pm-1am Tues.-Fri., 11am-1am Sat., no cover

BREWERIES AND BEER
Drunkendog

With over 30 beers of predominantly Mexican providence on tap, plus dozens more in the bank of refrigerators at the entrance, Drunkendog is the perfect place to get acquainted with some of the best brews in Mexico's booming craft beer movement. You can order in 150ml, 300ml, or 500ml (pint) glasses, giving you a chance to try a bunch of different styles and brewers. With green-tiled walls and a big wood bar, the place is definitively low-key, but stylish enough for a Saturday night.

MAP 5: Av. Nuevo León 4-A, tel. 55/4945-4273, www.drunkendog. mx; 2pm-midnight Mon.-Wed., 2pm-2am Thurs.-Fri., 10am-2am Sat., 10am-midnight Sun.; no cover

Patio Escondido

Set with picnic tables and shaded by trees, this relaxed beer garden is run by Monstruo de Agua, a Mexico City–based craft brewer that uses rainwater and sustainable practices in creating their beers, which are featured, alongside with guest brews, on the constantly changing menu. It can get crowded on the weekends, but is a very relaxed spot on a weekday afternoon. Look for this "hidden patio" tucked down an alley behind what appears to be a funky craft shop on Jalapa (from the street, the only indication that you've arrived is the sign above the door).

MAP 5: Jalapa 90, tel. 55/3226-6422; 2pm-9pm Wed.-Thurs. and Sun., 2pm-10pm Fri.-Sat.; no cover

Patio Escondido is a relaxed beer garden run by CDMX-based brewery Monstruo de Agua.

CANTINAS
El Centenario

Tucked between the stylish bars and restaurants of the Condesa neighborhood, this thoroughly unpretentious neighborhood cantina maintains a loyal clientele with its comfortable atmosphere, cheap drinks, and generally low-key patrons. The crowd is certainly a bit more gentrified than it was in the old days, but there's still a contingent of regulars chatting, playing dominoes, or watching a soccer match in the barroom.

MAP 5: Vicente Suárez 42, tel. 55/5553-5451; noon-1am Mon.-Wed., noon-2am Thurs.-Sat.; no cover; Metro: Patriotismo

Covadonga

This spacious cantina near the Plaza Río de Janeiro was once a quiet neighborhood watering hole where men gathered to play dominoes and sip tequila served from the fine old bar. In the past decade, however, it has also become popular with a hip Roma crew. Now, the seniors are joined by a bevy of artists and scenesters converging for drinks and Spanish food. It's a fun place for an evening out, uniting the old and new Roma.

MAP 5: Puebla 121, tel. 55/5533-2922; 1pm-2am Mon.-Sat., 1pm-7pm Sun.; no cover; Metro: Insurgentes

Riviera del Sur

This wonderful cantina in the southern Roma has an airy dining room decorated with wood paneling and filled with game tables, in the traditional CDMX style. There is sometimes live music in the afternoons and dominoes to play at your table. It's worth dining here, too; the kitchen makes lovely Yucatec-inspired food, including *sopa de lima* (lemon soup), *panuchos* (corn cakes topped with pulled pork), and *vaporcitos* (tamales in banana leaf).

MAP 5: Chiapas 174-B, tel. 55/5264-1552; 1pm-midnight Sun.-Wed., 1pm-2am Thurs.-Sat.; Metro: Centro Médico, Metrobús: Michoacán

TEQUILA AND MEZCAL

La Clandestina

As the name suggests, this tucked-away mezcal bar feels rather clandestine, though its dim, hole-in-the-wall appearance is stylish by design. Here, small-batch mezcal is served from big glass jugs lined up behind the bar; it's a good place to up your knowledge of the spirit, as the menu details each mezcal's producer, region, proof, flavor profile, and price. After a taste, you may want to pick up a bottle of their Enmascarado mezcal to take home.

MAP 5: Av. Álvaro Obregón 298, tel. 55/5525-1100, www.milagrito. com; 6pm-midnight Mon., 6pm-2am Tues.-Sun; no cover; Metro: Sevilla, Metrobús: Álvaro Obregón

Tlecan

One thing that distinguishes Tlecan from the many hot spots in the Roma neighborhood is the genuinely attentive and genial service. Bartenders and waitstaff are eager to talk about the small but beautifully curated list of mezcal, Mexican spirits, and mixed drinks on the menu, which includes more unusual offerings like tecuino, a fermented maize drink, and bacanora, a distilled spirit from Sonora. It's a dark, tiny spot that gets packed with patrons late in the evening, but the buzzy atmosphere is part of the fun.

MAP 5: Álvaro Obregón 228, no tel., https://tlecan.com; 6pm-2am daily; no cover

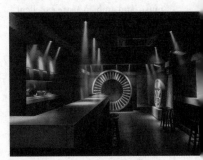

Tlecan

PULQUERÍAS
La Nuclear Pulquería

This sweet little bar maintains the mellow, neighborhood atmosphere typical to classic *pulquerías* while introducing a dose of Roma cool to the mix. Here, fresh flavored pulques are ladled into clay tumblers, which you can sip at one of the folding tin tables on the sidewalk or in the row of cozy wooden booths in the narrow back room, which is decorated with sepia-toned murals.
MAP 5: Querétaro 100, tel. 55/5574-5367; 5pm-midnight Mon., 4pm-midnight Tues.-Wed., 4pm-2am Thurs.-Sat., 4pm-10pm Sun., no cover; Metro: Insurgentes

LIVE MUSIC
Jazzatlan Capital

There's a bohemian feeling at this cozy Roma jazz club and cocktail bar, which features high-quality live music six nights a week. Though it's a relaxed environment, the bar can get quite crowded on the weekends, when there are bands playing both in the upstairs "club" and the downstairs "salon." Reservations are required for shows upstairs, and there is often a wait to get in (and standing room only) downstairs. It's worth the hassle/advance planning, as the music and ambience are excellent.
MAP 5: Guanajuato 239, reservations WhatsApp 52 551 390 1631, www.jazzatlan.club/capital; 6pm-2am Tues.-Sun., club shows generally start at 10pm; US$0-20; Metro: Insurgentes, Metrobús: Álvaro Obregón

La Bodeguita en Medio

A nod to the famous Havana bar of the same name, this Cuban spot has an upbeat atmosphere every night of the week, with party-happy patrons sipping the Bodeguita's signature mojitos, nibbling on rice, beans, and fried plantains, and shouting over the live band. Inside the multilevel, dimly lit space, the walls are scribbled with notes and photographs. For those who want to practice their groove, there are salsa classes at least once a week.
MAP 5: Cozumel 37, tel. 55/5553-0246, http://labodeguitadelmedio.com.mx; 1:30pm-1am Sun.-Wed., 1:30pm-2am Sat.; no cover; Metro: Sevilla

BILLIARDS AND GAMES
Salón Malafama

This attractive billiard hall is filled front to back with red-felt-topped pool tables, and it is always packed with a young crowd drinking and racking up games. It's a mellow place to pass several pleasant hours on a weekend night before going out, though it's lively enough to be a destination in itself. If you want to beat the crowds, go in the early afternoon, when there are usually free tables.
MAP 5: Michoacán 78, tel. 55/5553-5138, http://salonmalafama.com.mx; 5pm-midnight Mon.-Tues., 1pm-1am Wed.-Sat., 1pm-midnight Sun., no cover, billiards US$9/hour; Metro: Patriotismo, Metrobús: Sonora

Petanca Roma Club

The French garden game petanque has a small but enthusiastic following in Mexico City, and this relaxed bar and gathering place has become a favorite with locals who love to play. There are four petanque courts at this surprisingly spacious joint, which are available

CANTINA CULTURE

Sometimes historic, invariably low-key, and usually inexpensive, cantinas are quintessential places to eat and drink in Mexico City. Some cantinas are best for drinking and fill up at night, while others are family-friendly and popular for lunch. Most traditional cantinas offer free snacks, called *botanas,* with your drinks, which can range from a plate of peanuts to a three- or four-course meal, though some cantinas function more like restaurants. There are cantinas with food that rivals the best eateries in the city. Here's some noteworthy cantinas to check out.

La Bipo

OLD-SCHOOL CANTINAS

- **Bar La Ópera** (page 67), though still considered a cantina by most, is a full-service restaurant with a large menu of traditional Mexican food. It's historic, beautiful, and ideal for a shot of tequila accompanied by a *sangrita* chaser.

- **Covadonga** (page 193) is a classic spot. Though hipsters love it, lots of old-timers also come here for dominoes and drinks.

- **La Polar** (page 122) is a traditional cantina in the San Rafael that's famous for its *birria* (goat-meat stew).

- **La Valenciana** (page 216) is a pretty neighborhood cantina that draws Narvarte locals for food and drinks.

- **La Coyoacana** (page 239) in Coyoacán is a classic family-friendly cantina where musicians wander through the crowds on the weekends.

NEW-SCHOOL CANTINAS

- **Riviera del Sur** (page 193) is an upbeat spot in the Roma Sur with a menu of top-notch Yucatec food.

- **Salón Ríos** (page 126) has a classic feeling but a contemporary edge, with formal service but a modern take on food and drinks.

- **La Bipo** (page 239), an often-boisterous spot in Coyoacán, has a modern ambience but maintains the chill atmosphere typical of a cantina.

CANTINAS FOR DRINKING

- Traditional cantinas **Tío Pepe** (page 95) and **La Faena** (page 70) are best for a drink; kitchens aren't the attraction here.

- **El Centenario** (page 192), a long-running cantina in the Condesa, is an excellent place for cold beers and an unpretentious atmosphere in the afternoon or evening.

CURE THE *CRUDA*

If going out big is a way of life in Mexico City, it's no surprise that there are ample **hangover remedies** reputed to alleviate the post-party blues. If you've got a *cruda* (hangover) after a night out, here are some local solutions:

VUELVE A LA VIDA

One of the most popular hangover remedies is the famous *vuelve a la vida* (literally a "return to life"), a cold mixed-seafood cocktail, tossed with tomato, lime juice, cilantro, and lots of chile—the worse the hangover, the spicier you go to "sweat it out." Across Mexico, it's not uncommon to see bleary-eyed breakfasters lining up at seafood stalls in the early morning hours. Try it for yourself at **Jardín del Pulpo** in **Mercado Coyoacán** (page 237), the neighborhood's central food market.

BIRRIA

Birria, a goat-meat stew, is widely known as a hangover cure. Served boiling hot, then doused with chile and lime juice, it will certainly get you sweating. Try **La Polar** (page 122) in the San Rafael neighborhood for some of the city's best, and you'll find plenty of other diners, post-revelry, basking in the healing heat.

BARBACOA

Barbacoa, or slow-cooked lamb, is also a popular day-after remedy. Specifically, post-partiers seek out the pungent lamb broth served at most **barbacoa stands** (there is a popular spot on the corner of Cozumel and Durango, in the Roma, on Saturday and Sunday mornings) or at casual eateries like **El Hidalguense** (page 177). Spoon on some ultra-spicy salsa, top it off with white onions and cilantro, and sweat it all out.

POLLA

On the stranger end of the spectrum, a *polla* is a blended smoothie made from orange juice, *jerez* (sherry), a raw quail egg, and a touch of vanilla. It's sold at **street-side juice stands** throughout the city. The idea is to down your *polla* rapidly to alleviate your hangover lickety-split.

first-come, first-served and free of charge. If the courts are full, which is often the case in the evenings, it's just as fun to order some bar snacks, a craft beer, or a glass of wine on tap (a rarity in the capital) and watch the games.

MAP 5: Colima 124A, tel. 55/6586-0544; 5pm-midnight Tues.-Thurs., 1pm-midnight Fri.-Sat., 1pm-6pm Sun.; no cover; Metro: Insurgentes, Metrobús: Jardín Pushkin

Arts and Culture

CULTURAL CENTERS

Casa Lamm

An opulent Colonia Roma mansion, Casa Lamm was originally built by architect Lewis Lamm in 1911. Today, it's home to a small art school (which offers workshops, as well as undergraduate and graduate programs), a light-filled contemporary art gallery, and chic fusion restaurant **Nueve Nueve** (tel. 55/5525-9795, www.nuevenueve.com.

mx, 1:30pm-midnight Mon.-Sat., 1:30pm-7pm Sun.). In the basement, the well-stocked Biblioteca de Arte has a large selection of contemporary and modern art books.

MAP 5: Álvaro Obregón 99, tel. 55/5525-3938, www.casalamm. com.mx, www.galeriacasalamm. com.mx; cultural center 10am-11pm Mon.-Wed., 10am-midnight Thurs.-Sat., 10am-7pm Sun.; gallery 10am-7pm Mon.-Sat., 10am-5pm Sun.; free; Metro: Insurgentes

GALLERIES
Galería OMR

OMR has maintained a strong reputation for contemporary art in Mexico City since its founding in 1983. Preceding many of the popular galleries in the Roma, OMR has in many ways set the tone for the neighborhood, supporting emerging artists and avant-garde propositions. In 2016, it moved from its longtime space beside the Plaza Río de Janeiro to the Sala Margolin, which was, for 60 years, a wonderful bookstore and record shop that specialized in classical music—an attractive environment for the top-quality art on show.

MAP 5: Córdoba 100, tel. 55/5511-1179 or 55/5207-1080, https://omr.art; 10am-6pm Tues.-Thurs., 10am-4pm Fri., 11-4pm Sat.; free; Metro: Insurgentes, Metrobús: Álvaro Obregón or Parque Pushkin

Machete Gallery

There is a big picture window looking into the showroom of this contemporary art gallery, which is located on the ground floor of a beautiful Roma mansion and represents a varied roster of Latin American artists, both emerging and mid-career. Though the space is small, there's generally a lot of work on view, and the gallery maintains a stock of artwork at accessible prices aimed at young collectors.

MAP 5: Córdoba 25, tel. 55/5207-8779, https://macheteart.com; 11:30am-7:30pm Mon.-Fri., 11am-5pm Sat.; Metro: Insurgentes, Metrobús: Insurgentes

MUSEUMS
Museo del Objeto del Objeto (MODO)

This small museum, housed in a lovely Beaux-Arts mansion, focuses on the history of design and communications in Mexico City. Every few months, the museum inaugurates a new exhibit, dedicated to a theme like *lucha libre* or the history of the Roma neighborhood. Stories are often told via everyday objects, like matchbooks, enameled tin boxes, toys, watches, and posters, many of which are part of the museum's collection of over 100,000 design pieces.

Museo del Objeto del Objeto in the Roma

MAP 5: Colima 145, tel. 55/5533-9637, www.elmodo.mx; 10am-6pm Tues.-Sun.; US$3, US$1.50 students, teachers, and Roma neighborhood residents (with ID), children under 12 free; Metro: Insurgentes, Metrobús: Álvaro Obregón or Parque Pushkin

Museo Soumaya–Casa Guillermo Tovar de Tereza

Early 20th-century writer and historian Guillermo Tovar de Tereza was a chronicler of Mexico City and collector of art. His former home, a Porfiriato-era mansion in the Roma Norte, is now owned by Mexican billionaire Carlos Slim's Museo Soumaya. Free to enter and filled with Tovar de Tereza's collection of art, it's a petite but engaging spot that offers a nice glimpse into the life and interests of a preeminent Mexican intellectual.

MAP 5: Valladolid 52, tel. 55/1103-9800, www.museosoumaya.org; 10:30am-6:30pm daily; free; Metro: Insurgentes, Metrobús: Insurgentes

THEATER, CLASSICAL MUSIC, AND DANCE
Foro Shakespeare

Originally founded as a bookshop specializing in theater, the Foro Shakespeare eventually grew to include several performance spaces. Today, it's a nonprofit arts organization with a reputation for launching the careers of playwrights and actors. The 200-seat main venue puts on a range of musicals, comedies, and dramas (in Spanish), while you might find monologues or stand-up comedy in the smaller performance spaces.

MAP 5: Zamora 7, tel. 55/5256-0014, www.foroshakespeare.com; showtimes vary, but generally matinees 1pm, evening performance 7pm-10:30pm; US$8-25, Metro: Chapultepec

La Teatrería

See both well-known names and new talent in acting, direction, and playwriting at this active theater company, located on a quiet Roma street. For a small theater, the number of shows at La Teatrería produces is impressive, with new plays constantly opening, many by Mexican playwrights. There are occasional theater or music performances for children, as well as workshops in acting, ballet, yoga, music, and other creative arts in their upstairs studio.

MAP 5: Tabasco 152, tel. 55/5207-3234, www.lateatreria.com; box office 2pm-7pm Mon.-Fri., 11am-2pm and 4pm-7pm Sat.-Sun. showtimes vary, but are generally at 8:30pm or 9pm; tickets US$15-20; Metro: Insurgentes, Metrobús: Álvaro Obregón

Recreation

COMMUNITY CENTERS

★ Huerto Roma Verde

This wonderful ecological organization in the Roma has multiple facets. It maintains a large urban garden and chicken coop; hosts workshops in urban farming, composting, sustainable architecture, and other green topics; and oversees an ongoing program of ecology- and food-related events on the weekends, with themes ranging from edible insects to Mexican wines. If you stop by on the weekend, you can wander around the garden or have vegan snacks and craft beer on tap at one of the many shaded picnic tables.

the geodesic dome at Huerto Roma Verde

MAP 5: Jalapa 234, tel. 55/5564-2210, http://huertoromaverde.org; 10am-7pm Tues.-Sun..; Metro: Centro Médico, Metrobús: Campeche

Shops

ROMA SHOPPING DISTRICT

Álvaro Obregón has long been the heart of the Roma, and as the neighborhood becomes trendier, cute boutiques and galleries have cropped up alongside the avenue's old bookshops and ice-cream parlors. More recently, the parallel street Colima has become a hub of popular fashion design and concept shops, as has Córdoba, where you'll find everything from super-funky vintage clothing stores to a Doc Martens shop.

MAP 5: Colima between Insurgentes and Av. Cuauhtémoc, and Álvaro Obregón between Insurgentes and Av. Cuauhtémoc; Metro: Insurgentes

ANTIQUES AND COLLECTIBLES

Mercado de Cuauhtémoc

One of the funkiest vintage markets in the city is the weekly Mercado de Cuauhtémoc, in the Jardín Dr. Ignacio Chávez. Though the market also sets up on Sunday, you'll find the best vendors and largest selection on Saturday morning. Intrepid buyers with a good eye will stumble upon some real gems here, like mid-century furniture, eyeglasses from the 1950s and '60s, unusual vinyl records, desk lamps, vintage toy trains, and discontinued Lego sets.

MAP 5: Jardín Dr. Ignacio Chávez, Cuauhtémoc y Dr. Liceaga, Roma; 9am-3pm Sat.; Metro: Niños Héroes

BOOKS
Casa Bosques

It's pleasant to browse in this pretty second-floor bookshop, which has a range of well-selected titles in art, architecture, theory, and design, as well as independent magazines and artists' books, in both English and Spanish. The decor reflects the owners' interest in aesthetics, with pleasing white-painted floors, unusual wood bookshelves, and lots of natural light. The doors to the building are closed, even when the bookstore is open; ring the doorbell and the staff will buzz you in.

MAP 5: Córdoba 25, tel. 55/6378-2976, https://casabosques.net; 11am-7pm daily; Metro: Insurgentes, Metrobús: Insurgentes

Casa Bosques is a beautiful bookshop focused on art, architecture, photography, and design.

✪ Librería Rosario Castellanos

Run by the Fonda de Cultura y Económica (FCE), this bookshop has one of the best selections of Spanish-language titles in the city, including literature, culture, history, and sociology books published by the FCE. Located in the art deco Cine Lido building in the **Centro Cultural Bella Época**, the light-filled space has high ceilings decorated with glass panels by artist Jan Hendrix. There are comfy chairs throughout the stacks, a carpeted kids' section, and an in-house coffee shop.

MAP 5: Tamaulipas 202, tel. 55/5276-7110, www. fondodeculturaeconomica.com; 9am-11pm daily; Metro: Patriotismo

Under the Volcano Books

Named for the Malcolm Lowry novel about a British attaché living in Cuernavaca, this cozy English-language bookstore is on the second floor of the American Legion building in the Condesa. There's a wide selection of well-priced secondhand books in English, with an emphasis on fiction, though it also stocks poetry, history, essays, and more.

MAP 5: Celaya 25, http:// underthevolcanobooks.com; 11am-6pm Mon.-Sat.; Metro: Sevilla, Metrobús: Sonora

CLOTHING, SHOES, AND ACCESSORIES
180° Shop

Among the most well-stocked and charming of the Roma's many cool boutiques, 180° Shop sells a fun collection of urbanwear and accessories, like graphic tees, tennis shoes, skateboards, handbags, and design books and city guides, in addition to their proprietary line of hoodies, miniskirts, ball caps, T-shirts, and other hipster essentials. They

There's an excellent selection of home goods, clothing, and other design items at the Happening Store in the Roma Norte.

also carry a small line of children's clothes, including hand-embroidered shirts and adorable silkscreen tees.

MAP 5: Colima 180, tel. 55/5525-5626, www.180grados.mx; 10am-7:30pm Mon.-Sat., 10:30am-6pm Sun.; Metro: Insurgentes

Goodbye Folk

At this vintage shop and independent shoemaker, there are four floors of unique, specially tailored vintage dresses, blue jeans, button-downs, leather jackets, and more. The also have a line of shoes that mix both contemporary and old-timey aesthetics, you might find polka-dot beetle boots, aquamarine oxfords, or vintage-inspired lace-up leather booties.

MAP 5: Córdoba 55, tel. 55/5525-4109, http://goodbyefolk.com; 9am-9pm Mon.-Fri., 11am-8pm Sat.-Sun.; Metro: Insurgentes

DESIGN, ART, AND GIFT SHOPS

✪ Chic By Accident

This eye-catching design shop and gallery specializes in unique mid-century Mexican furniture and home accessories, in addition to showing a selection of artwork by contemporary artists. Occupying the second floor and rooftop terrace of an old Roma mansion, the space is gorgeous—don't miss the terrace, where there are more pieces on view and a lovely in-the-treetops feeling. Appointments are preferred, but if you drop by, buzz from the street to be let in.

MAP 5: Orizaba 28, tel. 55/3376-0412, www.chicbyaccident.com; 10am-8pm Mon.-Fri., 10am-6pm Sat.; Metro: Insurgentes, Metrobús: Insurgentes

Happening Store

This well-stocked design-centric home, clothing, and gift shop has a cool Roma vibe but a friendly and unpretentious attitude. It's a great place to pick up something that will remind you of CDMX, like graphic tees, leather handbags, colorblock swimsuits, journals, and colorful kids toys, among other cool home accents, clothes, and accessories, all designed in Mexico. The selection changes frequently, so it's worth a repeat visit.

MAP 5: Tabasco 210, tel. 55/5919-1254; 11am-7pm daily; Metro: Insurgentes, Metrobús: Durango

Hydra Foto

Part of the mission of this small photography gallery is to promote emerging photographers and to offer young collectors the opportunity to buy artwork at affordable prices. In addition to the rotating work hanging on its walls—much of it avant-garde, often by local artists, and usually well-priced—the gallery has a fine selection of photography books on sale, including a small selection published by their own imprint. The gallery also has a robust educational program, with frequent workshops in photography and design.

MAP 5: Tampico 33, tel. 55/6819-9872; http://hydra.lat; noon-7pm Tues.-Sat.; Metro: Chapultepec

La Canasta

Artes de Mexico is a small press that publishes a high-quality collectible magazine series covering Mexican traditions, culture, and people. At its headquarters in the Roma neighborhood, the press operates a lovely gift shop, where you can find a nice selection of handcraft from across the country, including wool textiles and embroidered blouses, traditional Mexican toys, handwoven baskets, and *alebrijes* (hand-painted wood animals from Oaxaca), in addition to a large selection of their magazine titles. It's a good spot to find a last-minute, thoroughly Mexican gift for a friend.

MAP 5: Córdoba 69, tel. 55/5525-5905; www.artesdemexico.com/la-canasta; 11am-7pm Wed.-Sun.; Metro: Insurgentes, Metrobús: Álvaro Obregón or Parque Pushkin

La Canasta sells well-priced traditional Mexican crafts.

GOURMET FOOD AND IMPORTS

Delirio

This popular bistro and deli sells a range of gourmet products, many with a Mexican heritage. You can pick up olive oil from Baja California, a bottle of wine from Casa Madero in Coahuila, or guava jam and dried-chile salsa, jarred under chef Monica Patiño's label. If browsing makes you hungry, order a fresh salad, a slice of quiche, and a cup of coffee from the deli, then grab a seat at one of the sidewalk tables. There is another Patiño-owned café and deli **Abarrotes** (Abarrotes Delirio, Colima 114, tel.

55/5264-1468), also in the Roma Norte, with a smaller selection of her products on sale.

MAP 5: Monterrey 116, tel. 55/5584-0870, www.delirio.mx; 8am-10pm Mon.-Sat., 9am-7pm Sun.; Metro: Insurgentes, Metrobús: Álvaro Obregón

MUSIC
Retroactivo Records

There are a surprising number of super-cool and well-stocked record shops in the Roma Norte, each with their own specialty. Retroactivo is among the most popular, catering to local vinyl collectors with rare and imported LPs among its tens of thousands of titles. The focus is on used records (they also buy and trade), representing a wide selection of eras, from the 1960s through the 1990s, and styles, from children's music to disco.

MAP 5: Jalapa 125, tel. 55/7158-5701, www.retroactivorecords.com.mx; 11am-8pm Mon.-Sat., 11am-4pm Sun.; Metro: Insurgentes, Metrobús: Álvaro Obregón

PUBLIC MARKETS
Mercado de Medellín

This neighborhood market in the Roma Sur is spacious and well-lit, with dozens of produce stands piled high with fresh fruits and vegetables, cheesemongers, and fresh tortillas on sale. Mercado de Medellín is known for its excellent seafood sold in bulk, as well as for the vendors selling goods from the Yucatán peninsula, like habanero salsas and pickled onions.

MAP 5: Medellín 234; 8am-5pm daily; Metro: Chilpancingo, Metrobús: Campeche

WINE AND LIQUOR
Sabrá Dios?

If you're looking for an unusual gift for an unusually discriminating friend, try this teensy shop in the Condesa, which specializes in small-batch spirits, including rare bottles of mezcal from Guerrero or Durango and *sotol*, a distilled spirit native to northern Mexico, made from the sotol plant. The knowledgeable staff can give you background on the production methods and provenance of everything on sale, and before you buy, you can taste from the bottles you're considering.

MAP 5: Veracruz 15-A, tel. 55/5211-7623; 9am-9pm Mon.-Sat.; Metro: Chilpancingo

Insurgentes Sur-Narvarte Map 6

Traveling south from the city center, Avenida Insurgentes is flanked on both sides by sprawling residential neighborhoods. Filled with family-friendly parks, tree-lined streets, and plenty of low-key eateries, these neighborhoods are becoming increasingly popular with visitors to the city, though they maintain a lovely local ambience. The tree-filled **Narvarte** is known for its many **taco stands** and **outdoor markets,** the expansive and largely residential **Colonia del Valle's** many mid-20th-century apartment buildings are complemented by ample greenery, and **Nápoles,** on the west side of Insurgentes, is a quiet but centrally located area. While there are some notable sights, these neighborhoods are best explored with the intention of experiencing everyday life in the capital.

TOP SIGHTS

- Site to See Before It's Gone:
  Centro SCOP (page 208)
- Art Meets Architecture: **Poliforum
  Siqueiros** (page 208)

TOP RESTAURANTS

- Best Traditional Breakfast:
  Fonda Margarita (page 210)
- Super Sinaloan Seafood:
  Mi Gusto Es (page 215)

TOP NIGHTLIFE

- Coolest Cocktails: **Kaito** (page 216)

TOP SHOPS

- Top Spot for Handcrafts: **FONART**
  (page 218)

GETTING THERE AND AROUND

- Metro lines: 3
- Metro stops: Etiopía, Eugenia,
  División del Norte
- Metrobús lines: 1
- Metrobús stops: Poliforum, Nápoles,
  Del Valle, Ciudad de los Deportes,
  Parque Hundido, Félix Cuevas, Río
  Churubusco, Teatro Insurgentes

1

2

3

SEE MAP 5

1

A

AVENIDA PROGRESO

VIADUCTO-PRESIDENTE MIGUEL-ALEMÁN

CALLE JOSÉ MARTÍ

AVENIDA REVOLUCIÓN

CALLE PUENTE DE LA MORENA

CALLE MINERÍA

XOLA

CALLE NICOLÁS SAN JUAN

B

COLONIA
NAPOLES

CALLE CHICAGO

CALLE DAKOTA

AVENIDA INSURGENTES SUR

6

Poliforum
Siqueiros
4

CALLE PEDRO ROMERO DE TERREROS

AVENIDA DIVISIÓN DEL NORTE

CALLE COYOACÁN

7

CALLE AMORES

GABRIEL MANCERA

CALLE TORRES ADALID

CALLE LUZ SAVIÑÓN

San Pedro
de los Pinos

CALLE 9

CALLE TEXAS

CALLE OKLAHOMA

CALLE LOUISIANA

CALLE ALABAMA

AVENIDA MAGDALENA

CALLE SAN FRANCISCO

CALLE PATRICIO SANZ

CALLE AGUSTÍN GONZÁLEZ COSSÍO

CALLE ADOLFO PRIETO

CALLE PROVIDENCIA

CALLE CONCEPCIÓN BEISTEGUI

CALLE 17

Jardín
Esparza
Oteo

CALLE PENNSYLVANIA

CALLE INDIANA

CALLE GEORGIA

CALLE ALABAMA

CALLE NEBRASKA

13

AVENIDA COLONIA DEL VALLE

AVENIDA DIVISIÓN DEL

C

CALLE KANSAS

CALLE MISSOURI

CALLE NUEVA YORK

AVENIDA EUGENIA

12

CALLE SAN
ANTONIO

AVENIDA SAN ANTONIO

CALLE SAN BORJA

San Antonio

CALLE

TINTORETO

ÁNGEL URRAZA

AVENIDA TOYOACÁN

CALLE AMORES

GABRIEL MANCERA

19

20

D

AVENIDA PATRIOTISMO

CALLE AUGUSTO RODÍN

AVENIDA INSURGENTES SUR

22

AVENIDA PORFIRIO DÍAZ

CALLE MATÍAS ROMERO

18

Jardín del Arte
Tlacoquemécatl

25

CALLE PILARES

Parque
Arboledas

26

CALLE JUAN FRANCISCO MILLET

Parque
Hundido
21

CALLE TLACOQUEMÉCATL

23

24

CALLE JOSÉ MARÍA PESTALOZZI

Mixcoac

Parque
San Lorenzo

MANZANILLO

27

CALLE MOLINOS

CALLE MIGUEL LAURENT

CALLE NICOLÁS SAN JUAN

CALLE JUAN SÁNCHEZ AZCONA

E

EXTREMADURA

CALLE PRESA

CALLE SAN FRANCISCO

CALLE PATRICIO SANZ

AVENIDA UNIVERSIDAD

CALLE ANAXÁGORAS

Insurgentes Sur

FÉLIX CUEVAS

CALLE ADOLFO PRIETO

CALLE DOCTOR ROBERTO GAYOL

SAN LORENZO

CALLE HERIBERTO FRÍAS

CUAUHTÉMOC

Hospital 20 de
Noviembre

28

CALLE PARROQUIA

Zapata

PORTALES
NORTE

F

CALLE PLATEROS

CALLE SAN FRANCISCO

JOSÉ MARÍA RICO

AVENIDA COYOACÁN

CALLE AMORES

AVENIDA POPOCATÉPETL

CALLE FELIX PARRA

Teatro de los
Insurgentes

31

30

SEE MAP 8

CALLE RODRÍGUEZ SARO

DISTANCE ACROSS MAP
Approximate: 3.5 mi or 5.6 km

SIGHTS

| 4 | B2 | Poliforum Siqueiros | 21 | D1 | Parque Hundido |
| 11 | B5 | Centro SCOP | 30 | F1 | Teatro de los Insurgentes |

RESTAURANTS

1	A3	La Secina	15	C4	Tacos Manolo
2	A5	Mi Gusto Es	16	C4	Mictlan Antojitos Veganos
3	A5	Peltre Ionchería	17	C4	El Vilsito
6	B2	Tacos Los Condes	23	D2	Fonda Margarita
7	B3	El Rey De Las Ahogadas	24	D2	Los Chamorros de Tlacoquemecatl
9	B4	Tacos Joven	25	D2	Hostal de Los Quesos
12	C2	Chiandoni	27	E2	Fonda 99.99
13	C2	Asador Libanés	28	E2	Tortas Don Polo
14	C4	Las Tlayudas, comida casual Oaxaqueña			

NIGHTLIFE

| 8 | B4 | Luvina Vegan Bar | 26 | D3 | Kaito Bar Izakaya |
| 10 | B5 | Cantina La Valenciana | | | |

SPORTS AND ACTIVITIES

| 19 | D1 | Monumental Plaza de Toros Mexico | 29 | E4 | Parque de los Venados |
| 20 | D1 | Estadio Ciudad de los Deportes | | | |

SHOPS

| 5 | B2 | Hotel Vermont | 22 | D2 | Hotel Diplomático |
| 18 | D1 | Fonart Patriotismo | 31 | F1 | City Express Plus |

SEE MAP 7

© MOON.COM

⭐ Poliforum Siqueiros

On Insurgentes Sur, in the shadow of the 50-story World Trade Center de México, this eye-catching arts complex is covered with huge three-dimensional murals created by artist David Alfaro Siqueiros. Commissioned by ex-revolutionary Manuel Suárez, the mural was originally intended for a building in Cuernavaca, but the project was relocated to its present site in 1965, opening in 1977.

Inside, in the second-floor Foro Universal, Siqueiros created a massive, three-dimensional mural entitled *La Marcha de la Humanidad* (The March of Humanity), a tribute to the people who fought to better society. On the ground floor, the there are often rotating exhibits by contemporary artists, and there's a nice café, if you want to linger. The building is currently undergoing extensive renovations with the plan to create an adjoining public plaza and cultural center, during which time there is no public access to the interior and some of exterior is also, unfortunately, out of view.

MAP 6: Insurgentes Sur 701, Col. Nápoles, tel. 55/5536-4520, www. polyforumsiqueiros.com; US$2 Foro Universal; gallery free; Metro: San Pedro de los Pinos or Eugenia, Metrobús: Poliforum

⭐ Centro SCOP

The headquarters of the Secretariat of Communications and Transportation, or Centro SCOP, is a functionalist office building covered in a breathtaking 20,000 square meters of volcanic-stone mosaics, created by 20th-century Mexican artists Juan O'Gorman, Jose Chavez Morado, and Arturo Estrada, among others. A landmark of midcentury architecture in Mexico City, it was conceived as part of integracion plastica, a movement to unite art and architecture in public spaces.

The top floors of Centro SCOP collapsed during the 1985 earthquake in Mexico City, and though the building was retrofitted, it was damaged again, this time irreparably, in the earthquake of 2017. The SCT announced that the building would be demolished, and after much public debate, the department began removing the murals from the edifice.

At press time, the relocation project had halted, and many key elements remain intact at the original site. Though you cannot access the building (it's unsafe and currently abandoned), many of the murals

Poliforo Siqueiros is an innovative union of art and architecture.

Centro SCOP, one of the most ambitious muralist projects in the city, is slated for relocation.

adjoin the sidewalk or are visible from the street, making it worth a trip to see this amazing half-toppled monument before it disappears into history.

MAP 6: Eje Central Lázaro Cárdenas and Xola, no tel.; free

Parque Hundido

On the weekends, this big urban park is a popular destination for local families, who come to buy ice cream, visit the playground, and take a ride on the small motorized "train" that weaves through the park. On the weekdays, it's much quieter, and a nice spot to take a stroll along the park's pretty footpaths, which are adjoined by about 50 reproductions of pre-Hispanic sculptures, including a large Olmec head. Across Insurgentes from Parque Hundido in the Colonia del Valle is the smaller Parque San Lorenzo (at the intersection of San Lorenzo and Fresas), which surrounds the Capilla de San Lorenzo Mártir, a small but beautiful 16th-century chapel.

MAP 6: Av. Insurgentes Sur between Porfirio Díaz and Millet; 24 hours daily; free; Metro: Mixcoac, Metrobús: Parque Hundido

Teatro de los Insurgentes

This prestigious theater on the southern stretch of Avenida Insurgentes, built in 1953, has a striking round facade decorated with a colorful mural by Diego Rivera entitled La Historia del Teatro (The History of Theater), which includes the portraits of many Mexican actors, including the beloved film star and friend of Rivera's Cantiflas. The theater generally puts on major dramatic productions by Mexican playwrights, many starring big-name actors.

MAP 6: Av. Insurgentes Sur 1587, tel. 55/5598-6894; shows usually Thurs.-Sun.; US$20-60 depending on seats; Metro: Barranca del Muerto, Metrobús: Teatro de los Insurgentes

Restaurants

PRICE KEY

$	Entrées less than $10
$ $	Entrées $10-20
$ $ $	Entrées more than $20

MEXICAN

✪ Fonda Margarita $

Even if you get there as dawn is breaking, you might still have to wait for a seat at this super-popular, ultra-casual breakfast spot, touted by many as the best traditional *fonda* in the city. As soon as you walk in, you'll see a row of clay pots filled with different Mexican dishes, gentling bubbling over an open charcoal fire. They sometimes run out of certain *guisos* (dishes) by midmorning, but you can't go wrong with anything on the menu. The famous *tortas de carne* (meat sandwiches) are a guaranteed way to fill your stomach till midday.

MAP 6: Adolfo Prieto 1354, tel. 55/5559-6358, http://fondamargarita. com; 5:30am-11:30am Tues.-Sun.; Metro: Insurgentes Sur, Metrobús: Parque Hundido

Fonda 99.99 $

Popular with Del Valle locals, this delicious and economical lunch spot specializes in food from the Yucatán peninsula, like puerco al pibil (pulled pork spiced with achiote seeds), sopa de lima (citrus soup), papadzules (egg-filled tortillas covered in a green pumpkin-seed sauce), and tacos stuffed with cazón (dogfish) or crab, all accompanied by fiery habanero salsa. During the daily lunch rush, servers in buttoned-up guayaberas rush trays to the flocks of diners chattering at the vintage Formica tables.

MAP 6: Moras 348, tel. 55/5559-8762; 1pm-7pm Tues.-Fri., 10am-7pm Sat., 1pm-6pm Sun.; Metro: Insurgentes Sur, Metrobús: Parque Hundido

La Secina $

In a bustling corner of the Colonia Narvarte, La Secina is a super low-key spot to unwind with drinks and generously served plates of antojitos (snacks) in the evening, when it's busy with neighborhood locals. The menu leans heavily on the namesake cecina (salt-cured beef), which the restaurant sources from Yecapixtla, Morelos, where some of the country's best cecina is produced. Try it in tacos, in Oaxacan-style tlayudas, or on sopes (round corn breads), or order some of the other delicious Mexican dishes on offer, like plate of grilled cactus with panela cheese.

MAP 6: Casa del Obrero Mundial, tel. 55/6730-2462, https://www.lasecina. com; 1pm-11pm Mon.-Wed., 1pm-2am Thurs.-Sat., 1pm-7pm Sun.; Metro: Etiopía, Metrobús: Obrero Mundial

Las Tlayudas $

If the no-frills dining room at Las Tlayudas doesn't initially strike you as promising, sit tight until the food comes. At this small, unpretentious, and surprisingly delicious Oaxacan restaurant, you'll find nicely rendered regional dishes like salsa de queso (Oaxacan cheese in a spicy red sauce) and tlayudas (giant corn

COFFEE EVERYWHERE

Mexico is a coffee-producing country, with high-quality beans cultivated in the mountains of Veracruz, Oaxaca, Chiapas, and Guerrero. In the capital, particularly in the Centro Histórico and the San Juan neighborhood, the scent of roasting beans is a regular delight.

a lovingly made latte

Third-wave coffee has arrived in Mexico with force, and you'll find outstanding coffee at shops like Cardinal (page 189), Camino a Comala (page 125), Café Avellaneda (page 236), and many, many more serving delightful gourmet coffee. Less avant-garde but just as wonderful, the city's oldest roasters, many established in the early 20th century, are also among the best places for a cup. Café Jekemir in the Centro Histórico is a good example, as is Café Emir (below).

If you're in a pinch for a place to work or a cup of something caffeinated, here are four good Mexican-owned coffee chains, which you'll see throughout the capital.

Tierra Garat (www.tierragarat.mx), owned by longtime Mexican coffee roaster Café Garat, sells Mexican coffee and espresso drinks, as well as a line of hot and cold drinks featuring Mexican chocolate, including chile-spiked hot cocoa. The shops all have a lovely dark-wood design and smell like the heavenly combo of coffee and chocolate.

Café Emir (www.cafeemir.com.mx), a small chain of cafés with a Middle Eastern influence, first opened in the Centro Histórico in 1936. Today, you'll find branches throughout the city, including the Roma Norte (Córdoba 113, tel. 55/5264-4577) and the San Rafael (Francisco Díaz Covarrubias 67, tel. 55/5535-8329).

Café Punto del Cielo (www.puntadelcielo.com.mx) is a Mexican-owned coffee franchise that sells Mexican beans and espresso drinks. You'll see their clean and modern shops in neighborhoods throughout the capital.

Cielito Querido is a chain of coffee shops selling only Mexican products, with a menu that mixes espresso drinks with traditional Mexican beverages, like *café de olla* (coffee boiled with cinnamon and raw cane sugar) and *horchata* (a sweetened rice drink). Their whimsically decorated shops, like the large branch in the Zona Rosa (Paseo de la Reforma 284, tel. 55/5533-9905), all take design cues from traditional *rotulistas,* or sign painters, in Mexico.

tortillas stuffed with beans, cheese, and, optionally, meat). There's a very nice selection of craft beer and legitimately tasty Oaxacan hot chocolate to accompany your meal.

MAP 6: Luz Saviñón 1161, Narvarte Poniente, tel. 55/6379-2496; 10am-6pm Sun.-Mon., 10am-10pm Tues.-Thurs., 9am-midnight Fri., 9am-11pm Sat.; Metro: Etiopía

Los Chamorros de Tlacoquemécatl $

There are a wide range of classic Mexican dishes on the menu at this old-school neighborhood eatery, which opened in 1974, like huazontles (a native Mexican green) with chile pasilla and meatballs in chipotle sauce. If you've come with an appetite, try the namesake chamorro: a

a beautiful breakfast at Peltre Lonchería

whole pig's leg, braised in its own fat and juices, carnitas-style, and delivered to your table as a drumstick fit for a Viking. They bring you a stack of tortillas and salsa, and you make the tacos.

MAP 6: Tlacoquemécatl 177, tel. 55/5575-0733; 9am-5pm daily; Metro: Insurgentes Sur, Metrobús: Parque Hundido

Mictlan Antojitos Veganos

An itsy-bitsy vegan eatery with just four sidewalk tables, Mictlan serves first-rate plant-based versions of classic Mexican snacks, like mushroom-stuffed gorditas made with heirloom corn and meat-free pambazos (a traditional chorizo-and-potato sandwich). Popular with neighborhood locals, there's often a wait in the afternoon, when the economically priced comida corrida (three-course lunch) is served. Top it off with a glass of their ultra-fresh pulque.

MAP 6: Xochicalco 341, Narvarte Poniente, tel. 55/4036-2821; noon-7pm Wed.-Sun.; Metro: Eugenia, Metrobús: Luz Saviñón

Peltre Lonchería $

While its geometric turquoise-and-white decor is indisputably contemporary, this low-key coffee shop and sandwich bar is unpretentious and inexpensive—as well as reliably delicious. It's a good place to start the day with a plate of fresh fruit with house-made granola, savory *enfrijoladas* (tortillas in bean sauce) topped with cream and avocado, and a tall glass of green juice or to wrap up an evening with a craft beer and grilled cheese. In addition to this spacious branch in the Narvarte, there are other branches in the Roma (Álvaro Obregón 85), the Cuauhtémoc (Río Lerma 213), and the Condesa (Saltillo 73).

MAP 6: Diagonal San Antonio 1810, Narvarte, tel. 55/5548-7899, https://peltre.mx; 7am-10:30pm Mon.-Fri., 8am-10:30pm Sat.-Sun.; Metro: Etiopía, Metrobús: Dr. Vertiz

MIDDLE EASTERN

Asador Libanes $

After decades in the neighborhood, this cozy Middle Eastern restaurant has become a Nápoles staple, serving delicious and well-priced Middle Eastern dishes like hummus, baba ghanouj, tabouli salad, and grilled meats and kebabs to neighborhood locals. Service has an old-school attentiveness and the ambience is cozy, with checkered tablecloths and a small bar in back. Quiet in the daytime, it livens up on the nights they host live music, from jazz to cello, or Middle Eastern music and dancers.

MAP 6: Kansas 19, Nápoles, tel. 55/6721-0127, www.asadorlibanes.com; 1pm-midnight Mon.-Sat., 1pm-10pm Sun.; Metrobús: Nápoles

TACOS, *TORTAS,* AND SNACKS

El Rey de las Ahogadas $

This old-school eatery specializes in deep-fried tacos called flautas, which are filled with cheese, potato, refried beans, or chicken and served piping hot and drowned ("ahogada") in a bowl of salsa verde. The satisfying crunch, the savory filling, and the tang of spicy salsa make for a delicious combination, but El Rey de las Ahogadas also serves nonfried snacks from the comal, including huaraches and quesadillas.

Open late, it's a popular spot for cheap meal.

MAP 6: Av. Coyoacán 360, tel. 55 5523 4989 www.elreydelasahogadas.com.mx; 11am-midnight Mon.-Thurs., 11am-1am Fri.-Sat., 11am-11pm Sun.; Metro: Etiopía, Metrobús: Poliforum

El Vilsito $

The Narvarte neighborhood is well-known for its excellent taquerias, and El Vilsito is widely regarded as offering one of the best (if not the very best) *pastor* tacos in the city, to which the nightly crowds attest. In a classic Mexico City twist, this evening-only joint is a mechanic shop by day, so head there well after the sun's gone down. It's as casual as they come—eat on the street, standing up—but a delicious, quintessential Mexico City experience.

MAP 6: Av. Universidad 248, Col. Narvarte, tel. 55/5682-7213; 8pm-3am Mon.-Thurs., 8pm-5am Fri.-Sat., 4pm-midnight Sun.; Metro: Eugenia, Metrobús: Dr. Vertiz or Luz Saviñón

Hostal de los Quesos $

This taco palace in the southern Del Valle neighborhood has been in business since the mid-20th century and serves such a wide range of tacos that it can be hard to limit your order. Among the options on offer are nopalitos (prickly pear), rib eye, *chuleta* (pork chop), liver and onions, chorizo, chicken, and legitimately delicious *pastor*, as well as pozole (hominy soup), *tortas*, *chicharron de queso* (crispy griddled cheese), tortilla soup, *frijoles charros* (stewed beans), and much more.

MAP 6: Pilares 205, tel. 55/5559-9651, www.hostaldelosquesos.com.mx; 8:30am-1am Mon.-Thurs., 8:30am-2am Fri.-Sat., 8:30am-midnight Sun.; Metro: División del Norte, Metrobús: Parque Hundido

Tacos Joven $

Throughout the city, you'll see locals lining up to buy tacos de canasta, tiny corn tortillas that are stuffed with simple fillings like potatoes or refried beans, cooked in oil, then piled into a basket, or canasta, to stay warm. These invariably inexpensive tacos are generally sold on street corners, in parks, or at very small street stands, like this one in the Narvarte neighborhood. Cheap, filling, and tasty, the only thing untraditional about Tacos Joven is the portion size: each of these tacos is at least three times the size of a classic taco de canasta.

MAP 6: Av. Universidad 199-B, tel. 55/5543-3366, www.tacosjoven. mx; 9am-2:30pm daily; Metro: Eugenia, Metrobús: Dr. Vertiz or Luz Saviñón

Simple yet filling tacos al vapor are the specialty at Tacos Joven.

Tacos Los Condes $

At this bright and friendly neighborhood taco shop, you can order a plate of perfectly seasoned pastor, suadero, or a much-beloved tripa (tripe), but you'll also find gorditas (round corn flatbreads) and quesadillas (both deep-fried and al comal) on the menu—with options for fillings like huitlacoche or poblano chiles that even vegetarians will love. Located on a tree-filled street corner, Los Condes has plenty of sidewalk seating and the service is genial.

MAP 6: Pedro Romero de Terreros 14, tel. 55/8661-0506; 9am-midnight Mon.-Wed., 9am-1am Thurs.-Sat.; Metro: Etiopía, Metrobús: La Piedad

Savory tacos and other delicious antojitos at Tacos Los Condes.

Tacos Manolo $

In the late afternoon, hours before the crowds descend, two huge spits of meat (or trompos) begin sizzling outside Tacos Manolo in preparation for the evening rush. One is bright red achiote-rubbed pastor, while the other is herb-flecked pork for tacos árabes. Both of these classic tacos are deliciously rendered at this no-frills traditional taco shop,

classic tacos al pastor and tacos árabes at Tacos Manolo

and you can accompany them with an agua fresca or a Mexican beer.

MAP 6: Luz Saviñón 1305, Narvarte Poniente, tel. 55/7095-8071; 2pm-midnight Sun.-Thurs., 2pm-2:30am Fri.-Sat.; Metro: Etiopía, Metrobús: Dr. Vertiz or Luz Saviñón

Tortas Don Polo $

While tacos get top billing, tortas (sandwiches made on a white roll called a telera) are another capital favorite, and this old-fashioned shop makes them in the traditional way: bread lightly toasted in butter, a thin spread of refried beans, and a range of fillings, like milanesa (breaded steak), pierna (pork leg), and quesillo (Oaxacan cheese) with avocado. The 1960-vintage original branch on Félix Cuevas is located just below the iconic apartment complex Multifamiliar Miguel Alemán, designed by an architectural team including Mario Pani. There's another branch across the street from Parque Hundido (Gral. Porfirio Díaz No. 534, Col. Noche Buena, tel. 55/5563-4242).

MAP 6: Félix Cuevas, tel. 55/5534-5760, www.tortasdonpolo.mx; 9am-9:30pm daily, 5pm close on Wed. only; Metro: Zapata, Metrobús: Félix Cuevas

SEAFOOD
✪ Mi Gusto Es $$

In the tree-filled Narvarte neighborhood, this ultra-popular Sinaloa-style seafood restaurant brings you as close to the beach as you can get in Mexico City, with flavorful marlin-stuffed chiles or incredibly fresh and spicy *aguachile verde*. There's often a wait at lunchtime, especially on the weekends, but you can sip a beer on the sidewalk in the meantime (there are coolers by the host station). Though they have other locations across the city, the Narvarte original remains the most fun.

MAP 6: Diagonal San Antonio 1709-C, Narvarte Poniente, tel. 55/5235-3217, http://migustoes.com.mx; noon-7:30pm Mon.-Thurs., noon-8pm Fri.-Sun.; Metro: Etiopía, Metrobús: Dr. Vertiz

SWEETS
Chiandoni $

In the heart of the Colonia Nápoles, this old-fashioned ice-cream shop is worth visiting for the authentic mid-century ambience, with a Formica-topped bar with turquoise barstools and a blue-and-white checkered floor. The ice cream is likewise old-fashioned, with classic flavors like vanilla, chocolate, and lemon served

old-fashioned ice cream shop Chiandoni

in small metal bowls at your table, in addition to a menu of nostalgic sundaes, like banana splits.

MAP 6: Pennsylvania 225, Nápoles, tel. 55/7592-0839; 11am-9pm daily; Metro: San Antonio, Metrobús: Colonia del Valle

Nightlife

BARS
✪ Kaito

This hip cocktail bar is tucked into a cozy barroom above Japanese restaurant Deigo in the quiet Del Valle neighborhood. Here, the woman-run bar team creates creative and often playful Japanese-inspired cocktails, like the Godzilla, which includes wasabi syrup and lemongrass, and is served with a side of wasabi peas. On weeknights, it's a popular dinner spot with neighborhood locals, but the quality has made it a destination for cocktail connoisseurs citywide. Make reservations for the nights when guest bartenders or DJs are in the house.

MAP 6: Enrique Pestalozzi 1238, Del Valle, tel. 55/9133-1476; noon-1:30am Tues.-Sat., noon-10:30 Sun.; Metro: División del Norte, Metrobús: División del Norte

Luvina Vegan Bar

On a weekend evening, in-the-know locals snatch up tables at this itsy-bitsy bar on a vibrant street corner in the Narvarte neighborhood. Specializing in creative gin-based cocktails, craft beer, and plant-based bar snacks (guacamole, potato wedges), it's as low-key as they come, with just a few outdoor tables and two inside, but the excellent drinks and affable service have made it a popular spot in the neighborhood.

MAP 6: Cumbres de Matrato 312 (entrance on Petén), no tel.; 3pm-10pm Sun.-Tues., 3pm-midnight Wed.-Sat.; Metro: Etiopía, Metrobús: Dr. Vertiz

CANTINAS
La Valenciana

For a long lunch or a leisurely food-and-drink session with a group of friends, this pretty tile-covered cantina is a great place for hours of easy-going fun. The place has a relaxed local-watering-hole vibe, catering to neighborhood families on the weekends. The specialty here is the molcajete, a stone bowl filled with a stew-like mix of meats, nopales (cactus), onion, and other savories. Even if you don't order anything off the menu, the kitchen will send out snacks to accompany your drinks, as is traditional in a cantina.

MAP 6: Av. Universidad 48, Narvarte Oriente, tel. 55/3330-7505; 1pm-2am Mon.-Sat., 1pm-8pm Sun.; Metro: Xola, Metrobús: Xola

Recreation

PARKS

Parque de Los Venados

This large and leafy park, which first opened to the public in the 1950s, serves neighborhood families with a large playground, an amphitheater that's popular for dance and Zumba classes, a running track, and lots of iron benches for relaxing. It's a nice spot to see local life in action. The park gets its name from the statue of an iron deer (venado) at its center.

MAP 6: Av. División del Norte s/n, Col. Santa Cruz Atoyac; 24 hours; Metro: División del Norte, Metrobús: División del Norte

SPECTATOR SPORTS

Estadio Ciudad de los Deportes

This attractive midsize stadium in the Colonia Nochebuena was long the home of soccer club Cruz Azul—in fact, it was generally referred to as "Estadio Azul" for years. Since 2019, however, Cruz Azul has been playing games in Estadio Azteca while Atlante, an expansion team, has continued using this stadium for games. At press time, it was widely expected that several major teams, including Cruz Azul rival Las Águilas de América, would be playing in the Ciudad de los Deportes while Estadio Azteca is remodeled in the summer of 2023 ahead of the World Cup in 2026. Whoever is playing, the small size and central location make this a good choice for a *fútbol* match while visiting Mexico City.

MAP 6: Indiana 255, Ciudad de los Deportes; hours vary; most games US$5-15; Metro: San Antonio, Metrobús: Ciudad de los Deportes

Monumental Plaza de Toros México

After years of activism in opposition to bullfighting in Mexico, a sport which had retained a small but passionate following in the capital, a federal judge permanently suspended all activities at the Monumental Plaza de Toros México in June 2022. Citing the cruel treatment of bulls used in the fights, the judge called the decision "a benefit to the whole society." Located right next to the soccer stadium in the Ciudad de los Deportes, the plaza will continue to be used as an attractive venue for concerts and other events.

MAP 6: Augusto Rodin 41, Ciudad de los Deportes; showtimes vary; Metro: San Antonio, Metrobús: Ciudad de los Deportes

The soccer stadium in the Ciudad de los Deportes is a great place for a match.

TIANGUIS, OUTDOOR MARKETS

Mesoamerican civilizations as far back as the early Olmecs on the Gulf Coast established open-air marketplaces for trade and commerce. After the Spanish conquest,
many important pre-Columbian markets continued to operate throughout the region,
including the giant market square in what is today the Zócalo.

In addition to neighborhood markets (see Public Markets on page 104), most
colonias also have one or two outdoor markets that set up once a week on a closed
street or sidewalk. Some are simple affairs, with 10-15 stands selling fruits and vegetables, meats, and cheese, as well as tacos and other street snacks. Others are massive 100-plus-vendor markets, where you can buy all your kitchen basics, as well as
picking up some of the city's best street snacks. Often referred to as **mercados sobre
ruedas (markets on wheels)**, or **tianguis** (from the Nahuatl word for an open-air
market), they can be wonderful places to shop, to munch, and to get a sense of a
neighborhood.

Most *mercados sobre ruedas* run from about 9am or 10am to 6pm, though they tend
to wind down after the *comida,* around 4pm. Here is a small selection of the dozens of
outdoor markets that set up across the city's central neighborhoods every day:

PACHUCA AND JUAN DE LA BARRERA, CONDESA

This bustling street market takes over Calle Pachuca in the northwest Condesa every
Tuesday. Come to shop for handmade tortillas, fresh fruit, herbs, vegetables, and
mushrooms—or simply to chow down at the many delicious street stands. You'll find
tacos, freshly fried flautas, handmade quesadillas, and *huaraches,* among other tasty
bites. At lunchtime, popular food stands are thronged by locals; many have tables and
chairs for dining.

TIANGUIS DEL ORO, GLORIETA DE LA CIBELES, AND CALLE DE ORO, ROMA

This open-air market, which sets up along Calle de Oro in the Roma on **Wednesday,
Saturday, and Sunday,** boasts a wide assortment of great grub, but particularly notable is the Argentine grill **Parrilladas Bariloche,** which serves South American steaks
to hungry crowds for very low prices.

TIANGUIS DE LOS JUEVES, CAROLINA AND HOLBEIN, NÁPOLES

A massive open-air market fills the streets between the Plaza de Toros and the Estadio
Azul in the Noche Buena neighborhood every **Thursday.** With hundreds of vendors,
it's a labyrinth of delicious aromas, tropical colors, and human traffic jams. Come for
the *gorditas,* the tacos, the *nieves,* and the excellent food shopping.

Shops

ARTS AND CRAFTS
✪ FONART

The Fondo Nacional para el
Fomento de las Artesanías
(FONART), a government branch
dedicated to supporting traditional artisans, runs a beautiful
shop on the Paseo de la Reforma.
This branch, on the busy avenue
Patriotismo, is much larger, with
a stunning selection of traditional
Mexican furnishings, Talavera ceramic work, textiles and handmade
clothing, dolls, toys, papier-mâché,

Flowers and clothing on sale at a street market in the Narvarte.

MERCADO EL 100, PLAZA DEL LANZADOR, ROMA
This ecological market's mission is to promote products that come from within 100 miles (160 kilometers) of Mexico City. You'll find fresh fruits and vegetables, local honey, jams, lead-free clay cookware, Mexican coffee, and other gourmet goods. Part of the growing organic and eco movement in the capital, this **Sunday** market in the Roma gets a lot of foot traffic from progressive locals. (Note that this market closes earlier than other *tianguis*, around 2pm or 3pm.)

OBRERO MUNDIAL, COLONIA DEL VALLE
On **Sundays,** a beautiful neighborhood market stretches along the street of Casa del Obrero Mundial from Monterrey to Amores. There are vendors selling tortillas, fruit, vegetables, and herbs, as well as flowers, plants, and clothing, among other sundries. Notable are the plethora of excellent and busy food stalls with their loyal clientele, including carnitas, barbacoa, handmade quesadillas, and more.

burnished clay urns and flatwear, and much more, representing artisans from across the republic. Prices are notably inexpensive when compared with the quality of the work.

MAP 6: Av. Patriotismo 691, Mixcoac, tel. 55/5093-6000;11am-7pm Mon.-Fri., 11am-5pm Sat.-Sun.; Metro: Mixcoac

Coyoacán

Map 7

Once part of a colonial-era settlement far outside the city limits, Coyoacán's **quiet plazas** and **cobblestone streets** are today a pleasant oasis within the capital. Lined with **restaurants** and **shops,** the twin squares at the center of Coyoacán, **Jardín Centenario** and **Jardín Hidalgo,** are often bustling with students, tourists, and local families on weekends. For visitors, Coyoacán is best known as the home of Mexican painter Frida Kahlo; her childhood home, now **Museo Frida Kahlo,** is today a moving museum that chronicles her life and work.

TOP SIGHTS
- Best Portrait of the Artist: **Museo Frida Kahlo** (page 228)

TOP RESTAURANTS
- Best Mezcal Pairings: **Corazón de Maguey** (page 232)

TOP NIGHTLIFE
- Top Spot for Beer: **Centenario 107** (page 238)

TOP ARTS AND CULTURE
- Ultimate Movie Destination: **Cineteca Nacional** (page 240)

TOP RECREATION
- Greenest Spot for a Stroll: **Viveros de Coyoacán** (page 243)

GETTING THERE AND AROUND
- Metro lines: 3
- Metro stops: Coyoacán, Viveros, Miguel Ángel de Quevedo, Copilco, Universidad
- Metrobús lines: 1
- Metrobús stops: La Bombilla, Dr. Gálvez, Ciudad Universitaria

COYOACÁN WALK

TOTAL DISTANCE: 4.5 kilometers (2.8 miles)
TOTAL WALKING TIME: 2.5 hours

There are no Metro stations in central Coyoacán, nor any major avenues passing through the neighborhood's charming **colonial-era** *centro*. As a result, a visit to Coyoacán often begins with a stroll. End your walk at **Museo Frida Kahlo,** one of the city's most moving art museums and a tribute to a truly original artist.

ALONG FRANCISCO SOSA

1 At a brisk pace, it takes 15 to 20 minutes to walk from **Metro Viveros,** on Line 3, to central Coyoacán, though considering how many lovely sights are dotted along the way, it's unlikely you'll make the journey so quickly. Departing the station, walk south along Avenida Universidad until you reach Avenida Francisco Sosa. Swing a left, and slow your gait: This historic, tree-lined avenue leads right into the heart of Coyoacán.

2 Within a block, you'll find the **Fonoteca Nacional,** an unusual public archive dedicated to documenting the unique music and sounds of Mexico. It's a fascinating project housed in Casa Alvarado, a brick-red 18th-century hacienda with strong Moorish and Andalusian influences. Wander through the lush gardens, where speakers play traditional music and sounds.

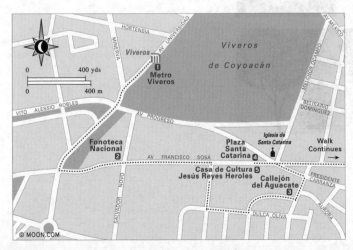

3 A few blocks later, you can continue along Francisco Sosa or make a small detour south along the street Tata Vasco to arrive in the **Callejón del Aguacate,** a historic and picturesque alleyway that is the subject of numerous legends and ghost stories. Whether or not the alley is haunted, it is worth seeing this pretty corner of the neighborhood, marked by a small altar to the Virgin Mary on its corner.

Iglesia de Santa Catarina

4 Once back on Francisco Sosa, backtrack a half block to the **Plaza Santa Catarina,** a serene colonial-era plaza, where paper flags flutter between leafy trees and the picturesque **Iglesia de Santa Catarina,** built in the 18th century.

5 Just across the street, the **Casa de Cultura Jesús Reyes Heroles** (Francisco Sosa 202) is a multipurpose cultural center, set in another lovely hacienda; join locals relaxing in the pretty coffee shop in back.

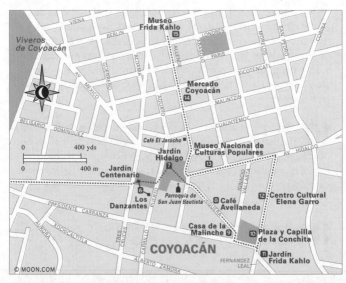

JARDÍN HIDALGO AND
THE PLAZA DE LA CONCHITA

6 Continue along Francisco Sosa until you arrive at **Jardín Centenario,** in the center of Coyoacán. As you arrive, you'll pass through two colonial-era archways that were once part of the massive Dominican convent that dominated central Coyoacán. Wander through the square, rest your legs on a bench overlooking its central fountain, or settle in for a drink at **Los Danzantes,** one of the many bars and restaurants that adjoin the plaza.

7 Just east, the **Jardín Hidalgo** is Coyoacán's central square, over which the historic **Parroquia de San Juan Bautista** presides. The first parish church was built here in 1528, atop a native school (the ruins of which still lie below the cloister), though the current edifice was constructed several decades later.

Jardín Hidalgo, the main square of Coyoacán

8 Behind the church, the small street Higuera cuts diagonally southeast from the Jardín Hidalgo. Stop into **Café Avellaneda** for a coffee to go, then continue down Higuera until you reach the end.

9 At the very end of Higuera, take note of the dark-red **Casa de la Malinche,** widely believed to be the house Cortés shared with his lover and interpreter Malintzin, better known as La Malinche. According to other legends, it is the house where Cortés's first wife, Catalina Suárez Marcayda, died, possibly by his own hand. Though historians entirely discredit these stories, the site is now a city landmark, though privately owned.

10 Just across the street, the quiet **Plaza y Capilla de la Conchita** is the setting for one of the earliest colonial-era chapels in Mexico. This fragile old church recently went through a complete renovation; admire its ornate (but still weathered) facade. According to archaeological evidence, this plaza may have been a central ceremonial space for pre-Columbian cultures in Coyoacán.

11 Walk through the plaza to the **Jardín Frida Kahlo,** a pretty public garden dedicated to the famous Coyoacán painter.

TO MUSEO FRIDA KAHLO

12 You can follow Higuera back to the plaza, but it's nicer to walk along the quaint and cobbled Fernández Leal, filled with the towering trees and country houses emblematic of residential Coyoacán. Stop at the cultural center and bookstore **Centro Cultural Elena Garro** for a coffee or to thumb through a book.

13 Heading back toward the center of town via Hidalgo, you'll pass coffee shops and taco stands, as well as the **Museo Nacional de Culturas Populares,** a craft museum, where a large ceramic *árbol de la vida* (tree of life) sits in the central courtyard.

Museo Frida Kahlo

locals outside Café El Jarocho

14 Continue along Allende, one of the neighborhood's main avenues, past locals sipping lattes at **Café El Jarocho.** A block farther, you'll likely notice a bit of bustle at the perennially popular seafood spot Jardín del Pulpo right on the corner of the **Mercado Coyoacán,** the neighborhood's municipal market. Wander amid flower vendors or stop to try one of Coyoacán's famous tostadas.

15 A few blocks farther, on the corner of Allende and Londres, Frida Kahlo's childhood home, now the **Museo Frida Kahlo,** is known as the "Caza Azul" or "Blue House" for its striking cobalt color.

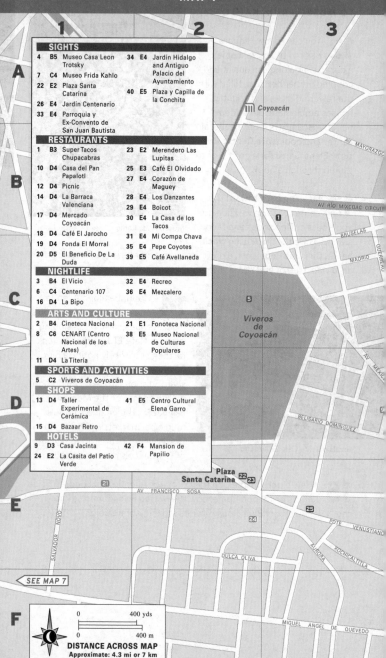

SIGHTS

4	B5	Museo Casa Leon Trotsky
7	C4	Museo Frida Kahlo
22	E2	Plaza Santa Catarina
26	E4	Jardin Centenario
33	E4	Parroquia y Ex-Convento de San Juan Bautista
34	E4	Jardín Hidalgo and Antiguo Palacio del Ayuntamiento
40	E5	Plaza y Capilla de la Conchita

RESTAURANTS

1	B3	Super Tacos Chupacabras
10	D4	Casa del Pan Papalotl
12	D4	Picnic
14	D4	La Barraca Valenciana
17	D4	Mercado Coyoacán
18	D4	Café El Jarocho
19	D4	Fonda El Morral
20	D5	El Beneficio De La Duda
23	E2	Merendero Las Lupitas
25	E3	Café El Olvidado
27	E4	Corazón de Maguey
28	E4	Los Danzantes
29	E4	Boicot
30	E4	La Casa de los Tacos
31	E4	Mi Compa Chava
35	E4	Pepe Coyotes
39	E5	Café Avellaneda

NIGHTLIFE

3	B4	El Vicio
6	C4	Centenario 107
16	D4	La Bipo
32	E4	Recreo
36	E4	Mezcalero

ARTS AND CULTURE

2	B4	Cineteca Nacional
8	C6	CENART (Centro Nacional de los Artes)
11	D4	La Titería
21	E1	Fonoteca Nacional
38	E5	Museo Nacional de Culturas Populares

SPORTS AND ACTIVITIES

| 5 | C2 | Viveros de Coyoacán |

SHOPS

13	D4	Taller Experimental de Cerámica
15	D4	Bazaar Retro
41	E5	Centro Cultural Elena Garro

HOTELS

9	D3	Casa Jacinta
24	E2	La Casita del Patio Verde
42	F4	Mansion de Papilio

Coyoacán

AV MAYORAZGO

AV RÍO MIXCOAC CIRCUIT

BRUSELAS

GUERRERO

MADRID

Viveros de Coyoacán

AV MÉXIC

BELISARIO DOMINGUEZ

Plaza Santa Catarina

AV FRANCISCO SOSA

SALVADOR NOVO

PTE VENUSTIANO

XOCHICALTILLA

AURORA

DULCA OLIVA

SEE MAP 7

MIGUEL ANGEL DE QUEVEDO

0   400 yds
0   400 m

DISTANCE ACROSS MAP
Approximate: 4.3 mi or 7 km

© MOON.COM

4   **5**   **6**

PUENTE XOCO

GRAL MANUEL RINCON

PALOMAR

DIVISION DEL NORTE

AV MEXICO COYOACAN

AV CARRILLO PUERTO

TETEPILCO

②

Panteón Xoco

INTERIOR

Museo Casa León Trotsky

④

AV RIO CHURUBUSCO

③

VIENA

To Ⓑ CENART
(Centro Nacional
de los Artes)

BERLIN

MORELOS

SAN PEDRO

ALDAMA

Museo Frida Kahlo

LONDRES

⑥ ⑦

ABASOLO

ALLENDE

PARIS

COYOACÁN

XICOTÉNCATL

CORTINA

⑳

⓪ ⑪

⑬

AGUAYO

MALINTZIN

⑭ ⑯ ⑰

⑫

CUAUHTÉMOC

⑮

⑱ **Jardín Hidalgo
and Antiguo
Palacio del
Ayuntamiento**

⑲

㉞ ㊳

AV HIDALGO

Jardín Centenario

㉗ ㉟

㉖ ㉝

IGNACIO VALLARTA

㊲

㉘

PUERTO

㉙ ㊱

⑪

⑨ ㉜

HIGUERA

㊴

TRES CRUCES

㉚
㉛

**Parroquía y
Ex-Convento de
San Juan Bautista**

**Plaza y
Capilla de la
Conchita** ㊵

CARRANZA

㊷

CARRILLO

ALBERTO ZAMORA

FERNANDEZ LEAL

Sights

TOP EXPERIENCE

✪ Museo Frida Kahlo

Frida Kahlo produced a small body of work during her lifetime, yet her paintings are so unique and powerful that she is now one of the most recognizable names in modern art. The Museo Frida Kahlo is located in the house where Kahlo grew up, lived with her husband, artist Diego Rivera, and died. Known as the Casa Azul for its cobalt color, this wonderful museum is both an art gallery and a re-creation of the home when Kahlo and Rivera lived there. It's an absolute must for Kahlo fans.

The ground-floor galleries exhibit some of Kahlo's work—including a lovely portrait she painted of her father, Guillermo—as well as some of her modern art collection. Perhaps the most moving rooms are upstairs, where visitors can see Kahlo's studio, with her wheelchair at the easel, as well as the bed where Kahlo spent so much time after a tragic trolley accident in her teenage years left her permanently disabled. Kahlo was a collector of traditional Mexican clothing and jewelry, which became a huge part of her public persona, as well as a key element in her artistic work. Many of her outfits are displayed throughout the museum.

Recently, the museum's collection became more robust after a remarkable discovery within its own walls.

Museo Frida Kahlo

In 2002, the home's bathrooms were unsealed, revealing a treasure of clothing, documents, toys, books, and other artifacts from the artists' lives. The collection was so extensive that the museum acquired the adjoining Porfiriato-era house to exhibit them. Advance tickets can be purchased via the museum's website. Only a limited number of tickets are sold each day, and there is often a wait to get in on weekends.

MAP 7: Londres 247, tel. 55/5554-5999, www.museofridakahlo.org.mx; 10am-6pm Tues. and Thurs.-Sun., 11am-6pm Wed.; US$12 Tues.-Fri., US$14 Sat.-Sun., US$3 students and teachers, US$1 children and seniors, free for children under 6; Metro: Coyoacán

Jardín Centenario

If you arrive in Coyoacán via Avenida Francisco Sosa, you will find yourself first at the Jardín Centenario, a shady plaza that adjoins the Jardín Hidalgo, another large plaza, to the west. The square is accessed via a lovely arched entryway, built by hand in the 16th century; it was once a part of the cloister of the San Juan Bautista monastery and church. The centerpiece of the garden is a circular stone fountain featuring bronze sculptures of two coyotes, a reference to the neighborhood's Nahuatl name, "Place of Coyotes." The fountain has become a symbol of Coyoacán. Both sides of the plaza are lined with restaurants and cafés, and there is often a friendly, upbeat vibe in the square, where students play guitars on park benches, intellectuals converse over coffees, and locals stroll along the stone paths with their dogs.

MAP 7: Carrillo Puerto and Tres Cruces; Metro: Viveros

Jardín Hidalgo and Antiguo Palacio del Ayuntamiento

Jardín Hidalgo is Coyoacán's lovely central plaza, bordered to the east by the impressive Parroquia de San Juan Bautista, one of the oldest churches in the city. Larger than the adjoining Jardín Centenario, this sun-drenched esplanade features an iron kiosk with a stained-glass cupola, constructed in France in the 19th century. Filled with benches and constantly patrolled by shaved-ice carts and toy vendors, this plaza is a popular place for a weekend stroll with the family.

Today, Coyoacán's main government offices are located in the Antiguo Palacio del Ayuntamiento de Coyoacán (Plaza Hidalgo 1), a rust-colored building constructed in 1755 and stretching across the entire north end of Jardín Hidalgo. Also known as the Casa de Cortés, the building stands on the site of what many historians believe to have been the administrative offices of Hernán Cortés, Marquis of the Valley of Oaxaca, in the 16th century.

MAP 7: Bordered by Felipe Carrillo Puerto and Caballocalco; Metro: Viveros

Parroquia y Ex-Convento de San Juan Bautista

One of the oldest Catholic churches in Mexico City, this huge baroque gem was originally built right after the conquest, in the mid-16th century, on land granted to the Franciscans by Hernán Cortés, and some elements of the original

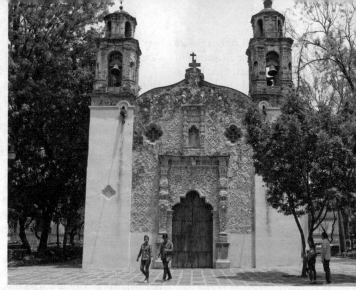
The Capilla de la Conchita is one of the oldest churches in Mexico City.

construction remain embedded in the building today. Like many churches of its era, it was once part of a much larger monastery complex at the center of Coyoacán, with buildings and gardens stretching all the way to the arches at the entrance to adjoining Jardín Centenario. The interior of the church was thoroughly and beautifully reconstructed, with the altars restored and recoated in gold leaf, and frescoes restored and added to the walls.

MAP 7: Jardín Centenario 8, tel. 55/5554-0560, 8am-7:30pm daily; free; Metro: Viveros

Plaza y Capilla de la Conchita

The colonial-era street Higuera cuts diagonally southeast from the Jardín Hidalgo, terminating at the picturesque Plaza de la Conchita. The chapel here, one of the oldest in the city, was originally constructed in 1521 by order of Hernán Cortés, though the facade that stands today dates from the 18th century. By some accounts, it was the site of the very first Christian church in Mexico. Although officially known as Capilla de la Purísima Concepción, the chapel and surrounding garden are more commonly known by the affectionate nickname La Conchita (the Little Shell). According to archaeological evidence, this plaza may have been a central ceremonial space for pre-Columbian cultures in Coyoacán.

On one corner of the Plaza de la Conchita, the brick-red Casa de la Malinche is said to be the house Cortés shared with his lover and interpreter Malintzin, better known as La Malinche. The story is likely apocryphal: Historians say the house was constructed many centuries after Cortés and La Malinche lived in the Valley of Mexico.

MAP 7: Fernández Leal and Vallarta; Metro: Viveros

Plaza Santa Catarina

A few blocks west of Jardín Centenario along Avenida Francisco Sosa is a lovely cobblestone square, fronted by the bright yellow Capilla de Santa Catarina and surrounded by restored colonial-era houses. On one side is the Casa de Cultura Jesús Reyes Heroles (Francisco Sosa 202, tel. 55/5658-7826; 8am-6pm daily), which often holds cultural events and art exhibits. Stop in to admire the rambling old hacienda, or enjoy the lush gardens in back, where there is also an attractive coffee shop with shaded tables. Back toward the center of Coyoacán, on Francisco Sosa, the Instituto Italiano di Cultura (Francisco Sosa 77, tel. 55/5554-0044, www.iicmessico.esteri.it) often hosts art exhibits and other special events.

MAP 7: Francisco Sosa at Tata Vasco; Metro: Viveros

Museo Casa Leon Trotsky

During the 20th century, Mexico's leftist government offered asylum to political exiles from many different countries, including anti-Fascist intellectuals from Spain and Cold War exiles from the United States. Following a power struggle with Josef Stalin, Russian Marxist revolutionary Leon Trotsky left the Soviet Union in 1929, eventually coming to Mexico with his wife, Natalia, in 1937, at the invitation of Frida Kahlo and Diego Rivera.

In 1940, a Spanish Stalinist named Ramón Mercader gained Trotsky's confidence, then fatally wounded him with an ice ax while Trotsky was in his study. Today, Trotsky's final home in Mexico City has been converted into an interesting museum that chronicles the rise of communism, Trotsky's life, and politics in Mexico and throughout the world, as well as exhibiting dozens of wonderful photographs of Trotsky and his Natalia with Mexican politicians, artists, and intellectuals. Many of the rooms in the home have been left entirely untouched since the day he died, giving a glimpse of Bolshevik revolutionary's documents, personal effects, and furnishings.

MAP 7: Río Churubusco 410, tel. 55/5658-8732 or 55/5554-0687, http://museocasadeleontrotsky.blogspot.com; 10am-5pm Tues.-Sun.; US$2; Metro: Coyoacán

The home where Leon Trotsky lived in Coyoacan is now a museum.

Restaurants

PRICE KEY

$ Entrées less than $10
$ $ Entrées $10-20
$ $ $ Entrées more than $20

MEXICAN

✪ Corazón de Maguey $$

This *mezcalería* and restaurant has a modern Mexican atmosphere and an ultra-fun menu of traditional food from across the republic, with a particularly strong emphasis on Oaxacan cuisine. On a leisurely afternoon in Coyoacán, this is a perfect place to order a flight of mezcal and a bunch of unusual bar snacks, like hibiscus-filled crispy tacos, guacamole with fried grasshoppers, or vegan ceviche.

MAP 7: Plaza Jardín Centenario 9A, tel. 55/7406-8199, corazondemaguey.com; 12:30pm-1am Mon.-Wed., 12:30pm-2am Thurs.-Fri., 9am-2am Sat.-Sun., kitchen closes about an hour before closing times; Metro: Viveros

Los Danzantes $$$

An elegant yet relaxed restaurant with a big outdoor dining area in the Jardín Centenario, Los Danzantes serves contemporary Mexican dishes with a strong emphasis on local Mexican ingredients and a notable influence from the culinary traditions of Oaxaca and other southern states. The appealing menu includes a range of interesting dishes, like duck enchiladas

dining alfresco at Corazón de Maguey

in *mole negro* and a green mole risotto. Los Danzantes is famous for its excellent line of Oaxacan mezcal, which, naturally, is served in-house.
MAP 7: Jardín Centenario 12, tel. 55/4356-7185, http://losdanzantes. com; 12:30pm-11pm Mon.-Thurs., 9am-midnight Fri.-Sat., 9am-11pm Sun.; Metro: Viveros

Fonda El Morral $$

This traditional Mexican restaurant is well suited to the old-fashioned ambience in Coyoacán, decorated with painted Talavera tile and wood furnishings and attended by a cadre of waiters in vests and bow ties. It's a good choice in the morning, when many beloved Mexican breakfast dishes are on offer, from *chilaquiles* to huevos rancheros. For lunch and dinner, plates like carne asada and chicken in *mole* are served with handmade tortillas. There are often mariachi musicians here on Sundays.
MAP 7: Allende 2, tel. 55/5554-0298; 8:30am-9:30pm Mon.-Thurs., 8am-10pm Fri.-Sat., 8am-9pm Sun.; Metro: Viveros

Papalotl Casa del Pan $

This long-running all-natural vegetarian and vegan café (which also has a branch in San Cristóbal de las Casas, Chiapas, and another in Cuicuilco, in southern Mexico City) serves house-baked breads and breakfast foods, baguette sandwiches, and other tasty fare, with an emphasis on local, organic ingredients. The small dining room opens onto the street, where sidewalk tables are filled with hippie-esque diners. The perfect spot to pass a Sunday morning with a cup of tea

and the paper, it often has a wait for weekend brunch.
MAP 7: Av. México 25, tel. 55/3095-1767, www.casadelpan.com; 9am-10pm daily; Metro: Viveros

Merendero Las Lupitas $

A *merendero* is a traditional restaurant serving light suppers, and though old-time Merendero Las Lupitas is open in the daytime (it started serving breakfast and lunch in the 1980s), it's nice to go in the evening, when the pleasant atmosphere, on the tranquil Plaza Santa Catarina, makes it the perfect place to wrap up the day. The menu includes a notable selection of dishes from northern Mexico, a surprising rarity in the capital. Try the *enchiladas potosinas* (fried-cheese enchiladas) or the burritos stuffed with *chilorio* (slow-cooked pork in chile sauce).
MAP 7: Plaza Santa Catarina 4, tel. 55/5554-3353; 8am-9:30pm Mon.-Thurs., 9am-11pm Fri.-Sat., 9am-8:30pm Sun.; Metro: Viveros

Merendero Las Lupitas

SEAFOOD

Mi Compa Chava - Coyoacán $

Roma neighborhood hot spot Mi Compa Chava opened a second branch of the superlative seafood restaurant in Coyoacán in the summer of 2022, providing a welcome culinary bump to a neighborhood that sometimes wavers on the food front. Though the space isn't as impressively big as the Roma original, you'll still find an incredibly upbeat vibe and some of the freshest and most delicious seafood in the capital at this central Coyoacán location.

MAP 7: Felipe Carrillo Puerto 31, reservations via WhatsApp 55/7838-5054; noon-8pm Tues.-Sun.; Metro: Viveros

TACOS, *TORTAS*, AND SNACKS

La Casa de los Tacos $

For a quick bite in central Coyoacán, this small and lively taqueria is conveniently located just down the street from Jardín Centenario. Here, you can get tacos filled with a range of ingredients, from "pre-Hispanic" choices like *chinicuiles* (the worm from the maguey cactus) to more standard fare like chorizo; however, the best bites might be those that come fresh off the *comal* (griddle) at the restaurant's entrance, like *gorditas* (thick round corn flatbreads). The salsas brought to each table are varied and delicious.

MAP 7: Carrillo Puerto 16, tel. 55/5554-9492, www.lacasadelostacos. com; 8am-11pm daily; Metro: Viveros

La Barraca Valenciana $

There are Spanish-style tapas on the menu—including classics like *tortilla española* (egg-and-potato omelet) and *patatas bravas* (fried and spiced potatoes)—but the thing to get at this low-key eatery is a *torta* (Mexican-style sandwich), served on a soft white roll. Try the breaded eggplant or the *jamon serrano* with cheese and chorizo, which come served (as any good *torta* should) with a bowl of pickled chiles. Big plus: The restaurant's owner is a craft beer aficionado, so there's always a nice selection of Mexican microbrews in the fridge.

MAP 7: Av. Centenario 91-C, tel. 55/5658-1880, www. labarracavalenciana.com; 1pm-9pm daily; Metro: Viveros

Pepe Coyotes $

With its massive spit of red-hued *pastor* spinning temptingly in the doorway, it's hard to miss Pepe Coyotes when walking up Avenida Hidalgo from the main plaza in Coyoacán. At this simple little eatery, you'll get filling tacos, *alambres* (stir-fried meat and vegetables), and savory pozole (a hominy soup) for very reasonable prices, and there's a full bar, if you'd like to accompany your food with a beer or a cocktail.

MAP 7: Av. Hidalgo 297, tel. 55/5659-8902, pepecoyotes. com; 8:15am-midnight Mon.-Sat., 8:15am-11pm Sun.; Metro: Viveros

Tostadas Amatista

Tostadas are a popular snack in Coyoacán, which you'll find in abundance at the public market and at street stands around the neighborhood. You can also get some delicious tostadas at this nice little shop, where you'll find the signature dish topped with seared tuna, chicken with *mole* and plantain, or roasted

ICONIC REGIONAL DISHES

There is a great deal of immigration to Mexico City from the greater republic, and, naturally, many of the capital's newer residents yearn for the flavors of home. Restaurants serving regional food are common in Mexico City, with some dishes becoming so popular that they are now mainstays in the city's cuisine. You'll find these regional dishes all over the city.

Chilorio and *machaca* tacos are served in flour tortillas.

CHILES EN NOGADA

Dressed in the colors of the Mexican flag, a *chile en nogada* is a large poblano pepper stuffed with ground meat, almonds, dried fruit, and spices, then topped with a creamy walnut sauce and dotted with fresh pomegranate seeds. It is generally served at room temperature. Mexico's national dish, *chiles en nogada* are typically made in celebration of Independence Day, in part because pomegranate comes into season in September. This popular take on the chile relleno can be found in restaurants throughout the city, but it's native to Puebla. They are traditionally available July to October.

Where to try it: Roldán 37 (page 66) or **Nicos** (page 267).

COCHINITA PIBIL

In the Yucatán, pulled pork is slow-cooked with citrus and ground seeds from the achiote tree. The bright red and very fragrant seeds give this dish its keynote flavor, popular throughout Mexico City. You'll see *cochinita* on restaurant menus, served in *tortas,* or rolled into tacos.

Where to try it: El Turix (page 150), **Cochinita Power** (page 122), or **Riviera del Sur** (page 193).

MOLE NEGRO

Moles are elaborate sauces ground from a mix of seeds, nuts, chile peppers, and spices, and there are different types of mole prepared throughout southern Mexico. *Mole negro* is a rich chocolate-based sauce that is traditionally served with chicken or turkey, and a signature dish from the state of Oaxaca.

Where to try it: Guzina Oaxaca (page 149) and **Los Danzantes** (page 232).

TLAYUDAS

A beloved street snack from the city and state of Oaxaca, tlayudas are giant corn flatbreads filled with refried black beans and Oaxacan cheese then toasted on a grill until crisp and toasted, and accompanied (optionally) by grilled meat like cecina or chorizo. Traditionally, a tlayuda is brushed with a thin layer of asiento (pig fat that drips off while making carnitas or chicharrón), which adds a delicious umami taste, but you can request your tlayuda without asiento to make it vegetarian.

Where to try it: Las Tlayudas (page 210) or **La Secina** (page 210), both in the Narvarte.

CHILORIO

A specialty of the northern Mexican state of Sinaloa, *chilorio* is pork slowly simmered with a mix of dried ancho chile peppers, oregano, cilantro seed, cumin, vinegar, and garlic. It is generally served in flour tortillas and surprisingly rare in Mexico City.

Where to try it: La Tonina (page 122) or **Merendero Las Lupitas** (page 233).

nopal and vegetables. The lunch special, which includes salad, soup, a tostada of your choice, a drink, and dessert is an excellent deal at about US$5, drawing a local crowd for lunch as the shop opens.

MAP 7: Centenario no. 31, tel. 55/672-9023, www.tostadasamatista.com.mx; 1:30pm-7:30pm Tues.-Thurs. and Sun., 1:30pm-9:30pm Fri.-Sat.; Metro: Viveros

Super Tacos Chupacabras $

One of the most famous taco stands in the city, this impressive street-side operation is a meat lover's dream, with busy *taqueros* rapidly plating orders for tacos filled with chorizo, *bistec* (beef), and *cecina* (salt-cured beef), as well as the signature taco "chupacabras," with its secret spices, to a swarm of customers. One thing that distinguishes Chupacabras from so many other taco stands is the variety of toppings—like potatoes, beans, and grilled prickly pear—lined up at the bar, which customers can pile onto their tacos.

MAP 7: Under the overpass at Lateral de Churubusco at Avenida México, no phone; 7am-3am Tues.-Sat., 7am-midnight Sun.; Metro: Coyoacán

COFFEE AND SWEETS
Boicot

There's a shaded rooftop terrace, breakfast served all day, and an extensive menu of caffeine-fueled beverages, from traditional (dripper, French press, espresso) to unusual (cold-brew frappé with peanut butter and chocolate), at this spacious café in central Coyoacán. There's always upbeat music on the sound system, plenty of tables for working

or chatting, and they're open late. They also serve Mexico City–brewed Cosaco beer on tap.

MAP 7: Felipe Carrillo Puerto 4, tel. 55/5663-7819, https://boicotcafe.com; 7:30am-10pm Sun.-Wed., 8am-midnight Thurs.-Sat.; Metro: Viveros

Boicot cafe

Café Avellaneda $

Serious coffee drinkers frequently point out the excellence of this itsy-bitsy café, just a block from the Plaza Hidalgo. It offers a selection of house-roasted beans from various Mexican coffee-growing regions, and a range of hot and cold coffee and espresso drinks, including some unusual offerings, like a cold-brew-based "oatmeal punch." There are two small tables inside the space and some stools at the bar, but it's just as nice to take your drink to the Plaza de la Conchita, a block and a half away.

MAP 7: Higuera 40, tel. 55/6553-3441, cafeavellaneda.negocio.site; 8am-9pm daily; Metro: Coyoacán

Café El Jarocho $

A neighborhood institution, the aromatic corner coffee stand Café El Jarocho is often jammed with neighborhood locals sipping inexpensive mochas and nibbling doughnuts. The only seating is the occasional milk crate outside or the iron benches along the sidewalk, where people gather for casual conversation throughout the week.

MAP 7: Calle Cuauhtémoc 134, tel. 55/5554-5418; 6am-midnight daily; Metro: Viveros

Café El Olvidado $

This perfect Coyoacán café, which overlooks the small plaza Fray Martín de Valencia, offers organic coffee drinks with beans from Veracruz, a large variety of teas, breads and pastries (like scones served with clotted cream and ginger cake), and an appealing menu of breakfasts, salads, and sandwiches. The space itself is lovely, with wood floors and tables, white walls, and lots of natural light.

MAP 7: Venustiano Carranza 267, tel. 55/7095-6125, https://elolvidado.com; 8am-9pm daily; Metro: Coyoacán

El Beneficio De La Duda $

After touring the Museo Frida Kahlo, it's a short stroll to this sweet café, where you can order a full meal from the menu of breakfasts, breads, and sandwiches, or just get a brownie and a cappuccino to enjoy on one of the sidewalk tables, where locals and their dogs often linger. The pretty country-style ambience feels nicely suited to a day in Coyoacán.

MAP 7: Valentín Gómez Farías 85, tel. 55/6724-9536; 8am-9pm Mon., 8:30am-10:30pm Tues.-Sun.; Metro: Viveros

Picnic $

If it's a warm day, stop for one of Picnic's creamy handmade ice creams in a classic (chocolate, vanilla, mint chocolate chip) or more experimental (pineapple-ginger, green tea, pear-anise) flavor; you can't go wrong with either. If it's a cool afternoon, try one of their delicious pecan-and-chocolate-chip cookies, a fresh-baked brownie, or whatever else they have on offer that day. There's another branch at Francisco Sosa 266-A.

MAP 7: Malintzin 205-2, tel. 55/5510-9209; 11am-7pm Wed.-Sun.; Metro: Viveros

MARKETS
Mercado Coyoacán $

A few blocks from Coyoacán's central plaza, this pretty covered market stocks fresh fruits, vegetables, and other kitchen staples, as well as flowers and handicrafts. It is particularly well-known for its *marisquerías,* seafood stands serving shrimp cocktails, ceviches, and fried fish. The most famous of these is Jardín del Pulpo, at the corner of Allende and Malintzin. Inside the market, there are also popular tostada stands, each offering *cazuelas* (clay pots) filled with an array of savory toppings.

MAP 7: Malintzin and Ignacio Allende, no phone; 7am-5pm daily; Metro: Viveros

Nightlife

BARS AND LOUNGES
✪ Centenario 107

This amiable spot in the heart of Coyoacán is a low-key place for a beer (there's an excellent selection of craft options on tap), a cocktail, or a shot of mezcal at any time of day. The spacious downstairs bar, with its high ceilings and big booths, is adjoined by a small outdoor patio, and there is an additional space upstairs. Chill and family-friendly during the day, the place gets busy with Coyoacán locals in the evenings.

MAP 7: Centenario 107, tel. 55/4752-6369, www.centenario107.com; 9am-11pm Mon., 9am-midnight Tues., 9am-1am Wed.-Thurs., 9am-2am Fri.-Sat., 10am-11pm Sun.; Metro: Viveros

Mezcalero

A relaxing bar just behind the Parroquia de San Juan Bautista, Mezcalero is a nice place to have a drink on the sidewalk tables in the late afternoon—or, alternatively, to stay up late partying, buoyed by the exuberance of Coyoacán's youthful night scene. As the name hints, there is a nice selection of mezcal, as well as beer and cocktails. If all the tables are full, grab a seat at La Celestina, another youthful cocktail bar, next door.

MAP 7: Caballocalco 14, tel. 55/5554-7027; 1pm-2am Fri.-Wed., 1pm-1am Thurs.; no cover; Metro: Viveros

Coyoacán is always bustling with visitors on the weekends.

CANTINAS

La Bipo

With a convivial local crowd and an atmosphere that blends new-school hip with quirky old-school kitsch, this casual nouveau cantina is a relaxed place to chat about parties or politics accompanied by an Indio on draft and a plate of fancy bar snacks, like fish tacos or hibiscus-filled quesadillas. Upstairs, there is an open-roof terrace where smokers converge, though the funky downstairs bar has more style.

MAP 7: Malintzin 155, tel. 55/5484-8230; 1pm-11pm Sun.-Tues., 1pm-midnight Wed., 1pm-2am Thurs.-Sat.; no cover; Metro: Viveros

La Coyoacana

Right in the heart of historic Coyoacán, this traditional cantina is a popular spot for families and day-trippers to have a few drinks and a bite to eat in the traditional dining room or on the pretty covered patio. On busy days, mariachi musicians mingle amid the diners and revelers. With its low cost, central location, and merry atmosphere, there is often a wait for a table on the weekends.

MAP 7: Higuera 14, tel. 55/5658-5337, www.lacoyoacana.com; 1pm-midnight Mon.-Wed., 1pm-2am Thurs.-Sat., 1pm-9pm Sun.; no cover; Metro: Viveros

LIVE MUSIC

El Vicio

A varied lineup can be found at this venue in Coyoacán, an incarnation of the long-running El Hábito, originally founded in 1954 by poet and essayist Salvador Novo. Often funny and irreverent shows include stand-up comedy, independent music, and monologues, and some performances benefit social organizations. As at many cabarets in Mexico City, you'll need proficient Spanish and some familiarity with Mexican politics and society to enjoy the show.

MAP 7: Madrid 13, tel. 55/3753-3529, www.elvicio.com.mx; shows generally Wed.-Mon., hours vary; tickets US$15-25; Metro: Viveros

BILLIARDS

Recreo

This spacious pool hall has been in operation for decades, with numerous gaming tables, foosball, and ping-pong, as well as a bunch of bar tables for groups waiting for a turn to play. The ambience has just enough style (tiled floors, hanging lamps) to make it attractive, but the atmosphere is zero percent pretentious. The crowd is likewise low-key, and the drinks are inexpensive, making Recreo a nice choice for a relaxed afternoon or evening.

MAP 7: Caballocalco 29, no phone; 1pm-10pm Tues.-Thurs., 1pm-11pm Fri., 1pm-midnight Sat.; no cover; Metro: Viveros

Cue up a game at billiard hall Recreo.

INDEPENDENT VENUES

- In the Roma Sur, **Cine Tonalá** (Tonalá 261, tel. 55/5264-4101, www.cinetonala.com) is an art house cinema, multidisciplinary performance space, and underground nightspot with an admirable focus on independent, director-driven films. The lineup changes weekly but usually includes four movies every day, with titles from across the world.

- The **Cineteca Nacional** (page 240) is the movie house par excellence in Mexico City. A much-anticipated second location of the Cineteca is currently under construction in the newly annexed Cuarta Sección of Chapultepec, with plans to open in late 2022 or early 2023.

- In addition to its own extensive programming, the Cineteca oversees programming at the Cine Lido in the Centro Cultural Bella Época, in the heart of the Condesa (Tamaulipas 202, tel. 55/5276-7110).

- A funky alternative cinema, **La Casa del Cine** (República de Uruguay 52, tel. 55/5512-4243, http://lacasadelcine.mx) was founded with the mission to promote young Mexican filmmakers. It shows works from international film festivals, independent Mexican films, and bigger-budget movies that are a few years old, in addition to participating in film festivals in the city.

- Located in the Santa María la Ribera's **Museo Universitario del Chopo** (page 129), **Cinematógrafo del Chopo** (Dr. Enrique González Martínez 10, www.chopo.unam. mx, functions usually at noon, 5pm, and 7:30pm, US$2, half price UNAM students) shows independent, avant-garde, and classic films throughout the week in the museum's small on-site cinema, curated by UNAM Filmoteca.

NOTABLE FILM FESTIVALS

- The **Festival Internacional de Cine UNAM** (www.ficunam.org) is a juried film competition overseen by the national university. It screens dozens of contemporary independent films during the second half of February and includes a prize category for feature-length Mexican films. Venues range from the university's cinemas to Cine Tonalá to outdoor plazas.

- An excellent annual documentary film festival, founded by Gael García Bernal, Diego Luna, and Pablo Cruz in 2006, **Ambulante** (tel. 55/5511-5073, http://ambulante.com. mx) shows over 100 international and national nonfiction films in movie theaters and *cineclubs* across the capital, with many free events during its springtime run.

Arts and Culture

CINEMA
✪ Cineteca Nacional

Founded in 1974, the Cineteca Nacional is a movie lover's paradise, with a lineup of international, independent, and art house films, shown by the dozens each week. Here you can see everything from experimental Mexican short films to an Akira Kurosawa retrospective to new blockbuster releases. The Cineteca maintains a huge film archive and publishes its own line of books on film. In 2012, the Cineteca buildings were renovated and expanded, including the addition of a new outdoor cinema that shows movies alfresco.

MAP 7: Av. México Coyoacán 389, tel. 55/4155-1200 or 55/4155-1190 (movie schedule), www.cinetecanacional.net; screenings generally begin at 2pm daily; US$3, US$2 students, people under 25, seniors, US$2 Tues.-Wed.; Metro: Coyoacán

documenting sound and hosts ongoing musical performances—all gratis—as well as guided listening tours of the archive.

MAP 7: Francisco Sosa 383, tel. 55/4155-0950, www.fonotecanacional.gob.mx; 10am-7pm Mon.-Fri., 9am-6pm Sat.; free; Metro: Viveros or Miguel Ángel de Quevedo

MUSEUMS

Fonoteca Nacional

The Fonoteca Nacional is a rather unusual project: Through a mix of recordings and audiovisual material, this archive seeks to preserve the unique sounds of Mexico, from the brassy tones of a band playing outside a Metro station to the sizzle of meat frying at a taco stand. Housed in Casa Alvarado, an 18th-century hacienda, the Fonoteca exhibits work by artists and historians

Museo Nacional de Culturas Populares

Dedicated to Mexico's diverse popular art and craft traditions, this museum is interesting from both an anthropological and aesthetic perspective. Overseen by the National Council for Culture and Arts, the museum doesn't have a permanent collection, instead organizing temporary exhibitions featuring work from specific regions or cultures, or around certain themes, like lunar

Fonoteca Nacional

metaphors or the milpa; it also occasionally exhibits work by Indigenous cultures from other parts of the world, in addition to hosting special events and performances in its back patio.

MAP 7: Av. Hidalgo 289, tel. 55/4155-0920, http://museoculturaspopulares.gob.mx; 10am-6pm Tues.-Thurs., 10am-8pm Fri.-Sun.; US$1, children under 12 and seniors over 60 free; Metro: Viveros

Museo Nacional de Culturas Populares

THEATER, CLASSICAL MUSIC, AND DANCE
CENART (Centro Nacional de los Artes)

Not far from central Coyoacán, CENART is a government-run institution dedicated to the study and promotion of performing, visual, and applied arts, from dance and circus arts to painting and architecture. The massive 12-acre campus, designed by a host of famous architects like Enrique Norten and Ricardo Legorreta, is visually striking, and includes five art galleries, an art store, three theaters, a library, a bookshop, a small café, and even

some landscaped green space. There are frequent musical and dance performances on the weekends, often presented by CENART students, from classic music and ballet to children's cinema.

MAP 7: Río Churubusco 79, Colonia Country Club, tel. 55/4155-0111, ticket office tel. 55/4155-0000, www.cenart.gob.mx; Metro: Viveros

the expansive campus of CENART

La Titería

This wonderful children's theater, which has a creative focus on puppetry and marionettes, presents colorful and joyous original shows every weekend. There's popcorn for sale in the patio outside, books and games for children to play with while they wait for the show to begin, and general good vibes from

the colorful patio of La Titería in Coyoacán, a puppet theater

the staff and actors. Productions here are in Spanish, but children who don't speak the language may be able to follow along with the upbeat programming.

MAP 7: Vicente Guerrero 7, tel. 55/5662-6952, www.latiteria.mx; shows noon and 2pm Sat.-Sun., as well as school holidays; tickets US$10; Metro: Viveros

Recreation

PARKS
❂ Viveros de Coyoacán
In 1901, architect and early environmentalist Miguel Ángel de Quevedo donated a hectare of land to the city to create a public nursery. Officially inaugurated in 1907, it was the first open space dedicated to growing trees and plants for public use in the city. Today, it's a popular place for neighborhood locals out for a stroll, especially during the early morning and late afternoon. Open yoga and tai chi classes are often held in the park.

MAP 7: Between Universidad, Madrid, Melchor Ocampo, and Pérez Valenzuela, www.viveroscoyoacan.gob.mx; daily 6am-6pm; free; Metro: Viveros

Shops

ARTS AND CRAFTS
Bazaar Reto
Bazaar Reto, a huge antiques vendor in the Portales neighborhood (Fernando Montes de Oca 391, tel. 55/3241-7243), operates a small but charming shop in central Coyoacán. Here, you'll find a selection of treasures like old maps, vintage artwork, mid-20th-century lamps and furnishings, old wall clocks, violins, and other curiosities. Half of the shop is dedicated to vintage clothing and shoes, in both men's and women's styles.

MAP 7: Centenario 25, tel. 55/4389-8422; 9am-6:30pm daily; Metro: Viveros

Taller Experimental de Cerámica
Visit this long-running open-air ceramics studio in downtown Coyoacán to browse a tiny, jumbled showroom of glazed handmade ceramic pieces created by the workshop's owners or find good bargains amid the dusty shelves of recently fired ceramic tableware, including mugs, plates, teapots, bowls, vases, and more. In addition to retail, the workshop offers ongoing classes in wheel throwing, sculpture, and glazing.

MAP 7: Centenario 63, tel. 55/5554-6960, www.ceramicadiazdecossio.com.mx; 10am-5pm Mon.-Fri.; Metro: Juárez

BEST SOUVENIRS

FOR THE HOME COOK

Lightweight **dried chiles,** of which you'll find a grand variety in Mexico City's markets, are the cornerstone of many Mexican salsas, and they can also be dropped into a pot of cooking beans to add both kick and flavor. **Mole paste** can be mixed with chicken or vegetable broth (or just water) to create a dish from this distinctively Mexican sauce.

traditional textiles from Oaxaca

Shopping tips: *Mole* can be bought in paste or powder, though it is generally easier and quicker to prepare from a paste. Note that *mole* paste may be confiscated by security at the airport, since some pastes are considered liquids. Pack it in your checked luggage to avoid problems.

Where to find it: The **Mercado San Juan** (page 105) is a favorite shopping spot for many chefs, both amateur and professional. The **Mercado de la Merced** (page 52) has a dizzying array of dried chiles, *moles,* spices, and other packable goodies.

FOR THE CAFFEINE LOVER

Mexico's southern states are major producers of high-quality **coffee beans** and **cacao.** Both beans have been consumed in Mexico for centuries, though you'll find hundreds of new artisanal chocolatiers and small-batch coffee roasters in the city today.

Shopping tips: Hip third-wave coffee roasters have taken over in the capital, but you'll also find excellent coffee beans for sale at some of the city's oldest shops, many of which have a Middle Eastern heritage.

Where to find it: Art bookshop **Casa Bosques** (page 200) carries a proprietary line of Mexican chocolate bars, some with unlike accents like wasabi and almond, rosemary, or cardamom. **Chocolatería La Rifa** (page 125) sells top-quality bars for eating and for hot chocolate, made with Mexican cacao. **Café Jekemir** (page 69) has been roasting coffee for almost a century, and still makes some of the city's best coffee. **Cafe Avellaneda** (page 236) roasts their own line of premium Mexican coffee beans.

FOR THE CREATIVE DECORATOR

From hand-loomed rugs to delicately embroidered blouses to warm wool ponchos, **traditional clothing** and **textiles** are produced in communities throughout Mexico. Some popular gifts are embroidered manta tunics and *huipiles* from Oaxaca, geometrically stitched Magdalena *huipiles* from Chiapas, and silk wraps or shawls from Tenancingo, Santa María del Río, and other regions.

BOOKS

Centro Cultural Elena Garro

Run by the Fondo de Cultura Económica, this multistory bookstore and cultural center is architecturally stunning. Here, a towering glass facade completely envelops the original early 20th-century mansion, creating an atmosphere both modern and historic. The bookstore is well-stocked, with a good selection of literature and children's

Shopping tips: Textiles made from hand-dyed, hand-loomed natural fibers are always the priciest, but the quality is also superlative. Look for wool dyed in the traditional style with cochineal, a crimson-colored tint derived from insects.

Where to find it: For the highest-quality pieces, try **Remigio** (page 78) at The Shops at Downtown. **FONART** (page 134) also has a fine selection of traditional textiles and clothing, as does excellent craft shop **Onora** (page 166) in Polanco. For a fun and contemporary twist on traditional Mexican clothing, try **Fábrica Social** (page 134) in the Juárez.

FOR THE SOPHISTICATE

There is a long tradition of silver design in Mexico, dating back to the early colonial era. Some of the Mexico's most famous **silverwork** comes from the former mining town of Taxco, Guerrero, much inspired by early 20th-century designer William Spratling.

Shopping tips: Though it's not an iron-clad guarantee, real silver will generally be stamped with *925, 920, MEX, or MEXICO.*

Where to find it: Tane (page 167) could be considered the Tiffany & Co. of Mexico, with multiple lines of high-quality silverwork from top designers, most contemporary in style. You can also find vintage silver at antiques market like the **Centro de Antigüedades Plaza del Ángel** (page 134).

FOR THE ECLECTIC COLLECTOR

There are endless finds, from splendid to quirky, at Mexico City's varied **antiques** and vintage markets. Shop for antique jewelry and watches, midcentury eyeglass frames, old enamel cookware, roller skates, Lego sets, Polaroid cameras, oil paintings, black-and-white photographs, vinyl records, used books, and other sundries.

Shopping tips: Before buying anything, take a quick turn around the entire market; you might find two vendors have similar products at different prices or with different quality. At all of Mexico City's antiques markets, serious buyers arrive early in the day to snag the best pieces. Prices are often negotiable for higher-priced items.

Where to find it: La Lagunilla (page 103), on Sunday mornings, is the biggest and most popular antiques market in the capital. **Centro de Antigüedades Plaza del Ángel** (page 134) has many upscale items on sale. **Mercado de Cuauhtémoc** (page 199) is a low-key and accessible place with some interesting vendors, especially on Saturday. There are antiques and other curiosities at **Bazaar Reto** (page 243) in Coyoacán.

FOR THE COCKTAIL ENTHUSIAST

Mezcal and **tequila** have become immensely popular internationally, and are now exported throughout the world, but you'll still find the best selection of Mexican liquors in Mexico.

Shopping tips: For the drinks connoisseur, bring home a lesser-known spirit, like *sotol*, or a bottle of mezcal distilled with a scorpion inside (it lends the spirit a bright, acidic taste).

Where to find it: Sabrá Dios? (page 203) has a unique high-end selection of Mexican spirits, including excellent rare mezcal.

books, though most titles are in Spanish. Even if you don't pick up a book, the adjoining garden café is a perfect place to rest your legs.

MAP 7: Fernández Leal 43, tel. 55/3003-4091, www.educal.com.mx/ elenagarro; 10am-9pm daily; Metro: Viveros

San Ángel and UNAM   Map 8

Upscale San Ángel is a colonial-era neighborhood with an old-fashioned feeling. Wander the streets around the main plaza to find **cobblestone streets** with marvelous **colonial-era homes and haciendas,** now inhabited by Mexico City's wealthier denizens, as well as some interesting museums, including the **Museo de Arte Carrillo Gil** and the **Museo de El Carmen.** The main plaza is also the site of a well-known Saturday craft market, the **Bazaar Sábado.**

Farther south, the Ciudad Universitaria is the main campus for the **Universidad Nacional Autónoma de México (UNAM),** the largest and most prestigious university in Mexico. The campus was

named a World Heritage Site for its **modernist architecture,** engineering, and landscape design, and it is home to one of the city's best contemporary art spaces, the Museo Universitario Arte Contemporáneo.

TOP SIGHTS

- Most Radical Spot: **Biblioteca Central** (page 249)

TOP ARTS AND CULTURE

- Best Contemporary Art: **Museo Universitario Arte Contemporáneo** (page 255)

TOP RECREATION

- Best *Fútbol* Stadium: **Estadio Olímpico Universitario** (page 257)

TOP SHOPS

- Best Browsing: **Bazaar Sábado** (page 258)
- Best Crafts: **Casa del Obispo** (page 259)

GETTING THERE AND AROUND

- Metro lines: 3
- Metro stops: Barranca del Muerto, Coyoacán, Viveros
- Metrobús lines: 1
- Metrobús stops: La Bombilla, Dr. Gálvez, Ciudad Universitaria

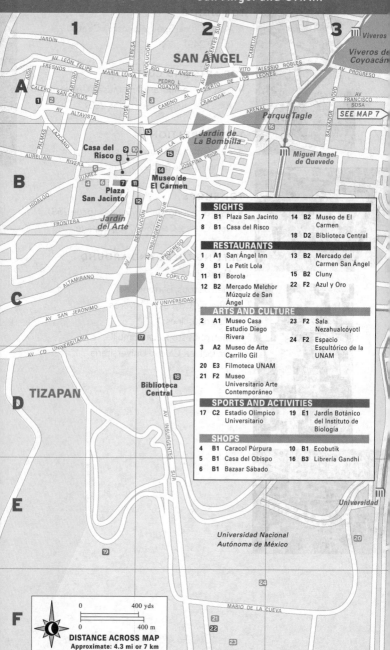

SIGHTS

7	B1	Plaza San Jacinto	14	B2	Museo de El Carmen
8	B1	Casa del Risco	18	D2	Biblioteca Central

RESTAURANTS

1	A1	San Ángel Inn	13	B2	Mercado del Carmen San Ángel
9	B1	Le Petit Lola	15	B2	Cluny
11	B1	Borola	22	F2	Azul y Oro
12	B2	Mercado Melchor Múzquiz de San Ángel			

ARTS AND CULTURE

2	A1	Museo Casa Estudio Diego Rivera	23	F2	Sala Nezahualcóyotl
3	A2	Museo de Arte Carrillo Gil	24	F2	Espacio Escultórico de la UNAM
20	E3	Filmoteca UNAM			
21	F2	Museo Universitario Arte Contemporáneo			

SPORTS AND ACTIVITIES

17	C2	Estadio Olímpico Universitario	19	E1	Jardín Botánico del Instituto de Biología

SHOPS

4	B1	Caracol Púrpura	10	B1	Ecobutik
5	B1	Casa del Obispo	16	B3	Librería Gandhi
6	B1	Bazaar Sábado			

DISTANCE ACROSS MAP
Approximate: 4.3 mi or 7 km

0   400 yds
0   400 m

© MOON.COM

Sights

⊛ Biblioteca Central

The Universidad Nacional Autónoma de México (UNAM), the country's oldest, largest, and most prestigious college, can trace its founding to the early colonial era. In its modern incarnation as the national university, it was inaugurated in September 1910 and granted its unique status as autonomous from the government in 1923. UNAM's main campus, built from 1949 to 1952 by more than 60 architects, engineers, and artists, is a UNESCO World Heritage Site. There are many architectural gems within the central campus, known as the Ciudad Universitaria, though none more iconic than the Central Library. All four sides of this million-plus-title library are covered in a dazzling mosaic made of colored volcanic stone. Designed by artist and architect Juan O'Gorman, the mural illustrates themes from Mexican history in four eras: pre-Hispanic, colonial, modern, and the present.

Just south of the library is the **Rectoría,** the campus's main administration building, whose south wall is covered with a three-dimensional mural by David Alfaro Siqueiros. Just below, **Museo Universitario de Ciencias y Artes CU** (Av. Insurgentes Sur 3000, tel. 55/5622-0206; 10am-7pm Mon.-Fri., 10am-6pm Sat.-Sun.) is a public museum that hosts free exhibits

Biblioteca Central

by predominantly Mexican artists. Across Insurgentes, the Estadio Olímpico is the home field for the Pumas soccer club, with a mosaic of the university's shield created in colored stones by Diego Rivera.

MAP 8: Circuito Interior, Ciudad Universitaria, tel. 55/5622-1603, http://bibliotecacentral.unam.mx; 8:30am-9:30pm daily; free; Metro: Copilco, Metrobús: Ciudad Universitaria

Plaza San Jacinto

The fine cobblestone plaza at the heart of San Ángel is ringed by cafés and restaurants. Although it's just a couple of blocks from a sea of traffic on Insurgentes and Avenida Revolución, wandering around the relaxed plaza makes it easy to imagine San Ángel as a village far from Mexico City, as it once was. On Saturdays, local artists sell work in the square, turning the plaza into a *jardín del arte* (art garden).

Up San Jacinto street, on the west side of the plaza, the Iglesia de San Jacinto was once part of a Dominican monastery built between 1564 and 1614. Notable are the principal retablo inside and the carved stone *cruz atrial* (atrium cross) standing in front of the church. The beautiful walled gardens are a favorite venue for weekend wedding parties.

MAP 8: Av. Madero at San Jacinto; Metro: Miguel Ángel de Quevedo, Metrobús: La Bombilla or Dr. Gálvez

Casa del Risco

The Centro Cultural Isidro Fabela, better known by its original name, Casa del Risco, is located in a 17th-century mansion, right in front of the Plaza San Jacinto in downtown San Ángel. Politician and judge Isidro Fabela donated the home, long a private residence and now a historic landmark, to the city in 1958, along with his collection of baroque European and colonial-era Mexican art and furnishings, including works by notable names from New Spain, like Miguel Cabrera. One of the most striking features of the museum is the large Mexican baroque wall fountain in the main courtyard, which is decorated with dozens of round Talavera ceramic plates, interspersed with hand-painted tiles and seashells. Admission is free.

MAP 8: Plaza San Jacinto 15, tel. 55/5616-2711, www.museocasadelrisco. org.mx; 10am-5pm Tues.-Sun.; free; Metro: Miguel Ángel de Quevedo, Metrobús: La Bombilla

Casa del Risco is a cultural center and art space in central San Angel.

Museo de El Carmen

A former Carmelite convent, established in 1615, is a fitting backdrop to the collection of Mexican colonial art and furniture at this wonderful museum. Including oil paintings, sculpture, and religious pieces from the 17th and 18th centuries, the large and interesting collection has been overseen by INAH (National Institute of Anthropology and History) since the 1930s; the organization opened the museum here in 1955.

Once the religious and economic center of San Ángel, the convent housed an order of Carmelite nuns. While touring the museum, note the vestry (where priests' robes were hung) with its elaborate gold-leaf carvings, the old bathroom and washbasins with Talavera-tile bowls, and the beautiful crypt downstairs, where naturally mummified bodies were discovered and are now on display in a somewhat macabre exhibit. Next door, the adjoining church, Iglesia de El Carmen, with its three beautiful tile-covered domes, was built in 1624.

MAP 8: Av. Revolución 4, tel. 55/5616-2816; 10am-5pm Tues.-Sun.; US$3.50 adults, free for students and teachers, free on Sun.; Metro: Miguel Ángel de Quevedo or Barranca del Muerto, Metrobús: La Bombilla or Dr. Gálvez

Restaurants

PRICE KEY

$	Entrées less than $10
$ $	Entrées $10-20
$ $ $	Entrées more than $20

MEXICAN

Azul y Oro $$

In the heart of the UNAM's cultural center, this contemporary Mexican restaurant occupies a former student cafeteria and adjoining outdoor patio. It's an unlikely setting for the restaurant's inventive Mexican menu, which draws much of its inspiration from the flavors of Yucatán, Oaxaca, and Veracruz, noted in dishes like duck-stuffed *buñuelos* in *mole* sauce or shrimp in *pipián* (a pumpkin-seed sauce). Because of its location on the university campus, no alcohol is served. At press time, it remained closed following pandemic restrictions, but was expected to reopen. Call ahead.

MAP 8: Centro Cultural Universitario, Insurgentes Sur 3000, tel. 55/5424-1426, www.azul.rest; 10am-6pm Mon.-Tues., 10am-8pm Wed.-Sat., 9am-7pm Sun.; Metro: Universidad, Metrobús: CCU

San Ángel Inn $$$

Built in the 17th century as a Carmelite monastery and later incorporated into a sprawling hacienda, the famed San Ángel Inn has more than three centuries of history behind it. Today, the historic building is still called San Ángel Inn, but it's a restaurant, not a hotel, serving traditional Mexican food in a truly old-fashioned atmosphere. The most famous items on the menu are undoubtedly the margaritas, served in little pitchers kept chilled in individual ice buckets.

MAP 8: Diego Rivera 50, tel. 55/5616-1402 or 55/5616-2222, www.sanangelinn.com; 8am-1am Mon.-Sat., 8am-10pm Sun.; Metro: Barranca del Muerto, Metrobús: La Bombilla

the communal patio at Mercado del Carmen San Ángel

Le Petit Lola $

This colorful, family-friendly restaurant is a nice place for a casual lunch in downtown San Ángel. You can order from the breakfast menu (served all day), which includes comforting items like baked eggs and waffles, but many come for the homemade pizzas and *tortas*, Mexican-style sandwiches served on a white roll called a *telera*. With big windows and bright, whimsical decor, it's popular with local families on the weekends.

MAP 8: Amargura 14, tel. 55/5550-8429, www.lepetitlola.com; noon-7pm daily; Metro: Miguel Ángel de Quevedo, Metrobús: La Bombilla

FRENCH
Cluny $$

This long-running French restaurant has a charming belle époque atmosphere and an appealing menu of bistro staples like quiche, salads, crepes, and steak frites. They've been in business in San Ángel since the 1970s, maintaining a dedicated clientele with fair prices and nicely prepared food. It's a cozy spot for a quiet evening out.

MAP 8: Av. de la Paz 57, tel. 55/5550-7350, www.cluny.com.mx; 12:30pm-11:30pm Mon.-Fri., 9am-11:30pm Sat.-Sun.; Metro: Miguel Ángel de Quevedo, Metrobús: La Bombilla

MARKETS
Mercado del Carmen San Ángel $

At this gourmet market and food court, opened in 2014 in central San Ángel, you'll find food stalls serving up ceviche, buffalo wings, and burgers, among other snacks. Order from whichever stand you wish, then take a seat at the long communal tables, which often get crowded on the weekends. A nice touch here are the two bars—El Bebedero, serving craft beer from Mexican producers, and

Onza, which serves beer, wine, and spirits.

MAP 8: Amargura 5, tel. 55/5256-4005; noon-11pm daily, hours vary by vendor; Metro: Miguel Ángel de Quevedo, Metrobús: La Bombilla

Mercado Melchor Múzquiz de San Ángel $

Along Avenida Revolución, this little neighborhood market is immediately recognizable for the colorful murals painted above the main arcades by artist Ariosto Otero. In 1958, the covered market was built on the site of what was once an open-air market, where it is rumored that Diego Rivera and Frida Kahlo did their shopping. It's an inexpensive spot for a traditional snack, like *tacos de guisado* or a seafood cocktail.

MAP 8: Av. Revolución and Melchor Múzquiz, tel. 55/4471-8834; 8am-5pm daily; Metro: Miguel Ángel de Quevedo, Metrobús: La Bombilla

Arts and Culture

CINEMA
Filmoteca UNAM

UNAM, the national university, has a major film program, which includes film studies, restoration, and a huge film library. The Sala Julio Bracho, Sala José Revueltas, and Sala Carlos Monsiváis, the university's three main screening rooms, are located on the university campus in the southern part of the city. Each month has a thematic focus, from movies featuring Mexican *luchadores* (wrestlers) to James Dean. In addition, UNAM runs screening rooms at the Museo Universitario del Chopo and at the Casa del Lago in Chapultepec.

MAP 8: Av. Insurgentes Sur 3000, Ciudad Universitaria in UNAM, tel. 55/5622-9374, www.filmoteca.unam. mx; hours vary; US$2, US$1 students; Metro: Universidad

MUSEUMS
Espacio Escultórico de la UNAM

A 1970s collaboration between artists including Federico Silva, Mathias Goeritz, Helen Escobedo, and Manuel Felguérez resulted in the national university's unique Espacio Escultórico, a monumental sculpture garden built within an open expanse of volcanic rock and scrubby brush. It is an iconic destination on the UNAM campus, drawing art and ecology into a

The Espacio Escultórico is a massive outdoor sculpture garden constructed in the 1970s.

unique dialogue. The keynote piece is a massive, circular concrete sculpture, which is often used for performances or student meetings.

MAP 8: Circuito Mario de la Cueva s/n, Ciudad Universitaria, tel. 55/5622-7003, www.cultura.unam.mx; 7am-4pm daily; free; Metro: Universidad, Metrobús: CCU

Museo Casa Estudio Diego Rivera

In 1931, artist Juan O'Gorman designed two small functionalist homes, joined by a footbridge, for Frida Kahlo and Diego Rivera. Kahlo lived there until 1941 and Rivera until his death, in 1954. The homes were opened to the public as a museum in 1986. Rivera's studio has been preserved as it was during his lifetime, providing an intimate look into the artist's enchanting personal aesthetics; some

of his pre-Columbian artifacts and Mexican handicrafts are also on display.

MAP 8: Av. Diego Rivera at Altavista, tel. 55/8647-5470, www.estudiodiegorivera.bellasartes.gob.mx; 11am-5pm Tues.-Sun.; US$2; Metro: Barranca del Muerto, Metrobús: La Bombilla

Museo de Arte Carrillo Gil

One of the nicest art museums in the city, the Carrillo Gil is housed in a modern, multistory stone building in San Ángel. The museum's permanent collection, originally donated by its namesake, includes work from modernist masters like Pablo Picasso and contemporary art stars like Gabriel Orozco. Even more interesting, the museum mounts ongoing large-scale exhibitions of artwork by current Mexican

Diego Rivera and Frida Kahlo's former home in San Ángel

and international artists, for which opening parties are usually packed to the brim.

MAP 8: Av. Revolución 1608, tel. 55/8647-5450, www. museodeartecarrillogil.com; 11am-4:30pm Tues.-Sun.; US$3, students, children under 12 free, free on Sun.; Metro: Barranca del Muerto, Metrobús: La Bombilla

✪ Museo Universitario Arte Contemporáneo (MUAC)

In the heart of the UNAM campus, this superb museum has consistently been one of the best places to see contemporary art in Mexico City since it opened in 2008. Designed by Teodoro González de León, the building is architecturally stunning and well situated for viewing art, with large glass walls flooding gallery spaces with indirect natural light. Frequently rotating exhibitions feature work from internationally recognized artists from Mexico and abroad, including recent exhibitions by celebrated British sculptor Anish Kapoor, Mexico City–based Belgian artist Francis Alÿs, and Mexican painter Manuel Felguérez.

MAP 8: Insurgentes Sur 3000, tel. 55/5622-6972, www.muac.unam. mx; 10am-6pm Wed., Fri., and Sun., 10am-8pm Thurs. and Sat.; Wed. and Sun. US$1.50, Thurs.-Sat. US$3.50, children under 12 free; Metro: Universidad, Metrobús: CCU

THEATER, CLASSICAL MUSIC, AND DANCE
Sala Nezahualcóyotl

In the heart of the university's cultural center, this picturesque and highly respected concert hall is the home of UNAM's philharmonic orchestra, and it also hosts national and international performers in jazz, chamber music, and other genres. Built in the mid-1970s, the theater was designed to resemble Amsterdam's Royal Concertgebouw theater, and there are excellent acoustics throughout the space. Balcony seats are often a bargain.

MAP 8: Insurgentes Sur 3000, tel. 55/5622-7125, www.musica.unam. mx; hours vary; US$5-15 depending on seats, half price for students and teachers; Metro: Universidad, Metrobús: Ciudad Universitaria

Festivals and Events

JULY
La Feria de Flores San Ángel
The annual Feria de Flores is celebrated in San Ángel's Parque de la Bombilla every July, when the plaza is filled with flower vendors, food and crafts stands, and live music throughout the day, as well as workshops and crafts for adults and children. Many families come out to hear Mexican ensembles like mariachi, *son jarocho*, and baile folklórico on the big stage. The fair was initially linked to the neighborhood's annual celebrations for the Virgen del Carmen, which take place every July 16, in the Ex-Convento del Carmen.

San Ángel: Parque de la Bombilla, Avenida de la Paz s/n, Chimalistac; mid-July

the annual Feria de las Flores in San Ángel

Recreation

PARKS
Jardín Botánico del Instituto de Biología

Operated by UNAM's biological sciences department, this expansive botanical garden, located in the southern stretches of the university campus, cultivates more than 1,600 plant species from Mexico's deserts, forests, and jungles as a part of its mission to promote the conservation of endangered and endemic species. There are frequent plant-related workshops, themed tours of the garden, and family-oriented activities on Saturday.

MAP 8: Tercer Circuito exterior, s/n, Ciudad Universitaria Coyoacán, tel. 55/5622-9047 or 55/5622-9063, www.ib.unam.mx/jardin; 9am-4:30pm Mon.-Fri., 9am-3pm Sat. winter, 9am-5:30pm Mon.-Fri., 9am-3pm Sat. summer; $3; Metrobús: Centro Cultural Universitario

SPECTATOR SPORTS
SOCCER
✪ Estadio Olímpico Universitario

This attractive and unusually intimate soccer stadium is home to the Pumas, a professional soccer team that is frequently among the best teams in the premiere league (though owned by UNAM and located on the university campus, students rarely play on the team). If you're interested in seeing a pro team play, Estadio Olímpico is easily accessible, and games are rowdy and fun. The Pumas have a fiercely loyal following and the *porras* (fan clubs) are known for their enthusiastic cheers at games.

MAP 8: Insurgentes Sur, just south of Eje 10 Sur, Ciudad Universitaria; hours vary; most games US$5-15; Metro: Universidad, Metrobús: Ciudad Universitaria

The Pumas are the home team at soccer stadium Estadio Olímpico at UNAM.

Shops

ARTS AND CRAFTS

⭐ Bazaar Sábado

Originally established in 1960, this is one of the nicest craft markets in the city, located in the courtyard of a 17th-century stone building and spilling out into the Plaza San Jacinto. You'll find traditional artisan work, including blown glass, jewelry, ceramics, traditional masks, paper flowers, and clothing, as well as some contemporary designers selling their work. It's a popular Saturday destination for both residents and tourists, often bustling with browsers and filled with cheerful marimba music.

MAP 8: Plaza San Jacinto 11, tel. 55/5616-0082; 10am-6pm Sat.; Metro: Barranca del Muerto or Miguel Ángel de Quevedo, Metrobús: La Bombilla

Caracol Púrpura

This small shop near the Plaza San Jacinto sells decorative crafts in a bright, gallery-like atmosphere. Some of the nicest pieces in the shop's collection include oversize beaded figurines made by the Huichol; delicately painted ceramics from Mata Ortiz, Chihuahua; and elaborate *árboles de la vida* (a ceramic sculptural tradition reaching back to the early colonial era) from Mexico state. There is another branch in The Shops at Downtown

Bazaar Sábado in San Ángel

258

(Isabel la Católica 30, tel. 55/5521-8000) in the Centro Histórico.

MAP 8: Juárez 2A, San Ángel, tel. 55/5550-1450; 11am-7pm Mon.-Fri., 9am-8pm Sat., 9am-7pm Sun.; Metro: Miguel Ángel de Quevedo, Metrobús: La Bombilla

✪ Casa del Obispo

Set in a colonial-era mansion, the Casa del Obispo is one of the most impressive craft shops in the city—with prices to match. If you'd like to browse high-quality works of folk art and artesanía, you will find many gorgeous pieces from across Mexico at this well-curated store, from ceramics from Mata Ortiz, Chihuahua, to splendid hand-painted wooden chests from Michoacán. The owner can give you background on any piece you're eyeing.

MAP 8: Juárez 1, San Ángel, tel. 55/5616-9079; 10am-6pm Mon.-Fri., 10am-7pm Sat.-Sun.; Metro: Miguel Ángel de Quevedo, Metrobús: La Bombilla

BOOKS

Librería Gandhi

This beloved bookseller is one of the best in the city, with a broad selection of fiction, nonfiction, children's titles, and travel guides, mostly in Spanish, in its 15 branches in the capital. One of the largest stores is on Miguel Ángel de Quevedo in Coyoacán, just a few steps away from where the original Gandhi opened in 1971. There's a smaller branch across the street from Bellas Artes (Juárez 4, tel. 55/5510-4231) in the Centro Histórico.

MAP 8: Miguel Ángel de Quevedo 121, Col. Guadalupe Chimalistac, tel. 55/2625-0606, www.gandhi.com. mx; Mon.-Fri. 9am-10pm Mon.-Fri., 10am-10pm Sat.-Sun.; Metro: Viveros

GREEN AND ECOLOGICAL SHOPS

Ecobutik

Specializing in ecologically responsible and organic products for the bath and home, this cute shop sells candles, essential oils, green cosmetics and cleaning products, handmade baby toys, reusable water bottles, and other smartly designed home goods. Run by organic food brand Aires de Campo, the store also has a small selection of kitchen and baking supplies, like vanilla beans, yuca flour, and coconut oil.

MAP 8: Amargura 14, No. 1, tel. 55/5550-9406, www.ecobutik.com; 9am-8pm Mon.-Fri., 11am-6pm Sat.-Sun.; Metro: Miguel Ángel de Quevedo, Metrobús: La Bombilla

Greater Mexico City   Map 9

It can take months to explore central Mexico City, but there is also a wide range of neighborhoods and experiences outside the city's most well-known districts, including **colonial-era neighborhoods,** memorable restaurants, and archaeological sites. If you are visiting Mexico City with a little extra time, it's worth it to visit **Xochimilco,** where you can take a flat-bottomed **boat tour** of the neighborhood's **centuries-old canals** and farmland. Almost every week, there are rowdy soccer matches at the massive **Estadio Azteca.** And there is always a colorful crowd at the **Basílica de Santa María de Guadalupe,** one of the world's most colorful and beloved Catholic pilgrimage sites.

TOP SIGHTS
- Best Floating Picnic: **Canals at Xochimilco** (page 263)

TOP RESTAURANTS
- Best Traditional Dining: **Nicos** (page 267)

TOP ARTS AND CULTURE
- Most Striking Architecture: **Museo Anahuacalli** (page 268)
- Best Spot for Diego-and-Frida Fans: **Museo Dolores Olmedo** (page 269)
- Best Mondays: **Museo del Juguete Antiguo México** (page 269)

TOP RECREATION
- Best *Fútbol* Stadiums: **Estadio Azteca** (page 271)

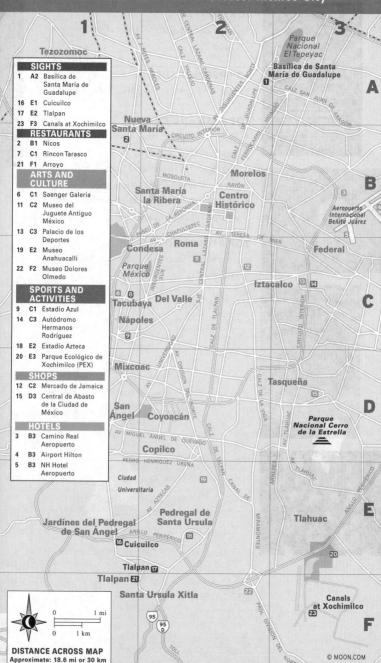

SIGHTS
1　A2　Basílica de Santa María de Guadalupe
16　E1　Cuicuilco
17　E2　Tlalpan
23　F3　Canals at Xochimilco

RESTAURANTS
2　B1　Nicos
7　C1　Rincon Tarasco
21　F1　Arroyo

ARTS AND CULTURE
6　C1　Saenger Galería
11　C2　Museo del Juguete Antiguo México
13　C3　Palacio de los Deportes
19　E2　Museo Anahuacalli
22　F2　Museo Dolores Olmedo

SPORTS AND ACTIVITIES
9　C1　Estadio Azul
14　C3　Autódromo Hermanos Rodríguez
18　E2　Estadio Azteca
20　E3　Parque Ecológico de Xochimilco (PEX)

SHOPS
12　C2　Mercado de Jamaica
15　D3　Central de Abasto de la Ciudad de México

HOTELS
3　B3　Camino Real Aeropuerto
4　B3　Airport Hilton
5　B3　NH Hotel Aeropuerto

Tezozomoc

Parque Nacional El Tepeyac

Basílica de Santa María de Guadalupe

Nueva Santa María

Morelos

Santa María la Ribera

Centro Histórico

Aeropuerto Internacional Benito Juárez

Condesa　Roma

Federal

Parque México

Iztacalco

Tacubaya　Del Valle

Nápoles

Mixcoac

Tasqueña

San Ángel　Coyoacán

Parque Nacional Cerro de la Estrella

Copilco

Ciudad Universitaria

Pedregal de Santa Ursula

Tlahuac

Jardínes del Pedregal de San Ángel

Cuicuilco

Tlalpan

Tlalpan

Santa Ursula Xitla

Canals at Xochimilco

DISTANCE ACROSS MAP
Approximate: 18.6 mi or 30 km

0　　1 mi
0　　1 km

© MOON.COM

Sights

Basílica de Santa María de Guadalupe

At every hour of every day, there are pilgrims arriving at the Basílica de Santa María de Guadalupe in northern Mexico City. It was here, on December 12, 1531, that Saint Juan Diego had a vision of a dark-skinned, Nahuatl-speaking Virgin Mary, whose image miraculously appeared imprinted on his cloak. Since the 16th century, numerous chapels have been built on the site—most recently, the modern basilica, designed by architect Pedro Ramírez Vásquez in 1976. Here, you can get a closer look at Juan Diego's cloak, which hangs behind the altar, where a moving walkway helps prevent human traffic jams. It is particularly crowded on and around December 12, the anniversary of the date when the Virgin appeared to Juan Diego.

You can reach the basilica via Metro to La Villa, or take the Metrobús along the Paseo de la Reforma to the Misterios stop.

MAP 9: Plaza de las Américas 1, Col. Villa de Guadalupe, tel. 55/5118-0500, www.virgendeguadalupe.org.mx; 6am-9pm daily; free; Metro: La Villa, Metrobús: Misterios

✪ Canals at Xochimilco

As early as the 13th century, people living in the community of Xochimilco began cultivating crops on *chinampas*, small patches

crowds at the Basílica de Guadalupe

263

The canals at Xochimilco are full of revelers on a sunny afternoon.

of farmland built atop the shallow lakes and marshes that covered the Valley of Mexico. Eventually, a massive system of canals, dams, and *chinampas* blanketed the valley—a sight that dazzled Hernán Cortés and his army when they arrived in 1519.

Though most of this unique agricultural system has since been destroyed, a network of canals and family-owned farms survives in the Xochimilco neighborhood, now a district in southern Mexico City. Visitors to Xochimilco can explore the main canals on colorful *trajineras* (flat-bottomed boats), which depart from the 10-plus public docks in the neighborhood. Saturdays and Sundays are the most spirited time to visit, when the waterways are crammed with families and revelers, steering past mariachi musicians and marimbas floating by on canoes. To see a quieter side of the neighborhood, request the four-hour "ecological tour" to visit the lesser-known farmland and residential areas along the waterways.

Food and alcohol are permitted on the boats, and many visitors pack elaborate meals to bring along. If you don't bring your own lunch, there are plenty of floating vendors offering handmade quesadillas, ears of corn, ice cream, beer, and other snacks.

To reach Xochimilco by public transportation, take Metro Line 2 to Tasqueña, then take the Tren Ligero (light-rail) to Xochimilco. Several *embarcaderos* (docks) are close to the Tren Ligero station, along Calle Violeta, off Avenida Cuauhtémoc. (Embarcadero Nativitas is about a 30-minute walk.)

Alternatively, you can take a taxi or car service to any *embarcadero* in Xochimilco. There are many different docks, and you can access the canals from any one of them; Nuevo Nativitas and Zacapa are considered the best launch points for a traditional tour of the canals. (Ignore the many "tour guides" along the route who tell you a dock is closed in attempt to lead you elsewhere; this is rarely the case.) To see the quieter side of Xochimilco at the Zona Natural Protegida (the nature preserve), go to Cuemanco.

MAP 9: Xochimilco; http://xochimilco. gob.mx; boats daily 8am-8pm; US$22 per hour for a boat that holds up to 12 people; Tren Ligero: Xochimilco

Cuicuilco

In the south of the city, the pre-Columbian settlement of Cuicuilco is the oldest archaeological site in the Valley of Mexico, built during the Pre-Classic period of Mesoamerican history, and the first major ceremonial center in the region. First established around 800 BCE, the settlement was once home to an estimated 40,000 inhabitants, though it was abandoned after the volcano Xitle erupted around 250 CE and lava covered the site. Today, the most notable structure is the settlement's expansive and unusual conical pyramid, which was built between 600 and 400 BCE and was once topped with a ceremonial altar.

The small site museum provides more information about Cuicuilco's inhabitants and displays some artifacts found at the site. Visitors can also walk along the footpaths in the small surrounding nature preserve. It's easiest to arrive via the Villa Olímpica Metrobús stop, but you can also take a bus marked Cuicuilco from the Universidad Metro station.

MAP 9: South of the intersection of Insurgentes and Periférico Sur, Col. Isidro Fabela, tel. 55/5606-9758; 9am-5pm daily; US$2.50; Metro: Universidad, Metrobús: Villa Olímpica

Tlalpan

Tlalpan is a lesser-known colonial-era settlement on the southern edge of the city, now part of the greater Mexico City urban area. Tlalpan's heart is the Plaza de la Constitución, a lovely public square with swaying trees and iron benches. On the east side of the plaza is the 17th-century Parroquia de San Agustín de las Cuevas, surrounded by well-kept gardens. Behind the municipal building, on the south side of the plaza, Mercado de la Paz is a large market good for a quick bite. Cross the street to have a drink at La Jaliscience, a charming old cantina. Next, follow Moneda east to the Capilla de las Capuchinas, designed by architect Luis Barragán.

Most visitors come by taxi, but the extension of the Metrobús

Parroquia San Agustín de las Cuevas in Tlalpan

XOCHIMILCO: UNIQUE URBAN FARMLAND

ORIGINS

Around the 13th century, people living in the pre-Columbian community of Xochimilco developed an ingenious farming system atop the broad lakes that covered almost all of the Valley of Mexico. Using tree limbs, reeds, and earth, the Xochimilcas created a network of "floating gardens," called *chinampas,* which benefited from the ample water and fertile soil beneath the lakes. The *chinampas* flourished, and the system spread to communities across the valley.

When the Mexica established the island city of Tenochtitlan in the 14th century, they also built an extensive network of *chinampas*. By 1519, the *chinampas* covered almost all of Lake Xochimilco (now central Mexico City), supporting a population of at least 200,000 (and by some estimates up to 350,000) people in Tenochtitlan.

DECLINE

After the Spanish conquest of Tenochtitlan, the lakes were slowly drained as the Spanish replaced the original system of dams and *chinampas* with plazas and avenues. Lake Xochimilco was channeled into canals that linked farmland to the center of capital.

With the creation of the huge drainage pipe in central Mexico City in the 1800s—designed to stop the flooding problems that plagued the capital—the lakes dried up almost entirely. Around the same time, the natural springs in Xochimilco were canalized belowground to channel water to central Mexico City.

As the canals and wetlands disappeared, *chinampas* were abandoned. Of the estimated 40,000 *chinampas* in Xochimilco at the beginning of the 18th century, only 15,000 were left when the 20th century began. Today, there are even fewer, as limited water supplies and severe groundwater contamination have made agriculture in the area unsustainable.

20TH-CENTURY TOURISM

In 1929, Xochimilco was officially incorporated into Mexico City. Around that time, the canals in Xochimilco became a popular tourist destination for Mexico City locals. Colorful flat-bottomed boats, called *trajineras,* began to carry picnickers along the canals, and Xochimilco earned the moniker "Venice of Mexico." Tourism remains one of the major industries in Xochimilco, and visiting the canals on a busy weekend is a highlight of a trip to the capital.

In 1987, along with Mexico City's Centro Histórico, Xochimilco and its canals were designated a World Heritage Site by the United Nations.

REFORESTATION AND THE FUTURE

Public and nonprofit organizations have recognized the vast historic value and ecological potential of Xochimilco's unusual urban farmland. In 1989, the federal government announced a plan to treat water supplies, revitalize agriculture, and promote conservation in the historic Xochimilco neighborhood. As part of that plan, the Parque Ecológico de Xochimilco, a 215-hectare botanical and wildlife reserve, was opened, and parts of the canals were declared protected areas.

Local organizations promote agricultural efforts in Xochimilco as a way to protect the ecosystem and provide sustainable produce to the city. **Yolcan** (http://yolcan. com) works with biologists and local farmers to restore the *chinampas* and to promote organic agricultural practices in Xochimilco. It operates a produce-sharing program that is popular with many high-end chefs as well as local residents. Another collective, **De La Chinampa** (www.delachinampa.mx), sells produce baskets, which come from a collective of farmers cultivating crops in Xochimilco in the traditional manner.

has made it relatively easy, albeit time-consuming, to get to Tlalpan via public transport. From anywhere along Insurgentes, take a southbound Metrobús marked El Caminero past the university to the Fuentes Brotantes stop; the center of Tlalpan is a few blocks east.

MAP 9: Between Insurgentes Sur and Calz. de Tlalpan, Calvario and Av. San Fernando; Metrobús: Fuentes Brotantes

Restaurants

PRICE KEY

$	Entrées less than $11
$ $	Entrées $10-20
$ $ $	Entrées more than $20

MEXICAN

Arroyo $$

Though a bit off the beaten path, this massive family-style restaurant in Tlalpan is hugely entertaining. Opened in the 1940s, the restaurant has an extensive menu of Mexican classics, from enchiladas to *mole*, though the best item is the flavorful *barbacoa* (lamb), slow-cooked in a brick pit on-site. There is a small playground for kids adjoining the two massive dining rooms, fluttering with paper flags, and, best of all, live music and dance shows take place throughout the afternoon on Saturday and Sunday.

MAP 9: Insurgentes Sur 4003, Tlalpan Centro, tel. 55/5573-4344; 8am-8pm daily; Metrobús: Fuentes Brotantes

✪ Nicos $$

This traditional family-style *fonda* in Azcapotzalco was doing its own thing for many years, drawing dedicated locals with its excellent traditional food and homey atmosphere. Word got out, and Nicos is now one of the most well-known restaurants in the city. Come here for a lovely, low-key Mexican breakfast, or make a reservation for *comida* (the midday meal) to try some of the restaurant's specialties, like the goat-cheese soup, organic *chamorro* (pork leg), or shrimp in chipotle. After, stroll around nearby Parque de la China and along Avenida Claveria.

MAP 9: Av. Cuitláhuac 3102, Clavería, tel. 55/5396-7090, www.nicosmexico. mx; 7:30am-7:30pm Mon.-Fri., 8am-7pm Sat.; Metro: Cuitláhuac

Rincón Tarasco $

Some of the best *carnitas* (slow-cooked braised pork) in the city can be had at this low-key restaurant in the Escandón neighborhood, just a short walk south of the Condesa. Order the soft *maciza* (shoulder), the excellent rib (served bone-in), or rich *panza* (belly)—or, if you're feeling more adventurous, try pig parts like *nana* (uterus) or *buche* (stomach), which aren't listed on the menu but available to those who ask. Tacos are generously served, in a perfect handmade corn tortilla.

MAP 9: Comercio 131, Escandón II Secc., tel. 55/5516-7802; 9:30am-4pm Wed.-Sun.; Metro: Patriotismo

Arts and Culture

CONCERT VENUES

Palacio de los Deportes

Major rock shows by major international groups touring in Mexico, like The White Stripes, Bon Jovi, Lenny Kravitz, and others, are often held at the "Sports Palace." The indoor arena was originally built for the 1968 Olympics and has a capacity of close to 20,000. Major concerts are also sometimes held at the outdoor Foro Sol in the adjacent Autódromo Hermanos Rodríguez car racetrack.
MAP 9: Av. Río Churubusco at Viaducto, tel. 55/5237-9999, www.ticketmaster.com.mx; hours and cost vary according to event; Metro: Velódromo

GALLERIES

Saenger Galería

For those with a deep interest in contemporary art, it's worth the extra effort to visit Saenger Galería, located in a tucked-away corner of the Tacubaya neighborhood. The space, which occupies two beautifully renovated floors and the rooftop terrace of an old office building, has gorgeous views, expansive galleries, and bright natural light—the ideal environment for the gallery's excellent shows of contemporary art. Call ahead to make an appointment or to let them know you're downstairs.
MAP 9: Manuel Dublan 33, Tacubaya, tel. 55/5516-6941, https://saengergaleria.com; 11am-7pm Tues.-Fri., 11am-4pm Sat.; Metro: Tacubaya

MUSEUMS

✪ Museo Anahuacalli

Diego Rivera was a prodigious collector of pre-Columbian art, and he constructed this pyramid-shaped museum to house his marvelous acquisitions. In addition to showcasing Rivera's varied art, artifacts, and sculpture from Mixteca, Mexica, Teotihuacán, and Veracruz cultures, among others, there are often contemporary exhibits in the space, as well as famously beautiful altars assembled in the courtyard for Día de Muertos. Admission to the Museo Frida Kahlo includes entry to the Anahuacalli, and the Fridabús provides transport between the two for about US$8.
MAP 9: Calle de Museo 150, Col. San Pablo Tepetlapa, tel. 55/5617-4310 or 55/5617-3797, www.museoanahuacalli.org.mx; 10am-6pm Wed.-Sun.; US$3, US$1 students under 16 and seniors, free for children under 6; Tren Ligero: Xotepingo

Museo Anahuacalli

✪ Museo del Juguete Antiguo México (MUJAM)

Avid toy collector Roberto Shimizu and his son, Roberto Jr., have united a huge collection of over 40,000 dolls, model cars and trucks, stuffed animals, wrestling figurines, and other curiosities in this unconventional and utterly delightful museum, which also functions as a cultural center and a laboratory for graffiti art and urban muralism. It's a short hop from the Roma into the more rough-around-the-edges Colonia Doctores to visit this unusual space—which, unlike many cultural institutions in the capital, is open on Mondays.

MAP 9: Dr. Olvera 15, Col. Doctores, tel. 55/5588-2100, www.museodeljuguete. mx; 9am-6pm Mon.-Fri., 9am-4pm Sat., 10am-6pm Sun.; US$4, Metro: Obrera

✪ Museo Dolores Olmedo

Dolores Olmedo Patiño was an art collector, philanthropist, and life-long friend of Diego Rivera. In the 1960s, Olmedo bought the marvelous 16th-century Hacienda La Noria in Xochimilco, which she later donated to the public to establish her namesake museum. Olmedo's collection of Riveras ranges from his earliest paintings to large-scale murals. With 25 pieces, the museum also holds the largest private collection of Frida Kahlo's work in the world, including *La Columna Rota* (*The Broken Column*).

MAP 9: Av. México 5843, Col. La Noria, tel. 55/5555-1221 or 55/5555-0891, www.museodoloresolmedo.org.mx; 10am-6pm Tues.-Sun.; US$3, free on Tues.; Tren Ligero: La Noria

Festivals and Events

FEBRUARY
Zsona MACO

Since 2004, Mexico City has been home to a prestigious five-day contemporary art fair known as Zsona MACO (México Arte Contemporáneo), with a roster of exhibitors coming from both the surrounding city and overseas, including some well-known names from the United States and Europe. It's a high-quality and well-attended event, held in early February at the Palacio de Cultura Banamex in the Lomas de Sotelo neighborhood. Complete visitor information is available on the website.

Greater Mexico City: Centro Citibanamex, Av. Del Conscripto 311, Lomas de Sotelo, Hipódromo de las Américas, tel. 55/5280-6073, www. zsonamaco.com; early Feb.

APRIL
Feria de la Flor Más Bella del Ejido

The southern neighborhood of Xochimilco celebrates the arts and floriculture with a weeklong festival every spring. Events include music and dance performances, a contest for the best-decorated *trajinera* (the traditional rafts used in Xochimilco's canals), and a local beauty pageant.

Greater Mexico City: Xochimilco's Centro Histórico, venues vary; early Apr.

Semana Santa

Easter week, or Holy Week, is one of the most important religious holidays of the year in Mexico. It is celebrated with enormous solemnity, tradition, and pageantry throughout the country, including in Mexico City—though many *capitaleños* also take advantage of the break in work or school to spend the week outside the city, at the beach, or in the country. During this time, traffic is subdued, museums are close to empty, and you'll rarely need a reservation at a restaurant—though you'll often find restaurant and bar owners close up shop for the week, too.

The celebrations (and vacations) officially begin on Domingo de Ramos, or Palm Sunday, when handwoven palm crosses and other adornments are sold outside the city's churches. The following Friday, Viernes Santo (Good Friday) is the single most important day of the season. (In fact, it's more likely that a restaurant or a shop will close on Good Friday than on Easter Sunday.) In Iztapalapa, a working-class neighborhood in southeast Mexico City, a very solemn and dramatic Passion Play is performed, with literally thousands of participants and even more spectators.

Greater Mexico City: Iztapalapa, Palm Sunday to Easter Sunday

DECEMBER

Día de Nuestra Señora de Guadalupe

The feast day of the Virgin of Guadalupe, December 12, is one of the most important holidays across Mexico. On the days and weeks leading up to it, groups of pilgrims can be seen walking toward the Basílica de Santa María de Guadalupe in northern Mexico City, often setting off noisy fireworks as they go. Special masses are held throughout Mexico, and in Mexico City, the area around the basilica is packed with thousands of pilgrims.

Greater Mexico City: Basílica de Santa María de Guadalupe, Plaza de las Américas 1, Col. Villa de Guadalupe, tel. 55/5118-0500, www. virgendeguadalupe.org.mx; Dec. 12

Recreation

PARKS

Parque Ecológico de Xochimilco (PEX)

This recreational park was founded as part of the Ecological Rescue Plan for Xochimilco, an ambitious program of water reclamation, agricultural reactivation, and historical and archaeological studies to restore and revitalize the historic Xochimilco community. The 189-hectare grounds consists of lakes, *ciénegas* (underground springs), canals, *chinampas,* and gardens. There are paddleboats for rent, lots of areas for picnicking, and a small train for children. The best way to get to the park, which is a couple of kilometers from downtown Xochimilco, is to take a taxi.

MAP 9: Periférico Sur at Canal de Cuemanco, Xochimilco, tel. 55/5673-7653, www.pex.org.mx; 9am-6pm Tues.-Sun. summer; 10am-4pm Tues.-Sun. winter; US$3 adults, US$1 over age 60, US$0.50 under age 12; Tren Ligero: Xochimilco station, then by taxi

canal in Xochimilco

SPECTATOR SPORTS

FORMULA ONE
Autódromo Hermanos Rodríguez

Ricardo and Pedro Rodríguez were stars of Formula One racing in Mexico during the 1960s, though both of their lives were cut short in racing accidents. The brothers lend their name to this racecourse in eastern Mexico City, where 15 Grand Prix championships were held, 1963-1970 and 1986-1992. In 2015, the Formula One Grand Prix returned to Mexico for the first time in more than two decades, as part of a five-year deal for continuing championships, with other car racing events throughout the year. If you're lucky, you may catch a race with Mexican sensation Checo Perez.

MAP 9: Av. Viaducto Río de la Piedad s/n, Iztacalco, tel. 55/5237-9920, www.autodromohr.com; tickets available through Ticketmaster; Metro: Ciudad Deportiva

SOCCER
✪ Estadio Azteca

Mexico's largest stadium, Estadio Azteca is a major concert and event venue in addition to being home to popular soccer clubs América and Los Rayos de Necaxa, both owned by media conglomerate Televisa. The national team also plays most of its important matches here. Opened in 1966, it was designed by architects Pedro Ramírez Vázquez and Rafael Mijares Alcérreca, with a capacity to seat almost 100,000. Despite the size, the field feels surprisingly

271

close, even in the cheaper seats, and the roar of the crowd can be exhilarating. Note that Estadio Azteca is slated to be closed in the summer 2023 for remodeling.

MAP 9: Calzada de Tlalpan 3465, Col. Santa Úrsula, www.clubamerica.com.mx; hours vary; most games US$5-15; Tren Ligero: Estadio Azteca

Estadio Azteca

Shops

PUBLIC MARKETS

Central de Abasto de la Ciudad de México

Covering three square kilometers in Iztapalapa, the Central de Abasto (Supply Center) is Mexico City's main wholesale market. It is the biggest food supplier in the country and the second-biggest point of commerce in Mexico, after the Mexican Stock Exchange. Around 30,000 tons of food are sold here daily, from banana leaves and sugarcane to dried chiles and grains. The nine-hectare seafood section called La Nueva Viga displays a huge variety of fish from across the country. By its own estimates, the market receives 350,000 visitors annually and employs more than 70,000 people. Though it's not the most atmospheric shopping area in the city, the sheer quantity of products will interest curious travelers.

MAP 9: Canal Churubusco and Canal Apatlaco, Iztapalapa, http://ficeda.com.mx; 24 hours daily; Metro: Aculco

Mercado de Jamaica

Mexico City's largest flower market, the Mercado de Jamaica is a colorful, sweetly scented destination. Here, you'll find stalls selling thousands of varieties of flowers, as well as potted plants, fruit, and (naturally) food stalls for snacking. Fresh flowers are used abundantly in Mexico for decoration, altars, religious services, birthdays, and other special occasions. Visit in the days leading up to Día de Muertos to see tremendous shipments of *cempasúchil* (marigold), the flower of the dead.

MAP 9: Guillermo Prieto 45, Venustiano Carranza, no phone; 8am-6pm Mon.-Fri., 7am-7pm Sat.-Sun., many flower vendors operate 24 hours; Metro: Jamaica

Flowers and piñatas are specialties of the Mercado de Jamaica.

MONDAYS IN MEXICO CITY

As in many major cities, most of Mexico City's important cultural institutions and galleries (and even some restaurants) are closed on Mondays. Here are a few options for a Monday in the capital.

DAY TRIP TO TEOTIHUACÁN

Teotihuacán, one of the largest and most spectacular archaeological sites in Mexico, is just an hour outside Mexico City by car or bus (page 299).
Hours: 9am-5pm daily

CUICUILCO

Cuicuilco is the oldest pre-Columbian settlement in the Valley of Mexico. Today, this unusual inner-city ruin, with its large circular pyramid, is an interesting half-day trip in the city's south (page 265).
Hours: 9am-5pm daily

PAPALOTE MUSEO DEL NIÑO

Though most museums in Chapultepec are closed on Monday, the city's delightful interactive children's museum is usually open and, if school is in session, often much quieter than it is on the weekends (page 162).
Hours: Hours vary, but generally 9am-6pm Monday-Friday

XOCHIMILCO ECOLOGICAL TOUR

If you'd like to see a quieter side of Xochimilco, you'll have the canals virtually to yourself on a Monday morning. It's an ideal time to take a longer tour of the waterways, reaching the residential areas and farmland that most tourists never see (page 263).
Hours: Boats leave from any dock after 8am daily

BASÍLICA DE SANTA MARÍA DE GUADALUPE

There are hourly masses and massive crowds every day of the week at this fascinating historic site and Catholic shrine in northern Mexico City (page 263).
Hours: 6am-9pm daily

TURIBUS

You can get the lay of the land, see some of the city's most iconic sights, and take some stunning pictures on the Turibus, which runs double-decker bus tours of the capital every day of the year (page 57).
Hours: 9am-9pm daily

WHERE TO STAY

Guesthouses have existed in Mexico City since the early colonial era, when Catholic missionaries and other Spanish settlers would arrive in the region

and take up temporary residence in the palaces along the Alameda Central. Perhaps this heritage has contributed to making Mexico City such a hospitable place for travelers. For a destination of its size and importance, Mexico City is filled with friendly, attractive, and surprisingly affordable hotels.

Mexico City offers a lot of variety when it comes to hotels, from creaky backpackers' favorites to full-service luxury high-rises that are destinations in themselves. Though once a rarity, there are an increasing number of charming bed-and-breakfasts in residential neighborhoods, as well as some new boutique hotels with popular nightclubs and design-centric hostels that cater to the Instagram-loving budget traveler.

the gorgeous glass ceiling at the Gran Hotel de la Ciudad de Mexico

The neighborhood you choose will be just as important in determining your experience as the place you stay. Many of the main attractions are located in the blocks surrounding the Zócalo, making the Centro Histórico and the area around the Alameda a good choice for first-time visitors. Given the capital's vast size, however, you're more likely to eat and go out in places near your hotel, which is one reason that travelers increasingly gravitate toward neighborhoods like the Roma and the Condesa. Polanco has always been a bastion of upscale, luxury hotels, and it remains so to this day.

All hotels charge a 15 percent IVA (value-added tax) and 2 percent city lodging tax. More expensive hotels may also tack on a 10 percent service

HIGHLIGHTS

✪ **MOST FASHIONABLE PALACE:** The gorgeous **Downtown Hotel** occupies the top floors of a colonial-era palace in the Centro. Ultra-modern decor complements the historic architecture (page 279).

✪ **BEST MIDRANGE HOTEL:** For a comfortable, reasonably priced space in the Centro Histórico, **Hotel Catedral** is the perfect choice (page 281).

✪ **MOST SOCIALLY MINDED SPACE:** More than an inexpensive crash pad, **Casa de los Amigos** is a social justice organization, a house for refugees, and a gathering place for socially minded people (page 282).

✪ **MOST COMFORTABLE LANDMARK:** A jewel of midcentury modernist architecture, **Camino Real Polanco México** is one of the city's most interesting buildings. Consider a drink in the lobby bar, even if you're staying elsewhere (page 285).

✪ **BEST BOUTIQUE HOTEL:** A quiet luxury hotel in Polanco, **Las Alcobas** delivers personable service and plenty of amenities, with zero pretension (page 287).

✪ **BEST GUESTHOUSE:** Tucked inside an early 20th-century Roma mansion, **Casa Nima** is a luxurious and intimate guesthouse in the city's trendiest neighborhood (page 287).

✪ **WARMEST ATMOSPHERE:** In the heart of the Condesa, the **Red Tree House** is famous for its friendliness, creating a spirit of camaraderie among its guests, who gather in the gardens during happy hour (page 290).

PRICE KEY

$	Less than $150 per night
$ $	$150-300 per night
$ $ $	More than $300 per night

Downtown Hotel

WHERE TO STAY IF...

In such a large, sprawling city, what neighborhood you stay in is often as important as the accommodations you choose. Depending on how you plan to spend your time, some neighborhoods will be better suited to your trip than others.

YOU ONLY HAVE A WEEKEND...

...stay in the **Centro Histórico,** where the city's most important sights and cultural institutions are walking distance from your doorstep.

YOU WANT TO GET AWAY FROM IT ALL (AND DON'T MIND PAYING FOR IT)...

...book a room along the park in **Polanco,** where fresh air, gorgeous views, and fancy service take the edge off city living.

YOU WANT TO PARTY...

...you won't be alone in the **Colonia Roma,** Mexico City's hippest neighborhood.

YOU'RE TRAVELING ON A BUDGET...

...look in the **Centro Histórico** or the **Tabacalera** neighborhood, where you'll find a higher concentration of hostels and budget hotels.

YOU AREN'T REALLY A CITY PERSON...

...**head south.** There aren't many hotels south of the Viaducto, but those who want a less urban environment will be happiest in the clean and sunny south.

A MORNING JOG IS PART OF YOUR ROUTINE...

...stay in **Polanco** and enjoy the proximity to the many trails snaking through the forested Bosque de Chapultepec.

YOU WANT THE LOCAL EXPERIENCE...

...book an Airbnb in the Nápoles, Narvarte, Del Valle, or one of the other beautiful residential neighborhoods south of the Viaducto.

YOU ARE A SERIOUS FOODIE...

...you're in luck. There are great eats in every neighborhood in the capital.

---

charge, as well as additional costs for amenities, like Internet service. When booking, ask whether tax and service are included in quoted rates.

CHOOSING WHERE TO STAY

Centro Histórico

The Centro Histórico is the heart of it all: dense, noisy, and pulsing with energy. Staying in the Centro is an excellent choice for **first-time visitors.** Plus, some of the very best breakfast options—from Sanborns de los Azulejos to El Cardenal to Café El Popular—are downtown. There are many excellent accommodations in the Centro in every price category. Though you'll find some new upscale options, the area remains a **backpacker's paradise,** with tons of cheap hotels and hostels scattered throughout the district.

Paseo de la Reforma

Mexico City's grand central avenue is known for its **luxury hotels,** anchored by the celebrated Four Seasons, just to the east of the Bosque de Chapultepec. Closer to the Centro, you'll find a few more inexpensive options along Reforma. The Tabacalera neighborhood, near the Monumento a la Revolución Mexicana, has long been hub of **inexpensive hotels.** There are many more options for this area beyond those listed in this book, though some are rather shabby, so check your room before you check in.

Zona Rosa and Cuauhtémoc

Central, safe, and tourist-friendly, the Zona Rosa has always been a popular place to stay, even if it isn't the city's most enchanting neighborhood. Here, you'll find hotels at a range of price points, a major public transportation hub at the Glorieta Insurgentes, and a late-night party scene that makes it safer to walk through the streets after dark (though nightclubs can also be a noisy nuisance for guests with street-view rooms). Just northwest of the Zona Rosa, the area around the U.S. Embassy is also a safe and central destination, with accommodation options near main thoroughfares Insurgentes and the Paseo de la Reforma, as well as plenty of dining and nightlife options.

Polanco

Affluent Polanco has some of the most luxurious hotels in the city, including the string of famous high-rises overlooking Bosque de Chapultepec from the street Campos Eliseos. Many of these establishments are favored by international businesspeople, though tourists also book in Polanco, particularly at the architecturally notable Camino Real or the party-centric W and Hábita.

Roma and Condesa

The hippest neighborhoods in Mexico City have become increasingly popular places to stay. There are no high-rise and few chain hotels in these residential districts,

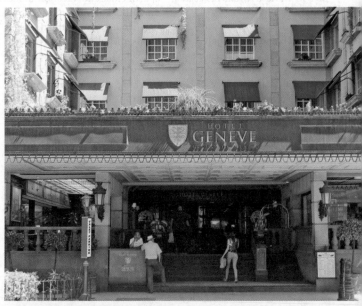

Hotel Geneve is an old-fashioned hotel in the heart of the Zona Rosa.

but in keeping with the neighborhoods' chic, independent reputation, there are boutique properties and bed-and-breakfasts. There is also a smattering of lower-priced hotels, some with A-plus locations, and an abundance of charming Airbnb and vacation rentals in the area, some basic and others downright luxurious.

Insurgentes Sur and Narvarte

Hotels in the sprawling residential neighborhoods along Insurgentes Sur generally cater to business travelers and families visiting the capital from other parts of Mexico. While they lack the panache of hotels in the city's central neighborhoods, there are some quiet, clean, and economical options in these safe and more peaceful parts of the city. They are also excellent places to look for a well-priced Airbnb or vacation rental.

Coyoacán and San Ángel

Mexico City's southern neighborhoods are greener and more peaceful than the city's urban heart. Yet with few businesses headquartered in the area and zoning restrictions making it more difficult to build, the south of the city has very few hotel options.

Travelers can find a few spots along Insurgentes Sur, though most will end up staying in the city center and visiting Coyoacán and San Ángel during day trips. If the hotels down south are booked, try Airbnb or another short-term apartment rental service.

Near the Airport

There are decent hotels near the airport (including a few nice options in the airport itself), but unless you have a very brief layover, you'll be much better off staying near the city center, even if it means taking a taxi there and back.

Alternative Lodging Options

Mexico City has a robust presence on Airbnb, with a range of well-priced options throughout the city. You can also find bedrooms, rental apartments, and vacation homes on VRBO and online hotel booking sites. In many central neighborhoods, including the Roma, hotels can sometimes beat the prices of an apartment rental, so it's worth checking all your options before booking. In the neighborhoods south of the Viaducto—Narvarte, Del Valle, Coyoacán, and San Ángel among them—Airbnb is a good option.

Círculo Mexicano $$

This elegantly minimalist hotel in the heart of the centro histórico provides a peaceful respite from its bustling environs. Located in a restored 19th-century residential building that was once the home of photographer Manuel Álvarez Bravo, guest rooms are arranged around a light-filled central patio and have high ceilings, white walls, and king-size beds. Breakfast is served in a glass-walled room on the upstairs terrace, with intimate views of the cathedral. MAP 1: República de Guatemala 20, tel. 55/9689-0543, www.circulomexicano.com; Metro: Zócalo

❂ Downtown Hotel $$

This small hotel in a stunning 17th-century palace makes wonderful use of its historic architecture through a simple yet elegant design that emphasizes the high ceilings and old stone walls of the original building. While there's no lobby, the hotel shares the palace with several restaurants and a lovely Mexican-design-centric shopping center, and the awesome rooftop bar and swimming pool are enviably cool places to relax. MAP 1: Isabel la Católica 30, tel. 55/5130- 6830, www.downtownmexico.com; Metro: Zócalo or Isabel la Católica

Gran Hotel de la Ciudad de México $$

Replete with tiered balconies and old steel-cage elevators, the art nouveau lobby at the Gran Hotel de la Ciudad is crowned by a vaulted Tiffany glass ceiling, made in Paris in 1908. Guest rooms, arranged around the central atrium, have an ultra-romantic vibe, with floral bedspreads and TVs hidden from view behind white-and-gold cabinets. Rooms overlooking the Zócalo are the most coveted; keep in mind that they can be noisy, too. MAP 1: 16 de Septiembre 82, tel. 55/1083-7700, www.granhoteldelaciudaddemexico.com.mx; Metro: Zócalo

Zócalo Central $$

On the northeast corner of the Zócalo, this contemporary hotel (formerly the Holiday Inn) has a perfect central location, with a bank of guest rooms looking directly over the Zócalo. Accommodations are clean and comfortable, with a conservative dark color scheme and marble baths, and the staff are accommodating and friendly. The same hotelier operates another similar property, Histórico Central (Bolívar 28, tel. 55/5521-2121), just a few blocks away, in a 300-plus-year-old building on Bolívar. MAP 1: Cinco de Mayo 61, tel. 55/5130-5138, www.centralhoteles.com; Metro: Zócalo

Downtown Beds $

At this hostel, hotelier Grupo Hábita mixes its signature design sense with low-key backpacker charm. Both dorms and private rooms are simple but sufficiently stylish, with whitewashed walls and brick ceilings. Amenities include an on-site movie-screening room, an inexpensive patio bar, and bike rental.

HOTEL BARS

Just because you aren't staying in a fancy hotel doesn't mean you can't enjoy some of its amenities. As in many big cosmopolitan cities, some of the capital's nicest bars are located in its upscale hotels. Here are a few of the best.

THE ROOFTOP BAR AT THE DOWNTOWN HOTEL
While taking a break from a tour around the Centro (or waiting for a table at Azul Histórico downstairs), head up to the shaded rooftop bar in the **Downtown Hotel**, where you can drink a cold margarita while looking out over the Porfiriato-era facade of the Casino Español across the street.

TERRACE BAR AT CÍRCULO MEXICANO
The rooftop terrace at **Círculo Mexicano** is relaxed and beautiful, with an intimate view of the bell towers and cupolas of the city cathedral. Rarely crowded, it's a great place for respite while touring the *centro*.

TERRAZA CATEDRAL AT MUNDO JOVEN
The casual backpacker bar on the roof of the **Mundo Joven** caters to the budget travelers, but the views (and low-key vibe) will appeal to any visitor.

TERRAZA RESTAURANT AND BAR AT THE GRAN HOTEL DE LA CIUDAD DE MÉXICO
At the bar and restaurant in the **Gran Hotel de la Ciudad de México**, the attraction is the view of the Zócalo (and the chance to walk through the Gran Hotel's gorgeous lobby). It offers a full menu and a buffet brunch on the weekends, but you can come for drinks in the afternoon.

KING COLE BAR AT THE ST. REGIS
Even if you aren't staying at the super-luxe **St. Regis,** you can experience the pleasures of being a guest at the King Cole Bar (daily 10am-2am), which serves the hotel's world-famous Bloody Marys. The decor is formal and elegant, and a terrace overlooks the Paseo de la Reforma.

LA TERRAZA AT CONDESA DF
It's no wonder the rooftop bar and Japanese fusion restaurant at the boutique **Condesa DF** is frequented by Condesa locals: The views of leafy treetops in Parque España make it the perfect place to unwind with a drink in the evening.

FIFTY MILS AT THE FOUR SEASONS
The posh cocktail bar **Fifty Mils** in the Four Seasons Hotel has become a city favorite for its creative cocktails and surprisingly fun crowd.

Plus, guests can use the posh rooftop pool at the Downtown Hotel upstairs (with a minimum purchase at the bar).
MAP 1: Isabel la Católica 30, tel. 55/5130-6855, www.downtownbeds.com; Metro: Zócalo or Isabel la Católica

Hostal Centro Histórico Regina $
Located in an 18th-century mansion, this hostel offers the perfect trio of great location, low nightly price, and a cool, youthful atmosphere. Dorm rooms, though a bit crowded, are clean and pretty, with parquet floors, high ceilings, and French windows overlooking the street below. Right on the Regina pedestrian corridor, it's a quick stumble from several neighborhood bars to the dorm, though you may be tempted to spend the evening "in" at the hostel's rooftop bar.

MAP 1: 5 de Febrero 58 at Regina, tel. and WhatsApp 55/4575-1835; www.hostalreginacentrohistorico.com; Metro: Isabel la Católica

Hostel Mundo Joven Catedral $

Just a block from the Zócalo, this popular hostel has dozens of dorm-style rooms with wood floors, in-room lockers, and clean bunk beds. A handful of private rooms have views of the Catedral Metropolitana (though note that street-facing rooms also get more ambient noise than interiors). On the top floor is a picturesque terrace bar, where guests convene to swap travel tips and snap photos of the back of the cathedral. It is best to reserve ahead for dorm beds and necessary for private rooms, which book well in advance.

MAP 1: República de Guatemala 4, tel. 55/5518-1726, https://mundojovenhostels.com; Metro: Zócalo

✪ Hotel Catedral $

Located right between the Zócalo and the Plaza Santo Domingo, Hotel Catedral is a great value, combining a wonderfully central location with comfortable modern guest rooms and genuinely affable service. The accommodating staff is always willing to call a taxi or give directions. It's popular with Mexican families, business travelers, and tourists, and there's always a pleasant buzz in the lobby.

MAP 1: Donceles 95, tel. 55/5518-5232, www.hotelcatedral.com; Metro: Zócalo

Hotel Gillow $

Run by the same owners as the Hotel Catedral, the Gillow is, like its sibling, a friendly and well-priced hotel in the heart of the Centro. Its crowning feature is a wholly perfect location, just a few blocks from the Zócalo and right between the pedestrian street Madero and bustling Cinco de Mayo. Exterior rooms with balconies, though slightly noisier, have beautiful views of the Centro's colonial palaces.

MAP 1: Isabel la Católica 17, tel. 55/5510-2636, www.hotelgillow.com; Metro: Zócalo

Hotel Isabel $

This rambling five-story hotel has long been a favorite with budget travelers, offering ramshackle charm at a low nightly rate. The 74 guest rooms vary widely in character (ask to see another if you don't like the accommodations you were assigned), though all have a scruffy old-fashioned feeling, with creaky wood furniture and high ceilings. You can shave a bit off the nightly price if you are willing to stay in a room with shared bath.

MAP 1: Isabel la Católica 63, tel. 55/5518-1213, www.hotel-isabel.com.mx; Metro: Isabel la Católica

Hotel Principal $

The friendly Hotel Principal is a budget-traveler favorite, offering small but clean rooms with a touch of charming colonial influence. Though the lobby is old-fashioned and dim, guest rooms are organized around four stories of bright, plant-filled courtyards. Double doors open onto each bedroom—though note that they have no windows and can get a bit stuffy during the warmest months.

MAP 1: Bolívar 29, tel. 55/5521-1333, www.hotelprincipal.com; Metro: Allende

Hotel Umbral $$

A 1920s-era office building has been converted into a contemporary four-story hotel, part of the Hilton's Curio Collection. The shadowy central atrium, which is serviced by the building's original elevator, has a moody urban feeling, but guest rooms are bright and airy, with high ceilings and spacious baths. Service is genuinely amiable and the location, within easy walking distance of all sights in the *centro histórico*, is ideal.

MAP 1: Venustiano Carranza 69, tel. 55/1203-2600, www.hotelumbral.com; Metro: Zócalo

Alameda Central — Map 2

Hilton Mexico City Reforma $$$

A high-rise hotel overlooking the Alameda Central, the Hilton is popular with business travelers, though tourists can also get good deals by booking rooms in advance. Accommodations are clean and modern, with a muted, rather corporate style. Request a room on a higher floor for wonderful views of the city (and less traffic noise from the street below).

MAP 2: Av. Juárez 70, tel. 55/5130-5300, www.hilton.com; Metro: Juárez or Hidalgo, Metrobús: Hidalgo

Paseo de la Reforma — Map 3

✪ Casa de los Amigos $

A guesthouse and social justice organization, Casa de los Amigos offers basic dorm accommodations and private rooms with shared bath. As part of its mission, Casa de los Amigos houses and acclimates political refugees, so you may be sleeping next to someone who's come to Mexico from very far away (in addition to meeting the long-term volunteers, who live on-site). A shared kitchen serves as an informal gathering spot, while the peaceful upstairs library was once the studio of muralist José Clemente Orozco, the home's former owner.

MAP 3: Ignacio Mariscal 132, tel. 55/70958094, www.casadelosamigos. org; Metro: Revolución, Metrobús: El Caballito

Casa González $

Close to the U.S. and British Embassies in the central Cuauhtémoc neighborhood, this friendly family-run guesthouse has 22 cheerful private bedrooms located in several buildings that share a plant-filled central courtyard.

Bedrooms are reasonably priced, cute, and clean, and some have private patios. Just a couple blocks from the Paseo de la Reforma, the hotel is perfectly central and an all-around good value.

MAP 3: Río Sena 69, tel. 55/5514-3302 www.hotelcasagonzalez.com; Metro: Insurgentes, Metrobús: Hamburgo

Casa Pani $$

Celebrated 20th-century architect Mario Pani lived in a quiet corner of the Cuauhtémoc neighborhood, and today his personal home has been converted into a stylish guesthouse that preserves and celebrates Pani's aesthetic principles, even in the parts of the hotel that have been remodeled and expanded. There are only six rooms, each nicely decorated in a style that is minimalist yet cozy. Despite the stylish atmosphere, the vibe is zero percent pretentious.

MAP 3: Río Po 14, tel. 56/2717-9260, www.casapani.com; Metro: Insurgentes, Metrobús: El Ángel

the downstairs common areas at Casa Pani

El Patio 77 $$

This small guesthouse is in a renovated mansion in a corner of the San Rafael neighborhood that is still largely off the beaten track for most tourists. Guest rooms are individually decorated yet consistently beautiful; color palettes are muted, and furnishings are a mix of antique and handcrafted. The suites are spacious, with light-filled bathrooms and street-facing balconies; there are also several reasonably priced rooms with shared bath. The eco-friendly hotel collects rainwater, recycles gray water, and heats showers with solar power.

MAP 3: Icazbalceta 77, tel. 55/5592-8452, www.elpatio77.com; Metro: San Cosme

Four Seasons Hotel $$$

The stately Four Seasons, ideally located near the main entrance to Chapultepec, has long been known as the premier high-end choice in Mexico City, consistently receiving high ratings in top travel magazines for its attentive service and luxury amenities. The eight-story hotel's guest rooms are elegant yet cozy, filled with armchairs, lamps, and writing desks; some have French doors opening onto the pretty central garden.

MAP 3: Paseo de la Reforma 500, tel. 55/5230-1818 or toll-free Mexico tel. 800/906-7500, www.fourseasons.com/mexico; Metro: Sevilla, Metrobús: Chapultepec

Hotel Carlota $$

In the spring of 2015, Hotel Carlota opened in what was formerly a family-friendly budget hotel, reinventing the space as a floor-to-ceiling showcase of contemporary Mexican design, with interiors and architecture by well-known Mexico City firms. There is original art in every room, and a hot in-house restaurant, Carlota, overlooks the sun-kissed central patio and glass-walled pool. Just a block from the Paseo de la Reforma, it's a central, chic place to stay.

MAP 3: Río Amazonas 73, tel. 55/5511-6300, https://hotelcarlota.mx; Metro: Insurgentes, Metrobús: Reforma

Hotel Geneve $$

Hotel Geneve seems trapped in time, from its pink facade to its turn-of-the-20th-century lobby, filled with overstuffed furniture, dark-wood bookshelves, and globe lamps. Guest rooms are not as opulent as the hotel's beautiful common areas suggest, lacking the polish and modernity of higher-end accommodations; however, they maintain a pleasantly old-fashioned feeling. Given the location and history, the rack rate isn't particularly high, but prices can drop much lower if you book ahead.

MAP 3: Londres 130, tel. 55/5080-0062 or 55/5080-0800, www.hotelgeneve. com.mx; Metro: Insurgentes, Metrobús: La Palma

Hotel Imperial Reforma $$

One of the most recognizable buildings on the Paseo de la Reforma, this beautiful wedge-shaped hotel, with a gold dome on the roof, has balconied bedroom windows overlooking the avenue. The interior of the hotel isn't quite as beautiful as the old-world exterior, but the 60 carpeted guest rooms are spacious and comfortable, if a tiny bit worn. The location on one of the city's iconic thoroughfares, close to the Centro, is convenient and charming.

MAP 3: Paseo de la Reforma 64, tel. 55/5705-4911 or 800/714-2909, www.hotelimperial.mx; Metro: Hidalgo, Metrobús: Glorieta Colón

Hotel Manalba $

The Tabacalera neighborhood, near the Monumento a la Revolución Mexicana, is a long-standing haven for good inexpensive accommodations, like Hotel Manalba. This small hotel has Mayan-themed decor in the lobby and small, modern rooms equipped with TVs, wireless Internet, and loud bedspreads. Some rooms can be a bit dark, but they're very quiet; for the price and comfort, it's a good-value spot.

MAP 3: Antonio Caso 23, tel. 55/5566-6066, www.hotelmanalba. com.mx; Metro: Revolución, Metrobús: Glorieta Colón

Hotel María Cristina $

In a lovely four-story colonial-style building just off the Paseo de la Reforma, the long-running María Cristina delivers a bit of old-world ambience without breaking the bank. The attractive lobby is filled with dark-wood furniture and iron chandeliers, and guest rooms surround the lovely interior gardens. The decor is rather dated, and some rooms feel more worn than others, but overall it's quaint and comfortable, best suited to those looking for a noncorporate, low-key hotel experience.

MAP 3: Río Lerma 31, tel. 55/5566-9688, www.hotelmariacristina. com.mx; Metro: Insurgentes, Metrobús; Hamburgo

St. Regis $$$

Every detail has been carefully considered at this five-star luxury hotel on the Paseo de la Reforma, a branch of the famed New York City establishment. This towering skyscraper, open since 2009, boasts breathtaking views of the city, which get better the higher you go. Rooms are subdued and elegant, with luxury bed linens and spacious baths. As in New York, you can find the King Cole Bar in the lobby, complete with its famous line of Bloody Marys.

MAP 3: Paseo de la Reforma 439, tel. 55/5228-1818, www.stregismexicocity. com; Metro: Sevilla, Metrobús: La Diana

the luxurious St. Regis hotel

Chapultepec and Polanco Map 4

✪ Camino Real Polanco México $$$

One of the most original architectural concepts in Mexico City,

the Camino Real Polanco México

famed architect Ricardo Legorreta's Camino Real is a marvel of mid-20th-century design, from its pink sculptural wall at the entryway to its royal-blue lobby lounge. On top of that, the Camino Real is a luxury establishment, known for its fine service and amenities. It has three swimming pools, rooftop tennis courts, and numerous in-house eateries, including a branch of the world-famous restaurant Morimoto.

MAP 4: Av. Mariano Escobedo 700, Col. Anzures, tel. 55/5263-8888 or U.S./Canada tel. 800/722-6466, www.caminoreal.com/mexico; Metro: Chapultepec, Metrobús: Gandhi

Hotel Hábita $$$

Open since 2000, this boutique hotel is still one of the chicest places to stay in the city. Behind its frosted-glass

The grand JW Marriott, the W, and the Presidente Intercontinental overlook Chapultepec from Polanco.

facade, designed by Enrique Norten and Ten Arquitectos, the 36 guest rooms are elegantly minimalist, with classic modern furniture in dark neutral tones, long glass desks, and, in most, small terraces. It features a cool lobby restaurant and a glassed-in exercise room upstairs; the signature establishment, however, is the popular rooftop nightclub and bar.

MAP 4: Av. Presidente Mazaryk 201, tel. 55/5282-3100, www.hotelhabita.com; Metro: Polanco, Metrobús: Auditorio

InterContinental Presidente Mexico City $$$

The InterContinental Presidente is the oldest of the grand park hotels, originally built in 1977. Its multistory pyramid lobby, topped with an immense skylight, is impressive, though the 660 rooms are more modern and subdued. The hotel is known for its dining, with six restaurants and a bar, including Au Pied de Cochon, a French restaurant that is open 24 hours, and the Balmoral tea room, with English-style afternoon tea and snacks.

MAP 4: Campos Eliseos 218, tel. 55/5327-7700 or U.S./ Canada tel. 800/327-0200, www. presidenteicmexico.com; Metro: Auditorio, Metrobús: Auditorio

JW Marriott $$$

Like the InterContinental Presidente, the JW Marriott overlooks the Bosque de Chapultepec from Campos Eliseos in Polanco, and it's the favored choice of many travelers for its genial service. The hotel's comfortable rooms were renovated in 2013, and they have a homey feeling, with wood furnishings, lamps, and carpeting, though no major emphasis on design. Most impressive are the views, which get better the higher you go.

MAP 4: Andrés Bello 29, tel. 55/5999-0000 or U.S./Canada tel. 888/813-2776, www.marriott.com; Metro: Auditorio, Metrobús: Auditorio

⊙ Las Alcobas $$$

In the heart of Polanco, this boutique hotel has enough style to warrant its chic zip code, but its intimate size distinguishes it from nearby establishments. The 35 elegant guest rooms are warm and modern, with rosewood furniture and huge plate-glass windows allowing in ample natural light (but, fortunately, not much sound from the street below; the glass is double-paned). Details are taken seriously: Beds are dressed in Italian linens, flat-screens are equipped with home-theater sound systems, and marble baths have rain showers stocked with handmade soaps.

MAP 4: Presidente Masaryk 390A, tel. 55/3300-3900, www.lasalcobas.com; Metro: Polanco, Metrobús: Auditorio

W Mexico City $$$

The W Mexico City underwent a massive renovation in 2015, reopening with an artsy new design that includes an ultra-modern cocktail bar in the lobby. The bold new look extends to the guest rooms, which have splashy colors and white polished floors. Fortunately, some things haven't changed: Most bedrooms have remarkable views of the surrounding city or Chapultepec park, and the in-house bar retains the buzzy atmosphere that made the W hotel chain famous worldwide.

MAP 4: Campos Eliseos 252, tel. 55/9138-1800, www.wmexicocity.com; Metro: Auditorio, Metrobús: Auditorio

Wyndham Garden Polanco $$

This hotel typically attracts business travelers, but the price and quality make it a good choice for any visitor to the city. Rooms are modern and functional, though a bit nondescript; on the higher floors, however, you'll have lovely views of the park. For those who like the Polanco neighborhood, it's a good alternative to the pricier hotels that dominate the skyline along the Bosque de Chapultepec.

MAP 4: Tolstoi 22, tel. 55/5262-0844, www.wyndhampolanco.com; Metro: Chapultepec, Metrobús: Chapultepec

Roma and Condesa   Map 5

⊙ Casa Nima $$$

This perfect four-room guesthouse is housed in a gorgeous early 20th-century mansion, right in the heart of the Roma. Each of the rooms is warmly decorated, with king-size beds, blackout curtains, Netflix-equipped TVs, and French doors opening onto the home's central atrium or a street-view balcony. Guests can relax with a drink in the cozy living room or on the upstairs roof deck, which is filled with plants and flowers (there are honor bars in both). The warm, solicitous service and generous morning breakfast top off the experience.

the facade of charming four-room guesthouse Casa Nima

Colima 236, tel. 55/7591-7175, http://nimalocalhousehotel.com; Metro: Insurgentes, Metrobús: Álvaro Obregón

Condesa Haus $$

On a quiet residential street in the southeastern Condesa, a beautiful old mansion has been turned into a bed-and-breakfast that offers plenty of modern comforts while ably preserving the building's historic ambience, from original ceramic-tile floors to the soaring ceilings in the lobby. Each room is individually decorated around a theme, like the lovely Porfirio room, which takes its cues from late 19th-century Mexico, with a claw-foot tub, Juliet balconies, and a decorative iron headboard on the queen-size bed. MAP 5: Cuernavaca 142, tel. 81/1769-2769, www.condesahaus. com; Metro: Chilpancingo, Metrobús: Campeche

Condesa DF $$$

Located in a fine triangular mansion overlooking the tree-filled Parque España, this design-centric boutique hotel is beloved by bloggers, neighborhood hipsters, and chic travelers who place equal value on comfort and aesthetics. Here, 24 modern guest rooms and 16 suites surround a central atrium with an in-house restaurant and lobby, stylishly decorated with globe lamps, an eclectic mix of tables and chairs, and an aqua-and-white color scheme. MAP 5: Av. Veracruz 102, tel. 55/5241-2600, www.condesadf.com; Metro: Sevilla, Metrobús: Sonora

Distrito Condesa $

A pleasant and affordable little inn in a converted family home, Distrito Condesa has an enviable location, just blocks from Parque México and a stone's throw from the neighborhood's many nightlife and dining options. With its friendly staff and accessible price, it's a good choice for independent travelers who are looking for a convenient place to stay, with small, basic, but attractive rooms with wood floors and modern baths.

MAP 5: Cholula 62, tel. 81/1769-2769, www.distritocondesa.com; Metro: Chilpancingo, Metrobús: Campeche

Hippodrome Hotel $$$

This discreet 16-room hotel is in the Edificio Tehuacan, a lovingly restored 1930s art deco building a half block from Parque España in the Condesa. The rooms are quite small by Mexico City standards, but the interiors were carefully chosen to complement the building's inherent charms, with art deco finishes in the bedrooms and period-style furnishings. Flat-screen TVs, 600-thread-count sheets, goose-down pillows, and other modern luxuries are nonetheless abundant. Top-floor suites have gorgeous, plant-filled terraces overlooking architectural landmark Edificio Balmori.

Hippodrome Hotel

MAP 5: Av. México 188, tel. 55/6798-3974, https://hippodrome.mx; Metro: Sevilla, Metrobús: Sonora

Hotel Milan $

The Milan has long been a favorite with visitors for its surprisingly nice rooms and undeniably awesome location, right on the Roma's main corridor, Álvaro Obregón. Rooms have TVs and Wi-Fi. There is room service from the downstairs restaurant, which has long maintained a good reputation in the neighborhood (you'll see plenty of locals lunching there midweek). Street-facing rooms are more atmospheric, but you'll have to deal with some ambient noise.

MAP 5: Álvaro Obregón 94, tel. 55/5584-0222, www.hotelmilan.com.mx; Metro: Insurgentes, Metrobús: Álvaro Obregón

Hotel Milan

Hotel Stanza $

At the easternmost end of Álvaro Obregón, this nice midrange hotel isn't known for its contemporary design, but its well-priced and quiet guest rooms are comfortable and generally quiet, and the downstairs restaurant and bar is surprisingly pleasant, overlooking Jardín

Pushkin. Though it's a step up in price from the budget hotels in the city, Stanza delivers an overall nicer environment and better service than many of its neighbors.

MAP 5: Álvaro Obregón 13, tel. 55/5208-0052, http://stanzahotel.com; Metro: Niños Héroes or Insurgentes, Metrobús: Parque Pushkin

Ignacia Guest House $$$

There are a multitude of restaurants and bars along Jalapa and Chiapas, but once you step inside Ignacia Guest House, the noise and bustle are behind you. Located in a renovated 20th-century mansion, the hotel's four lovely color-themed rooms overlook an interior garden. Guests can use the main living room for reading or relaxing. The amiable staff will help you make plans around the city or set up Mexican cooking classes with the chefs next door, who designed the hotel's signature breakfasts.

MAP 5: Jalapa 208, tel. 55/5584-2681, http://ignacia.mx; Metro: Hospital General, Metrobús: Sonora

La Valise $$$

There are only three rooms at this teensy Roma hotel, but each feels like its own ultra-spacious, super-chic apartment. Taking advantage of the mansion's original details, the rooms have high ceilings and French doors, elements complemented by the modern furnishings curated by well-known Mexico City-based design firm Chic by Accident. Each has an ample living room with comfortable chairs and couches, baths with claw-foot soaking tubs, plus a small kitchen.

MAP 5: Tonalá 53, tel. 55/5286-9560 or U.S. tel. 305/999-1540, www.lavalise. com; Metro: Insurgentes, Metrobús: Álvaro Obregón

❂ Red Tree House $$

A lovely bed-and-breakfast in the heart of the Condesa, Red Tree House occupies a converted family home, with comfy guest rooms opening onto the central garden. The genuinely friendly staff and relaxed atmosphere—which is plenty stylish but still cozy—seem to instill a sense of community among guests, who often gather in the common areas or enjoy a glass of wine together during complimentary afternoon happy hours. It's one of the most popular spots in the capital, so make reservations well ahead.

MAP 5: Culiacan 6, tel. 55/5584-3829, http://theredtreehouse.com; Metro: Chilpancingo, Metrobús: Chilpancingo

Villa Condesa $$

This discreet bed-and-breakfast occupies a lovely old mansion on a tree-filled residential street, just a block away from the Parque España. Rooms are warmly decorated, some with romantic private balconies and French doors. There's no nightclub or buzzy rooftop bar (though there is a restaurant for hotel guests, where some in-the-know locals drop in), but that's exactly the charm of this little spot: It's a tucked-away, quiet place to stay, with no sign on the door or the flashy lobby.

MAP 5: Colima 428, tel. 55/52114892, www.villacondesa.com.mx; Metro: Sevilla, Metrobús: Álvaro Obregón

City Express Insurgentes Sur $

City Express is a small Mexican-owned chain of pod-style hotels, which are designed for convenience and low cost. Rooms are very small, with everything, from the showers to the TVs, in reduced sizes. It caters principally to business travelers, though tourists can also get good deals here. This branch is close to the Teatro de los Insurgentes, putting UNAM and San Ángel within striking distance.

MAP 6: Av. Insurgentes Sur 1581, tel. 55/5482-0280, www.cityexpress.com; Metro: Barranca del Muerto, Metrobús: Teatro Insurgentes

El Diplomatico $

There are few nice places to stay in Mexico City's quieter southern neighborhoods. This glass-fronted hotel, on the southern stretch of Avenida Insurgentes, is an exception. Rooms are impeccably clean and spacious, all equipped with Wi-Fi, coffeemakers, air-conditioning, and cable TV. Though a bit off the beaten path for most visitors, it's close to San Ángel and Coyoacán, and a quick ride on Insurgentes Metrobús if you want to head downtown.

MAP 6: Av. Insurgentes Sur 1105, Col. Noche Buena, tel. 55/5563-6066, www. eldiplomatico.com.mx; Metro: San Antonio or Insurgentes Sur, Metrobús: Parque Hundido

Hotel Vermont $

Just behind the World Trade Center Mexico, the unassuming Hotel Vermont mostly caters to Mexican travelers visiting the city on business or attending a convention at the WTC, but its proximity to Insurgentes Sur makes it a convenient place to stay for tourists as well. The carpeted guest rooms are a bit dated, but they are quiet and neat.

MAP 6: Vermont 29, Nápoles, tel. 55/5543-3700, https://hotelvermont. com.mx; Metrobús: La Piedad

Coyoacán   Map 7

La Casita del Patio Verde $$

There are only three rooms in this itty-bitty bed-and-breakfast, located on a charming cobblestone street. The largest room is in its own detached cottage, with two double beds and a fireplace. In the main house, there are two considerably smaller but lovely bedrooms on the second floor. For those who want to experience life in this quiet neighborhood, La Casita is one of the few options—and fortunately, it's a lovely choice.

MAP 7: Callejón de la Escondida 41, tel. 55/4170-3523, http://la-casita-del-patio-verde.mexico-hotels-mx.com; Metro: Viveros

Casa Jacinta $$

This neat, friendly, and well-located bed-and-breakfast occupies a pretty little house in residential Coyoacán. Cozy wood-floored guest rooms have French doors or windows that open onto the garden and patio and private baths with colorful tiles. A freshly prepared breakfast is included in the nightly price and served on the pretty back patio—a lovely way to begin a day in the south of the city.

MAP 7: 2da. Cerrada de Belisario Domínguez 22, tel. 55/7098-9384, www. casajacintamexico.com; Metro: Viveros

Mansion de Papilio $$

Delightfully, there is a flock peacocks wandering around the gardens of this Coyoacán guesthouse, located in a beautiful belle époque mansion just a few blocks from Jardín Hidalgo. Like the birds, the common areas have a quirky but cool charm, while spacious guest rooms lean more modern. While the environs feel a bit formal, this is a more informal establishment without a traditional lobby or front desk.

MAP 7: 5 de Febrero 28, La Concepcion, tel. 55/1324-6308, www. mansiondepapilio.com; Metro: Viveros

Mansion de Papilio

Airport Hilton $$$

This Hilton is built on top of the international terminal—take the elevator up to the fourth floor, and you will be in the lobby. The hotel's rooms all have 24-hour housekeeping, minibars, and free wireless Internet. It's pricey for what you get, but that's to be expected for the convenience of staying in the airport terminal.

MAP 9: Benito Juárez International Airport Terminal 1, Capitan Carlos León and Blvd. Puerto Aérea, tel. 55/5133-0500, www.hilton.com; Metro: Terminal Aéreo

Camino Real Aeropuerto $$$

Connected to the domestic terminal via a pedestrian bridge, the Camino Real is a large, comfortable hotel. Amenities include a health club and pool, several good restaurants, and friendly service. Rooms are nothing special for the price, but they're more spacious than the Hilton. Though it's the same hotel chain as the famous Camino Real in Polanco, this branch is more about comfort and convenience than high-end luxury.

MAP 9: Puerto México 80, tel. 55/3003-0033, www.caminoreal.com; Metro: Terminal Aéreo

NH Hotel Aeropuerto $$

The only hotel in the newly constructed Terminal 2 at Benito Juárez International Airport, the NH has almost 300 rooms, with a clean, modern design and enough amenities to justify its decent nightly price. Its chief attraction, however, is its proximity to the airport. For those flying Aeroméxico, Delta, or other airlines that leave from the newer wing of the airport, it couldn't be more convenient: There is an entrance directly inside the terminal.

MAP 9: Benito Juárez International Airport Terminal 2, Eje 1 Nte. and Blvd. Puerto Aérea, tel. 55/5786-5750, www.nh-hotels.com; Metro: Terminal Aéreo

DAY TRIPS

Mexico City is propitiously located in one of the most densely populated and diverse regions in the country. From the capital, you're within a few

Puebla's baroque downtown

hours of impressive ancient ruins, snowcapped volcanoes, enchanting small towns, and bustling colonial-era cities. With efficient buses and well-maintained highways radiating out from the city in every direction, it's easy to plan a change of scenery.

For most first-time visitors to Mexico City, a day trip to the pyramids at Teotihuacán is a must. Just an hour east of the city, Teotihuacán is the most visited archaeological site in Mexico, an awe-inspiring example of city planning in 5th-century Mesoamerica. Those with a strong interest in pre-Columbian history, however, will find a number of remarkable destinations in and around the Valley of Mexico, including the well-preserved fortified city of Xochicalco near Cuernavaca. In some cases, beautiful archaeological sites are adjoined by charming small towns; such is the case in Tepoztlán, a popular weekend destination that boasts pre-Columbian ruins in addition to lovely colonial architecture and abundant natural beauty.

Puebla is one of the most rewarding destinations near the capital, just 90 minutes south. Boasting a gorgeous *centro histórico*, Puebla is also known throughout Mexico for its inventive cuisine and its traditions in handicrafts, particularly Talavera pottery.

HIGHLIGHTS

✪ **CLOSEST TO THE GODS:** For its scale and beauty, the ancient city of Teotihuacán was named "place of gods" by the Nahuatl-speaking people in the Valley of Mexico. Walk through history in the plaza between the Pirámide de la Luna and the 75-meter-high **Pirámide del Sol,** the most iconic structure in Teotihuacán (page 302).

✪ **BEST PLACE TO START THE DAY:** The heart of Puebla's gorgeous colonial downtown, the **Zócalo** is adjoined by the city's impressive cathedral and surrounded by sidewalk cafés, perfect for sipping a coffee while planning your walking tour of the city's *centro histórico* (page 308).

✪ **MOST IMPRESSIVE REGIONAL MUSEUM:** There is an excellent collection of pre-Columbian art along with interesting temporary exhibits at Puebla's top-notch **Museo Amparo** (page 309).

✪ **BEST EARLY COLONIAL MONUMENT:** An early Spanish settlement and former home of Hernán Cortés, Cuernavaca has many impressive early colonial-era buildings, of which the austere and beautiful 16th-century **Catedral de la Asunción** is a must-see (page 318).

✪ **MOST INSPIRING LOOKOUT:** Ascend through lush forests to the pre-Columbian **Pirámide de Tepozteco,** on a bluff overlooking the tiny town of Tepoztlán, Morelos. The views of the valley below, together with the adrenaline of the climb, will take your breath away (page 326).

Puebla at night

Day Trips

To Querétaro

57D

TULA
Tula
126

Jilotepec

10

57D

55

15D

11

Tlalpujahua
El Oro

Atlacomulco

Tepotzotlán

55

55D

57D

55

85D

15

134

MEXICO CITY

Toluca

Parque Nacional Desierto los Leones

48

15

La Marquesa

Parque Los Dinamos

Lago Avándaro

Parque Nacional Nevado de Toluca

Raíces

TEOTENANGO

Tenango de Arista

Parque El Ajusco

95D

Valle de Bravo

Nevado de Toluca ▲ 4,691 m

95

Los Saucos

134

Tres Marías

3

550

55

CATEDRAL DE LA ASUNCIÓN

Texcaltitlán

12

Malinalco

MALINALCO

Chalma

Cuernavaca

160

Sultepec

Ixtapan de la Sal

XOCHICALCO

Temixco

95D

Las Grutas de la Estrella

Parque Nacional Las Grutas de Cacahuamilpa

14

55

Lago Tequesquitengo

95

95D

Taxco

85

Ixcateopan

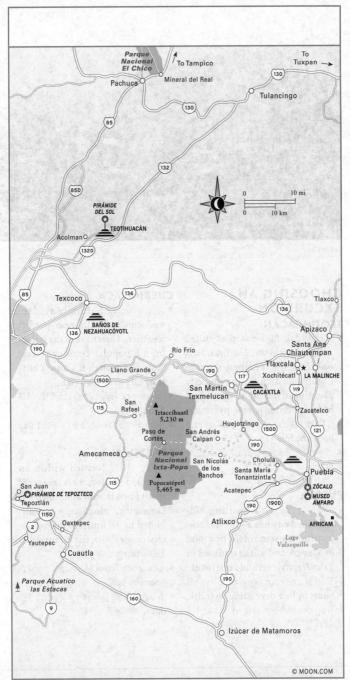

Tepoztlán

CHOOSING AN EXCURSION

TEOTIHUACÁN

- Why visit? Mexico's most visited archaeological site, Teotihuacán is one of the finest examples of pre-Columbian architecture and city planning in the country, crowned by two towering temple-pyramids.
- Distance from Mexico City: 1.5 hours by bus
- Suggested length of visit: 2-4 hours

PUEBLA

- Why visit? This bustling old-fashioned city has a splendid *centro histórico,* some of the best food in Mexico, and a long tradition of Talavera-style ceramic craftwork.
- Distance from Mexico City: 1.5 hours by bus, depending on traffic
- Suggested length of visit: 1-3 days

CUERNAVACA

- Why visit? Naturally verdant and known for its near-perfect weather, Cuernavaca has long been a popular country retreat from the capital. It's now a bustling city in its own right.
- Distance from Mexico City: 1.5 hours by bus
- Suggested length of visit: 1 day

TEPOZTLÁN

- Why visit? Nestled within an emerald valley, this magical small town is built around an old Dominican monastery and adjoined by an unusual hilltop archaeological site, the Pirámide de Tepozteco.
- Distance from Mexico City: 1.5 hours by bus
- Suggested length of visit: 1-2 days

Teotihuacán

Little is known about the people who built the ancient city of Teotihuacán in the northern Valley of Mexico. The name itself, which means "the place of gods" in Nahuatl, was given to the ancient city several centuries later. What the people of Teotihuacán called their city, what language they spoke, and what ethnic heritage they came from remain unknown. One of the largest archaeological sites in the Americas, Teotihuacán is known today for its towering temple-pyramids, as well as for its impressive city planning and architecture.

Though the area in the northern Valley of Mexico was inhabited long before Teotihuacán was settled, construction of the major buildings in Teotihuacán took place between 100 BC and AD 250. The population increased rapidly as the city-state grew powerful; by the 4th century, Teotihuacán's cultural hegemony was evident in cities throughout Mesoamerica. Anthropologists estimate that, at its height, Teotihuacán was home to as many as 150,000 people and covered over 20 square kilometers, forming the largest city in the Western Hemisphere at the time. Under unknown circumstances, Teotihuacán began to decline in the 7th century AD, possibly under attack from nearby tribes; the city was largely abandoned, leaving

the Pirámide del Sol (Pyramid of the Sun) in Teotihuacán

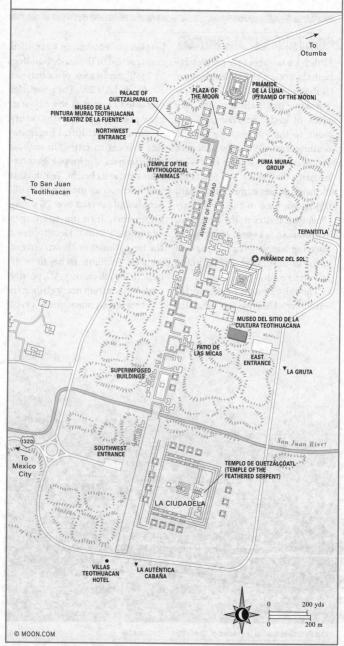

Teotihuacán

To Otumba

PLAZA OF THE MOON

PRIÁMIDE DE LA LUNA (PYRAMID OF THE MOON)

PALACE OF QUETZALPAPALOTL

MUSEO DE LA PINTURA MURAL TEOTIHUACANA "BEATRIZ DE LA FUENTE"

NORTHWEST ENTRANCE

PUMA MURAL GROUP

TEMPLE OF THE MYTHOLOGICAL ANIMALS

To San Juan Teotihuacan

AVENUE OF THE DEAD

TEPANTITLA

PIRÁMIDE DEL SOL

MUSEO DEL SITIO DE LA CULTURA TEOTIHUACANA

PATIO DE LAS MICAS

EAST ENTRANCE

LA GRUTA

SUPERIMPOSED BUILDINGS

San Juan River

132D

To Mexico City

SOUTHWEST ENTRANCE

TEMPLO DE QUETZALCÓATL (TEMPLE OF THE FEATHERED SERPENT)

LA CIUDADELA

VILLAS TEOTIHUACAN HOTEL

LA AUTÉNTICA CABAÑA

0   200 yds

0   200 m

© MOON.COM

only 30,000 residents through the Late Classic period. By 900, the city was almost entirely empty.

With its impressive architecture and proximity to Mexico City, it's not surprising that Teotihuacán is the most visited archaeological site in Mexico. It is particularly popular on the spring equinox, when thousands of people assemble at the ruins to absorb the special energy of the sun.

SIGHTS

Calzada de los Muertos (Avenue of the Dead)

Teotihuacán's principal artery, the Calzada de los Muertos, runs two kilometers south to north between La Ciudadela and the Pyramid of the Moon. The avenue is impressive at its current scale, but archaeological evidence suggests it originally ran another kilometer farther south during Teotihuacán's height. It's flanked on either side by pyramid-shaped residences.

La Ciudadela (The Citadel)

On the south end of the Avenue of the Dead, there is a large, fortresslike enclosure, once located at the geographic center of the city. Archaeologists surmise that this area, called the Main Plaza, was where ritual performances took place. At the southeast end of the plaza is the impressive Templo de Quetzalcóatl (Temple of Quetzalcóatl or, as it is sometimes called, the Temple of the Feathered Serpent), which is decorated with elaborate stone carvings of serpents' heads protruding from the facade.

The remains of more than 200 men and women were found buried

Calzada de los Muertos from the Pyramid of the Moon

here. Evidence suggests they were sacrificed during the construction of the pyramid. The corpses were placed in pits with thousands of pieces of worked shell and numerous obsidian blades and points, suggesting that they may have been Teotihuacano warriors, rather than prisoners from neighboring tribes.

Museo del Sitio de la Cultura Teotihuacana

Just beside the Pirámide del Sol, the Museo del Sitio de la Cultura Teotihuacana (Site Museum) contains a collection of artifacts excavated from the site (though the best collection of art and artifacts from Teotihuacán is in the Museo Nacional de Antropología in Mexico City). The building also has a snack bar, a bookshop, and restrooms, as well as a small but nicely tended botanical garden, right beside the Pyramid of the Sun. Admission is included in the cost of your ticket, and the museum is open the same hours as the archaeological site.

WALMART AND TEOTIHUACÁN

In 2004, Walmart de México, the largest subsidiary of the massive U.S. retail outlet Walmart (and the biggest private employer in Mexico), began construction on a new mega-supermarket in the community of San Juan Teotihuacán. The supermarket, part of Walmart's Bodega Aurrerá chain, was about a kilometer from the great ruins of Teotihuacán. INAH, the National Institute of Anthropology and History, officially stated that the construction would not affect the ancient site, despite its location within the outer limits of a protected zone, and Walmart appeared to have legal paperwork to support the new construction. People of the town, however, were outraged at not only the proximity of the new store to the ruins but the way their small-business-based community would be affected by the giant retailer. When a little pre-Columbian altar and some artifacts were discovered in what is now Bodega Aurrerá's parking lot, it helped galvanize opposition to the project.

Townspeople accused the local authorities of corruption for allowing construction on protected lands, and pointed fingers at INAH for jeopardizing a historic monument. Showing fierce pride in the ruins, as well as in their community, Teotihuacán locals organized months of protests against the megastore, and their efforts were eventually joined by high-profile Mexican intellectuals, including Oaxacan painter Francisco Toledo and essayist Elena Poniatowska. At one point, several protesters went on a week-long hunger strike.

Although the protests received a great deal of national and international press, Walmart prevailed: The Bodega Aurrerá opened in 2005, and it hasn't lacked clients. However, the people of San Juan Teotihuacán weren't far off the mark: An exhaustive 2012 investigation by the New York Times uncovered more than US$200,000 in bribes paid to Teotihuacán's mayor and other government authorities to make concessions on laws and alter the town's zoning map; according to the Times report, it was part of a larger trend within the company to offer payouts for building permits in Mexico. Investigations into the case are ongoing.

Museo de la Pintura Mural Teotihuacana "Beatriz de la Fuente"

Opened in 2001, this small museum contains interesting murals excavated from the archaeological site, as well as anthropological exhibits detailing religion and customs in the ancient city. Admission is free with your ticket to the ruins; it operates daily 8am-5pm.

✪ Pirámide del Sol (Pyramid of the Sun)

One of the largest, most impressive pyramids in the world, the Pirámide del Sol measures just under 70 meters in height. Until recently, it was possible to ascend to the top of the pyramid via a steep stone staircase, a challenging but rewarding climb

that was undertaken by hundreds of people every day. At the beginning of the pandemic lockdown in 2020, access to the pyramid was closed and will remain closed indefinitely. Though disappointing for visitors, archaeologists and cultural advocates have long worried that the constant foot traffic was causing irrevocable damage to the pyramid. The deterioration of the staircase was evident, even to nonexperts. Today, you can admire this impressive monument from below, as the ordinary citizens of Teotihuacán would have done.

In 1971, a long stairway was discovered that ended in a four-chamber lava cave, 100 meters long, under the pyramid. Archaeologists surmise that the cave was considered by the city's builders to be a sacred entryway to another world, which is why they chose the location to build their largest pyramid.

Pirámide de la Luna (Pyramid of the Moon)

At the north end of the Calzada de los Muertos is the beautiful Pyramid of the Moon, centered on the Plaza of the Moon, which, along with the Main Plaza at the Ciudadela was one of the principal ritual areas in the city. Built later than the other principal monuments in the city, the Pyramid of the Moon is 46 meters high. When approaching the pyramid along the Avenida de los Muertos, note how the outline of the structure mirrors that of Cerro Gordo, the mountain behind it.

Palace of Quetzalpapalotl and Patio of the Jaguars

Just to the west of the Pirámide de la Luna, the impressive Palacio de Quetzalpapalotl is far more ornate than other dwellings in the city and was likely the home of a ruler or priest of Teotihuacán. In the main patio, principally excavated in the 1960s, there are beautiful stone columns carved with bas-relief butterflies and birds in profile. The roof was partially reconstructed by anthropologists in a style thought to be consistent with Teotihuacán's original architecture.

Just behind the palace, the Patio of the Jaguars is a small rectangular room that still retains its original red-tinted frescoes, depicting jaguars with conch shells in their mouths.

carved stone column in the Palace of Quetzalpapalotl

RESTAURANTS

There are lots of casual places to eat around the ruin site, catering to families and day-trippers. There are several places near the main entrances along the west side of the site, but the highest concentration of eateries is located on the east side of the pyramids, near parking lot 5. Of these, the most distinctive is undoubtedly La Gruta (tel. 55/5531-4877 or 594/956-0127, reservations via WhatsApp 55/5191-9799, http://lagruta.mx; 10am-4pm daily; US$10). The menu covers Mexican basics without much inspiration, from sopa de tortilla (tortilla soup) to grilled meats, as well as daily specials. The setting is the real attraction: The restaurant is in

La Gruta

an underground cave, lit by candles, just behind the Pirámide del Sol. Come for a snack and a beer to enjoy the unique ambience.

There are dozens of other ultra-casual family-style eateries east and south of the archaeological site, many offering similar menus of grilled meats, *barbacoa* (slow-cooked lamb), and *antojitos* (snacks) like quesadillas. One such spot, La Auténtica Cabaña (Circuito Piramides 24, tel. 56/1168-4227 or 56/2740-8824, www.laautenticaca-bana.com; 8am-6pm daily; US$5), has an appealing menu of traditional Mexican cuisine and a decent touch with food, but it's the beautiful country setting that recommends this place. If it's a warm day, order a cold drink and sit on the restaurant's *palapa*-shaded (thatched palm roof) patio, from which you can see the pyramids of Teotihuacán.

WHERE TO STAY

Though most people make the trip to and from Teotihuacán in a single day, staying the night can give you a little more time to explore the archaeological site—and, if you're an early riser, the opportunity to get there right as the gates open, when there are few people in the park. A nice option for an overnight is the Villas Teotihuacán Hotel (tel. 55/5836-9020, www.villasteo.com; US$70-100), located on the ring road south of the ruins. The rooms are out of date and a bit dark, but the lovely grounds make up for those shortcomings. There's a big swimming pool in the central patio, a nice restaurant on-site (the weekend brunch buffet is particularly good), huge lawns, and a small playground for children. Located south of the pyramids, there is also a small ruin site on the property. It's less than a kilometer from entrance 1, but if you don't want to walk, there are often taxis waiting just outside the main entrances.

PRACTICALITIES

The Teotihuacán archaeological zone (Ecatepec Pirámides km 22 + 600, Municipio de Teotihuacán, Estado de México, tel. 594/956-0276, www.teotihuacan.inah.gob.mx; 9am-5pm daily; US$5, children under 13, students, teachers, seniors, and people with disabilities free) has five entrances, three on the west side and two on the east. They are each adjoined by a parking lot (US$4 per car), and they all have public restrooms. The traditional place to start your tour is at the southern entrance (no. 1), visiting the Ciudadela before heading north along the Calzada de los Muertos to the pyramids. Buses will drop you off here. For a shorter tour, the second entrance is just in front of the Pirámide del Sol.

Wear good walking shoes for exploring the site. A hat, sunblock, and water are musts to carry with you. If you want to experience the site in relative peace, arrive early, when the ticket-takers open the gate. The tour buses start arriving around 10am. Weekends are the busiest, especially on Sunday, when admission is free for nationals.

TRANSPORTATION

The ruins lie about 45 kilometers northeast of Mexico City. Autobuses Teotihuacán (tel. 55/5767-3573, www.

autobusesteotihuacan.com.mx) buses depart the Terminal Central del Norte (Eje Central Lázaro Cárdenas 4907, www.centraldel-norte.com) every 15 minutes 6am-2pm and return every 15 minutes from the ruins to the terminal until 8pm. The trip to Teotihuacán takes about an hour. Ask for the bus to Los Pirámides, not Teotihuacán or you may end up in the town of the same name. It costs about US$6 round-trip. If you want to skip the bus, you can ask Taxis Radio Union to take you all the way to the pyramids and back. For trips out of the city, they charge about US$10/hour (three-hour minimum trip).

Turibus (tel. 55/51411365, ext. 2, www.turibus.com.mx; US$50) operates daily guided tours to Teotihuacán, departing from the Auditorio at 8:30am and from the Zócalo at 9am every morning. (This company also offers the double-decker sight-seeing rides around Mexico City.) The tour bus stops at the Basílica de Santa María de Guadalupe before heading to the pyramids; the cost includes guide service (in Spanish), admission to the archaeological site, and lunch. Capitalbus (WhatsApp 55/6676-8033 or 55/5208-2505, https://www.capitalbus.com.mx; US$50) offers a similar service.

Puebla and Vicinity

Though the city of Puebla is a popular day trip from the capital, it is nonetheless surprising that this big and beautiful metropolis remains largely off the beaten track for most foreign visitors, despite its fine architecture, celebrated cuisine, and wonderful traditions in art and craftwork. Though close to Mexico City, it has a very different ambience than its neighbor to the north. It's more old-fashioned, with a family-oriented downtown district filled with funky small businesses, a more visibly Catholic population, and air clean enough to provide intermittent glimpses of the volcano Popocatépetl rising to the west.

Many people come to Puebla to eat and with good reason. Though famous *poblano* dishes like *chiles en nogada* and *tinga* are prepared

throughout the country, they rarely reach the sublime perfection achieved in their native home, and street snacks here are both uniquely prepared and utterly delicious. At the same time, many visitors will find the city's architecture and history to be just as rich and enthralling as its culinary traditions. Puebla has a long and important history in Mexico, founded in the early colonial era. It's one of the few cities in Mexico that wasn't built directly atop an existing native community, and its beautifully preserved historic center is filled with some of the most impressive colonial churches, palaces, and ex-convents in the country, replete with ornate gold-leaf trimmings, magnificent stonework, and Puebla's distinct signature, Talavera tile.

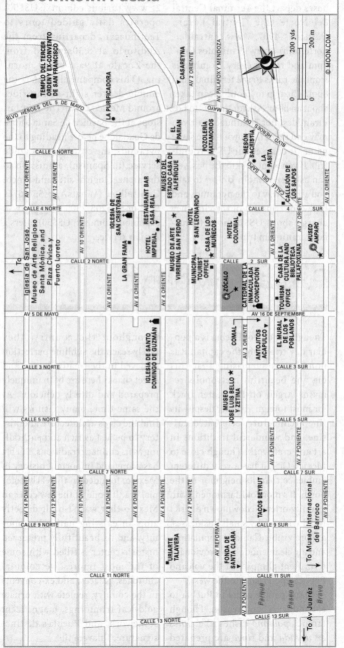

Downtown Puebla

ON THE ROAD TO PUEBLA: TWIN PEAKS

Popocatépetl and Iztaccíhuatl

Twin volcanoes rising between Puebla and Mexico City, Popocatépetl and Iztaccíhuatl are the most recognizable and striking natural landmarks in the region. Often shortened to Popo and Izta, the volcanoes' Nahuatl names mean "the smoking mountain" and "the white woman," respectively, and they were the subject of great fascination and various legends in pre-Columbian Mexico. Today, these beautiful peaks are the crown jewels of a national park, Parque Nacional Izta-Popo, a surprising refuge of natural beauty located in the middle of the most densely populated region in Mexico.

A symmetrical cone and the second-highest peak in Mexico, Popo has become all the more picturesque, but perhaps a touch more troublesome, since it woke from a decades-long slumber in 1994. In the year 2000, the largest eruption in 1,200 years occurred on the mountain, and it remains one of Mexico's most active volcanoes, frequently spewing smoke and ash into the air. Craterless Izta, just 16 kilometers north, lies dormant beside it.

Both Popo and Itza are blanketed with pine and oak forests, as well as alpine prairie, at lower elevations. Izta has permanent glaciers at its peaks, a rarity in Mexico (only the country's highest mountain, the Pico de Orizaba, also claims them)—though these have been diminishing rapidly and are expected to disappear altogether. The wilderness surrounding the volcanoes was among the earliest designated nature preserves in the country, receiving national park status from President Lázaro Cárdenas in 1935.

Occupying a unique place right between Mexico's great plateau and the subtropical southern states, the Izta-Popo National Park extends into the states of Mexico, Morelos, Puebla, and Tlaxcala. It is home to at least 48 types of mammals and more than 150 bird species, as well as a multitude of plants and mushrooms (many of which are edible and popular for soups and quesadillas in the pueblos that surround the volcanoes). Several endemic species inhabit the park, including the rather charming *zacatuche*, or volcano rabbit, which was named for its habitat amid the *zacates*, or tall grasses, of the park.

SIGHTS

✪ Zócalo

The Zócalo (Palafox y Mendoza and Av. 16 de Septiembre) is Puebla's main public plaza, facing the cathedral and bordered on three sides by 16th-century *portales* (arcades). Once a bustling marketplace, it is today a nice park, with towering trees and lots of benches, surrounded by sidewalk cafés, restaurants, shops, and newspaper stands. It's always bustling with activity and a great place for sipping a coffee or simply enjoying quality people-watching.

Catedral de la Inmaculada Concepción

On the south side of the Zócalo, Puebla's Catedral de la Inmaculada Concepción (Av. 16 de Septiembre and Av. 5 Oriente, tel. 222/232-2316; 8am-7:30pm daily; free) is one of the most beautiful churches in Mexico, first begun in 1575 by Francisco Becerra and completed almost a century later, in 1664. The tile-domed facade, adjoined by the two highest church towers in the country, is a mix of medieval, Renaissance, and baroque styles, and inside, you'll even notice a few neoclassical touches in Manuel Tolsá's marble and onyx altar.

Casa de la Cultura and Biblioteca Palafoxiana

Formerly the archbishop's palace, the Casa de la Cultura (Av. 5 Ote. 5, tel. 222/246-3186; 9am-8pm Mon.-Fri., 10am-5pm Sat.-Sun.; free) was originally constructed in 1597. Today, the building is a cultural center with exhibition spaces, a cinema, and a café, as well as the home of the

Puebla's bustling Zócalo

Biblioteca Palafoxiana (10am-5pm Tues.-Sun.), one of the oldest libraries in the Americas. In 1646, Bishop Juan Palafox y Mendoza donated the first 5,000 volumes, including works of philosophy, theology, and history, some printed as early as the 15th century.

Iglesia de Santo Domingo de Guzmán

Three blocks north of the plaza on Cinco de Mayo lies what remains of the fine baroque Dominican monastery Iglesia de Santo Domingo de Guzmán (Av. 5 de Mayo and Av. 6 Ote., tel. 222/268-7232; 8am-2pm and 4:30pm-8pm daily; free), constructed in the mid-16th century and consecrated in 1690. Inside the spacious, highly ornamented church, the exceptional Capilla del Rosario stands out, with walls that are covered with gilded floor-to-ceiling carvings, tiles, and cherubs.

Iglesia de San Cristóbal

Constructed in the 17th century, the Iglesia de San Cristóbal (Calle 4 Norte at Av. 6 Oriente, tel. 222/235-9645; 7am-2pm and 4pm-8pm daily; free) is another wonderful example of baroque architecture in Puebla, with a beautifully carved sandstone facade and an interior filled with elaborate relief figures (though not, as in many churches, gilded).

✪ Museo Amparo

The Museo Amparo (Av. 2 Sur 708, tel. 222/229-3850, www.museoamparo.com; 10am-6pm Wed.-Sun., 10am-9pm Sat.; US$2) is an excellent anthropology and art museum with a gorgeous rooftop café located in two adjoining colonial-era buildings

three blocks from the Zócalo. The museum's permanent collection contains more than 2,000 pieces of pre-Columbian and colonial art, including outstanding artifacts from the Maya, Olmec, Zapotec, and Mixtec cultures, as well as paintings, pottery, crafts, and furniture created in Puebla during the viceroyalty. Though best known for its permanent collection, the museum also hosts nice temporary exhibits, often exploring themes in modern and contemporary art.

Museo de Arte Religioso Santa Mónica

Museo de Arte Religioso Santa Mónica (Av. 18 Pte. 103 at 5 de Mayo, tel. 222/232-0178; 10am-5pm Tues.-Sat.; US$4) was founded as a convent in 1610. The building was converted to a religious art museum and taken over by INAH in 1940, exhibiting work by many well-known colonial-era artists divided over two stories of exhibition spaces. Just as interesting, the museum offers a look at the living quarters and daily life of the nuns who once lived here.

Museo José Luis Bello y Zetina

José Luis Bello, a wealthy *poblano* businessman, spent his riches on

the roof cafe at the Museo Amparo

elegant furnishings and art from Mexico, Europe, and Asia, including porcelain, glass, Talavera ceramics, wrought iron, religious vestments, and clothing. Today, the Museo José Luis Bello y Zetina (Av. 5 de Mayo 409, tel. 222/232-4720, www. museobello.org; 10am-4pm Tues.-Sun.; free) displays that massive collection in a historic building that was once part of Puebla's large Dominican convent.

Museo Universitario Casa de los Muñecos

An unusual colonial-era building, the Casa de los Muñecos (2 Norte 2, tel. 222/246-2899; 10am-6pm Tues.-Sun.; US$2, free on Wed.) is famous for its brick facade, which, according to legend, is adorned with satirical portraits of the town fathers, who wouldn't let the owner construct a third floor (though he eventually gained permission to do so). Today, it houses a small museum with a permanent collection of colonial-era oil paintings, vintage scientific tools and musical instruments, prints, and other historic artifacts owned by the Universidad Autónoma de Puebla.

Museo del Estado Casa de Alfeñique

The intricate baroque facade of Museo del Estado Casa de Alfeñique (Av. 4 Ote. 416, tel. 222/232-0458; 10am-5pm Tues.-Sun.; US$2) is a classic example of the *alfeñique* architectural style, named for a white sugar candy made in Puebla, which the trim on this building resembles. Built in 1790, it now houses the state museum, with old manuscripts related to Puebla

history, ethnography on different Indigenous groups in the state, and colonial clothing. It's worth the entrance fee to see the beautiful interiors.

Plaza Cívica and Fuerte Loreto

To the north of the *centro histórico*, Puebla's civic center is adjoined by the historic military Fuerte Loreto (Fort Loreto) and the Museo de la No Intervención (Calz. de los Fuertes s/n, Centro Cívico 5 de Mayo, Zona Histórica de los Fuertes, tel. 222/234-8513; 10am-4:30pm Tues.-Sun.; US$3, free Sun.), located on the site of the famous Battle of Puebla, in which local troops defeated French invaders, celebrated annually on May 5—or, as it is better known, Cinco de Mayo. The fort is a lovely place to spend an afternoon, with a coffee shop on-site, plenty of public spaces, and great views of the city below.

Parque Conmemorativo del 150 Aniversario de la Batalla de Puebla

Though it is a bit outside the Centro, those interested in contemporary design will want to walk a few extra blocks to see the Parque Conmemorativo del 150 Aniversario de la Batalla de Puebla (Centro Cívico 5 de Mayo, Av. Ejército de Oriente; free), an innovative new park and monument designed by famed Mexico City architect Enrique Norten in 2012, as part of a larger renovation of Puebla's Plaza Cívica and the historic Fort Loreto and Fort Guadalupe. The unusual public space is composed of undulating wooden decks with lovely views of the surrounding city.

Museo Internacional del Barroco

In 2016, the city of Puebla inaugurated the Museo Internacional del Barroco (Vía Atlixcáyotl 2501, Reserva Territorial Atlixcáyotl, tel. 222/326-7130, http://mib.puebla. gob.mx; 10am-5pm Tues.-Sun.; US$5), a museum dedicated entirely to baroque art and architecture. The biggest reason to visit is the museum's striking contemporary design by Pritzker-winning Japanese architect Toyo Ito. If you can take your eyes off the architecture, the most interesting rooms are those dedicated to Puebla's baroque *centro histórico*. The museum is about seven kilometers outside the city center; the easiest way to get there and back is with ride-hailing app Uber.

RESTAURANTS

Start your food tour at one of Puebla's oldest markets, the Mercado Melchor Ocampo El Carmen (21 Oriente 209; 7am-7pm daily). This is the place to try *cemitas,* Puebla's version of the *torta,* or sandwich, filled with meat and often garnished with the fragrant herb *pápalo.* The market is packed during the lunch hour.

Another quick bite, *tacos árabes* are a fusion of Mexican and Middle Eastern traditions, and they are a specialty in Puebla: crispy spit-roasted pork served in a pita, sometimes with *jocoque,* an acidic strained-yogurt spread. One of the best places to try these uniquely delicious tacos (or, if you're vegetarian, an excellent falafel wrap) is

casual late-night spot Tacos Beyrut (Av. 5 Poniente 718, tel. 222/232-3040, www.tacosbeirut.com; 6pm-midnight Mon.-Sat.; US$3).

There are no tables or barstools and little ceremony at Antojitos Acapulco (Av. 5 Pte. 114; 9am-midnight daily, www.antojitosaca-pulco.com, US$3), but you don't need anything more than a plate and a dollop of spicy salsa to fully enjoy this tiny storefront's flautas and *molotes,* a crisp deep-fried corn flatbread stuffed with fillings like potato, *tinga* (spiced and shredded meat), and cheese. Though they're open all day, it's the perfect late-night, post-bar snack, as the crowds attest.

Simple yet remarkably good, the Pozolería Matamoros (Palafox y Mendoza 6, tel. 222/237-6365; 1:30pm-8:30pm Mon.-Tues. and Thurs.-Sun.) is just a few blocks from the main square. The namesake dish—a rich hominy soup called pozole—is excellent, but the menu also includes a number of *poblano* specialties, like chalupas (hand-rolled corn cakes topped with red or green salsa, shredded chicken, and diced onions). Head to the more spacious upstairs dining room, where you can order a beer and enjoy a leisurely lunch.

Just across the street from the city cathedral, the bustling two-story eatery Comal (16 de Septiembre 311-b, tel. 222/688-4888, 8am-midnight Mon.-Thurs. and Sun., 8am-2am Fri.-Sat.) is a colorful and contemporary spot to try excellent versions of poblano staples like enmoladas, pipían, memelas, cemitas, and chiles en nogada, along with a craft beer or a glass of mezcal. Try the trio of

PUEBLA: A CULINARY CAPITAL

Cemitas are a traditional poblano sandwich.

Puebla has a remarkable culinary tradition, noted for its complex flavors and for its use of centuries-old heirloom recipes. Uniting pre-Columbian and Spanish ingredients and preparations with a touch of French and Middle Eastern influence, food in Puebla is delicious and very much a part of the cultural experience of visiting the city.

MOLES

Moles—thick, heavily spiced sauces (often served over poultry)—are prepared throughout the country, with many famous versions produced in the state of Oaxaca. According to legend, however, *mole* was first created by the nuns of the Convento de Santa Rosa in Puebla, during the 16th century.

Puebla's signature version of the dish, **mole poblano,** usually combines dozens of ingredients, including chocolate, dried chile peppers, onion, garlic, peanuts, raisins, cinnamon, coriander, peppercorns, and sesame seeds. In Puebla, you'll find *mole* piled onto sandwiches, slathered over turkey, or stuffed into tamales.

Variations on *mole* are served in restaurants throughout the city. **Pipián,** sometimes called *mole verde,* is a flavorful sauce made with green pumpkin seeds and

Comal is an upbeat poblano restaurant with lovely views of the city cathedral.

moles on enchiladas for a taste of Puebla's diverse flavors. For the high quality of the food and service, the prices are surprisingly accessible— which means there is often a wait for a table.

One of the nicest places for a traditional meal is the lobby restaurant in the Hotel Colonial (Calle 4 Sur 105, tel. 222/246-4612; 7am-10pm daily; US$8), which offers a daily three-course *comida corrida* (lunch special) for a reasonable price. The menu changes daily but

spices, ground till smooth; it is also considered a specialty in Puebla, though you'll see it prepared in the traditional cuisine of other regions, like Yucatán. *Pipián rojo* is a variation, made with tomatoes and dried chiles.

POBLANOS

Popular throughout Mexico, **chiles en nogada** are a highly distinctive *poblano* creation. Traditionally prepared during the fall harvest season and served as a part of the Independence Day holidays in September, a *chile en nogada* is a large green poblano pepper stuffed with beef or pork, almonds, fruit, and spices, which is then bathed in a creamy walnut sauce and showered with pomegranate seeds. Another rich regional dish, **tinga poblana** is slow-cooked shredded pork in a stew of chipotle chiles and vegetables. It is usually served with tortillas and rolled into tacos.

STREET FOOD

Some wonderful quick bites and street foods are also typical to Puebla. A popular appetizer or snack, **chalupas** are small, handmade corn tortillas that are deep fried in *manteca* (lard) or hot oil, then doused in spicy salsa and topped with shredded pork and onions. Puebla's version of the *torta* is the **cemita,** a sandwich made on a sesame-studded roll also called a *cemita. Cemitas* are piled with meat, string cheese, lettuce, tomato, and onion, then garnished with *pápalo,* a fragrant Mexican herb. Another *poblano* sandwich, the **pelona** is served on a soft, lightly fried bun, layered with beans, meat, and cheese. **Tacos árabes** are a Middle Eastern–inspired taco made with spit-roasted meat served in a warm pita and topped with lime and chipotle salsa.

DULCES

Puebla is also famous throughout the country for its traditional *dulces* (sweets). On the highways outside town, vendors sell bags of the city's famous candy to motorists idling at the tollbooths. Among the most typical sweets in Puebla are starchy treats made with *camote* (sweet potato). Sweet potatoes are cooked, sweetened, and flavored, then rolled into soft, cigar-shaped tubes. Also typical to Puebla are **macarrones,** a type of *dulce de leche* (milk candy), and **mueganos,** a fudgelike cake made with flour, egg, butter, and unrefined sugar. Sweets made with pumpkin seeds are a regional specialty; try **tortitas de Santa Clara,** a small cookie topped with pumpkin-seed cream, or **jamoncillo,** a fudgelike treat garnished with nuts. Many of these sweets (like much of Puebla's famous food) were originally created by nuns, who sold candies and eggnog (*rompope*) to support their convents, as they continue to do today.

almost always includes the option of ordering the restaurant's delicious *mole poblano* with chicken breast or thigh. The pretty dining room, illuminated by a skylight, is popular with local families and can get quite crowded on the weekends.

The elegant restaurant **Casareyna** (Privada 2 Oriente 1007, tel. 222/232-0032, ext. 406; 8am-10pm daily; US$12), located in the ground floor of the Casareyna hotel, makes a wonderful version of *mole poblano*, widely cited as among

Modern Casareyna is a boutique hotel with a famed in-house restaurant.

the best in the city, and local diners flock here for chiles en nogada in the late summer and early fall, when this dish is in season. These two dishes are standouts, but don't let that limit your order: The restaurant's menu of *poblano* cuisine is, across the board, creative yet traditional, and it is all nicely matched to the intimate stone-walled interior dining room. Make a reservation for lunch on the weekends.

The legendary Fonda de Santa Clara (Av. 3 Pte. 307, tel. 222/232-7674, and Av. 3 Pte. 920, tel. 222/246-1919, www.fondadesantaclara.com; 7am-10pm daily; US$10) is a traditional *poblano* restaurant serving regional food, like *mixiotes, tingas,* and mole in a delightfully old-fashioned dining room decorated with Puebla's famous Talavera tile. Many people come here to try the *chiles en nogada*, one of Puebla's signature dishes and one of the restaurant's specialties.

A sophisticated, upscale spot preparing creative *poblano* cuisine, El Mural de los Poblanos (16 de Septiembre 506, tel. 222/225-0650, www.elmuraldelospoblanos.com; 8am-midnight daily; US$12) serves regional dishes made with local ingredients. Everything on the menu, from the creative soups to the range of heirloom moles, is served with unique style and pretty, inventive presentations. Appropriately, they also have a great list of small-batch mezcal and Mexican artisanal beer.

SHOPS

The city and surrounding state of Puebla are well known for fine artisan products and craftwork, which include sculpted onyx, *papel amate*

(handmade bark paper), *papel picado* (decorative cut-paper flags), handmade furniture, wool rugs, silverwork, and, most famously, Talavera pottery, which is principally made in the city of Puebla and nearby Cholula.

To browse a selection of handicrafts from Puebla and beyond, stroll the outdoor market El Parian (Calle 6 Nte. between Av. 2 Ote. and Av. 6 Ote., 9am-7:30pm daily), where rows of craft shops are housed in a former 18th-century clothing warehouse. Just a few blocks from the Zócalo, the market's specialty is Talavera, and there are numerous stalls selling colorful painted wares of varying quality and prices, from huge urns to little keepsakes and tiles.

Perhaps the most famous—and certainly the most historic—Talavera shop in Puebla is Uriarte (Av. 4 Pte. 911, tel. 222/232-1598, http://uriartetalavera.com.mx; 10am-7pm daily), originally founded in 1824. Uriarte's delicately painted pottery, including dishes, trays, tea sets, urns, tiles, and more, is all handmade and very high quality; if you buy more than you can pack in your suitcase, they can help arrange shipping.

You'll have to travel a bit outside of the central area to visit the factory store of Talavera de la Reyna (Lateral Sur Recta a Cholula 3510, tel. 222/225-4058, http://talaveradelareyna.com.mx; 10am-7pm Mon.-Fri., 9am-3pm Sat., 11am-3pm Sun.), another very high-quality artisan producer of Talavera. At their Cholula-based factory, these artisan producers sculpt, glaze, and paint everything by hand, creating

shopping for handcraft in Puebla

gorgeous traditional as well as more modern designs.

Puebla is famous throughout the country for its traditional handmade candies. In the Centro, old-fashioned sweet shops, or *dulcerías,* line Calle 6 Oriente between 5 de Mayo and 4 Norte. One of the most historic spots is **Dulcería La Gran Fama** (Calle 6 Ote. 208, tel. 222/242-3316, www.lagranfama. com; 9am-8pm Mon.-Sat., 10am-6pm Sun.), which carries traditional sweets from the region, including *camotes* (a flavored sweet-potato candy), *tortitas de Santa Clara* (a round pumpkin-seed-cream-topped cookie), *dulce de leche* (milk candy), and much more. Many of these unique treats have been made in Puebla since the colonial era.

Puebla is also well known as a place for hunting antiques, with some very interesting vintage pieces (and occasionally some priceless antiques) showing up in the weekend flea market along the street of **Callejón de los Sapos** (Calle 6 Sur between Av. 5 Ote. and Calle 3 Sur; 10am-5pm Sun.). Here you'll find everything from old maps and silverwork to jewelry and vintage magazines, as well as the occasional religious artifact or saint—which will come with a hefty price tag. The numerous permanent shops along the alleyway offer some very nice collections of Mexican antiques.

Near Los Sapos, the tiny, folkloric shop **La Pasita** (Calle 5 Ote. 602; officially 1pm-6pm Fri.-Wed., though hours vary) sells bottles and serves shots of house-made liqueurs in flavors like almond, coconut, and fancifully named *sangre de la bruja,* or witch's blood (blackberry and hibiscus). The drink of the house is the sweet, dark raisin liqueur *pasita,* served in a shot glass with a piece of cheese on a toothpick floating inside.

WHERE TO STAY

A block from the plaza and across from a picturesque little square, the well-priced Hotel Colonial (Calle 4 Sur 105, tel. 222/246-4612 or 800/013-0000, www.colonial.com.mx; US$60-80) is very convenient for exploring downtown and has, as the name suggests, a lovely historic colonial ambience. The rooms are fairly large and comfortable, though most are also creaky and dated. It's a popular spot with European travelers.

The Hotel San Leonardo (Av. 2 Ote. 211, tel. 222/223-6600, www.hotelsanleonardo.com.mx; US$70-175) has comfortable, clean, remodeled rooms, some with stunning views of the volcanoes outside Puebla (though note that rooms with views cost quite a bit more than interior accommodations). The real highlight of this hotel is the elegant old French-colonial building in which it's housed, decorated with antiques and oriental rugs, and only a few steps from the Zócalo.

A charming option on a quiet street in the Centro, the Mesón Sacristía de la Compañía (Calle 6 Sur 304, tel. 222/232-4513, www.mesones-sacristia.com; US$120) has just eight rooms, each carefully decorated with antiques and collectibles. An antiques store, the excellent Restaurante Sacristía, and Bar El Confesionario are all within the 18th-century building that houses the hotel.

Designed by architect Ricardo Legorreta, Casareyna (Privada 2 Ote. 1007, tel. 222/232-0032, www.casareyna.com; US$85) is a gorgeous hotel that brings the architect's signature modern vision to several renovated historic buildings on the southeastern edge of the *centro histórico*. The spacious, quiet rooms all have Saltillo tile floors, king-size beds, and high ceilings. Upstairs, the rooftop pool deck is a nice place to relax in the afternoons, and the in-house restaurant is excellent (a small breakfast is included in the price).

Puebla's chicest accommodations are at La Purificadora (Callejón de la 10 Nte. 802, Paseo San Francisco, Barrio Alto, tel. 222/309-1920, www.lapurificadora.com; US$100-130), a hotel from the same group that operates Hotel Hábita, Downtown Hotel, and Condesa DF in Mexico City. Blending 19th-century architecture with modern design, the guest rooms have wood floors, fluffy white bed linens, and lots of natural light.

INFORMATION AND SERVICES

The Puebla tourism office (Av. Don Juan de Palafox y Mendoza 14, tel. 222/122-1100, ext. 6418; 10am-6pm daily) in the Zócalo can offer maps and information on upcoming festivals, art exhibits, and other municipal goings-on in Puebla city and state.

TRANSPORTATION

First- and second-class buses depart Mexico City's Terminal TAPO (Calz. Ignacio Zaragoza 200) for Puebla almost constantly, day and night, with lines ADO, Cristóbal Colón, and Estrella Roja offering first-class service to CAPU, a large bus terminal north of the city center in Puebla (Calle 11 Nte. and Blvd. Atlixco, www.capu.com.mx). The trip takes about 90 minutes and runs around US$5 one way, depending on bus line and service class.

A slightly more expensive but more convenient option is to take Ebus (http://ebus.mx) from Mexico City's central neighborhoods to the smaller and more central Terminal de Autobuses Puebla 4 Pte. (4 Poniente 2110, Col. Amor, tel. 222/273-8300) in Puebla. There are several daily departures from the Ángel de la Independencia on the Paseo de la Reforma and from the World Trade Center (Montecito 38, Nápoles), just off Insurgentes, in the Nápoles neighborhood. Tickets are about US$16 one-way. If the Ebus website doesn't accept your reservation, give them a call to reserve a ticket; the buses fill up.

Estrella Roja (tel. 222/273-8300, www.estrellaroja.com.mx) runs the express bus direct from both Terminal 1 and Terminal 2 of the Mexico City airport to CAPU and to the Terminal de Autobuses 4 Pte. hourly. ADO has service buses, roughly once an hour, from Terminal 1 of the Mexico City airport to the Terminal de Autobuses Puebla 4 Pte.

NEAR PUEBLA
Zona Arqueológica de Cholula
What appears to be a large church-topped hill in the center of Cholula is actually the largest pyramid in the continent by volume, with a base measuring 450 meters on each side. Construction on this massive structure began in the 3rd century BC and continued for almost a thousand years. The pyramid was first thoroughly explored in 1931, revealing altars with offerings, floors, walls, and buried human remains. You can visit the pyramid and part of the excavation site at the Zona Arqueológica de Cholula (Av. 8 Nte. 2, San Andrés Cholula, tel. 222/247-9081; 10am-5pm Tues.-Sat.; US$3). To get to the beautifully gilded Capilla de la Virgen de los Remedios (8am-4pm daily), first built in 1594 and rebuilt after an earthquake in the mid-19th century, follow the steep path to the top of the hill. On clear days, views of Popocatépetl are spectacular.

Estrella Roja operates multiple direct buses (US$9-11) between Mexico City's TAPO and the Cholula bus terminal, though it's generally most convenient to get to Cholula via Puebla. Minibuses leave central Puebla from Avenida 2 Poniente at Calle 3 Sur. The trip costs about US$2. A taxi or Uber from the *centro* costs around US$10 and takes about 30 minutes, depending on traffic.

A view of the church-topped pyramid in Cholula.

Cuernavaca

An easy drive an hour south of Mexico City, Cuernavaca shares many cultural similarities with the capital, and it has long been a favored retreat for harried big-city residents. With its verdant vegetation and temperate climate, Cuernavaca has attracted many of Mexico's most powerful politicians and businesspeople, who built luxury villas here for their weekend getaways. In fact, Cortés was the first of many Mexico City residents to keep a vacation home in Cuernavaca; his was built out of the ruins of the city pyramid. Since the 1980s, many Mexico City residents have made the move permanently, giving this medium-size metropolis a pleasant, cosmopolitan atmosphere. Unfortunately, *chilangos* have brought some of their problems with them: crime, traffic, and air pollution are now common in Cuernavaca.

SIGHTS
✪ Catedral de la Asunción
Cuernavaca's keynote sight is the austere Catedral de la Asunción (Hidalgo at Juan Ruiz de Alarcón, tel. 777/312-1290; 9am-2pm and 4pm-7pm Mon.-Fri., 9am-7pm Sat.-Sun.; free). Surviving since the very early colonies, it was part of a Franciscan monastery originally founded in 1526. Inside, note the wonderful early colonial murals in the main nave depicting the

Cuernavaca's picturesque city center

Cuernavaca

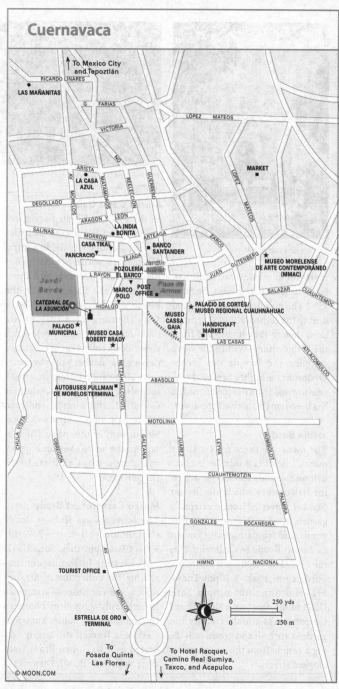

↑ To Mexico City
and Tepoztlán

RICARDO LINARES

LAS MAÑANITAS

G FARIAS

VICTORIA

LÓPEZ MATEOS

ARISTA

LA CASA
AZUL

DEGOLLADO

SALINAS

ARAGON Y LEON

MORROW

CASA TIKAL

PANCRACIO

Jardín
Borda

CATEDRAL DE
LA ASUNCIÓN

HIDALGO

PALACIO
MUNICIPAL

Museo Casa
ROBERT BRADY

AUTOBUSES PULLMAN
DE MORELOS TERMINAL

MARKET

AV MORELOS

MATAMOROS

REELECCIÓN

GUERRERO

LA INDIA
BONITA

ARTEAGA

BANCO
SANTANDER

TEJADA

Jardín
Juárez

POZOLERÍA
EL BARCO

L RAYON

MARCO
POLO

POST
OFFICE

Plaza de
Armas

MUSEO
CASSA
GAIA

ZARCO

JUAN

GUTENBERG

★ MUSEO MORELENSE
DE ARTE CONTEMPORÁNEO
(MMAC)

SALAZAR

CUAUHTEMOC

★ PALACIO DE CORTÉS/
MUSEO REGIONAL CUAUHNÁHUAC

HANDICRAFT
MARKET

LAS CASAS

ATLACOMULCO

NETZAHUALCOYOTL

ABASOLO

MOTOLINIA

GALEANA

JUAREZ

LEYVA

HUMBOLDT

CHULA VISTA

OBREGON

CUAUHTEMOTZIN

PALMIRA

GONZALES

BOCANEGRA

HIMNO

NACIONAL

TOURIST OFFICE

ESTRELLA DE ORO
TERMINAL

AV MORELOS

To
Posada Quinta
Las Flores

To Hotel Racquet,
Camino Real Sumiya,
Taxco, and Acapulco

0   250 yds
0   250 m

© MOON.COM

Cuernavaca cathedral

Jardín Borda is a green respite in central Cuernavaca.

martyrdom of Mexican saint San Felipe de Jesús in Nagasaki, Japan, in 1597. The murals were rediscovered during the cathedral's 1957 renovation, though they likely date from the 17th century. Within the same complex, the Templo del Tercer Orden has a highly ornate, 18th-century gilded altarpiece, which has been remarkably well preserved.

Jardín Borda

The owner of Taxco's great silver mines, José de la Borda, built a luxurious hacienda in Cuernavaca in the 18th century, which later his son Manuel converted into an extensive garden filled with footpaths, fishponds, and fountains, today known as Jardín Borda (Av. Morelos 271, tel. 777/318-6200, www.jardinborda.com; 10am-5:30pm Tues.-Fri. and Sun., 10am-6pm Sat.; US$3 adults, free Sun.). Showing off Cuernavaca's natural fecundity, the gardens are lush and green, providing a respite from the city's traffic-clogged streets.

Museo Cassa Gaia

In the 1950s, celebrated actor, comedian, and filmmaker Cantiflas bought a country home in central Cuernavaca, which became a popular retreat for artists and intellectuals of the time. In 2021, the house opened as Museo Cassa Gaia (Benito Juárez 102, no tel., noon-6pm Tues.-Sun., free), which showcases a collection of paintings, drawings, and other works by prominent 20th-century Mexican artists, including Diego Rivera, Mathias Goeritz, Carlos Mérida, and Juan O'Gorman, among others. A notable curiosity of the space: The mosaics in the house's swimming pool were designed by Cantiflas's friend Diego Rivera.

Museo Casa Robert Brady

The Museo Casa Robert Brady (Nezahualcóyotl 4, tel. 777/318-8554; 10am-6pm Tues.-Sun.; US$2) is a charming little museum containing the collection of art, antiques, and furniture of American Robert Brady at his former home in Cuernavaca. The house, known as Casa de la Torre, is still largely decorated as it was when Brady lived there, with more than 1,000 works of native art from across the world, as well as colonial antiques and paintings by well-known artists such as Frida Kahlo, Rufino Tamayo, and Miguel Covarrubias.

Museo Morelense de Arte Contemporáneo (MMAC)

Opened in 2018, the **Museo Morelense de Arte Contemporáneo** (Dr. Guillermo Gándara s/n, Col. Amatitlán, tel. 777/608-3350 or 777/608-3351; 11am-5pm Thurs.-Sun., free) is a thoughtfully designed contemporary art museum, with three large exhibition spaces showing a rotating lineup of work by contemporary artists, both international and local. A highlight of the museum is the sculpture garden featuring lush vegetation and work by Mexican artist Juan Soriano. The museum operates a large two-story library with titles focusing on modern and contemporary art, and it runs an incredibly robust roster of concerts, performances, dance, and workshops for children and adults on-site.

the sculpture garden at the Museo Morelense de Arte Contemporáneo

Museo Regional Cuauhnáhuac (Palacio de Cortés)

One of the oldest colonial-era buildings in Mexico, the **Palacio de Cortés** (Leyva 100, tel. 777/312-8171; 9am-5pm daily; US$4 palace and museum) runs along the Plaza de Armas. After the conquest, Hernán Cortés lived in this huge fortresslike palace, built in the early 1520s. The building remained in the Cortés family through 1629. Today, the palace contains the attractive **Museo Regional Cuauhnáhuac**, a museum that details the history of Mexico and the state of Morelos, with an emphasis on the local Tlahuica people, as well as murals by Diego Rivera that trace the history of Cuernavaca from the Spanish invasion to the present.

Plaza de Armas and Jardín Juárez

Cuernavaca's two **central plazas** (bordered by Blvd. Benito Juárez, Miguel Hidalgo, Ignacio Rayon, and Galeana) are filled with trees and often bustling with locals buying newspapers, getting their shoes shined, relaxing on benches, or chatting. **Plaza de Armas** is the larger of the two, adjoined by the **Jardín Juárez**, with its late 19th-century kiosk supposedly designed by French architect Alexandre Gustave Eiffel. The majority of buildings surrounding these two plazas are modern, so they lack a bit of the colonial charm of many central squares in the region.

RESTAURANTS

Catering to locals and visiting *capitaleños*, Cuernavaca has a nice assortment of places to eat, though the restaurants here don't rival the color and diversity of the food in Mexico City. Close to the main square, **La India Bonita** (Dwight Morrow 15-B, tel. 777/312-5021, www.laindiabonita.com.mx; 8am-6pm Mon.-Thurs. and Sun., 8am-9pm Fri.-Sat.; US$10) is a classic old-time Cuernavaca restaurant that opened in 1933. The pretty, tree-filled patio is the perfect setting for a top-shelf tequila and a plate of *sopes* (round corn cakes topped with beans and shredded chicken) or stuffed chile peppers.

A favorite with Cuernavaca's creative class, the colorful and eclectically decorated dining room at **Casa Tikal** (Comonfort 13, 777/202-9063; 9am-6:15pm daily) is full of Mexican handcraft and contemporary art. It's a quirky backdrop for the traditional Mexican menu, which features food from the states of Morelos, Oaxaca, and Yucatán, from pork shoulder in mole coloradito to papatzules (egg-stuffed tortillas in pumpkin-seed-sauce). The lunch special, which includes soup of the day, agua del día, and a main dish, is an excellent value. The restaurant is often packed on the weekends.

Both the charming tile-floored dining room and the pretty court-yard seating recommend a meal at Spanish-style restaurant **Pancracio** (Ignacio López Rayón 22, Local 18, tel. 777/202-4948, http://pancraciocvca.com; 8:30am-11pm Mon.-Sat., 9am-10pm Sun.) in the heart of the centro histórico, where you'll find good versions of Iberian staples like gazpacho and patatas bravas on the menu, along with ceviches, meats, and pastas. There's a beautiful bar in the restaurant's entrance on Rayón that is a nice place for a drink in the evening.

For a more casual meal, try **Pozolería El Barco** (Rayón 3, tel. 777/314-1020; 11am-10pm daily; US$5), a simple place with garden seating specializing in pozole, a hearty hominy soup served with pork or shredded chicken and garnished with chopped onions, oregano, radishes, and chiles. Pozole is a specialty of the state of Guerrero, served in three different styles here (red, green, or white), each seasoned differently. They also serve tacos, chalupas (thick corn cakes topped with meat and salsa), and pig's-feet tostadas, among other dishes.

There are intimate views of Cuernavaca's historic cathedral from the second-floor balcony at Italian restaurant **Marco Polo** (Hidalgo 30, tel. 777/312-3484 or 777/318-4032, www.marco-polo.com.mx; 1pm-10:30pm Mon.-Thurs., 1pm-midnight Fri.-Sat., 1pm-10pm Sun.;

Marco Polo is an old-fashioned Italian restaurant with an appealing terrace dining room.

US$6), a supremely pleasant place to fill up on a plate of the restaurant's homemade pastas and decent thin-crust pizzas, along with a glass of wine and a craft beer.

WHERE TO STAY

Posada Quinta Las Flores (Tlaquepaque 1, Col. Las Palmas, tel. 777/314-1244 or 777/312-5769, www.quintalasflores.com, $50) is a well-run and well-priced family-friendly hotel, located within walking distance of Cuernavaca's centro histórico—though the many Mexican families staying here choose to skip sightseeing in the centro and spend the whole day at the small pool and on-site restaurant. Guest rooms are quiet and impeccably neat, with modern baths, and there is a generous full breakfast included in the nightly price, which makes this hotel an excellent value.

If you've come to Cuernavaca to escape the city, there are old-fashioned family-style resort-hotels where you can spend the weekend floating in the pool, as they did in mid-20th-century Mexico. One of these is the Hotel Racquet (Av. Francisco Villa 100, tel. 777/101-0350 or 800/002-5425, www.hotel-racquet.com; from US$65) in the pretty Rancho Cortés neighborhood, which originally opened in 1939. It features tennis and racquet-ball courts, a pool, several restaurants and bars, and an on-site spa.

For modern luxury, the Camino Real Sumiya (Col. José Parras, in Jiutepec, near the highway exit to Tepoztlán and Cuautla, tel. 777/329-9888, www.caminoreal.com; US$100-150) was originally constructed as a residence by American heiress Barbara Hutton, who designed the space with Japanese-style interiors, verdant gardens, and walking paths. Rooms are clean and comfortable, also with an Asian theme, and equipped with flat-screen TVs and Wi-Fi.

Las Mañanitas (Ricardo Linares 107, tel. 777/362-0000, www.lasmananitas.com.mx; from US$250), a 15-minute walk from the city center, is a super-luxe place to stay, with resident peacocks and flamingos roaming the tropical gardens, an elegant swimming pool, and on-site spa. Rooms are cleanly decorated yet charming, and some have private terraces. Around the grounds, there are plenty of intimate nooks to sit and enjoy the ambience.

TRANSPORTATION

Cuernavaca is on the Acapulco-México highway, south of Mexico City. On the toll road, it takes less than an hour to get there, if there's no traffic. If you're driving to Cuernavaca, take Insurgentes Sur all the way south until it departs the city, following signs for the Cuernavaca *cuota* (toll road).

From Mexico City, buses to Cuernavaca depart from the Taxqueña bus terminal (Av. Taxqueña 1320). With departures every 15 minutes from about 5:30am to 7pm, Autobuses Pullman de Morelos (tel. 55/5445-0100, www.pullman.mx) runs buses into two terminals, Cuernavaca Centro (Abasolo 12, tel. 777/312-6001) and Cuernavaca Casino (Plan de Ayala 102, tel. 777/318-9205). You can also take Estrella de Oro (tel. 800/900-0105, www.estrelladeoro.com.mx) to Cuernavaca. It takes about an hour and a half to get there by bus and costs roughly US$8-10 each way.

NEAR CUERNAVACA
Zona Arqueológica Xochicalco

After the decline of Classic Zapotec and Mayan cities to the south, the population in Mesoamerica largely dispersed, creating both competition and instability throughout the region and giving rise to great fortified settlements in central Mexico. Located on a natural hilltop southwest of Cuernavaca, the remarkably well-preserved ruins at the Zona Arqueológica Xochicalco (Carr. Federal Xochicalco-Tetlama, Xochicalco, Miacatlán, tel. 737/374-3090; 9am-5pm daily; US$5) were a fortress city and ceremonial center. Xochicalco's extensive systems of defense, which included walls, trenches, and moats, helped it maintain and protect trade routes as it grew to prominence in the 7th century.

Xochicalco is one of the most densely built pre-Columbian cities in Mexico, and among the many temples and pyramids at this site, perhaps the most outstanding structure is the Pyramid of the Plumed Serpent, its sloped base decorated with intricate geometric patterns and stone reliefs of sinuous serpents and men with plumed headpieces. On the back side of the main acropolis is a tunnel leading to a constructed cave, first used to mine rock and later employed by the priests of Xochicalco as a subterranean observatory.

Autobuses Pullman de Morelos (www.pullman.mx) offers buses to Xochicalco every half hour from its Cuernavaca Centro terminal (Abasolo 12, tel. 777/312-6001), as well as from Mexico City's Taxqueña terminal (Av. Taxqueña 1320). The archaeological site is not usually the bus's final destination, so ask at the ticket desk and let the driver know that you plan to get off at the ruins. It is often more convenient to hire a taxi from Cuernavaca to the ruins.

Tepoztlán

Tucked into a lush valley bordered by a dramatic wall of cliffs, Tepoztlán is a ruggedly beautiful little town in the mountains of Morelos. Adjoined by an unusual mountaintop archaeological site, it is the mythical birthplace of the Mesoamerican god Quetzalcóatl, and even today, older residents still speak Nahuatl.

For centuries a sleepy little village, Tepoztlán has become a favorite weekend getaway for Mexico City residents, as well as a bit of an artist community with a hippie sensibility. Although the people of Tepoztlán (frequently shortened to "Tepoz") seem content enough with all the cafés, art shops, and weekend visitors, they keep tourism on their own terms, and the town retains an old-fashioned, easygoing atmosphere.

Tepoztlán

- To ★ PIRÁMIDE DE TEPOZTECO
- MUSEO EX-CONVENTO DE TEPOZTLÁN (MUSEO DE LA NATIVIDAD)
- EL CIRUELO
- SUSTANCIA
- TEMPLO Y EX-CONVENTO DE LA NATIVIDAD
- To La Buena Vibra, Amomoxtli and Mesa de Origen
- POSADA DEL TEPOZTECO
- Mercado de la Plaza Municipal
- MUSEO DE ARTE PREHISPÁNICO COLECCIÓN CARLOS PELLICER
- POSADA MAHE
- TEPOZNIEVES
- LA SOMBRA DEL SABINO
- To Casa Bugambilia
- 0   200 yds
- 0   200 m
- POSADA SARITA

© MOON.COM

Parroquía de la Natividad in Tepoztlán.

SIGHTS

Museo de Arte Prehispánico Colección Carlos Pellicer

The small **Museo de Arte Prehispánico Colección Carlos Pellicer** (Pablo González 2, tel. 739/395-1098; 10am-6pm Tues.-Sun.; US$1), just behind the Templo de la Natividad, houses a nice collection of pre-Hispanic pottery from Totonac, Maya, Zapotec, and Olmec cultures, from the collection of poet Carlos Pellicer, who lived in Tepoztlán. Take note of the fine Mexica statue of the god Ometochtli. At press time, it remained closed indefinitely following the pandemic lockdown of 2020.

Museo Ex-Convento de Tepoztlán (Museo de la Natividad)

After sustaining serious damage in the 2017 earthquake that affected the state of Morelos and Mexico City, Tepoztlán's historic Dominican monastery, the **Museo Ex-Convento de Tepotzlán** (Plaza

inside the 17th century Dominican convent in the center of Tepoztlán

Municipal, Revolución and Pablo González; tel. 739/395-0255, 10am-5pm Tues.-Sun., free) was restored and reopened in December 2021. Keep an eye out for the easy-to-miss entrance on Zaragoza street, from which you can enter the former convent and see its historic interiors, many of which retain vestiges of 16th-century Dominican frescoes, which include images of flowers, religious figures, and Dominican symbolism. There's a lovely bookstore and gift shop run by publisher Educal on the ground floor.

Parroquía de la Natividad

Parroquía de la Natividad (Plaza Municipal, Revolución and Pablo González) dominates central Tepoztlán with its crumbling bell towers and striking austere facade. It was built in 1555-1580 and, along with its cloisters (today the Museo Ex-Convento de Tepoztlán), was declared a World Heritage Site by the United Nations in 1994. The church is undergoing restoration of its delicate almost-500-year-old structure and isn't always open to the public. During the pandemic, an outdoor chapel was erected in the church's courtyard for masses.

✪ Pirámide de Tepozteco

Perched on a ledge in the hills 400 meters above Tepoztlán (and over 2,000 meters above sea level), the **Pirámide de Tepozteco** (Cerro del Tepozteco, via Avenida del Tepozteco; 9:30am-6pm daily; US$3.50), dedicated to Ometochtli, the Mesoamerican god of plenty and the legendary creator of pulque, occupies one of the most spectacular spots in the region. The pyramid itself is not much to see, but the chance to hike up into the hills and catch views of the Tepoztlán valley below makes it worth the rigorous trek to the top.

From the town square it's an ascent of about two kilometers to the pyramid. To find the start of the trail, just follow the Camino del Tepozteco directly north from the main square and you'll hit the bluffs. Although plenty of nonathletes make their way up to the top, be prepared for a good hour's workout. Wear sturdy shoes and sunscreen.

RESTAURANTS

Located in a lush agricultural region, Tepoztlán is blessed with wonderful fresh foods, which you can get a taste of at the **Mercado de la Plaza Municipal** (Plaza Municipal, between Revolución and Envila; 8am-7pm daily). In this picturesque outdoor market, myriad stalls sell excellent *barbacoa* (slow-cooked lamb) and set-price *comidas corridas* (lunch specials), though it's particularly worth trying the popular regional snack called *itacate,* a thick, toasted, wedge-shaped corn cake stuffed with meat or veggie fillings.

One of Tepoztlán's most famous spots is the colorful scoop shop **Tepoznieves** (Av. 5 de Mayo 21, www.nieves-tepoznieves.com; 8am-8pm daily), which sells traditional Mexican *nieves* (similar to a sorbet or ice milk) in a staggering array of flavors, like coconut, corn, tequila, strawberry, walnut, pistachio, and more. There are now branches of Tepoznieves in Mexico City, Cuernavaca, and other Mexican cities, but the original spot still does robust business in central Tepoztlán.

In addition to the patio seating, there are wooden chairs scattered throughout the expansive garden at ultra-relaxing **La Sombra del Sabino** (Av. Revolución 45, tel. 739/596-0998, http://lasombradel-sabino.com.mx; 10am-6pm Wed.-Sun.), a lovely bookstore and café just outside of Tepoztlán's bustling centro. There are plenty of vegetarian dishes on both the breakfast and lunch menus (which focus on sandwiches), plus nice black teas, a range of sweets, and artisanal beer. Pick up a book at the on-site shop and linger longer.

An elegant yet family-friendly restaurant right in the center of town, **El Ciruelo's** (Zaragoza 17, tel. 739/395-1203 or 739/395-1037, www.elciruelo.com.mx; 1pm-6pm Mon.-Thurs., 1pm-11pm Fri.-Sat., 1pm-7pm Sun.; US$10) plant-filled outdoor patio is set against the breathtaking backdrop of green mountains towering over Tepoztlán. The creative Mexican menu includes many beautifully plated and well-prepared dishes like *enchiladas de pato* (duck enchiladas) or chicken breast in mole. Accompanied with

Prehispanic food vendors at Tepoztlán's central market

OFF THE BEATEN TRACK: MALINALCO

Set amid dramatic scenery in a remote corner of the mountains between Toluca and Cuernavaca, Malinalco was once off the beaten path for most tourists. Today, it's become a weekend destination for Mexico City residents and a smattering of foreigners, but nonetheless it retains an authentic small-town atmosphere. In addition to enjoying the rural setting, there are a few sights worth visiting here: the 16th-century convent at the heart of Malinalco and the impressive archaeological site on a hill just outside the town.

SIGHTS

At the heart of Malinalco, the impressive Augustinian monastery **Ex-Convento Agustino** (Plaza Central, 10am-5pm Tues.-Sun., free) dates from the 1540s. Similar in style to the convent in Tepoztlán, the main **church** (El Templo del Divino Salvador) is largely unadorned yet imposing, while the cloister to the side is divided into two levels and surrounds an open garden. Decorating the walls of the cloister are beautiful murals of flowers and animals. Note an obviously pre-Columbian carved rock sitting on a stump in front of the church. On Wednesday an **open-air market** takes over the center of town. Vendors arrive in Malinalco from the surrounding communities, selling everything from tamales and handmade tortillas to clay pots and wood utensils.

The **Zona Arqueológica de Malinalco** (Amajac s/n, Col. Santa Monica, tel. 722/215-7080, 9am-5:30pm Tues.-Sun., US$4) sits on a bluff about one kilometer west of the town of Malinalco, all uphill on a dirt road. The small but impressive site, also known as Cuauhtinchan or Cerro de los Idolos, was built in the Late Classic period. The six monuments are carved directly out of the mountain rock, the only place in central Mexico where the Mexica used this technique. The post was a tribute to Malinalxochitl, the Mexica goddess and sister of Huitzilopochtli. The long stairway up to the ruins is a bit of a slog, but it's broken up with interesting write-ups (in three languages: English, Spanish, and Nahuatl) on the site itself and local history, culture, and environment. Views from the ruins across the town and surrounding countryside are magnificent.

GETTING THERE

It's not easy to get to Malinalco via public transport. Most people rent or drive their own car to town. The drive takes about two hours. If you'd like to visit without a set of wheels, you can take a bus from Observatorio to Tenango, letting the driver know that you want to get off at the stop for the combis (collective vans) to Malinalco.

a tamarind margarita or a glass of mezcal, the experience is ideal.

Inside the luxe hotel Amomoxtli and overlooking its lush gardens, the elegant restaurant **Mesa de Origen** (Amomoxtli, Prolongación Matamoros 115, tel. 739/395-0012, https://mesadeorigen.com, 8am-noon and 1pm-midnight daily, US$25) serves seasonal and creative takes on traditional food from the region, like tacos stuffed with hibiscus, local trout in green mole, or pozole (a traditional hominy soup) with local mushrooms, though

you'll also find wood-fired pizzas on the menu (likewise served with local ingredients, like squash blossom). Everything is beautifully presented and delicious.

SHOPPING
Sustancia

A little craft shop that specializes in burnished clay pottery from Puebla, Oaxaca, and Chiapas, Sustancia (Av. Ignacio Zaragoza 2, tel. 55/3717-0690, https://sustanciamexico.design; noon-6pm Wed.-Fri., 11am-7pm Sat.-Sun.) has a small but lovely selection of mugs, bowls, dinner plates, playful mezcal cups, and other kitchen staples. Everything is made with a centuries-old technique that uses natural clay and stone polishing for a naturally shiny and elegant product.

Weekend Market

The street Revolución in the center of Tepoztlán turns into one big craft market on weekends. Vendors sell Mexican handicrafts, as well as jewelry, art, and clothing from around the world, in outdoor stalls on the streets and in front of the church. If you don't make it to Tepoz on a Saturday or Sunday, there is a smaller artisan market just east of the Capilla de Nuestra Señora de la Asunción, selling jewelry, textiles, leather goods, and other handicrafts every day of the week.

WHERE TO STAY

So close to the capital and Cuernavaca, Tepoztlán is a hugely popular weekend destination. During the week it's usually no problem to show up without reservations, but you'll want to book ahead if you're staying on a Friday or Saturday night.

A good low-budget choice is the small and friendly **Posada Mahe** (Paraíso 12, tel. 739/395-3292; US$35), on a cobbled street just above the town center. Quiet and clean, it has cozy, brightly painted rooms with tile floors and teeny but nice private bathrooms. There's a small patio and pool in back.

Another budget option, **Posada Sarita** (Allende 26, tel. 739/395-0635, www.posadasarita.com; US$40-60) is located just south of the central square, with nondescript

the weekend craft market in Tepoztlán

but spacious rooms, some overlooking the quiet central courtyard and others facing the street below, with nice views of the surrounding town and mountains. There's a small pool with shaded tables, hammocks for lounging, and a friendly staff.

Just outside the city center in the Valle de Atongo neighborhood, Casa Bugambilia (Callejon Tepopula 007, Valle de Atongo, tel. 739/395-4229, www.casabugambilia.com; US$100) is a comfortable and family-friendly hotel with a warm and peaceful ambience. Guest rooms, arranged around the expansive central lawn and gardens, are comfortable and classically Mexican in style, with tile floors and wood furnishings. There's a small pool with lawn chairs and a decent on-site restaurant for breakfast in the morning or a beer in the afternoon.

One of the nicest hotels in town is the enchanting Posada del Tepozteco (Paraíso 3, tel. 739/395-0010, www.posadadeltepozteco.com.mx; from US$180). It's perched just above the main square, and from the gardens and guest rooms, there are breathtaking views overlooking the town and valley, as well as the towering bluffs to the north. The garden patio is a supremely pleasant place to sip a drink, and there's a pretty pool where you can swim on warm days. Accommodations are full of old-fashioned Mexican charm, with tiled walls and vintage wooden furnishings.

A great place to soak up the positive energy that abounds in Tepoztlán, La Buena Vibra (San Lorenzo 7, tel. 739/395-1491, www.hotelbuenavibra.com; from US$200) is a bit out of the center of town, but the point of staying here is precisely to get away from it all. Overlooking the bluffs of El Tepozteco, the ultra-relaxing grounds and gardens include a pool, a meditation room, and a spa. Beautiful guest rooms are designed with a touch of Asian aesthetic, including Buddha statues.

With incredibly lush, oasis-like gardens and striking views of the surrounding mountains, Amomoxtli (Prolongación Matamoros 115, Valle de Atongo, tel. 739/395-0012, https://amomoxtli.com, $250) is a destination in itself. Spacious guest rooms have an earthy elegance that befits their Tepotzlán location, some with private patios or balconies. The on-site restaurant is also among the town's best, and guests can order a private dinner in their room or at the pool bar. Note that this is an adults-only property.

TRANSPORTATION

Autobuses Pullman de Morelos (Av. 5 de Mayo, tel. 739/395-0520 or 55/5549-3505, www.pullman.mx; US$7) and Omnibuses Cristóbal Colón (operated by ADO, www.ado.com.mx; US$10) run regular buses every 30 minutes 6:30am-9:30pm to and from the Taxqueña terminal in Mexico City (Av. Taxqueña 1320). The trip takes about 1.5 hours, and drops you off just outside of town (take a taxi to the center of town from there). By car, it's an easy hour drive from the capital, departing via Insurgentes Sur.

BACKGROUND

The Landscape

GEOLOGY

Mexico City is located in the Valle de México, an alpine basin surrounded by volcanic mountains, which measures a considerable 2,200 meters at its lowest point. The valley is on the southern edge of a great plateau known as the Mexican Altiplano, which extends from the United States border to the Trans-Mexican Volcanic Belt, just south of Mexico City. Several of Mexico's highest peaks—including the famous twin volcanoes of Popocatépetl (5,465 meters) and Iztaccíhuatl (5,230 meters)—rim the valley to the south and southeast.

Bucarelli Fountain in a traffic circle on the Paseo de la Reforma

The Valle de México was once covered by a series of broad, shallow lakes, which have been largely drained in the past 500 years; today, much of the city is built atop spongy dry lakebed. The unstable earth makes the city more susceptible to damage during seismic tremors. Earthquakes are frequent throughout the region, largely generated by the subduction of the Cocos tectonic plate beneath the North American plate, on Mexico's Pacific coast. Because of the interaction between earthquake wave movement and the valley's weak subsoil, Mexico City sometimes feels the effects of a coastal quake more than places closer to the quake's actual epicenter. Such was the case in the deadly 1985 earthquake, the epicenter of which was more than 160 kilometers away.

SEPTEMBER 19: A CITY CHANGED

Volunteers staff an emergency command center following the 2017 earthquake in Mexico City.

SEPTEMBER 19, 1985

At 7:18am on September 19, 1985, Mexico City trembled violently for more than three full minutes, as an 8.1 magnitude earthquake rippled across central Mexico. In Mexico City, where the water-rich sediment below the streets is highly susceptible to movement, the ground trembled so violently that it led to soil liquefaction, creating waves of movement that were, ominously, particularly traumatic to taller buildings.

In those three minutes, hundreds of buildings came crashing to the ground while drainage pipes and gas mains burst beneath the streets, contaminating the water supply and causing fires and explosions throughout the city. The death toll was massive, though never definitively determined, with estimates ranging from at least 10,000 to more than 35,000. Tens of thousands more were injured and over 100,000 left homeless. Exacerbating the situation, important medical centers were among the 3,000-plus

Contributing to seismic activity, the Trans-Mexican Volcanic Belt remains active, with eruptions from nearby volcanoes sending tremors (as well as toxic dust) through the capital. The main culprit is Popocatépetl, the most active volcano in the region, which has had several notable eruptions since the 1990s, requiring the evacuation of people living in its foothills. In July 2013, the volcano spewed enough dust and ash that airlines had to cancel their flights for 24 hours.

HYDROLOGY

Before the Mexica arrived in the Valley of Mexico and began the centuries-long projects of damming its lakes, the water level fluctuated dramatically throughout the year, depending on rainfall. In the late 15th century, Nezahualcóyotl, the poet-king of Texcoco, oversaw the construction of a massive dike dividing Lake Texcoco into two halves, one salty and one fresh, as a means of controlling floods. In Tenochtitlan, a system of canals was built for drainage control and transportation, while freshwater

buildings that were seriously damaged during the quake. Just a day later, a massive aftershock of almost equal magnitude amplified the destruction.

The federal and municipal governments were overwhelmed by the scale of the tragedy, and the people of Mexico City became important first responders, with civilians risking their lives to dig through the rubble of fallen buildings to find survivors. Citywide, and with uncharacteristic disregard for social divisions, people offered homes to neighbors, distributed food, and helped to bring order to the devastated city.

The earthquake of 1985 left a lasting mark on Mexico City. In 2010, the city commemorated the earthquake's 25th anniversary in a ceremony overseen by the head of government Marcelo Ebrard and President Felipe Calderón. They dedicated a plaque to the victims along the Alameda Central, where the historic Hotel St. Regis stood before crashing to the ground during the earthquake.

SEPTEMBER 19, 2017

Every September 19 at 11am, in commemoration of the 1985 earthquake and to test the city's first-response system, there is an official earthquake safety drill throughout Mexico City. On September 19, 2017, the drill was performed with particular solemnity, as an 8.1 magnitude earthquake had recently hit the Mexican coast near Oaxaca, shaking the capital violently and destroying coastal towns along the Isthmus of Tehuantepec.

Incredibly, just a few hours after the drill, a 7.1 magnitude earthquake hit central Mexico, with an epicenter just 120 kilometers outside the city, in the state of Puebla. Schools, offices, and apartment buildings in the Roma, Condesa, Del Valle, Tlalpan, Iztapalapa, Coyoacán, and Xochimilco neighborhoods collapsed during the quake, while thousands more structures were declared uninhabitable in the days that followed, leaving many people homeless. As in 1985, the most important first responders were the people of Mexico City, who organized rescue efforts in fallen buildings (successfully pulling many survivors from the rubble), delivered supplies across the city via bicycle brigades, and operated emergency shelters and collection centers around the clock. Many of the young people who enthusiastically volunteered during the aftermath of the earthquake were the sons and daughters of the very same people who volunteered after the 1985 quake.

was brought in by aqueduct from Chapultepec.

As part of his final assault on the Mexica in 1521, Cortés ordered the breaching of Tenochtitlan's dams in an attempt to destroy the city. After the Mexica defeat, the Spaniards left the dike in ruins when they rebuilt the city, and as a result saw their new colonial capital flooded repeatedly. It was not until 1900, with the construction of the Gran Canal de Desagüe (Great Drainage Canal) under President Porfirio Díaz, that the waters of Lake Texcoco were finally emptied.

Currently the only major bodies of water in the valley are small tracts of Lake Xochimilco in the south, the lakes in Chapultepec, and the remnants of Lake Texcoco northeast of the city, in the state of Mexico. The rivers that once flowed into the valley from the western mountains—such as Río Mixcoac, Río de la Piedad, Río Tacubaya, and Río Churubusco—still exist but are canalized and sealed under major avenues, eventually draining into one of the five canals on the east side of the city, which in turn flow out of the valley to the northeast.

The soggy earth below the city has contributed to the capital's rapid sinking: In the Centro Histórico, you may notice old stone buildings are cracked or tilting, some to the point of becoming uninhabitable. Some neighborhoods have dropped an estimated 7.5 meters in the last century alone! Air quality is also affected; the dried lakebeds in the northeast part of the valley create swirling clouds of dust that are swept up into the atmosphere and moved to the southwest directly across the city by the prevailing winds, worsening the air pollution.

CLIMATE

Altitude tempers Mexico City's tropical location, creating a remarkably pleasant climate year-round. During the spring and fall, daytime temperatures generally hover 22-23°C (72-73°F), dropping to 10-12°C (50-54°F) in the evening. The short winter season usually runs between December and February, and the weather is cooler throughout those months, especially at night. April, May, and early June are typically the warmest months, when the temperature slowly climbs until the rainy season begins.

As in most of central Mexico, Mexico City's climate can be divided into two distinct seasons: the dry season, which runs from November to May, and the shorter rainy season, from June to October. During the rainy season, flash floods, furious downpours, and even hailstorms pummel the capital, bringing everything to a halt. In most cases, these storms rarely last longer than an hour or two, and they help moderate the heat of the summer.

ENVIRONMENTAL ISSUES

Mexico City's 20-million-plus population has had a substantial impact on the environment in the Valle de México. There is a growing environmental consciousness in the capital, and there have been some modest improvements in recent decades, but environmental problems remain one of the most substantial issues facing the city.

AIR QUALITY

A semiopaque haze of yellowish smog lingers above Mexico City most days, blocking the view of the surrounding mountains. The city's well-publicized air pollution problems hit an all-time high in the late 1980s and early 1990s; though the city has made progress in improving the environment, air quality is an ongoing problem in the capital. The winter months are the worst, when there are fewer and lighter air currents.

Automobile traffic is the number one contributor to air quality problems in the greater Mexico City metropolitan region. To help address air quality, the local government has implemented several programs, including tighter vehicle emissions checks, reforestation projects, and a program to restrict driving, called "Hoy No Circula," which restricts the number of cars on the road.

Mexico City surveys its Metropolitan Air Quality Index (Índice Metropolitana de Calidad de Aire, or IMECA) every day, measuring the city's levels of ozone, carbon monoxide, carbon dioxide, lead, sulfur, and other contaminants. You can track the daily IMECA readings in most local newspapers or on-line or at the website maintained by the Mexico City Secretaría de Medio Ambiente (Environment Secretariat) at www.sma.df.gob.mx.

WATER

Mexico City consumes 3.5 million cubic meters of water every day, twice the level of many industrialized countries. Poor infrastructure is an unfortunate contributor to usage; it is estimated that 40 percent of the city's water supply is lost through leaky pipes before it reaches household taps.

Because of the dwindling aquifers, about 20 to 30 percent of the city's water is pumped uphill 1,000 meters from the Lerma and Cutzamala Rivers, 100 kilometers to the west. As a result, not only is the Mexico City water table dropping, but water shortages are increasing all around central Mexico. About 20 percent of Mexico City's residents do not have consistent access to tap water, with some residents relying almost entirely on water delivered by truck. A reforestation program along the banks of the dwindling Lago de Texcoco has helped to cut back on dust and to recycle carbon dioxide, and it may also speed efforts to reclaim more rainwater in the lake basin.

History

PRE-COLUMBIAN HISTORY
EARLY CIVILIZATIONS

More than 30,000 years ago, the majority of the North American continent was covered in sheets of ice. Amid this forbidding landscape, the first human settlers are believed to have migrated from Siberia to North America via a narrow land bridge across the Bering Strait. These first people were followed by another wave of migrants, likely of Asian descent, who eventually migrated to the southern reaches of the Andes Mountains of South America.

Eventually, tribes of hunter-gatherers began to organize into communities—there is evidence of living sites dating back over 20,000 years—in a region known as Mesoamerica, a culturally linked swath of territory that covers southern Mexico, Belize, Guatemala, Honduras, El Salvador, and Nicaragua. Although the American population was now physically isolated from Eurasia, they independently developed farming techniques, with maize cultivation dating back 9,000 years.

THE FIRST INHABITANTS OF THE VALLEY

Groups of nomads arrived in the Valle de México sometime around 20,000 BC. Over the next several thousand years, the valley's population grew to rely on gathering fruits and grains, especially maize, until agricultural societies established themselves in the third millennium BC.

The agricultural revolution created profound changes in social

NEZAHUALCÓYOTL: THE POET, THE CITY

a statue of Nezahualcóyotl in Chapultepec park

When the city of Tenochtitlan rose to power during the 15th century, the Mexica formed a strategic alliance with the Nahuatl-speaking people of Tlacopan and Texcoco on either side of their island city. At that time, the great Nezahualcóyotl ruled the Acolhua people of Texcoco. As *tlatoani* (monarch), Nezahualcóyotl was a visionary city planner and engineer, responsible for designing the massive dam in Lake Texcoco that prevented the annual flooding in Tenochtitlan, as well as the aqueduct that brought freshwater to the city from Chapultepec. He was reputed to be a great lover of nature,

organization. Between 1500 and 650 BC, the villages around the valley's lakes grew. The first full-fledged city to develop was Cuicuilco, centered around a pyramid site located at what is now the junction of Insurgentes Sur and Periférico Sur. By 100 BC a second city was growing at Teotihuacán in the north. Cuicuilco had already begun to decline when its existence was dramatically cut short when Volcán Xitle exploded and covered Cuicuilco with beds of lava.

TEOTIHUACÁN AND THE CLASSIC PERIOD

Characterized as an era of great human advancement, the Classic period in Mesoamerica began about AD 250-300. During the early Classic period, an unknown people founded the city of Teotihuacán in the Valley of Mexico. Teotihuacán's largest structure, the 70-meter Pyramid of the Sun, was completed around AD 100, though the city reached its peak several hundred years later. With an estimated population reaching 150,000 (and possibly more), Teotihuacán's influence reached throughout Mesoamerica. It was overtaken and destroyed around AD 800, though its lofty pyramids remain standing today.

As Teotihuacán declined, the great Maya and Zapotec people flourished in the south of Mexico, from AD 200 to 1000. Though their city-states and vast empires had little direct influence on the Valley of Mexico, the Maya aesthetic and

and some of the oldest *ahuehuetes* (cypresses) in the Bosque de Chapultepec were said to have been planted by Nezahualcóyotl during his lifetime. He is also remembered, perhaps most reverently, as a great poet and philosopher. Much of the classic Nahuatl verse has been attributed to him, often ruminations on war, the divine, and the ephemeral nature of human life. Many of Nezahualcóyotl's moving *cantos* (songs) have been etched into the stone patio at the Museo Nacional de Antropología.

Today, not far from where he once ruled the Acolhua, a massive urban settlement bears the poet-king's name. Ciudad Nezahualcóyotl, located on the southeast fringe of Mexico City, was built atop the drained bed of Lake Texcoco in the early 20th century, right after the Xochiaca Dam was erected, exposing new dry land for development. Urban services were slow to arrive in the area, but people were not. Even without electricity, by the 1950s the suburban community had a population of 40,000, comprising mostly poor immigrants from the rural countryside. Despite ongoing problems with land titles in the area, Ciudad Neza continued to grow unchecked throughout the 20th century, finally garnering some public services like paved roads and potable water when it became an official municipality in the 1960s, though even these basic services weren't a given.

Ironically, Nezahualcóyotl the man is a symbol of high-mindedness and visionary leadership, while the city that bears his name characterizes the modern metropolis's failures in urban planning. In Ciudad Neza, massive immigration and a lack of city services gave way to slumlike conditions for many residents during the late half of the 20th century. With a population of well over a million people, it is now one of Mexico's biggest cities (though considered part of the greater Mexico City metropolitan region), but it has long been plagued by poverty, extortion, drugs, and gang wars. In recent decades, Neza has begun to modernize, and there is new industry in the area, but it remains a place largely representative of the massive and uncontrolled settlement of the city.

philosophical legacy, as well as their skill in astronomy and mathematics, had a notable impact throughout the region.

THE TOLTECS AND THE POST-CLASSIC

After AD 1000, Maya and Zapotec cities began to decline, as new tribes descended from the north. Among these, a bellicose people known as the Toltec dominated central Mexico about AD 800-1000, controlling trade routes from the huge city-state of Tollan, now called Tula, in present-day Hidalgo. The Toltecs controlled the Valley of Mexico, though their reach extended as far north as Zacatecas and as far south as Guatemala. Similarities in the architecture of post-Classic Maya cities and Tula have also prompted debate about the interaction between these peoples, suggesting that the Toltec may have been involved in the building of great post-Classic cities like Chichen Itzá.

The Toltec civilization never reached the heights achieved by Teotihuacán and began to decline after AD 1200. After suffering successive invasions from the Chichimeca tribes to the north, Tula was eventually abandoned.

THE MEXICA AND EL GRAN TENOCHTITLAN

After the decline of Tula, there was increased migration into the Valley of Mexico. In 1250, the powerful cities of Azcapotzalco, Culhuacan, and Texcoco controlled much of the area when a nomadic northern tribe known as the Mexica (pronounced meh-SHEE-ka) arrived in the valley. According to legend, these people originally came from the city of Aztlán, thought to be on the coast of modern-day Nayarit; for that reason, historians began calling them the Aztecs, though the Mexica people never used that name.

After years of enslavement and attacks on their settlements, the Mexica eventually founded a city on an uninhabited island not far from the shore in Lake Texcoco, which they named Tenochtitlan. According to legend, the Mexica knew that they were meant to settle the island when they saw an eagle perched on a cactus with a snake in its beak (a rendering of that vision is at the center of the Mexican flag). Courageous warriors, the Mexica eventually gained dominance over the valley, vanquishing their chief rivals, the Tepanecs, with the assistance of the great Nezahualcóyotl of Texcoco, and establishing a strategic triple alliance with the cities of Texcoco and Tlacopan under their fourth emperor, Itzcóatl.

In the generations following Itzcóatl's rule, the Mexica started to rewrite their own history, identifying the Toltecs as their spiritual ancestors and downplaying their nomadic past. Moctezuma I, who took power in 1440 after Itzcóatl's death, embarked on an expansionist program that brought much of the Valley of Oaxaca and the Gulf Coast regions under Mexica control. During the next generations of Mexica rulers, almost all of central Mexico fell under their sway, with the exception of a few regions

that maintained their independence, notably the Tlaxcaltecas and Chollulans to the east. By the time Moctezuma Xocoyotzin, or Moctezuma II, took power, in 1502, the Mexica were the ruling power in Mesoamerica.

As the center of the empire, the city-state of Tenochtitlan grew rich and splendid, demanding lavish tributes of food, clothing, tools, and jewelry from the hundreds of cities it controlled. Upper-class Mexica dressed in embroidered tunics decorated with feathers, and their boys were sent to schools called *calmécac* (children of regular civilians were also sent to vocational schools, to learn the craft of their community, in addition to natural history and religion). Adjacent to Tenochtitlan, and eventually linked to it by continual landfill projects, the smaller island of Tlatelolco was the empire's principal market center, ruled by its own line of kings.

Tenochtitlan itself was large, orderly, and clean. Laid out in an organized grid pattern, it was crisscrossed by a system of canals, which allowed for drainage during the flood season and also provided the principal means of transportation to and from the mainland via canoe. At the center of the city was a stepped pyramid-temple, today called the Templo Mayor, which was the principal religious monument in the city. Indeed, religion was central to life in Tenochtitlan. Huitzilopochtli, the god of war, and Tlaloc, the god of rain, were central figures in their pantheon. The Mexica fed Huitzilopochtli's favor by performing human sacrifices in their temples—a practice common throughout Mesoamerica but brought to new heights in Tenochtitlan. The Mexica often sacrificed prisoners of war brought home from their many battles, with massive sacrifices taking place on festival days.

SPANISH CONQUEST AND THE COLONIAL ERA
THE CONQUEST

After Christopher Columbus's 1492 voyage to the Indies, Iberian conquest of the Americas swiftly began. The Spaniards first took control of several Caribbean islands, principally Hispaniola and Cuba, where the native population was enslaved and largely died out after a few generations, owing to disease and depression. During that time, several Spanish envoys discovered the existence of richer "islands" to the east, populated by civilizations more advanced than those in the Indies. Rushing to gain control of these new territories, Cuban governor Diego Velázquez chose a young Spaniard named Hernán Cortés from Medellín, Spain, to lead a reconnaissance expedition to the Mexican coast.

Cortés accepted the post, amassing a huge group of volunteers to accompany him on the voyage. Sensing Cortés's growing power and insubordination, Velázquez attempted to cancel Cortés's appointment, but Cortés sailed anyway, bringing 11 ships and close to 500 men with him. He landed first in Cozumel, then touched down along the Gulf Coast, where he battled local Chontol Maya people, who didn't comply with Cortés's repeated demands for food and gold. It was here that Cortés first heard of the Mexica and Emperor Moctezuma.

After destroying his boats (thereby forcing dissenting Spanish soldiers to join the conquest), Cortés made his way to Tenochtitlan, gathering Mexica enemies as his allies along the way. Moctezuma had already received detailed reports about the Spanish arrival, and descriptions had led him to fear Cortés was the embodiment of the god Quetzalcóatl. When the Spanish arrived in Tenochtitlan, Moctezuma allowed them to enter the city as protected guests.

Several weeks went by without event, but tensions brewed. When Cortés returned to the Gulf Coast to fight off a brigade of soldiers sent by Velázquez, Pedro de Alvarado was left in charge, and he led a misguided massacre of 200 Mexica nobles at the festival of Tóxcatl. Cortés returned, but the situation between the Spanish and the Mexica was now irreparable. During this time, Moctezuma was also killed under unknown circumstances while being held hostage by the Spanish. Trying to escape under the cover of darkness and in possession of as much gold and jewelry as they could carry, the Spanish lost hundreds of soldiers to angry Mexica attackers while trying to flee the city in a massacre remembered as the Noche Triste (Night of Sorrows).

Playing on the widespread resentment of the Mexica throughout the region, the Spanish recruited help from many tribes near Tenochtitlan and regrouped their forces. The Spanish were further assisted by the smallpox virus, which they had unwittingly introduced to the Americas. In a matter of weeks, thousands of native people fell sick and died, including Moctezuma's successor, Cuitláhuac.

After months of preparation, the Spanish launched a waterborne attack on Tenochtitlan in 1521. Months of conflict ensued, concluding with a siege of the city. Led by Moctezuma's cousin, Cuauhtémoc, the Mexica resisted the Spanish, even as they ran low on both food and water supplies. Finally, Cortés and his military forced the Mexica to flee to the adjoining community of Tlatelolco, where they were overcome. The Spanish razed Tenochtitlan and built a new city on its ruins. Victorious, the Spanish named their new city Mexico, capital of New Spain. In 2021, Mexico City observed 500 years since the conquest and the founding of the modern city.

NEW SPAIN

Under the direction of Alonso García Bravo, a new Spanish city was constructed, borrowing much from Tenochtitlan's highly organized street plan. As they worked, the Spanish built a temporary capital in the community of Coyoacán, which had been an ally during their siege of Tenochtitlan. The first viceroy of Mexico, Don Antonio de Mendoza, took his post in 1535.

The conquest and colonization were brutal for native people, both physically and culturally. Where they encountered resistance, the Spanish used ruthless tactics to subdue native tribes. Many Indigenous people were enslaved, while others succumbed to foreign disease. As a result of these changes, the native population dropped significantly during the early years of New Spain.

Fifteenth-century Spain was a deeply Catholic place, entrenched in the Inquisition at the time Cortés conquered Tenochtitlan. Converting the native population to Catholicism was a top priority for the Spanish crown (and a justification for colonization), and as early as the mid-1520s, missionaries had founded settlements in Mexico City and in the surrounding communities.

In addition to seeking converts, the Spanish came to Mesoamerica in search of wealth and fortune. To encourage settlement, the crown doled out land grants throughout the territories, and Spanish families established large haciendas, clearing the native land for agriculture and cattle grazing. Having admired the gold and silver jewelry worn by Mexica nobles, the Spanish aggressively sought precious metals within the craggy Sierra Madre. Fortuitously, a Spanish expedition discovered a large silver vein outside the modern-day city of Zacatecas in 1546. Several more bountiful silver veins were discovered shortly thereafter.

The discovery of silver changed the power dynamic in the colonies, giving the colonies massive trading power with Europe. All of the immense quantities of silver mined in New Spain passed through Mexico City, where merchants had an official monopoly on all trading in the colony. As a result of these advantages, the city grew immensely wealthy and came to be known throughout Europe as *la ciudad de los palacios* (the city of palaces). With the decline of the silver industry in the late 17th and early 18th centuries, Mexico City's economy stagnated, though the last decades of the 18th century saw a burst of reformist zeal under the new Bourbon kings.

Throughout the colonial era, society was highly stratified: Spaniards born in Spain were afforded the highest place in society and were consistently appointed to all of the most important political posts. Mexican-born people of Spanish heritage were referred to as *criollos* and, despite their common heritage, had a lower social and political standing. *Mestizo* people of mixed ethnic heritage held a far lower place in society, only better than the abysmal position of Indigenous workers and slaves.

INDEPENDENT MEXICO

THE WAR OF INDEPENDENCE

After close to 250 years of Spanish rule in the Americas, Bourbon king Charles III ascended the Spanish throne. A believer in "enlightened absolutism," he made dramatic changes to the governance of New Spain. Undermining the colony's economic autonomy, he established royal monopolies on seminal industries like tobacco, gunpowder, and mercury (needed for silver extraction). He also forbade church loans, which were a major source of credit within Mexican communities. Finally, he expelled the highly popular Jesuit order from Mexico. For many Mexicans—especially those who had already come to resent the colony's strict hierarchies and distant authority—these changes bred deep resentment.

Mexico's struggle for independence began on September 16, 1810, when Padre Miguel Hidalgo y Costilla gave his famous *grito de la independencia* (cry of independence) from a church in Dolores, Guanajuato, where he and a group of *criollos* led the insurrection. After Hidalgo's capture and assassination, José María Morelos took charge of the army. He in turn was captured and executed. The battles continued for almost a decade until the government of Ferdinand VII was overthrown in Spain. As a result of the change in Spanish governance, Colonel Agustín de Iturbide, a fierce royalist, switched sides to join the Mexican army. With Iturbide at the helm, Mexico achieved independence with the Treaty of Córdoba in 1821. Mexico City, home of wealthy nobles, remained a royalist holdout during the struggle, firmly opposed to independence.

EARLY INDEPENDENT MEXICO

The end of the war was the beginning of a century of political unrest and instability in Mexico. After signing the Treaty of Córdoba, Mexico took its first steps toward establishing autonomy. Twenty-four states were named in the First Mexican Empire, with independence leader Agustín de Iturbide crowning himself emperor of Mexico. In 1824, Mexico City was officially designated the seat of the federal government.

Just eight months after Iturbide took control of the government, Vicente Guerrero and Antonio López de Santa Anna led a successful revolt against the government.

They established the first Mexican republic, and another hero of the War of Independence, Guadalupe Victoria, became the country's first president. Amid turmoil, Vicente Guerrero assumed the post of president when Guadalupe Victoria stepped down, though the conservative forces of General Anastasio Bustamante quickly ousted him.

MEXICAN-AMERICAN WAR

In 1831, Antonio López de Santa Anna was elected president. During this time, the United States was aggressively expanding westward, and U.S. citizens had begun to settle in Texas. When Mexico's constitution centralized power and abolished slavery in 1835, Texas declared independence. In response, Santa Anna sent troops to Texas. He sustained a major victory at the Alamo, but the brutality of the fighting galvanized Texans against the Mexican president. After numerous confrontations, the Texan army overpowered Santa Anna's forces.

On June 16, 1845, the United States annexed Texas, though the state's independence was never formally recognized by the Mexican government. When a skirmish broke out between Mexican forces and the U.S. military along the Texas border, President James Polk asked Congress to declare war. Aggressively recruiting new soldiers to join the effort, the United States advanced into Mexico under General Winfield Scott. After battles through the north, the army captured the important central city of Puebla, from which Scott's army launched an offensive on the capital. After numerous battles, Scott took control of Mexico City during the Battle of Chapultepec, when American forces invaded the castle on the Cerro de Chapultepec and raised their flag over the city.

The capital of Mexico was temporarily relocated to Querétaro, where Santa Anna signed the infamous Treaty of Guadalupe, which ceded half of Mexico's territory to the United States, including California, New Mexico, Arizona, Texas, Colorado, and Nevada.

REFORM AND FRENCH RULE

Santa Anna returned to power after the war, but he was overthrown in 1855 by a Zapotec lawyer named Benito Juárez. Among his most significant acts, Juárez abolished church property and amended the constitution to officially recognize freedom of religion. Juárez's presidency was repeatedly threatened by conservative and royalist forces, though he is remembered today as one of Mexico's most just and visionary presidents.

Juárez had a great impact on the layout and power structures in Mexico City. When he took the presidency, much of the Centro Histórico was controlled by large convents, including San Agustín, San Francisco, Santo Domingo, and La Merced. After seizing church properties under the Reform Laws, city officials demolished large parts of these religious compounds and repossessed their land. Remnants of the old convents still stand, but none are fully intact today.

Failing to oust liberals from power, conservative leaders conspired with the government of

VIRGEN DE GUADALUPE: A MARÍA FOR THE PEOPLE

According to oral history, on December 12, 1531, the image of a dark-skinned Virgin Mary appeared to Juan Diego Cuauhtlatoatzin, speaking to him in his native Nahuatl language and asking him to build a shrine in her honor on the hill at Tepeyac, previously the site of a Mexica pyramid dedicated to the goddess Tonantzin. Church authorities initially ignored Juan Diego's entreaties, but the Virgin appeared to him again, instructing him to gather roses in his cloak and carry them to the bishop.

Following her instructions, Juan Diego returned to the bishop and opened his cloak before the assembled clergymen; inside, there was a detailed image of the Virgin Juan Diego had described. The bishop was dazzled, declaring it a miracle, and construction of the church at Tepeyac began. Today, Juan Diego's cloak hangs in the modern **Basílica de Santa María de Guadalupe.**

image of the Virgen de Guadalupe in Basilica de Santa María de Guadalupe

The story of a Nahuatl-speaking Mary is believed to have been a watershed moment for Christianity in the Americas, inspiring mass conversion to Catholicism in Mexico City. Thereafter, miracles were repeatedly attributed to the Virgin's influence, and the Virgen de Guadalupe became a symbol of the colonies. During the Mexican War of Independence, famous insurgent Miguel Hidalgo used a banner with the image of the Virgin of Guadalupe as a flag to lead the Mexican army into battle against the Spanish.

While the power of the image is immense, the truth of the origin story is debated. Little is known about the life of Juan Diego, and neither the Virgin of Guadalupe nor Juan Diego are mentioned in the surviving early colonial accounts from Mexico City. Some historians and authorities have questioned if Juan Diego existed at all. On the other hand, there are numerous curiosities on the cloak itself. According to some studies, the 47 stars in the image represent the exact constellations seen over Mexico on the night of the winter solstice in 1531. The pigments are also of unknown origin and unusual for the time period in which the narrative took place.

Today, the shrine to the Virgin of Guadalupe is the second-most-visited Catholic pilgrimage site in the world, after the Vatican, with an estimated six million people visiting each year (including 300,000 visitors arriving on her feast day, December 12). Saint Juan Diego was canonized by Pope John Paul II on July 31, 2002, as the first Indigenous American saint.

France to overthrow Juárez's government. France invaded Mexico under Napoleon III and, after a disastrous defeat in Puebla, came back to successfully overwhelm Juárez's forces. The French established the Second Mexican Empire, placing Emperor Maximilian I of Austria in charge. During his brief rule, Maximilian and his wife, Carlota, claimed the Castillo de Chapultepec as their residence, redesigning it in a grand European style. To link the new palace with downtown, the Paseo de la

Reforma (originally the Paseo de la Emperatriz), now the city's broadest boulevard, was laid out.

In 1867, there was yet another successful uprising by the liberals; Maximilian was executed in Querétaro. Benito Juárez returned to the presidency, and he remained in power until his death in 1872.

MODERN MEXICO CITY
THE PORFIRIATO

Not long after Juárez's successor, Sebastián Lerdo de Tejada, had won his second election, army general Porfirio Díaz took office in a coup. A hero in the war against the French, Porfirio Díaz was a liberal from Oaxaca, but his politics changed in office. He became a powerful and conservative political leader with a strong military outlook. Fascinated by European aesthetics, he spent lavishly on city infrastructure and architecture in the European style.

Under Díaz, Mexico City began to expand beyond the Centro Histórico. The first neighborhoods established outside downtown were Guerrero and San Rafael, north and west of the Alameda, in the 1850s and 1860s, followed by the development of the San Cosme and Santa María la Ribera farther west, and later the Juárez and Cuauhtémoc on either side of the newly chic Paseo de la Reforma. The Colonia Roma, just to the south, followed.

Díaz held the presidency for 26 consecutive years, a period known as the Porfiriato. Under Díaz's dictatorship, Mexico entered into an era of relative stability, though the regime's despotic tendencies did not play out positively for the majority of Mexicans. While the country's wealth increased, social conditions for the poor worsened under Díaz's iron-fisted control.

THE MEXICAN REVOLUTION

After almost 30 years of the Porfiriato, wealthy politician Francisco I. Madero announced his presidential candidacy, in opposition to Díaz. President Díaz jailed him, and in return, Madero declared a revolt against the Díaz government on November 20, 1910, now remembered as the Day of the Revolution.

The Mexican Revolution was helmed by some of Mexico's most colorful personalities. Leading the *división del norte* (northern division), the wily and charismatic bandit Pancho Villa recruited thousands to the revolutionary cause. From the state of Morelos, Emiliano Zapata was a middle-class landowner who joined the revolution to promote land reform among peasants. Zapata rode to war dressed as a traditional Mexican *charro* (cowboy), with a wide-brim sombrero and thick moustache. He is still revered for his populist politics and his strong commitment to rural people and land rights.

Within six months, the people's army defeated Díaz's military. Madero initially took the presidency, but Victoriano Huerta ousted Madero in a coup. In response, Venustiano Carranza, Álvaro Obregón, Pancho Villa, and Emiliano Zapata led yet another revolt against Huerta's government. Villa and Zapata toppled Huerta's regime in August 1914.

Venustiano Carranza made a bid for the presidency, initially opposed by both Villa and Zapata. However, Carranza was able to win a broad base of support by promising constitutional reform. He oversaw the writing of the Constitution of 1917, which included land, law, and labor reforms. Carranza was eventually forced out of power by General Álvaro Obregón.

POST-REVOLUTIONARY MEXICO CITY

The post-revolutionary period was a time of great progress, culture, and intellectual achievement in Mexico. During Obregón's presidency, José Vasconcelos served as the secretary of public education, overseeing the establishment of the National Symphonic Orchestra as well as the famed Mexican mural program. Music and cinema flourished during the 1930s and 1940s, with Mexican movies outselling Hollywood films during World War II. During and after the Spanish Civil War, many European intellectuals took up residence in Mexico, adding to the thriving art and cultural community. Always the center of the republic, Mexico City was at the heart of this cultural movement, its artists, writers, thinkers, musicians, and actors gaining national and world-wide fame.

In a watershed moment in Mexican politics, Lázaro Cárdenas was elected to the presidency in 1937. Unlike his predecessors, Cárdenas enacted land reform and redistribution as laid out in the Constitution of 1917. In a move that would serve as a model for other oil-rich nations, Cárdenas expropriated oil reserves from the private companies that had been running them. He established Petróleos Mexicanos (Pemex), concurrently founding the National Polytechnic Institute to ensure a sufficient engineering force in the country.

EXPANSION AND POST-WORLD WAR II BOOM

Mexico City's population exploded during the 20th century. In 20 years alone, the population doubled, from 906,000 in 1920 to 1,757,000 in 1940. To cope with its new residents, the city expanded in all directions, with little planning. The government turned a blind eye to the impromptu settlements set up by rural immigrants, which would eventually become entire cities in their own right, and freely gave out permits to build new, upscale neighborhoods for the wealthy.

The construction of the new national university complex in the early 1950s, along with the expansion of Avenida Insurgentes to connect it to the city center, led to the buildup of the entire southwestern quadrant of the city in just a few short years. Wide-open fields south of the Roma were quickly converted into the Del Valle and Nápoles neighborhoods. In the early postwar years the formerly outlying villages of Mixcoac, San Ángel, Tacuba, Tacubaya, and Coyoacán were formally incorporated into the city limits. To the north, the industrial areas grew quickly. When the middle-class suburb Ciudad Satélite was built with great optimism in the late 1950s, it was surrounded by open land; in the years that followed, the city swallowed it completely.

The poor, rural immigrants flooding into the city didn't have money to buy property or houses, and so they simply erected shanty-towns in the less desirable, eastern side of the valley, once under the waters of Lake Texcoco. Over the years, these *ciudades perdidas* (lost cities) have become permanent cities. The classic *ciudad perdida* is Ciudad Nezahualcóyotl, which saw its population increase from 65,000 in 1960 to 650,000 in 1970 to over a million by the 1990s, making it one of the largest cities in the country.

THE 1960S AND THE TLATELOLCO MASSACRE

Mexico City was selected to host the Olympic Games in 1968. For Mexico's government, the Olympic Games were a major financial investment, as well as an important opportunity to boost the nation's economy and bring Mexico to the world stage. Mexican students saw the international publicity as an opportunity to draw attention to Mexico's one-party-rule government. There were widespread protests against the government in the months preceding the opening ceremony, many drawing tens of thousands of protestors.

Ten days before the Olympic Games were set to begin, thousands of students marched in protest to the Plaza de las Tres Culturas in Tlatelolco. The gathering was meant to be peaceful, but armed military troops were sent in, firing indiscriminately on the crowd. While the government stated that only four students had been killed, eyewitnesses saw hundreds of bodies. The official events were never fully uncovered, yet the massacre

a memorial to the massacre of 1968 in Mexico City's Zócalo in 2022

permanently tarnished the government's reputation with the people of Mexico City.

ECONOMIC CRISIS, NAFTA, AND THE ZAPATISTA MOVEMENT

In the early 1980s, falling oil prices and high worldwide interest rates created a massive recession in Mexico. President Miguel de la Madrid was forced to drastically cut government spending, the economy stagnated, and unemployment soared. Recovery was incredibly slow, with the GDP growing just 0.1 percent per year until 1988. The situation worsened for the capital after a massive earthquake on September 19, 1985. Measuring an 8.1 on the Richter scale, the quake shook Mexico City for three full minutes, during which time hundreds of buildings collapsed to the ground and around 10,000 people were killed (though some estimates put the number of fatalities much higher). There was major damage to infrastructure, leaving tens of thousands without potable water and hospitals inoperable.

Economic recovery began under the next president, Carlos Salinas de Gortari, who renegotiated the country's external debts and embarked on a policy of trade liberalization. By 1994, Mexico was economically stable enough to sign on as a member of the North American Free Trade Agreement (NAFTA). However, shortly after PRI president Ernesto Zedillo was sworn into office, Mexico's currency collapsed and recession returned. The U.S. Treasury and the International Monetary Fund put together a massive financial bailout. Under NAFTA, Mexico's economy has continued to grow annually, and trade between NAFTA nations has more than tripled.

The same morning that NAFTA went into effect, a small Indigenous army called the Ejército Zapatista de Liberación Nacional (Zapatista Army of National Liberation), or EZLN, took armed control of several cities in the southernmost state of Chiapas, including the historic capital of San Cristóbal de las Casas. Known as the Zapatistas (in a nod to Revolution hero Emiliano Zapata), this small but well-organized group of largely Indigenous revolutionaries declared war on the Mexican government, citing the years of poverty and oppression suffered by the country's native people. In response to the uprising, the Mexican government quickly dispatched thousands of troops to Chiapas, pursuing the EZLN as they retreated into the southern jungles, where the rebel army suffered heavy casualties.

This rebellion was small in scope but wide-reaching in consequences, inspiring support for Indigenous causes throughout Mexico—and the world. The army's unofficial leader, Subcommandante Marcos, became a national spokesperson for the Indigenous cause and, along with a convoy of EZLN leadership, met repeatedly with Mexican government leaders. In 2000, they marched peaceably to Mexico City, where they met with the federal government and were greeted by thousands of supporters.

PRI OPPOSITION: THE PRD AND THE PAN

In 1988, leftist politician Cuauhtémoc Cárdenas, son of post-Revolution president Lázaro Cárdenas, split from the monolithic ruling Partido Revolucionario Institucional party and announced his candidacy for president against Carlos Salinas de Gortari. Cárdenas was defeated in a highly suspect election, during which the voting systems failed to function for several hours. He lost another race against the PRI in 1994 but was elected mayor of Mexico City two years later, bolstering the notion that Mexico was ready for a change from the one-party system that had ruled since the early 20th century.

In the meantime, the conservative Partido Acción Nacional (PAN) had made inroads into politics. In the elections of 2000, popular support began to rally around the tall, mustachioed Vicente Fox Quesada, a former Coca-Cola executive. Campaigning on a ticket of change, Fox won a much celebrated victory over PRI candidate

Francisco Labastida. The PAN did not control the Congress, however, and Fox's presidency was marked by inefficiency. Fox's PAN successor, President Felipe Calderón, was elected in 2006, taking the office after winning by just one percentage point over the Party of the Democratic Revolution (Partido de la Revolución Democrática; PRD) candidate, Andrés Manuel López Obrador, in an election that was mired by controversy.

During his presidency, Calderón declared a war on drugs as a major spike in drug-related violence plagued much of northern Mexico, causing widespread instability and fear along the border with the United States, among other areas. Capitalizing on dissatisfaction with the PAN and the violence in Mexico, the PRI regained control of the executive branch with the election of Enrique Peña Nieto, former governor of the state of Mexico, to the presidency. Like his predecessor, Peña Nieto won over PRD candidate López Obrador, and protests against his legitimacy, though less widespread, were also fierce.

AYOTZINAPA

Violence, organized crime, and corruption continued to plague Mexico throughout Peña Nieto's presidency, with journalists, activists, and ordinary citizens the targets of extortion, murder, and disappearance. On September 26, 2014, university students from the Ayotzinapa teacher's college in the state of Morelos—an activist educational institution dedicated to teaching and advocating for the rural poor—boarded chartered buses to Mexico City, where they planned to attend a political protest commemorating the 1968 student massacre in Tlatelolco. In circumstances that have never been fully uncovered, their buses came under armed attack by police and organized crime in the city of Iguala. Six students died and 43 went missing without a trace.

Despite widespread public outrage and years of demonstrations, both national and international, there has never been a full account of what happened, and many continue to question the government's official version of events on the night of September 26, 2014. That said, the events of Ayotzinapa became a galvanizing moment in Mexican history, sparking massive public protest against Peña Nieto's government and human rights abuses in Mexico. For more information about this pivotal event in recent Mexican history, Reveal from the Center for Investigative Reporting and Adonde Media produced a three-part 2022 podcast "After Ayotzinapa" that chronicles the tragedy, the national reaction, and the investigation that followed, as well as the relationship between Ayotzinapa and the U.S. war on drugs.

MORENA AND AMLO PRESIDENCY

During his candidacy and controversial loss in the 2012 presidential elections, former Mexico City head of government and two-time PRD presidential candidate Andrés Manuel López Obrador founded a new leftist opposition party, Movimiento Regeneración Nacional, or Morena. López Obrador, popularly known as AMLO, entered the

2018 presidential race as Morena's candidate and won the presidency.

Claudia Sheinbaum, who was the secretary of the environment during AMLO's term as head of government in Mexico City, won the election to become the head of government in the capital, establishing Morena's newfound dominance in national politics.

Government and Economy

GOVERNMENT
THE FEDERAL REPUBLIC

As laid out in the Constitution of 1917, Mexico is a democratic republic. It is divided into 31 individually governed states, plus one *distrito federal* (federal district) in Mexico City. The federal government is divided into three branches: executive, legislative, and judicial. State governments are similarly divided into three branches and are elected locally.

LA CIUDAD DE MÉXICO

After independence, Mexico City was declared the seat of the national government. Though technically federal land, the Distrito Federal was divided into independent *municipios* throughout the post-Independence era. President Álvaro Obregón abolished the *municipios* altogether, dividing the city into *delegaciones* and uniting political power into a single body run by the federal government. Thereafter, the head of government of Mexico City was appointed directly by the president of the Mexican republic.

After seven decades as a badly managed appendage of the federal government, Mexico City's political reform began in 1989 with the birth of the Asamblea de Representantes del Distrito Federal (Legislative Assembly), housed in the old federal Congress in the Centro. After arduous negotiations, the city took its first step in modern democracy by voting for the first full elections of the assembly and *jefe del gobierno* (head of government, similar to a mayor) on July 6, 1997.

In Mexico City's first open elections for governor of the city, Cuauhtémoc Cárdenas won 47 percent of the vote. On top of that, Cárdenas's leftist Partido de la Revolución Democrática (PRD) swept every single assembly district in direct vote. The PRI, PAN, and the smaller parties were able to capture seats only by proportional representation. Two years later, Cárdenas stepped down to pursue a run for the presidency and was followed in the mayoralty by another leftist PRD politician, Andrés Manuel López Obrador.

Since the beginning of elections for *jefe del gobierno* in Mexico City, the post has always been filled by PRD politicians. Though they are not without controversy, the party's progressive, populist politics have made some notable changes to the Distrito Federal, such as the introduction of the new aboveground bus system called Metrobús, the development of a financial assistance program for single mothers and other vulnerable groups, and the restoration of much of the Centro Histórico. The PRD is also known for its socially progressive positions, which have led to the legalization of both same-sex marriage and abortion in the past decade.

In early 2016, the government announced that the Distrito Federal would now officially be named Ciudad de México, and that the city would be granted greater autonomy and more state-like powers, including the creation of a local congress and the drafting of a city constitution.

POLITICAL PARTIES
Movimiento Regeneración Nacional (Morena)
The Movimiento Regeneración Nacional, or Morena, was founded by then-presidential candidate Andrés Manuel López Obrador and his supporters in 2011 in response to corruption within the PRD party. It was officially registered as a political party in 2014 and quickly became a major national force, with candidates taking the presidency and the head of government in Mexico City in 2018. The most left-leaning of the major parties, Morena advocates environmental stewardship and human rights, including LGBTQ+ rights and the decriminalization of abortion, and opposes neoliberal economic policies.

Partido Revolucionario Institucional (PRI)
Although the Institutional Revolutionary Party no longer maintains unilateral power in Mexican politics, it remains one of the most important political parties in the country. After its losses in 2000, it regained majority in the legislature in 2003 and retook the presidency in 2012. The PRI was traditionally considered a leftist party, espousing many of the socialist viewpoints common to Latin American governments. Over time, it has become more centrist, especially in its new role as an opposition party.

Partido Acción Nacional (PAN)
The National Action Party is a traditionally conservative party, established in the 1930s to protect the rights of the Catholic Church. Economically, the PAN generally supports a market economy and free trade, and socially, they also toe a traditionally conservative line, opposing both same-sex marriage and abortion. The PAN grew strong among conservative voters in northern Mexico, and PAN candidates won the national presidency in 2000 and 2006.

Partido de la Revolución Democrática (PRD)
Until the founding of Morena, the Party of the Democratic Revolution was the most leftist of the major political parties in Mexico. The PRD grew out of the leftist opposition to the PRI, originally led by Cuauhtémoc Cárdenas. The party maintains an important presence throughout the country. It gained a national reputation through leadership in Mexico City, where PRD heads of government have instituted strong urban-planning programs.

Other Parties

Aside from the three major political organizations, smaller parties in Mexico include the Labor Party and the Green Party, which also have representation in the Congress. In many cases, these smaller political organizations will work together with one of the three major parties to back a candidate. In 2005, the Labor Party officially backed PRD presidential candidate Andrés Manuel López Obrador. In 2000 the Green Party joined the PAN in supporting Vicente Fox Quesada.

ECONOMY

Mexico City produces over 20 percent of Mexico's entire gross domestic product. Since the 1950s, Monterrey and Guadalajara have been developing industrial bases of their own, and in more recent decades, cities such as Puebla, Querétaro, Aguascalientes, Tijuana, and Toluca have been rapidly industrializing as well. But Mexico City completely controls the financial sector, as it's home to Bolsa Mexicana de Valores (the Mexican stock exchange) and all major banks and insurance companies. It also plays a big role in the service economy and is the headquarters of all of the dominant media and communications conglomerates.

THE INFORMAL ECONOMY

As they have for generations, many new immigrants to the city begin their new urban lives hawking their modest wares from any street corner not already occupied by another seller. Driven in part by a desire to clean up the downtown area, city authorities have begun regular patrols to evict unlicensed vendors in the city's central districts. In addition to *ambulantes,* there are thousands of housekeepers, nannies, cooks, chauffeurs, and other household employees working throughout the city as a part of the informal economy.

POVERTY

Mexico is a wealthy nation with abundant natural resources. Yet wealth is poorly distributed throughout the population, and vast extremes in the standard of living define the modern social landscape. Mexico City resident Carlos Slim was named the world's wealthiest person by *Forbes* magazine in 2010, yet 10 percent of Mexicans do not have access to sufficient food or medical care. According to government figures, more than 40 percent of Mexico's population lives below the poverty line. Mexico City, like the rest of the country, is a place of great extremes. You will see fashionable people dining in restaurants on a Monday afternoon, while children beg for change at a nearby traffic stop.

Local Culture

POPULATION

Accurate population statistics for Mexico City are difficult to obtain. According to the official 2020 census conducted by the National Institute of Statistics and Geography (Instituto Nacional de Estadística y Geografía; INEGI), there are 9,209,944 people living in Mexico City proper. If you extend the range to the entire metropolitan zone (which includes many densely populated areas of the state of Mexico adjacent the city, like the million-plus municipalities of Ciudad Nezahualcóyotl and Ecatepec de Morelos), the number is much higher. According to the Population Division of the Department of Economic and Social Affairs at the United Nations, the entire Mexico City metropolitan region has an estimated population of 21,581,000 inhabitants, making it the fifth-largest city in the world, just behind São Paulo.

Mexico City's growth has slowed considerably since the 1970s, when its population was expanding at an average rate of 4.5 percent per annum. Throughout the 2000s, the city's population grew negligibly (and more slowly than the country-wide growth rate of 1 percent), and the most recent census numbers even show more people emigrating from the city than immigrating to it. In general, the population growth of the past 30 years has been in the outer edges of Mexico City, while the population of the inner core has been declining steadily.

CLASS AND ETHNICITY

A large and multiethnic country, Mexico has suffered from racial and class divisions throughout most of its history. In the colonial era, Mexican society was highly stratified: The most privileged class was the *peninsulares,* pure-blooded Spaniards born in Spain, followed by *criollos,* pure-blooded Spaniards born in Mexico. *Mestizos,* of mixed Indian-Spanish heritage, and *indios* (Indigenous people) were afforded a lower social status and little political power.

Today, the vast majority of Mexicans are *mestizo,* or mixed race. Genetic studies have confirmed that most Mexicans are predominantly a mix of Spanish and Indigenous American heritage; however, *mestizo* implies a mixed ethnic background, and it may include other ethnicities. To a much smaller extent than in the United States or the Caribbean, some enslaved Africans were brought to New Spain during the colonial era, and they also mixed with the population. Mexicans of strictly European heritage, comprising about 10 percent or less of the population, are generally Spanish descendants, though there have also been other waves of European migrants to Mexico over the course of the country's history, including Irish, German, and French, among others.

In the country at large, about 8-10 percent of the population identifies as Indigenous, with around 6 percent speaking a native language.

Nahuatl, the modern version of which is similar to the language spoken by the Mexica and many other people in the Valley of Mexico and the surrounding regions before the Spanish conquest, is the most widely spoken Indigenous language in Mexico. Nonetheless, it's been more or less erased in the capital; fewer than 2 percent of people in Mexico City speak a native language.

Today, social stratifications are not entirely ossified, but social mobility is highly limited. In Mexico, your economic class will determine a great deal about your possibilities in life. Lack of opportunities and hard economic realities make it far more difficult for the rural or urban poor to improve their economic situation.

INDIGENOUS PEOPLE AND CULTURES

An estimated 30 million people were living in Mesoamerica when the Spanish arrived in the 15th century. Immediately following the conquest, the native population was drastically reduced, both through violence and through diseases introduced by European settlers. Though many ethnic groups disappeared entirely, a significant Indigenous population has survived to the present day, with the largest communities living in Oaxaca, Chiapas, Yucatán, Quintana Roo, Hidalgo, Puebla, and Morelos. About 6,700,000 people in Mexico speak an Indigenous language, and many communities in remote or rural areas have maintained native customs, craftwork, and dress.

Mexico City draws a large number of Indigenous immigrants, though their presence is largely subdued. You will rarely see people dressed in traditional clothing or speaking native languages, though there are some historic Nahuatl-speaking communities in the state of Mexico, as well in some of the small towns to the south of the city. For more information about Mexico City's Indigenous communities, the Asamblea de Migrantes Indígenas de la Ciudad de México (Assembly for Indigenous Migrants to Mexico City) hosts educational events, cosponsors conferences, and gives workshops, including classes in native languages, in support of native people living in the capital (http://indigenasdf.org.mx).

While most Mexicans are fiercely proud of the advanced societies of pre-Columbian Mexico, native people have been highly marginalized since the beginning of the colonial era. Today, predominantly Indigenous communities suffer from a lack of basic resources, education, and infrastructure. They are at a further disadvantage from a deeply embedded racism that has been perpetuated since the colonial area. Today, 75 percent of Indigenous people live below the poverty line.

WOMEN

In Mexico, women and men share equality under the law. Second-wave feminism arrived in Mexico in the 1960s, and there are numerous nonprofit organizations working to improve conditions for women, socially and politically. In 1994, the EZLN's rebel army included male and female soldiers and commanders and listed women's rights within its agenda for social justice. At the same time, the feminist movement in Mexico has never received a wide base of support.

There has traditionally been a large gender gap in Mexico's workforce, as many women leave school early in order to help out at home. In today's Mexico, economic realities, social changes, and increased education have changed women's relationship to the workforce, with women taking jobs in all sectors of society, from the small entrepreneur who cleans homes to the high-ranking political leader, as you'll see amply illustrated in Mexico City's workforce. At the same time, women earn less than men across the board and continue to play a larger role in the household.

HOMOSEXUALITY

Mexico is a generally accepting society, and most people are unlikely to raise a fuss about someone else's business. At the same time, the Catholic Church has traditionally opposed gay and lesbian relationships, making it less acceptable for homosexuals to come out within conservative Catholic households. Today, as in many aspects of society, Mexican attitudes toward homosexuality are becoming more liberal. In the capital, gay marriage was legalized in 2008, and gay couples may legally adopt children. Popular support for same-sex marriage is split, with about half the country backing it.

Generally speaking, the gay community is more visible and comfortably accepted in Mexico City than in most parts of Mexico. More and more, it is common to see same-sex couples holding hands while walking down the street or snuggling on a park bench.

RELIGION

After Cortés vanquished the city of Tenochtitlan, the Spanish razed the Mexica temples and built Catholic churches atop their remains. Coming from a deeply religious atmosphere in Spain (where the Inquisition was in full effect), colonial missionaries were active throughout New Spain, establishing an abundance of churches, Catholic schools, and hospitals. Throughout Spanish rule of Mexico, the Catholic Church was one of the country's biggest landowners and a major player in politics. There were massive conversions among the Indigenous population to Catholicism, which are said to have spiked after the apparition of the Virgin of Guadalupe in Mexico City in 1531. Today, according to INEGI, close to 85 percent of Mexicans identify as Catholic.

The Catholic Church continues to hold a very important place in Mexican society, even for those who aren't actively religious. Throughout the country, Catholic schools are among the best and most popular options in private education, while Catholic mass is the traditional celebration for life's milestones: baptism, important birthdays, marriage, and death. Catholic holidays are widely and exuberantly celebrated, with the entire country taking a vacation for Holy Week and Easter.

One religious icon common to all of Mexico is the Virgin of Guadalupe. Worship of the image began in the early colonial era, after Juan Diego Cuauhtlatoatzin was said to have witnessed a dark-skinned Virgin Mary in a series of three visions at Tepeyac, a hill in northern Mexico City. Today, many Mexican churches are named for Our Lady of Guadalupe, who has become fused with Mexican identity. The official feast day for Guadalupe, December 12, is widely celebrated in Mexico City and throughout the country. After years of controversy, Juan Diego, the Mexica man who saw the vision of the Virgen de Guadalupe, was declared a saint in 2002.

OTHER RELIGIOUS GROUPS

Mexicans who don't identify as Catholic are generally Protestants and Evangelicals, who number at about 7.5 percent of the population. The country also has a small historic Jewish community. The majority of Jewish immigrants arrived in Mexico from Syria, the Balkans, and Eastern Europe at the end of the 19th century and beginning of the 20th century. Today, an estimated 90 percent of the 40,000-50,000 Mexican Jews live in Mexico City, with notable communities in the Condesa, Polanco, and Santa Fe, among other areas. The Comite Central Israelita de México (www.tribuna.org.mx) is the best source of news, information, and statistics about Mexico City's Jewish community.

LANGUAGE

Mexico is the largest Spanish-speaking country in the world. The type of Spanish spoken in Mexico is usually referred to as Latin American Spanish, in contrast to the Castilian Spanish spoken in Spain. Still, the Spanish here differs significantly from that of even other Spanish-speaking countries in the Western Hemisphere. While English is widely spoken in the service industry, first-time visitors are often surprised by how little English one hears in Mexico City compared to what might be encountered at popular beach resorts in Mexico. Visitors should take the time to learn at least enough Spanish to conduct everyday transactions, like ordering food in restaurants or paying for a bus ticket.

Mexican Spanish, and especially Mexico City Spanish, is extremely rich with slang expressions, unique tones of voice, and hilarious wordplay, and it is immediately recognizable to any other Spanish speaker, both because of its distinct character and also because of the prevalence of Mexican television and movies throughout Latin America. Many anglicisms have crept into the Mexican language. For example, the common Latin American Spanish term for car is *coche,* but in Mexico you'll often hear *carro.*

Another distinctive aspect of Mexican Spanish is the great number of words incorporated from Indigenous Mexican tongues, particularly Nahuatl, the language spoken by the Mexica. Among notable examples, the word *chocolate* comes from the Nahuatl word *chocolatl. Coyote* is a derivation of the term *coyotl,* also from the Nahuatl. (Both of these words have also been transferred from Nahuatl to English.) In Mexico, many indigenous plants or animals, like the *guajolote* (wild turkey) and *mapache* (raccoon), are still more commonly referred to by their

Indigenous names. In addition, Mexico retained many Indigenous place-names after the conquest. Oaxaca, Guanajuato, Tlaxcala, and Cancún are a few of the many cities that have Castellan versions of the Nahuatl place-name—not to mention the name México itself, which took its name from the Mexica people of Tenochtitlan.

The Arts

Mexico has rich and varied traditions in music, literature, visual arts, architecture, and film, as well as robust traditions in popular art, textiles, craft, and clothing. Both traditional and contemporary forms are celebrated in Mexico City, with fine art museums, popular art museums, concert halls, galleries, and festivals enthusiastically attended by locals.

FILM

Though Mexicans have been making films since the genre was invented, the 1930s and 1940s are known as the golden age of Mexican cinema. During this era, Mexican directors prolifically produced feature films, even surpassing Hollywood in international success during World War II. The glamorous and charismatic film stars of the golden age—Mario Moreno Cantiflas, Tin-Tan, Dolores del Rio, Pedro Infante, and Maria Felix, among others—are some of the country's most beloved personalities. In the 1940s and 1950s, Spanish filmmaker Luis Buñuel made many of his most celebrated films in Mexico, including *Los Olvidados*. Mexican film output began to decline by mid-century, though a few experimental young filmmakers contributed to the country's canon, including Arturo Ripstein and Mexico-based Chilean-French filmmaker Alejandro Jodorowsky.

In the 21st century, Mexican film and filmmakers have made a prominent resurgence. In 2000, Alejandro González Iñárritu's widely acclaimed *Amores Perros* was heralded as the beginning of a new era in Mexican filmmaking, focused on gritty modern themes. The following year, Alfonso Cuarón's film *Y Tu Mamá También* was nominated for several Golden Globes and Academy Awards. Cuarón and González Iñárritu, like many of Mexico's filmmakers and actors, work extensively in Hollywood; González won Best Director at Cannes for his 2006 release *Babel,* while Cuarón took home the same prize for *Gravity* in 2014. Another lauded director from Mexico, horror film director Guillermo del Toro, won major accolades for 2008's *El Laberinto del Fauno (Pan's Labyrinth)* and 2017's *The Shape of Water.*

In 2018, Alfonso Cuarón put Mexico City in the spotlight for his Best Picture–winning movie *Roma*, a tribute to his childhood, featuring many scenes in the city's Roma, Condesa, and San Juan neighborhoods, including extensive footage of the house at 22 Tepeji Street in the Colonia Roma, located directly across from Cuarón's childhood home.

POPULAR ART AND CRAFTS

Mexico has celebrated traditions in popular art and handicrafts, or *artesanía*. Most Mexican craftwork relies on centuries-old techniques that unite pre-Hispanic and Spanish aesthetics. Among other disciplines, Mexico is famous for textiles, weaving, embroidery, ceramics and pottery, blown glass, baskets, woodworking, toy-making, hammered tin, lacquered wood, shoemaking, and tooled leather.

Like most aspects of Mexican culture, traditional handicrafts are highly specific to the region in which they are produced. In Puebla, for example, the Spanish introduced tin glazes and kiln-firing to skilled Indigenous potters. The resulting blend of traditions created a novel version of Spain's decorative Talavera ceramics, but with more color and whimsy. In Tonalá, Jalisco, artisans create an entirely different line of burnished and painted pottery, much of which can be used for cooking.

LITERATURE

Elaborate hieroglyphic books and a priest-dominated literary tradition existed in Mesoamerica before the arrival of the Spaniards. Writing in the beautiful Nahuatl language, the poet-king of Texcoco, Nezahualcóyotl, was a prolific crafter of verse, with many poems written by or attributed to him surviving today.

The fantastic chronicles of Spanish soldiers, explorers, and priests in the Americas show early expression of many enduring Mexican themes. Two examples of this genre, widely available in English translation, make for compelling reading. Bernal Díaz del Castillo's *Conquest of New Spain* is the memoir of a foot soldier in Cortés's military campaign against the Mexica empire. A very different view can be found in Bartolomé de las Casas's *Brevísima relación de la destrucción de las Indias* (Brief Account of the Devastation of the Indies), which details the astounding brutality that the invaders visited upon the people of what was then called "the New World." De las Casas, a priest who accompanied many expeditions, raised the first voice of protest against Spanish destruction of native peoples and cultures.

After the conquest, Mexican-born writers continued to make a distinguished contribution to literature in Spanish. Baroque dramatist Juan Ruiz de Alarcón and writer Carlos de Sigüenza y Góngora were two important literary figures during the colonial era, but they are both surpassed in reputation by the beloved baroque poet Sor Juana Inéz de la Cruz. *Respuesta a Sor Filotea* (Reply to Sister Philotea), in which she defends a woman's right to education, is a classic.

During the 20th century, Mexico's national character was more strongly reflected in its literary traditions. Writers like Rosario Castellano and Juan Rulfo began to describe a distinctly Mexican environment, exploring the country's identity and consciousness. Rulfo's most famous work, *Pedro Páramo,* influenced writers not only in Mexico but in all of Latin America.

In the 1990s, Mexican poet and essayist Octavio Paz received the Nobel Prize in literature. His meditation on the Mexican people, *The Labyrinth of Solitude,* is his most famous work, though he is also remembered as an able poet. Another excellent observer of Mexican character and society is Carlos Monsiváis, whose *Rituales del Caos* is a collection of essays on life in Mexico City; it's available in Spanish only.

Two Colombian writers, Gabriel García Marquéz and Álvaro Mútis, garnered international acclaim for their fiction, which was set in Latin American locales and imbued with a distinctly Latin perspective. The fact that these two literary stars chose to live and write in Mexico City says much about the capital's intellectual environment. Another novel by a Latin American literary star that takes place mainly in Mexico City is *Los Detectives Salvajes,* by Chilean expatriate Roberto Bolaño. It offers a surprisingly accurate portrait of the city's subcultures.

A new generation of young Mexican writers has begun to leave a mark on the literary scene. Notably, Jorge Volpi, a fiction writer and essayist, has not only reached a worldwide audience, he is now the head of culture at the Universidad Autónoma de México, overseeing the university's wide-reaching programs in the visual arts, music, dance, literature, and cinema.

MUSIC AND DANCE

Native Mesoamerican, African, and European musical traditions all contributed to the development of unique music and dance traditions. In Mexico, folk musical styles, or *sones,* developed in various regions, with diverse rhythms and instrumentation. From these *sones,* various genres of Mexican music flourished. Such song forms, like *huapango* from the Huasteca region, are still very popular throughout the country, though not often heard in Mexico City.

Mariachi, Mexico's most well-known musical ensemble, is a derivation of *son jarocho,* the musical genre from the state of Jalisco. Mariachi is characterized by its brassy sound and robust vocal style, as well as its impressive visual presentation. Dressed in formal *charro* suits and large sombreros, mariachi bands usually feature a lineup of violins, trumpets, guitars, bass guitars, and *jaranas* (a slightly larger five-string guitar). Mariachi music is a fixture at special events, like weddings or birthday parties, throughout Mexico.

Mariachis often play *rancheras,* traditional Mexican ballads, often covering nostalgic or patriotic themes. This song style became very popular in the late 19th and early 20th centuries, and again flourished in the 1940s and 1950s with popular *trío* bands such as Los Panchos and Los Diamantes.

One of Mexico's most popular and distinctive genres, *norteño* music grew out of the traditional *conjunto norteño,* an ensemble noted for its inclusion of the *bajo sexto* (a 12-string guitar) and the button accordion, an instrument that was introduced by German immigrants to northern Mexico. European styles, like polka and waltz, also influenced *norteño* music. Similar to *norteño*, the popular *banda* style incorporates more brass sounds. *Norteño* and *banda* groups, like the world-famous Los Tigres del Norte, have a massively popular following in both Mexico and the United States.

VISUAL ART AND ARCHITECTURE

Though most pre-Columbian cities were abandoned or destroyed by the 16th century, their ruins offer a glimpse into the accomplished architecture, city planning techniques, and artistic achievements of early Mesoamerica. The most distinctive features of Mesoamerican cities are the stepped temple-pyramids, seen in the Valley of Mexico at sites like Teotihuacán, which are often surrounded by wide public plazas and palaces.

As the Spanish began to colonize the Americas, they built new cities in the European style. Catholic missionaries and Jesuit educators were active throughout the country, and wealthy benefactors helped support their efforts by funding massive religious projects. Baroque art and design, which originated in Italy, formed the dominant aesthetic during the colonial era. Inside chapels, religious oil paintings and elaborate retablos (altarpieces) show enormous creativity and skill on the part of Mexican artists. Among the most famous names of the era, Indigenous artist Miguel Cabrera contributed hundreds of religious paintings to chapels in Mexico City, Guanajuato, and other colonial capitals.

The French occupation and the ensuing dictatorship of Porfirio Díaz also left a mark on the country's architecture, especially in the capital. Emperor Maximilian oversaw the construction of the Paseo de la Reforma in Mexico City, a large and central avenue that was designed to resemble a Parisian boulevard. During his decades of presidency, Porfirio Díaz followed in the emperor's footsteps, investing in buildings, monuments, and sculptures that would transform Mexico City into a European-style capital, which also included neoclassical buildings.

At the same time President Díaz was constructing marble monuments, a new and more national strain of art was emerging in Mexico. The wildly original printmaker José Guadalupe Posada produced political and social satire in lithography, woodcut, and linocut for local publications, often depicting Mexican aristocrats as *calaveras* (skeletons). His wry wit and whimsical aesthetic would become synonymous with Mexico, and today, his pieces are often used as illustration during Day of the Dead.

After the Revolution of 1910, art, culture, and intellectual thought flourished in Mexico. Through progressive movements in government, the folk arts began to receive institutional support, while a new, government-sponsored public murals program brought artists Diego Rivera, José Clemente Orozco, and David Alfaro Siqueiros to a greater public and international fame. American photographer Edward Weston spent extensive time living and working in Mexico, not long before Manuel Álvarez Bravo began photographing nationalistic scenes in Mexico, rising to international prominence. A fixture in Mexico City's political circles, Frida Kahlo was another expressive oil painter of the post-revolutionary era; she became internationally renowned for a series of powerful self-portraits.

Today, Mexico has a vibrant and growing contemporary art scene. Mexico's most celebrated international artist, Gabriel Orozco, presented a massive retrospective at the New York Museum of Modern Art in 2009, not long after he opened the gallery Kurimanzutto in the capital with a team of partners. The wildly famous British artist Damien Hirst lives part-time on the Mexican coast (and has exhibited in Mexico City), while Belgian artist Francis Alÿs lives and works in Mexico City. Collectors have also been important in stimulating Mexico's art scene, particularly Eugenio López Alonso, the owner of the Colección Jumex, a vast and important collection of Latin American and contemporary art.

ESSENTIALS

Getting There

AIR
AEROPUERTO INTERNACIONAL BENITO JUÁREZ DE LA CIUDAD DE MÉXICO

The Aeropuerto Internacional Benito Juárez de la Ciudad de México (tel. 55/2482-2424 or 55/2482-2400, www.aicm.com.mx) is on the east side of the city near Lake Texcoco. Both domestic and international flights leave from either of two main wings, Terminal 1 and Terminal 2, each used exclusively by different airlines. A light-rail track connects the terminals in case you end up on the incorrect side of the airport, though they are fairly distant; before leaving for the airport, check with your carrier to see which terminal your airline operates from.

Ecotaxi in Mexico City

Though it rarely gets much attention, inside the "Sala B" in Terminal 1, there is a mural by Mexican artist Juan O'Gorman illustrating the history of flight, from a Mexica nobleman eyeing the wings of a bat with curiosity to the Wright brothers and Charles Lindbergh.

AEROPUERTO INTERNACIONAL FELIPE ÁNGELES (AIFA)

In 2022, President Andrés Manuel López Obrador inaugurated a new airport 20 kilometers from the city center in the community of Santa Lucía in the state of Mexico, with the intent to reduce the congestion at AICM, which has long been running at maximum capacity. Two Mexican carriers, Volaris and Viva Aerobus are both running national flights out of the airport, to Cancún, Tijuana, Guadalajara, and Monterrey. At press time, Aeroméxico also had plans to begin operating national flights to and from Santa Lucía. No international flights are currently slated to open. There are plans to build a light-rail line connecting AIFA to Mexico City's center should boost the number of flights in and out of the new facility.

ALTERNATIVE AIRPORTS

In some cases, you can save a little bit of money by traveling to an airport near the capital, rather than flying directly into Mexico City itself. Notably, the international airport in Toluca (www.vuelatoluca.com) has become a popular inexpensive alternative for travelers heading to Mexico City from national destinations like Cancún, Acapulco, Guadalajara, and Los Cabos. You may also be able to find international flights to and from the city of Puebla on major carriers, though they are rarely much cheaper than flights directly to the capital.

GETTING TO AND FROM AEROPUERTO INTERNACIONAL BENITO JUÁREZ

Taxi

Registered taxis operate out of the airport, with service 24 hours a day, 365 days a year. Official airport taxis are more expensive than regular cabs, but they are the only legal option available (non-airport taxis

are not allowed to pick up passengers within the terminals).

There are several safe, registered taxi companies that operate out of the domestic and international wings in Terminal 1 and Terminal 2, which offer flat-rate prices to destinations throughout the city. There is little difference between one airport taxi company and another. Buy a ticket from one of the booths inside the airport terminal, then take your ticket curbside to the queue of waiting taxis, where attendants will take you to a car and help you load your luggage (it's customary to offer a small tip to the porters). Generally, taxis costs about US$15-20 to most central neighborhoods and several dollars more if heading south to Coyoacán or San Ángel.

Metro and Metrobús

If you're arriving in Mexico City between 6am and midnight and don't have a lot of baggage, you can take the Metro into town from the Terminal Aéreo station on Line 5. The station is just outside Terminal 1, on the Boulevard Puerto Aéreo, at the corner of Avenida Capitán Carlos León González. (Follow the signs for the Metro out of the airport; they look like a stylized letter *M*.)

The Metrobús also connects to the airport via an extension of Line 4. There are stops for the Metrobús heading into the city center at door 7 in Terminal 1 and at door 2 in Terminal 2. The first major hub on Metrobús Line 4 is the San Lázaro station, which connects to the Terminal Central del Norte bus station, as well as to the Metro. You can also continue on Line 4 to the Buenavista train terminal, which offers connecting service to the Metro, to Metrobús Line 1, or to the suburban trains to the state of Mexico. Metrobús operates roughly from 5am to midnight.

Intercity Bus

Several bus companies offer direct routes from the airport to the nearby cities of Toluca, Pachuca, Puebla, Cuernavaca, and Querétaro. They depart from the international wing of Terminal 1 and from the ground floor of Terminal 2. Follow the signs to the ticket counters. Most buses run every half hour or hour throughout the day, with more limited but continuing service at night. Rates and schedules are available on the airport's website (www.aicm.com.mx).

Driving

The airport is just off the eastern side of the Circuito Interior, an intercity highway that is easily accessible from most major neighborhoods in the center, west, and south of the city. The best route from most central neighborhoods is via the Viaducto, a highway that cuts east to west across the center of the city; just south of the airport, there is a left-hand exit onto the Circuito. Once on the Circuito, the airport exit is clearly marked, but follow signs to make it to the correct terminal and wing. There are parking lots in the domestic and international wing of Terminal 1 and in Terminal 2, with rates of about US$4 per hour and US$25 for 24 hours.

BUS

For both visitors and Mexicans, buses are the most popular and economical way to travel around Mexico. Dozens of private companies offer service to almost every corner of the country, with literally hundreds of buses leaving from and arriving in Mexico City every hour.

Unless you are going a very short distance, first-class or executive-class bus service is generally faster and more comfortable than second-class service. First-class buses have more comfortable seats, fewer stops, and in-cabin bathrooms—some even offer snacks and drinks for the ride. Second-class buses are 20 to 40 percent cheaper than first-class buses, and they are generally comfortable and safe. The disadvantage of second-class buses is that they rarely offer direct service between two cities. Instead, they stop at rural towns along their route to pick up and drop off passengers, adding considerably to travel time.

That said, second-class buses can be more convenient for shorter trips, with many bus lines offering frequent and inexpensive service between neighboring towns. In some cases, they are the only option to a more off-the-beaten-path destination.

INTERCITY BUS STATIONS

There are four major bus terminals in Mexico City, located at the four major exits from the city. Each is accessible by Metro, and some by Metrobús.

For northern destinations,

including Querétaro, San Miguel de Allende, Guanajuato, Zacatecas, Chihuahua, Monterrey, and Tijuana, buses depart from the Terminal Central del Norte (Eje Central Lázaro Cárdenas 4907, www.centraldelnorte.com). The Terminal Central del Norte is accessible via the Autobuses del Norte station on Metro Line 5.

Terminal Central Sur "Taxqueña" (Av. Taxqueña 1320) is a smaller station serving southern destinations, like Cuernavaca, Acapulco, and Taxco, accessible via Metro Line 2 Tasqueña station. Taxqueña also connects to the Tren Ligero (light-rail) to the southern neighborhoods of the city.

Terminal de Autobuses de Pasajeros de Oriente, better known as "TAPO" (Calz. Ignacio Zaragoza 200), offers service to eastern and southeastern cities, like Oaxaca and Puebla. To get there, take Metro Line 1 or Metrobús Line 4 to the San Lázaro station.

Terminal Centro Poniente (Av. Sur 122) has departures to Toluca, Valle de Bravo, Morelia, Guadalajara, and Puerto Vallarta and is connected to the Observatorio Metro station on Line 1.

When you are arriving by bus, all stations have authorized taxi services operating in the terminal, with fixed rates to different neighborhoods in the city. Only authorized taxis are legally permitted to pick up passengers at a bus station; however, you can get an Uber from any bus terminal if you leave the station and walk out to the curb (often, if you can't locate your car, the driver will call you to coordinate).

BOOKING BUS TICKETS

For trips to major cities nearby (such as Puebla, Toluca, or Cuernavaca), buses depart from Mexico City every 20-30 minutes throughout the day, so it's generally unnecessary to make advance reservations for travel. If you are going to destinations with less frequent service or are traveling during the holidays, it's best to get your ticket beforehand.

You can buy bus tickets at any OXXO convenience store (www.oxxo.com), which has thousands of locations throughout the city. OXXO represents 18 bus lines, including Primera Plus, ETN, Turistar, Futura, Chihuahuenses, Costa Line, Transportes del Norte, and TAP. The store charges a small commission, payments must be made in cash, and the ticket is nonrefundable—though, in most cases, the tickets are transferrable if you change your departure beforehand. There is also an ETN office in the Hotel Benidorm (Frontera 217, tel. 55/5264-4173, 5:30am-2pm, 2:30-11pm daily, though hours may vary) in the Roma Norte.

You can also purchase bus tickets in advance via the internet or by telephone, though note that websites may not be equipped to process foreign credit cards. Contact ADO (tel. 55/5784-4652, www.ado.com.mx) for Oaxaca, Puebla, Chiapas, Veracruz, Yucatán, and other southern destinations. Autobuses Pullman de Morelos (800/022-8000, www.pullman.mx) runs buses to Cuernavaca and Acapulco. For northern destinations, including Guadalajara, San Miguel de Allende, Guanajuato, Zacatecas,

Puerto Vallarta, and more, use ETN (800/800-0386, www.etn.com.mx) or Primera Plus (800/375-7587, www.primeraplus.com.mx).

DRIVING
QUERÉTARO AND POINTS NORTH

Take Paseo de la Reforma west past Chapultepec to the Periférico, turn north on the Periférico, and follow it all the way past Ciudad Satélite and Tlalnepantla, keeping an eye out for Querétaro signs. It's also possible to follow the Eje Central north from downtown, but this is sometimes more complicated and with more traffic. Returning to the city, stay on the Periférico around the northwest side of the city and either get off at Paseo de la Reforma (for Polanco, the Zona Rosa, and the Centro) or continue farther south on the Periférico for San Ángel and Coyoacán.

TOLUCA AND VALLE DE BRAVO

Paseo de la Reforma and Avenida Constituyentes (a major avenue parallel to Reforma but farther south) both lead directly to free and toll highways to Toluca. The toll road costs US$5 for the 16-kilometer stretch to La Marquesa (one of the most expensive tolls in the country for the distance), where it meets back up with the free road. Coming in from Toluca, keep an eye out for signs directing you to Reforma (for Polanco, Paseo de la Reforma, or the Centro Histórico) or Constituyentes (for Condesa,

Roma, or anywhere in the south of the city).

CUERNAVACA AND ACAPULCO

Both Avenida Insurgentes and Calzada Tlalpan (the southern extension of Pino Suárez, the road on the east side of the Zócalo) lead directly to both the free and toll highways to Cuernavaca. Tlalpan is usually faster as there are more lanes and fewer stoplights, but Insurgentes is simpler. Follow signs for the *cuota* or toll road; it costs about US$8, bypassing the scenic yet incredibly slow and somewhat dangerous free highway.

PUEBLA AND OAXACA

The easiest way to get to the exit to Puebla is to take Pino Suárez and Tlalpan south, turn off on the Viaducto Miguel Alemán heading east, and follow the signs to Puebla. Returning to the city, paradoxically, it's a bit of a trick to find the entrance to the Viaducto, whereas following Izazaga and then Fray Servando into the city center is fairly straightforward. The toll road to Puebla costs US$5 and allows you to avoid all the curves and slow trucks on the free highway.

TEOTIHUACÁN

Getting out on the highway to the ruins northeast of Mexico City is simple: Take Avenida Insurgentes north and keep going straight. At the first tollbooth, Pachuca drivers stay to the left, while those going to Teotihuacán stay to the right.

Getting Around

Depending on where you're going, there are ample transport options, including buses, microbuses, taxis, Uber, Metro, Metrobús, and light-rail. Getting around Mexico City on public transportation is cheap, efficient, and generally safe. Within each neighborhood, walking is the best way to see everything.

METRO

Mexico City's extensive underground Metro system (www.metro.df.gob.mx) is a reliable, ultra-cheap, and safe way to travel both short and long distances. Almost all of the city's central districts have at least one Metro stop in the vicinity, and daytime service on most lines is frequent, with one train arriving minutes after another has departed the station.

Mexico City's Metro is incredibly easy to use. The system's 11 color-coded lines run in a web across the city, intersecting at key points, with each stop marked by a visual icon as well as a name. In the station, signs marked Correspondencia indicate the walking route to transfer train lines; to know where to go, look for the name of the final station in the direction you are going.

You buy individual tickets for each ride on the Metro at in-station *taquillas* (ticket counters). At a cost of US$0.25 per ticket, it is the most inexpensive major urban subway in the world, and the second-busiest, after Tokyo. It runs 5am-midnight on weekdays, 6am-midnight on

Saturday, and 7am-midnight on Sunday.

PEAK HOURS

Riding the Metro can be considerably more difficult when the trains are full. Peak hours vary by line, but most tend to get shockingly crowded at centrally located stations at the beginning and the end of the workday. Sometimes, it can be close to impossible to board, and the crowds of waiting passengers on the platform simply watch a series of full-to-the-brim trains pass by. In general, riding the Metro is particularly challenging during the weekday morning rush hour, 7am-9:30am, and in the evenings 5:30pm-7:30pm.

CUSTOMS AND SAFETY

Unfortunately, getting on and off a train is a bit of a free-for-all, especially during rush hour. Riders are not known for their courtesy when boarding crowded cars, so you need to be proactive if you want to exit. Pickpockets are also not unknown on the Metro, particularly at busy stations. When riding the Metro, keep purses, backpacks, and cameras close to you, and be aware of anything valuable in your pockets, especially when boarding a train or when standing in a crowded car. There has been a very active pickpocketing ring working at the Pino Suárez Metro stop. Despite word-of-mouth reports and published newspaper stories exploring the problem, the police have been unable or unwilling to stop the crime.

WOMEN'S CARS

Women traveling alone, both foreign and Mexican, may receive unwanted attention on the Metro. Particularly disturbing, some women are groped on crowded subway cars. To avoid these problems, there are train cars specially designated for women and children only, which operate during peak hours on some Metro lines, generally located at the rear of the train.

METROBÚS

Metrobús (www.metrobus.cdmx. gob.mx) is a high-speed bus service that runs on dedicated lanes along major city avenues. For destinations along Insurgentes, including Roma, Condesa, San Ángel, and UNAM, the Metrobús can be a far more convenient option than the Metro.

The first line of the Metrobús opened on Avenida Insurgentes in 2005. There are five more Metrobús lines, which may come in handy if traveling beyond the regular central neighborhoods. Particularly, the circular route that runs between the TAPO bus station and the Buenavista train station passes a number of popular attractions on its way through the Centro Histórico and past the Alameda Central.

Note that in order to service the most popular stations along these routes, not every bus that runs along a Metrobús line covers the full route. Along Insurgentes, for example, some buses will only go as far as the Glorieta Insurgentes or the Buenavista train station before returning south. Look for the bus's end point posted above the windshield.

Most Metrobús lines operate 5am-midnight Monday-Friday and 6am-midnight on the weekends, though hours vary slightly by route. Like the Metro, the Metrobús can become intolerably packed during peak hours. Though it is slightly less hectic than the belowground free-for-all, it is nonetheless more comfortable to avoid the Metrobús 7am-9am and 5:30pm-7:30pm.

The fare for Metrobús is about US$0.50 flat rate, with free transfer between lines. Unlike for the Metro, you do not buy individual tickets for each ride but a prepaid electronic Metrobús card, which you fill up with credit and then scan at the entrance. There are machines where you can buy or refill a Metrobús card in each station.

SUBURBAN LIGHT-RAIL

Some outlying neighborhoods in the north and south are serviced by light-rail lines. In the south, the Tren Ligero (www.ste.df.gob.mx) departs from the Tasqueña Metro station, running to Estadio Azteca and Huichapan 6am-7pm Monday-Saturday and 7am-8pm Sunday and from Tasqueña to Xochimilco 6am-11pm Monday-Saturday and 7am-11pm on Sunday.

The Ferrocarril Suburbano de la Zona Metropolitana (Estación Terminal Buenavista, Av. Insurgentes Norte and Eje 1 Norte, tel. 55/1946-0790, www.fsuburbanos.com) offers frequent passenger train service to the Valley of Mexico, to points between Cuautitlán and the Buenavista train terminal,

It's always safer to take registered or *sitio* taxis than to hail cabs on the street in Mexico City. Like regular taxis, *sitios* and radio taxis run on a metered rate, with a base cost and per-kilometer charge that is slightly more expensive than the regular cabs circulating in the street. Where can you find a *sitio*?

Sitios operate at Benito Juárez International Airport and inside each of the four major bus stations. At the airport and bus stations, you buy your ticket and prepay for the ride before heading to the queue on the street, where you will be escorted to a taxi. Within the city, you can always ask a hotel or restaurant to call you a secure taxi; most have a company they use often and trust. Alternatively, you can go directly to a *sitio* or call a cab yourself. There are often sitios outside large shopping centers or popular destinations, like Parque México. (Note that there are few sitios in the Centro Histórico, so it's best to ask a hotel or restaurant to call you a car.) A few good options for citywide travel are Radio Union, with one base of operations at Colima and Av. Cuauhtémoc in the Roma Norte (55/5514-7709) and Taxi Mex (55/7059-9854), also with a kiosk in the Roma Norte on Colima and Av. Oaxaca.

- **Taxis Moliere:** Moliere at Horacio, tel. 55/5280-9153
- **Radio Union:** Colima at Av. Cuauhtémoc, Col. Roma Norte, tel. 55/5514-7709 or 55/5514-8074
- **Servi Taxis:** Various locations, including Parque España y Veracruz, Col. Condesa, tel. 55/5516-6020 or 55/3626-9800
- **Taxi Radio Mex:** Various locations, including Merida at Guanajuato, Col. Roma Norte, tel. 55/5574-3368 or 55/5574-3520
- **Sitio Parque México:** Michoacán at Avenida México, tel. 55/5286-7129 or. 55/5286-7164

located at Avenida Insurgentes Norte in Colonia Buenavista (and accessible via Metro Buenavista).

TAXI

There are three types of taxis in Mexico City: *taxis libres,* which are hailed on the street; *sitio* taxis, which are based at a fixed station and can be either called or picked up from their home base; and radio taxis, reached by telephone. By law, all taxis (except for private car services, which sometimes operate from high-end hotels) are equipped with *taxímetros* (taximeters).

TAXIS LIBRES

Metered *taxis libres* roam the streets picking up passengers. Most are painted white and pink, per city regulation, though you'll still see some

red-and-gold (the previous color scheme) sedans circulating as well. Taxis hailed on the street in Mexico City have a shaky reputation, with reason. Though not particularly common, *taxis libres* have been involved in armed muggings and kidnapping of both foreigners and locals. In almost any circumstance, it is better to take a registered taxi, either a *sitio* or a radio taxi.

In the case that you do take a street taxi, check that the driver has a taximeter and *tarjetón* (identification card) in the window with a license number, keep the window rolled up and doors locked (most robberies involve an accomplice), and give clear directional instructions to the driver. Be sure the driver turns on the meter as soon as you start driving.

Street taxis charge US$0.80 (about 9 pesos) as a base rate, then about a peso per 250 meters or 45 seconds—roughly US$0.40 per kilometer. After 11pm and until 6am, taxis are legally allowed to charge an additional 20 percent on the fare. Most have special meters with a night setting. If it's late, taxi drivers may refuse to turn on their meter and will instead want to negotiate a price. Although this is technically illegal, it's not uncommon.

SITIO, RADIO, AND HOTEL TAXIS

Safer alternatives to street cabs are the city's abundant *sitio* (pronounced SEE-tee-yoh) taxis and radio taxis, which operate with a fleet of registered drivers. You'll find *sitios* all over the city, except in the Centro Histórico. *Sitios* often have a curbside kiosk nearby where dispatchers log the taxis in and out, though some do not. *Sitios* are legally allowed to charge a slightly higher price than *libres,* with a base fare of about US$1.50 and an additional US$0.50 per kilometer. There are *sitios* at all four major bus terminals in Mexico City, as well as a number of *sitios* operating at Benito Juárez International Airport. Radio-dispatched *sitios,* or radio taxis, reached by telephone, with service to and from anywhere in the city, are considered the safest way to travel. Radio taxis charge a base rate of about US$2.50 and about US$0.60 per kilometer or 45 seconds.

In addition to city-licensed taxis, most high-end hotels work with private car services; these are the most expensive cabs by far, usually charging a flat rate between destinations,

though they are safe and can be very comfortable. The cars are usually unmarked four-door sedans, and the drivers often speak some English. Some are licensed tour guides as well, who will offer a flat rate for a day trip to places like Teotihuacán or Xochimilco with tour services included.

RIDE-HAILING SERVICES

Uber (www.uber.com) operates in Mexico City, and is generally a safe, pleasant, and inexpensive way to get around. Uber charges a flat rate between destinations and often arrives within minutes. In order to use the service, you need to use the Uber app on your phone, which is connected to a credit card. Download it, and make sure you have roaming capabilities on your phone.

BUS

In addition to the Metro and Metrobús, there are several types of buses in the city, from large city buses to smaller microbuses called *peseros.* In general, visitors to the city will not need to use regular city buses to reach destinations in the central districts, but they can come in handy if you are traveling to La Villa or other destinations in greater Mexico City.

To find the right bus for your destination, start by looking at the placards posted in the front window. Usually, only the end of the route is listed (along with, in some cases, major destinations along the way), so you most likely will have to ask drivers where they stop. At the end of each Metro line, huge corrals of *peseros* and smaller VW bus *combis* depart for destinations around the edge of the city.

CAR

Driving in Mexico City can be a challenge at first, particularly because of the city's size and circuitous topography. Not to mention, maddening traffic jams can halt your progress for hours on end. Fortunately, *chilangos,* though perhaps a little heavy-footed on the gas, aren't particularly reckless drivers. Armored cars, city buses, and taxis can occasionally be aggressive (practice defensive driving!), but those who have driven in other large, chaotic cities will find Mexico City negotiable with the proper maps or GPS navigator in tow.

If driving, choose your hours carefully. Mornings (8am-10am) can be very congested, while midday traffic is usually reasonable until around 4pm. During the week, late afternoon and early evening are the worst, particularly on the main commuter routes in and out of the city and in the Centro. Traffic begins to dissipate around 9pm or earlier in the city center. The worst traffic of all occurs on Friday afternoon, and even worse still if it's a *viernes quincena,* a Friday that coincides with the twice-monthly payday. Unpredictable demonstrations in various parts of the city—but particularly on Paseo de la Reforma, on Paseo Bucareli, and in the city center—also regularly tie up traffic, as does the weekly closing of Paseo de la Reforma on Sundays for cyclists.

NAVIGATION

As might be expected, learning your way around an urban area

of several million inhabitants can be a bit confusing, but being familiar with a couple of major avenues can help you stay oriented. Avenida Insurgentes is the longest boulevard in the city and a major north-south route crossing Mexico City. To the northeast, Insurgentes takes you to the exit for Pachuca and Teotihuacán, while to the south it continues past San Ángel to UNAM and the exit to Cuernavaca and Acapulco. Paseo de la Reforma is a broad avenue punctuated by large traffic circles (called *glorietas*) running northeast-southwest from the exit to Toluca to the Basílica de Santa María de Guadalupe.

The city is circled by two ring highways, the inner Circuito Interior and the outer Periférico. The Circuito makes a complete loop, although it changes names (Río Churubusco, Patriotismo, Revolución, and Circuito Interior) along the way. There are no freeways passing through the center of town, so the city has developed a system of *ejes viales* (axes), major thoroughfares that cross the city, with traffic lights (somewhat) timed, either east-west or north-south. *Ejes* are numbered and given a reference of *norte* (north), *sur* (south), *oriente* (east), or *poniente* (west). Other important roads that are not technically *ejes* are the east-west Viaducto Miguel Alemán and the south-to-center Avenida Tlalpan, both of which are major two-way arteries.

In addition to a good GPS system, the best tool for drivers is the *Guía Roji,* a bright red book of maps and indexes of the city. It can be found in Sanborns department stores, as well as at many street corner newsstands, for about US$20.

HOY NO CIRCULA

Mexico City's "Hoy No Circula" ("Don't Drive Today") program has made strides in reducing automobile emissions in the Valley of Mexico. All 16 boroughs in the capital and 18 municipalities in Mexico state participate in the program, which prohibits cars from circulating on certain days of the week, based on the last letter of their license plate. Foreign-registered cars are not exempt from the program, nor are cars from other states of the republic. Failure to comply can result in hefty fines and even towing and impoundment of your car. Even for foreigners, there is no opportunity to claim ignorance; every driver has the responsibility to comply with the restrictions.

In 2016, the government extended restrictions, including Sunday for the first time. The rules are constantly changing and being updated, and in the case of pollution alerts. Be sure to check www.sedema.df.gob.mx for updated information.

The schedule is as follows for license plates registered in Mexico City or the state of Mexico. Driving is prohibited from 5am to 10pm for cars with the following license plates:

- **Monday:** No driving if final digit is 5 or 6, yellow sticker.
- **Tuesday:** No driving if final digit is 7 or 8, pink sticker.
- **Wednesday:** No driving if final digit is 3 or 4, red sticker.
- **Thursday:** No driving if final digit is 1 or 2, green sticker.
- **Friday:** No driving if final digit is 9 or 0, and those with letters only or temporary plates, blue sticker.
- **Saturday:** On the first and third Saturday of the month, no driving for cars with hologram 1 if final digit is 1, 3, 5, 7, or 9. On the second and fourth Saturday of the month, no driving for cars with hologram 1 if final digit is 0, 2, 4, 6, or 8. Cars with hologram 2 are not permitted to drive on any Saturdays.
- **Saturday:** No driving for cars with hologram 2.
- **Sunday:** In most cases, all vehicles may drive. Check www.sedema.df.gob.mx for updated information.

Local cars are required to have a decal bearing a 0, 1, or 2. A 0 or 00 means the car is exempt from any days off, regardless of the license number, because it has passed emissions tests. A 1 hologram requires the car to not circulate on one day, regardless of the conditions; and a 2 means the car cannot circulate on two days of the week.

For cars with foreign plates, or for cars registered in states other than the state of Mexico or Mexico City, there are additional restrictions. The rules are as follows:

- No driving on one weekday, as corresponds to the final number on your license plate (as listed above).
- No driving on any Saturday from 5am to 10pm.
- No driving Monday, Tuesday, Wednesday, Thursday, and Friday from 5am to 11am.

Foreign-registered cars are not required to have decals, though like local cars, they may apply for exemption from the Hoy No Circula rules by passing emissions tests and receiving a "0" or "00" hologram from Centros de Verificación (Verification Centers) run by the Secretaría del Medio Ambiente del Gobierno (the Environment Secretariat).

On rare occasions (such as for Christmas holidays), cars from outside Mexico City may be exempt from the circulation rules. Other times, when pollution levels are high, additional restrictions may be added to the program. Full schedules and rules are available (in Spanish) at the Environmental Secretariat's website: www.sedema.df.gob.mx.

OFFICIALS

Traffic cops, or *transitos,* respond to traffic accidents and issue citations for moving violations. When you're driving in Mexico, the transit cops may stop you. However, if your car is in Mexico legally, the papers are in order, and you haven't broken the law, it should be a fairly easy interaction. If you did break the traffic rules in some way, you will be issued a citation and fine, which you will pay in the transit office.

In addition to city police, there are *policía federal,* or federal police, patrolling the intracity highways. Federal police can be helpful in the case of a roadside emergency or accident. If pulled over by a federal officer, you should have little problem if you have all your paperwork in order.

Another official service on the streets of the city is Apoyo Vial

(Road Support), men and women in bright yellow uniforms driving motor scooters. Funded jointly by the city and federal governments, Apoyo Vial helps out with emergency breakdowns, traffic accidents, and directing traffic in congested areas. Their services are free.

BRIBES

Mexico has developed a bad and not undeserved reputation for police corruption. The famous *mordida,* or bribe, has become so legendary that many foreigners reach for their wallet as soon as they see flashing lights in their rearview mirror. In reality, not every interaction with a traffic cop will necessarily end in extortion. In some cases, you will just receive a warning, and in others, a legal citation.

That said, extortion does happen. If you have committed a traffic violation, you may find yourself threatened with going to the *delegación,* the precinct house, if you don't pay a "fine" there and then—in other words, paying off the cop instead of dealing with the paperwork of an actual moving violation.

If you find yourself in this position, you can insist on following proper legal channels and go to the *delegación* with the cop, or you can pay the bribe and go on your way. If you are confident of having done nothing wrong and insist on being taken to the *delegación,* there is a chance the cop will give up and allow you to go without any fine. If you did do something wrong, you can still insist on doing everything by the books, though going down to the *delegación* is a several-hour ordeal.

CAR RENTALS

There are many car rental offices throughout the city and in the airport, as well as in the lobbies of some of the bigger hotels. In general, rental car prices are much more expensive in Mexico than in the United States. Mandatory insurance packages (which you are required to buy when you go to pick up the keys, even if they don't appear in an online booking) can triple the price of the rental. All told, a small car with unlimited mileage will run US$50-80 a day, sometimes less if you shop around. International companies operating in Mexico include Avis (www.avis.com.mx), Budget (www.budget.com.mx), and Dollar (www.dollarmexico.com.mx).

Many local rental agencies offer cars at lower prices than the U.S. agencies. A good option is Casanova Renta de Automoviles (Chapultepec 416, tel. 55/5514-0449 or 55/5207-6007, 8am-6pm Mon.-Fri., 8am-1:30pm Sat.; Patriotismo 735, Col. Mixcoac, tel. 55/5563-7606, 8am-6pm Mon.-Fri., 8am-1:30pm Sat.; www.casanovarent.com.mx), offering no-frills cars for 20-30 percent cheaper than big car rental companies. Be sure to reserve ahead of time, as their good prices mean that they often sell out of options, and be sure to check with them about requirements to rent, which may include a proof of residence.

Visas and Officialdom

TOURIST PERMITS AND VISAS

Immigration paperwork is fairly straightforward for residents of most countries, whether they are planning a short-term or long-term stay in Mexico. For more detailed information, visit the website of the Secretaría de Relaciones Exteriores (www.sre.gob.mx/en) or the Instituto Nacional de Migración (www.inm.gob.mx).

ENTRY REQUIREMENTS

No advance permission or visa for travel to Mexico is required for the citizens of about 40 countries, including the United States, Canada, most of Europe and Latin America, New Zealand, and Australia. Citizens of these countries need only a valid passport to enter Mexico. A tourist permit will be issued to visitors of these countries at the point of entry.

TOURIST PERMITS

Visitors who do not require a visa to visit Mexico are granted a six-month travel permit, officially known as the forma migratoria multiple (FMM) but unofficially referred to as a "tourist card," at the airport or border. If arriving by air, you'll receive the paperwork on the plane and your card will be ratified at the immigration desk when you land. If driving, stop at the immigration office at the border to get a tourist card.

Tourist cards are valid for travel in Mexico for up to 180 days. In most cases, the immigration official will automatically award you 90 or 180 days when you enter (you can request the full 180, if you need it). If you only get 90 days and need to extend your time, you can do so free of charge at any immigration office.

If you lose your tourist card while you are in Mexico, you can report it at an immigration office and pay a fine to replace it, or you can wait and pay the fine at the airport. If you choose to do the latter, leave ample extra time to check in and visit immigration before your flight.

CHILDREN TRAVELING ALONE OR WITH ONE PARENT

Children under the age of 18 entering Mexico unaccompanied by either parent must present a letter translated into Spanish and notarized by a Mexican embassy or consulate that gives the consent of both parents for the trip. The letter should include the dates of travel, the reason for the trip, airline information, and the name of the child's official guardian. The U.S. State Department further recommends that unaccompanied minors travel with a copy of their birth certificate or other documents that prove their relationship. In cases of divorce, separation, or death, the minor should carry notarized papers documenting the situation.

Rules regarding minors were originally established to help combat human trafficking and are therefore rather strict. Current information on minors traveling to Mexico can be obtained from the Mexican Embassy (http://embamex.sre.gob.mx/eua) in the United States.

TOURIST VISAS

If you do not live in one of the 40 countries exempt from visa requirements, it is necessary to apply for a tourist visa in advance of arrival in Mexico. If you apply in person at a Mexican consulate, you usually can obtain a tourist visa on the day of application, although for some countries it can take a couple of weeks. Legal permanent residents of the United States, regardless of nationality, do not need visas to visit Mexico for tourism.

BUSINESS VISAS

Citizens of Mexico's NAFTA (North American Free Trade Agreement) partners, the United States and Canada, are not required to obtain a visa to visit Mexico for business purposes. Business travelers must solicit a business permit, or FMM, at the point of entry; it's valid for 30 days. To ratify your FMM, you must present proof of nationality (a valid passport or original birth certificate, plus a photo identification or voter registration card) and proof that you are traveling for "international business activities," usually interpreted to mean a letter from the company you represent, even if it's your own enterprise. Those who arrive with the FMM and wish to stay over the authorized period of 30 days must replace their FMM with a temporary resident visa form at an immigration office in Mexico.

Citizens of non-NAFTA countries who are visiting for business purposes must obtain an FM3 visa endorsed for business travel, which is valid for one year. Visitors to Mexico coming as part of human rights delegations, as aid workers, or as international observers should check with a Mexican embassy about current regulations.

OVERSTAYS

If you overstay your visa, the usual penalty is a fine of about US$50 for overstays up to a month. After that the penalties become more severe. When crossing a land border, it's rare that a Mexican border official asks to see your FMM or visa. The best policy is to stay up to date in spite of any laxity of enforcement.

NONIMMIGRANT VISAS (*RESIDENTE TEMPORAL*)

Far and away the most popular visa option for foreign residents of Mexico is the *residente temporal*, or temporary resident visa. There are several categories, but all of them classify holders as nonimmigrant residents of Mexico. These are the type of visa issued to most retirees, employees, and business owners. The benefit is that it allows you to come and go from Mexico as you please, and there is no minimum residency requirement.

You must apply for a visa at the Mexican consulate in your home country. The applicant must submit a proof of citizenship (passport), proof of residence, three months of bank statements, five color photos measuring 2.3 by 3 centimeters (three looking directly at the camera and two in profile), and a proof of income.

STUDENT VISAS

Students who will be in Mexico for fewer than six months can use a tourist visa for the length of their stay. No special visa is required. Those planning to study in Mexico for a longer period of time may need to apply for a student visa, which is a variation of the temporary resident visa (application procedures are roughly analogous).

CUSTOMS
BASIC ALLOWANCES

Customs, or *aduana,* allows visitors to Mexico to enter the country with personal items needed for their trip, as well as duty-free gifts valued at no more than US$500. Personal effects may include two photographic or video cameras and up to 12 rolls of film, up to three cellular phones, and one laptop computer. The full list of permitted items is available at the Customs Administration, or La Administración General de Aduanas (www.aduanas.gob.mx). Most animal-derived food products are not permitted, including homemade foods, pet food or dog treats, fresh or canned meat, soil, or hay. Other food products are permitted.

If you are arriving by air, you will be given a customs declaration form on the airplane and will pass through the customs checkpoint right after immigration. Customs checks are performed by random selection. After collecting your luggage, you will be directed to a stoplight and asked to press a button. If you get a green light, you can pass. If you receive a red light, customs officials will open your luggage to inspect its contents. In larger airports, luggage is often passed through an X-ray machine, and passengers may be detained if a possible contraband item is detected.

There are severe penalties for carrying firearms to Mexico. Also note that narcotics are heavily regulated in Mexico, so if you have a prescription for painkillers or other controlled substances, carry what you'll need for personal use, along with an official note from your doctor. Sudafed and all pseudoephedrine-based decongestants are illegal in Mexico, so leave those at home.

Customs regulations can change at any time, so if you want to verify the regulations on a purchase before risking duties or confiscation at the border, check with a consulate in Mexico before crossing, or look on the customs website (in Spanish): www.aduanas.sat.gob.mx.

PETS

Mexico, the United States, and Canada share land borders, and therefore, as long as a cat or dog is in good health, there are no quarantine requirements between those countries. If you are bringing a cat or dog to Mexico, the animal must be accompanied by a certificate of health, issued by a licensed international veterinarian no more than 10 days before arrival in Mexico, and proof of a current rabies vaccination. Further, rabies vaccinations must be issued at least 15 days before entry but can be no more than a year old. If you're not coming from the United States or Canada, you must also present proof that the animal has been treated for worms and parasites. Bring a copy of your pet's vaccination record; customs officials may request it. If your pet does not meet health standards, it may be detained at the airport.

EMBASSIES AND CONSULATES

Most foreign embassies are located near the city center, with the majority of embassies concentrated in the Polanco and Cuauhtémoc neighborhoods, including the United States Embassy (Paseo de la Reforma 305, Col. Cuauhtémoc, tel. 55/5080-2000, http://mexico.usembassy.gov), the Canadian Embassy (Schiller 529, Col. Bosque de Chapultepec, tel. 55/5724-7900, www.canadainternational.gc.ca), Australian Embassy (Ruben Dario 55, Col. Polanco, tel. 55/1101-2200, www.mexico.embassy.gov.au), and the British Embassy (Río Lerma 71, Col. Cuauhtémoc, tel. 55/1670-3200, www.gov.uk/government/world/mexico). If you have trouble with the law while you are in Mexico or your citizenship papers have been lost or stolen, you should contact your embassy right away.

POLICE

Officers in blue fatigues patrolling streets or parks are a part of the Protección Civil (Civil Protection), the local police force. In Mexico City, they are generally around to keep the peace in public spaces, as well as to respond to emergencies, break-ins, or other complaints. The police officers stationed in the Centro Histórico or along the Paseo de la Reforma are generally happy to answer questions or give directions to tourists as well.

Conduct and Customs

BUSINESS AND ETIQUETTE

TERMS OF ADDRESS

Mexicans are generally polite and formal when interacting with people they do not know well. When speaking to an elder or to someone with whom you will have a professional relationship, it is customary to use the formal pronoun *usted* instead of the informal *tú*. If you are unsure which pronoun a situation requires, you can always err on the side of caution by using *usted* with anyone you've just met.

It is also common practice to speak to someone you've just met using a polite title, such as *señor* for a man, *señora* for a married or older woman, and *señorita* for a young woman. When speaking with a professional, Mexicans may also use the person's professional title, such as *doctor/doctora* (doctor), *arquitecto/arquitecta* (architect), or *ingeniero/ingeniera* (engineer).

GREETINGS

When greeting someone in Mexico, it is customary to make physical contact, rather than simply saying "hello." A handshake is the most common form of greeting between strangers, though friends will usually greet each other with a single kiss on the cheek. The same physical gestures are repeated when you say good-bye. When greeting a group of people, it is necessary to greet and shake hands with each person individually, rather than address the group together.

If you need to squeeze past someone on a bus or reach over their shoulder at the market, it is customary to say *"con permiso"* (with your permission). If you accidentally bump into someone (or do anything else that warrants a mild apology), say *"perdón"* (sorry).

TIME AND APPOINTMENTS

Mexico has a well-earned reputation for running on a slower clock. Certainly, there is less urgency in Mexico, and it is not considered excessively rude to arrive tardy to a social engagement. In fact, guests are usually expected to run about a half hour (or more) late for a party at a friend's home. However, when it comes to doctor's appointments, business meetings, bus schedules, or any other official event, punctuality is just as important in Mexico as it is anywhere else.

When it comes to social engagements, Mexicans will typically accept an invitation rather than decline, even if they don't plan to attend. Some Mexicans feel more self-conscious refusing an invitation than not showing up later.

TABLE MANNERS

When you are sharing a meal, it is customary to wish other diners *"buen provecho"* before you start eating. *Buen provecho* is similar to the well-known French expression *bon appetit*. If you need to leave a meal early, you should excuse yourself and again wish everyone at the table *"buen provecho."* Charmingly, many

ESSENTIALS

CONDUCT AND CUSTOMS

people will also wish other diners in a restaurant *"buen provecho"* on their way out. As in most countries, when sharing a meal, it is customary to wait for everyone to be served before starting to eat.

When dining out with friends or acquaintances, Mexicans rarely split the bill. Usually, one of the parties will treat the others. If you were the one to invite a friend or business associate to a meal, you should also plan to treat. Usually, whomever you've treated will pick up the tab the next time.

TIPPING

In a restaurant, waitstaff receive a tip of 10-15 percent on the bill, though foreigners are generally expected to tip on the higher end of the scale. In bars, a 10 percent tip is standard.

Tips for hotel housekeeping is optional according to Mexican custom—some guests tip, and some don't, and it is less common in budget hotels. However, it is appreciated. It is customary to tip porters at an airport or hotel several dollars per bag, or about US$5-10, depending on how far you are going and the size of your load. In nicer hotels, it is necessary to give a higher tip.

Though it is not necessary to tip a taxi driver when traveling within city limits, tips are always graciously welcomed. At gas stations, a small tip of about 5 percent of the sale is customary for gas station attendants (all gas stations are full service in Mexico).

BARGAINING

When shopping, it is not common practice to bargain or ask for lower prices on goods in shops and stores in Mexico City. Some vendors may offer a small discount for bulk purchases or for cash payments, but these are offered at the shop owner's discretion. Don't expect employees at a brick-and-mortar store to bargain on prices.

In an artisan or craft market, such as the Mercado de la Ciudadela or the Bazaar Sábado in San Ángel, or at an antiques market like La Lagunilla or the Saturday market on Avenida Cuauhtémoc, prices for goods may be more flexible. It is customary to ask the vendor for the price of the item (they are rarely marked with price tags), and the vendor may then offer you a lower price as you think it over. This is particularly true for large purchases. In general, these discounts are not significant (don't expect to pay half of the price initially quoted) and aggressive haggling is not common, nor is it particularly fruitful. If you do wish to bargain on a price, do so politely.

Do not bargain at food markets, even if you are buying a substantial quantity. Usually, the prices at food markets are low to begin with, and few vendors can afford to drop their prices further.

SMOKING

Smoking tobacco (including electronic cigarettes) is prohibited in restaurants and bars throughout Mexico City. Though many people still smoke, they are required by law to smoke outside (patios, sidewalk seating, and open-air terraces located inside restaurants are all places where smoking is permitted). When the antismoking laws first went into effect, tough fines on establishments violating the policy helped ensure its widespread adoption throughout the city. However, as time passed, many establishments opened open-roofed segments of their restaurants or allowed patrons to smoke near entryways, leading to more lax rules.

DRESS

Mexicans are not particularly concerned with how visitors dress, but you will probably feel more comfortable if you conform to some basic standards. In Mexico City almost no one ever wears shorts; although this is mainly because of the cool year-round climate, it also demonstrates that *capitaleños* tend to be more formal in dress than Mexicans in other cities, especially those on the coast. Upon entering a church or chapel in Mexico, visitors are expected to remove their hats.

BUSINESS HOURS

Standard business hours are 8am to 6pm Monday through Friday, with lunch breaks taken between 1 and 3pm. Banks are usually open from 9am to 5pm Monday through Friday, though hours may be longer and include Saturday at some branches. Though lunch breaks are common in a corporate environment, many small business owners will work in their shop from morning to night, without so much as a coffee break.

No matter what hours are posted for small businesses, the actual opening and closing times may vary with the whims of the proprietors. This is also true for tourist information offices. Banks usually follow their posted hours to the minute.

Health and Safety

FOOD AND WATER
FOOD SAFETY

Getting sick from a serious food-borne illness or parasite isn't particularly common in Mexico City, especially if you take some precautions when eating. However, some travelers do experience gastrointestinal distress or diarrhea while visiting Mexico.

Changes in the food you eat and the water you drink, changes in your eating and drinking habits, and a new overall environment can cause unpleasant diarrhea, nausea, and vomiting. Because it often affects Mexico newcomers, gastrointestinal distress is called *turista* (tourist) in Mexico, and "traveler's diarrhea" in English. In many cases, *turista* can be effectively treated with a few days of rest, liquids, and antidiarrhea medication, such as Pepto Bismol, Kaopectate, or Imodium.

To avoid *turista,* eat and drink with moderation, and go easy—at least at first—on snacks offered by outdoor street vendors or market stands, where food is exposed to the elements. It's always a good idea to choose street stands where you see a lot of other clients, which is a

THE SEISMIC ALARM

Though highly susceptible to earthquakes, Mexico City is not on a fault line. In most cases, earthquakes originate from faults along the Pacific coast, with seismic waves traveling hundreds of miles to reach the capital. As a result, there is often a substantial minute-or-more delay between the time an earthquake begins off the coast and when its tremors can be felt in Mexico City.

Using this delay to its advantage, Mexico City initiated the **Sistema de Alerta Sísmica Mexicano (Mexican Seismic Alert System),** a citywide earthquake warning system, which is linked to a series of seismic sensors along the Pacific coast and in the state of Guerrero. Whenever the sensors detect a tremor of 6 magnitude or higher, a pulsating siren sounds on loudspeakers throughout the city. The siren, though distinctive, can sound a bit like a home or car alarm, so pay attention if you think you hear it. In addition to the siren, a voice repeats the words alerta sismíca (seismic alert). You can listen to the sound of the seismic alarm online to familiarize yourself with it.

Many of Mexico City's residents also use seismic alarm apps on their smartphones, which operate using the same model as the municipal system. You can install these apps on your phone, then modify them to only sound an alarm when earthquakes reach a certain intensity. The most popular options are SkyAlert and Alerta Sísmica DF, both available for iOS and Android.

Though the alarm system is a lifesaving innovation, note that when an earthquake's epicenter is closer to the capital, the alarm system may not sound in time for you to safely evacuate your building. On September 19, 2017, most of the capital's residents only heard the alarm after the ground had already begun to shake.

good indication of the food's quality. Some people consume street food from all over the city with no incident; others become ill after eating in markets or on the street. Use your discretion.

If the symptoms are unusually severe or persist for more than a few days, see a doctor. It could be a case of amoebic or bacterial dysentery. Most hotels can arrange a doctor's visit.

WATER QUALITY

Mexican tap water is treated and potable, yet it is generally considered unsafe for drinking, in part because of the unknown condition of most buildings' plumbing and water tanks. Hotels and restaurants serve only purified drinking water and ice. Bottled water, like all bottled beverages, is readily available and safe for drinking. You can also make tap water safe for drinking by boiling it for several minutes to kill any bacteria or parasites.

ALTITUDE SICKNESS

At 2,250 meters (7,380 feet) Mexico City is at a high elevation. Some visitors experience mild altitude sickness shortly after arrival. Symptoms include headache, shaky stomach, breathlessness, and general malaise. The body needs time to acclimate to the change in barometric pressure and lesser amounts of oxygen, and the air pollution can exacerbate the symptoms. If you feel ill, take it easy for a while: no running, no climbing pyramids, no alcohol. Some people find it takes two or three days to fully adjust to the elevation when flying in from places at or near sea level.

DEHYDRATION

At a high altitude, it's important to drink plenty of water and other fluids to avoid dehydration. Alcohol and caffeine increase your potential for dehydration. Symptoms of dehydration include darker-than-usual urine or inability to urinate, flushed face, profuse sweating or an unusual lack thereof, and sometimes a headache, dizziness, and general feeling of malaise.

EARTHQUAKES

Earthquakes are common in Mexico City, and occasionally deadly. In the wake of the massive 1985 quake, building codes were updated and many unsafe structures were demolished. In fact, Mexico has some of the strictest seismic building codes in the world, making most newer buildings very safe, even during big earthquakes. That said, tens of thousands of older structures are not up to code and remain vulnerable to damage or collapse during a quake, as was demonstrated during the devastating 7.1 magnitude earthquake on September 19, 2017.

When checking in to your hotel or apartment rental, it's a good idea to ask about emergency exits and evacuation plans. In some cases, it is safest to evacuate to the street when you hear the seismic alarm or feel tremors; in other cases it is safer to stay put, especially if you are on the fourth floor or above. If you are outside, stand in the middle of an intersection (you'll likely see many other people gathered there), away from tall buildings.

After the trembling has stopped, go outside until your hotel or building has had a preliminary structural inspection. Do not light cigarettes or candles, even if the power goes out, and remain alert to the smell of gas leaks.

INFECTIOUS DISEASE

No vaccines are required for travel to Mexico City, though it's always a good idea to be up to date on routine vaccines. Some doctors recommend the hepatitis A vaccine for travel to Mexico. Hepatitis A affects the liver and is contracted from contaminated food or water. Symptoms may resemble the flu, though they are severe and may last several months. Typhoid is also contracted through contaminated food or water, though it's more of a concern in rural areas.

H1N1, or swine flu, was a major health concern in Mexico City in the spring of 2008, but it is no longer a major health concern in Mexico.

To date, the mosquito that carries the Zika virus is not found in Mexico City, owing to the city's high altitude.

COVID-19

At the time of writing in the fall of 2022, Mexico City had mostly stabilized from the effects of the coronavirus, but the situation is constantly evolving. Now more than ever, Moon encourages readers to be courteous and ethical in their travel. Get vaccinated if your health allows, make an effort to follow all Mexican health protocols and customs, and if possible, test regularly before, during, and after your trip to ensure you continue to test negative for COVID-19.

It is currently not necessary to

provide proof of vaccination or a negative Covid test result to enter Mexico. Although Mexico suspended indoor masking requirements in the fall of 2022, wearing a mask or facial covering remains an important measure in slowing the spread of COVID-19 and other infectious disease, and you may still be asked to wear a mask in some establishments, or when riding in a taxi or Uber. Please note that passengers traveling to Mexico on Mexican airlines, like Aeromexico, are required to follow Mexican guidelines for masking while onboard, regardless of their country of origin.

If you are experiencing symptoms of COVID or require a rapid COVID test to return to your home country, you may make an appointment online at Farmacias de Ahorro (www.fahorro.com) or Farmacias San Pablo (www.farmaciasanpablo.com.mx), both large pharmacy chains, which can administer and provide certified results of COVID antigen tests. Facial coverings, including N95 and KN95 masks, are widely available from street vendors and at almost any pharmacy, including the pharmacies listed above.

More information about the current situation, as well as lists of COVID test providers, can be found at the US Embassy in Mexico's website (https://mx.usembassy.gov) or at local consulate sites. The Mexican government provides health and safety updates (in Spanish) at https://coronavirus.gob.mx. You can also get updated Coronavirus stats at the World Health Organization's Mexico Coronavirus Dashboard (https://covid19.who.int).

MEDICAL ASSISTANCE

The quality of basic medical treatment, including dentistry, is high in Mexico City. Large hotels usually have a doctor on staff or a list of recommended physicians in the neighborhood. Polanco is the best area for private medical clinics, where a consultation will run US$25-60. Another good option is to call the Hospital ABC, which has a referral service for quality doctors of different specializations.

EMERGENCIES

In case of emergency, dial 911 from any telephone to reach an emergency dispatcher.

DOCTORS AND HOSPITALS

Hospital American British Cowdray (ABC) (Calle Sur 136, No. 116, tel. 55/5230-8000 or 55/5230-8161, www.abchospital.com), at the corner of Avenida Observatorio, south of Bosque de Chapultepec in Colonia Las Américas, is considered one of the best hospitals in the city, and prices are accordingly high. Another well-regarded hospital is Hospital Español (Ejército Nacional 613, Polanco, tel. 55/5255-9600 general information, www.hespanol.com).

PRESCRIPTIONS AND PHARMACIES

Visitors to Mexico are permitted to carry prescription medication for preexisting conditions among their personal effects. Generally, they can bring no more than a three-month supply of medicine with them, and it should be accompanied by documentation from a doctor. (There can be strict penalties, including incarceration, for tourists who are suspected of drug abuse.) Most common over-the-counter medication is available in Mexico. Drugs in Mexico are regulated and safe; there are also generic brands.

If you need to purchase prescription medication while you are in Mexico, you can visit a doctor, who will write you a prescription. Most Mexican pharmacies do not ask for prescriptions for the majority of medication, except for certain oft-abused substances. However, it is usually a better idea to get a prescription for medication, as the brands and dosages may differ in Mexico. If you'd like to take your meds home, rules for export depend on your home country.

There are pharmacies, or *farmacias,* throughout the city. Many are open 24 hours a day. All Sanborns department stores have an in-house pharmacy.

CRIME CONCERNS

Until the 1980s, Mexico City was known as one of the safest large cities in the Americas. The image suffered a reversal after the economic crisis of 1994-1995, when the peso plummeted, unemployment soared, and some urban residents began resorting to robbery and kidnapping. Since then, the city has maintained a poor image with regard to crime, which is not totally undeserved. Fortunately, the city has become much safer, and with reasonable precautions, most visitors will feel entirely comfortable and safe throughout their stay.

PRECAUTIONS

In most cases, crime in Mexico City is economic—in other words, theft, break-ins, mugging, and pickpocketing are the most common problems. Crime can occur anywhere in Mexico City, even in affluent neighborhoods, but you can reduce the dangers by traveling by day or on well-lit roads, keeping an eye on your wallet and camera in crowded subway cars or busy markets, carrying a cell phone, and always taking registered taxis.

There have been rare but very troubling cases of taxi-related muggings and kidnappings, wherein taxi drivers shuffle unsuspecting passengers down dark side streets, where they are assaulted and robbed by organized gangs. To avoid taxi-related crimes, take registered taxis, called *sitios,* or get a car with a ride-hailing app like Uber. There are safe, registered taxi stands in the airport, in bus terminals, and in every major neighborhood, and dozens of independent companies that will pick you up anywhere in the city.

After dark, you should be more cautious, especially when walking through unpopulated areas. The Centro Histórico is now patrolled by police officers in the evening, but it is best to stick to the areas to the west of the Zócalo, along the Alameda Central, or near the pedestrian street Regina if you are going out at night. After dark, avoid walking alone through the Doctores, Santa María la Ribera, Tabacalera, Guerrero, the areas around Plaza Garibaldi, and most of the Juárez until you are better acquainted with the city. In the Roma, Condesa, and

Polanco neighborhoods, there is less crime in the evening, especially in popular areas where crowds of diners and partygoers make the streets safe for walking. Nonetheless, it is wise to be on guard in the evenings, no matter where you are, and to avoid deserted streets or very late hours.

It's a good idea to carry limited cash and credit cards—no more than you need for an outing—when moving about the city, and don't wear ridiculously expensive-looking clothes or jewelry. Keep money and valuables secured, either in a hotel safe or safe deposit box, and lock the doors to your hotel room and vehicle.

When using ATMs as a source of cash, do so during the day or in well-lit, well-trafficked places. One reliable option is to use the Inbursa ATMs located inside Sanborns department stores. In general, don't change too much money at once.

Finally, if confronted by someone intent on robbing you, don't resist. Most Mexican thieves are simply out for quick cash. Violence is usually a problem only if you don't cooperate.

Travel Tips

STUDYING IN MEXICO
SPANISH LANGUAGE AND MEXICAN CULTURE

Mexico City is an excellent place to study Spanish, even if it hasn't traditionally been a popular choice with language learners. One of the major advantages of studying Spanish in Mexico City is having the opportunity to interact with a largely Spanish-speaking population on a daily basis. Here, using Spanish is a necessity in daily transactions, which is a huge asset to anyone with a serious drive to learn the language. There are also some excellent language school options.

One of the best options is the prestigious Universidad Nacional Autónoma de México's Centro de Enseñanza Para Extranjeros (Center for Instruction for Foreigners), or CEPE, which offers blocks of intensive introductory, intermediate, and advanced Spanish-language classes, as well as culture and history courses. The programs enjoy a very good reputation and are divided among six departments: Spanish, art history, history, social sciences, literature, and Chicano studies.

Universidad Nacional Autónoma de México (UNAM) also runs special training programs for teachers of Spanish as a Second Language (SSL). For all courses, tuition is reasonable, and CEPE can arrange housing either with local families or in dormitories. UNAM/CEPE also has a branch in Taxco (Ex Hacienda El Chorrillo s/n, Barrio del Chorrillo, Apartado Postal 70, Taxco, tel. 762/622-0124, www.cepetaxco.unam.mx).

Universidad La Salle (Benjamin Franklin 65, Col. Condesa) offers inexpensive Spanish group classes and language certificate programs for foreigners. It is closer to the center of the city than UNAM. It is closer to the center of the city than UNAM and can also arrange homestays and cultural experiences in addition to language classes.

ACCESS FOR TRAVELERS WITH DISABILITIES

Although the government has made some efforts to improve the situation, Mexico City is not an easy place for travelers with disabilities, particularly people with a limited range of movement. Many of the old, colonial-era structures that house hotels, restaurants, and museums do not have ramps or wheelchair access, nor do they have elevators inside the building. Using the Metro system can also be a challenge; currently only six stations (on Lines 3 and 9) have special platforms for people in wheelchairs. That said, there have been some positive developments in the city. The newer Metrobús system is a big improvement on the Metro, with ramps leading into all stations, audio-signaled pedestrian crossings, and information printed in Braille. Many public museums and cultural centers have added ramped entrances. With a little advance planning, visitors can also find a number of hotels and restaurants that have made special accommodations for visitors with disabilities.

TRAVELING WITH CHILDREN

Mexico City is a surprisingly kid-friendly, family-oriented place. There are plenty of great activities for kids in the city, from the wonderful children's museum in Chapultepec park to the colorful Ballet Folklórico performances at the Palacio de Bellas Artes. Most restaurants welcome children, and you will see plenty of other kids touring museums and cultural centers with their parents. A few hotels do not allow children under a certain age, but others are more than happy to accommodate children with foldout beds in the rooms. Children under 5 ride for free on the Metrobús.

WOMEN TRAVELING ALONE

Women traveling alone will generally feel safe and comfortable in Mexico City, though they should take the same safety precautions they would in any large city. Mexico is a social place, and unaccompanied women may be approached by men when dining alone at a restaurant or having a beer in a cantina—or even wandering through a museum. In most cases, curiosity and the chance to flirt drive most of these interactions, and most would-be suitors will leave you alone if you aren't interested in chatting. That said, unaccompanied foreign women may also experience unwanted catcalling from men in the street. Generally, these interactions will not escalate, so the best tactic is to simply ignore the catcaller. In the rare case that you do feel unsafe, look for a nearby police officer or enter a well-lit restaurant or business.

LGBTQ+ TRAVELERS

LGBTQ+ visitors will find a generally accepting, cosmopolitan environment in the capital. There is a large and visible gay population in the city, with an ever-increasing acceptance of diverse sexuality, gender expression, and queerness. Although many Mexico City residents are still relatively conservative, the attitude throughout the city is definitively one of tolerance; it is not uncommon to see same-sex couples holding hands or kissing in public.

TRAVELERS OF COLOR

In Mexico City, like all of Mexico, most people are from a mixed-ethnic heritage, predominantly a mix of Spanish and Indigenous American. On the whole, other ethnic groups are in the minority and less visible in Mexico City, especially outside the city's central neighborhoods like the Roma, Condesa, and Centro Histórico.

Mexico City has become increasingly diverse in the past two decades. There has been a notable influx of Indigenous, mixed-race, and Afro-Latino people from Central America. There are large Korean and Japanese communities in the city, as well as a large and multiracial expatriate community from the United States living in the Roma, Condesa, Juárez, Santa María, and other central neighborhoods. South Americans and Europeans also have a long presence in the city. Owing to the increasing diversity, travelers of color

will generally not stand out or receive unwanted notice in Mexico City, and most will find the city is a welcoming and friendly place for people of color. That said, Mexico has a long history of racial inequality running all the way back to the conquest and enslavement of the native people by the Spanish. Issues of racial discrimination and prejudice persist, which travelers may or may not witness or experience.

In some cases, Mexican customs and attitudes toward race may differ from what you've experienced in your home country. One noticeable example of this is that terms that would be considered derogatory in the United States are still somewhat commonly used (without derogatory intent) in Mexico, e.g. addressing or referring to someone Black or dark-skinned as *negrito*, addressing someone who is Asian (of any background) as *chinito*.

There are online and on-the-ground resources for travelers of color who are visiting Mexico City, including a guide to Mexico from **Diversity Abroad** (https://www.diversityabroad.com). **Blackvoyageurs** (http://blackvoyageurs.com), an online booking platform and travel planner, offers guided tours and itinerary planning in Mexico City. There are also blogs and travel guides to the city written by people of color, including **Black Girls Who Brunch** (blackgirlswhobrunch.com).

Information and Services

MONEY
CURRENCY
The unit of currency in Mexico is the peso, which comes in paper denominations of 20, 50, 100, 200, and 500. Coins are available in denominations of 5, 10, 20, and 50 centavos, and 1, 2, 5, 10, and 20 pesos. The $ symbol denotes prices in pesos. While it's highly unlikely you'll ever confuse dollar and peso prices because of the differing values, you should ask when in doubt.

Paying in Dollars
A few commercial establishments in Mexico City will accept U.S. dollars as well as pesos. Paying with pesos, however, usually means a better deal when the price is fixed in pesos; if you pay in dollars for a purchase quoted in pesos, the vendor can determine the exchange rate.

Sales Tax
An *impuesto al valor agregado* (IVA, or value-added tax) of 16 percent is tacked onto all goods and services, including hotel and restaurant bills as well as international phone calls. Hotels may add a further 2 percent lodging tax. Most budget hotels include the IVA and hotel tax in their quoted prices.

CHANGING MONEY
ATMs
The best way to get pesos is with an ATM card; they are accepted in *cajeros automático* (ATMs) in all Mexican and foreign-owned banks and invariably offer the best and most up-to-the-minute exchange rate. Some charge a rather hefty handling fee, however, so pay attention when clicking through the screens.

When using your ATM card, always choose an official bank (like Banamex, Santander, Scotiabank, Inbursa, Banorte, HSBC, or BBVA Bancomer). Recently, there have been reports that ATM and credit card numbers have been stolen and used for illicit withdrawals in Mexico. If you are dealing with an official bank rather than a stand-alone ATM, it will be easier to get the money credited back to your account in the unfortunate case that your number is used fraudulently.

Banks
While banks are the best place to withdraw money from an ATM machine, they will no longer change dollars or other foreign currency into pesos unless you are an account holder. In most cases, you will need to visit a casa de cambio (see below) if you are carrying cash.

Casas de Cambio
In most cases, the only place to change cash is at a *casa de cambio,* or private money-changing office. Nowadays, these are far less common as most travelers carry ATM cards, but you can still see them in the airport and in popular tourist neighborhoods like the Centro Histórico, the Zona Rosa, and the Condesa.

If you're going to change money at an exchange house, it pays to shop around for the best rates, as some places charge considerably more than others. The rates are usually posted; *compra,* always the lower figure, refers to the buying rate (how many pesos you'll receive per dollar or other foreign currency), while *vende* is the selling rate (how many pesos you must pay to receive a dollar or other unit of foreign currency).

MAPS AND TOURIST INFORMATION

MAPS

Most tourist-information kiosks offer small foldout maps of the city that point out noteworthy sites. You can pick them up for free at any tourist information booth you see. For a highly accurate and detailed map of the city, the best option is the excellent *Ciudad de México Area Metropolitana,* a massive flipbook street atlas published by Guía Roji (www.guiaroji.com). It covers every corner of Mexico City and includes two complete indices, one by street name and one by *colonia* (neighborhood). You can buy the Guía Roji in many corner newsstands or in a Sanborns store, or order online from Mexico Maps (www.mexico-maps.com).

Those planning to spend time on Mexico's back roads should buy a Mexican road atlas. The best available is the annual 127-page *Guía Roji por las Carreteras de México,* published in Mexico and available at newsstands and at Sanborns department stores. This atlas covers the entire country, including downtown maps of major city centers and a fairly complete network of unpaved roads, villages, and *ejidos* (communal farmlands).

TOURIST INFORMATION

Mexico City has its own tourist office, the **Secretaría de Turismo de la Ciudad de México** (Av. Nuevo León 56, 9th fl., Col. Hipódromo Condesa, tel. 55/5286-9077, fax 55/5286-9022, www.mexicocity.gob.mx). For the most part this is an administrative office, so if it's information you need, you're better off visiting one of the several tourist suboffices (*módulos de información turística*) around the city and at the airport. These small offices usually stock a variety of free brochures, maps, hotel and restaurant lists, and information on local activities and are staffed by Mexicans who are trained to handle visitor queries. Some speak very good English.

TIME, POWER, AND MEASUREMENTS

TIME

Mexico City time coincides with central standard time in the United States and is six hours ahead of Greenwich mean time (GMT -6). Between the first Sunday in April and the last Sunday in October each year, Mexico City changes by one hour to central daylight saving time.

Time in Mexico is commonly expressed according to the 24-hour clock, from 0001 to 2400 (one minute past midnight to midnight).

ELECTRICITY

Mexico's electrical system is the same as that in the United States and Canada: 110 volts, 60 cycles, alternating current (AC). Electrical outlets are of the American type, designed to work with appliances that have standard double-bladed plugs.

MEASUREMENTS

Mexico uses the metric system as the official system of weights and measures. This means the distance between Nogales and Mazatlán is measured in kilometers, cheese is weighed in grams or kilograms, a hot day in Monterrey is 32°C, gasoline is sold by the liter, and a big fish is two meters long.

COMMUNICATIONS AND MEDIA

POSTAL SERVICE

Correos de Mexico (www.correosdemexico.gob.mx), Mexico's national postal service, is known to be both erratic and slow. It can be reliable, if sluggish, for simple communications, like postcards. However, larger and more valuable items are at risk of loss or seizure. If they do arrive, months of delay are not uncommon. While it is certainly possible that the postal service will successfully deliver your package or letter, it isn't a particularly reliable way to communicate. If something absolutely must arrive in the hands of the recipient, you should pay more for a private service.

The Mexican post office offers a more reliable express mail service called Mexpost. International rates are relatively high, but it is a good option for mailing communications within Mexico. The most atmospheric place to send a postcard is doubtlessly the grand old Palacio Postal (Tacuba 1, 9am-6pm Mon.-Fri.), which also has Mexpost services.

COURIER SERVICES AND SHIPPING COMPANIES

In most cases, you will have better luck shipping packages with private companies. They offer more reliable and faster (though also more expensive) ways to send letters and packages within Mexico and internationally. DHL, UPS, FedEx, and Mexican-owned Estafeta all offer national and international expedited shipping. In Mexico, DHL tends to be the most widely used and reliable service.

Though these companies have branches throughout the city, some convenient locations include DHL Internacional de México (Madero 70, Col. Centro, tel. 55/5345-7000, www.dhl.com), Federal Express (República de Uruguay 17, Col. Centro, and Puebla 46, Col. Roma, tel. 800/900-1100, www.fedex.com), and UPS de México (Paseo de la Reforma 34, Col. Juárez, tel. 800/7433-877, www.ups.com).

The courier Estafeta Mexicana (Av. Insurgentes 105-9, Col. Juárez, tel. 55/5511-0206) is an official agent of the U.S. postal service, which makes for reliable, lower-priced service to the United States.

TELEPHONE SERVICES

Ground lines are becoming increasingly uncommon in Mexico, as many people switch to the relative ease and lower upfront costs of cellular telephones. If you need to make local calls while you're visiting, many hotels will include calls to Mexico City landlines in the cost of a room. Because Mexico's cellular phone service operates on a different system, called El Que Llama Paga (Whoever Calls, Pays), calling a cell phone will incur an additional charge.

On the street, if you aren't using a cell phone, the best option is to use the public pay-phone service called Ladatel (an acronym for Larga Distancia Teléfono). Though they are increasingly going out of service, there are still plenty of Ladatel phones in the central districts. To use a Ladatel phone, you buy a card (for sale in pharmacies, stationery stores, bus terminals, supermarkets, or convenience stores) with prepaid credit, which you can then use at public phone booths.

International Calls
To direct-dial an international call via a landline, dial 00 plus the country code, area code, and number. Note that long-distance international calls are heavily taxed and cost more than equivalent international calls from the United States or Canada. Confirm prices with your hotel before dialing internationally.

The cheapest way to make long-distance international calls is via the Internet, using Skype or some other service, though most U.S. and Canadian carriers offer economical short-term service for visitors to Mexico.

FOREIGN CELL PHONES IN MEXICO
Considering the high costs of domestic telephones and cellular service, it is not surprising that roaming charges can be particularly high for foreign cell phones in Mexico. U.S. cell phones are generally locked to their carrier, so you will have to activate an international plan with your usual company if you want to use your U.S. cell phone in Mexico. If you plan to use Uber or navigation apps, be sure to purchase international data coverage as well.

If you have an unlocked phone, you can buy a SIM card to use in Mexico. Once you have a Mexican chip, you can buy credit for your phone and make local calls. There are cell phone outlets throughout the city that will be happy to help you get it set up; they will sell you credit directly, or you can have credit charged directly to your phone at the register in OXXO or other convenience stores.

National Cell Phones
You can buy a new Mexican cell phone in Mexico City for about US$65, with call credit already on it—not an entirely unaffordable option if you're going to be making a lot of calls. When your credit expires, you can buy more credit at one of the thousands of cell-phone outlets throughout the city or at the checkout counter at OXXO, Su Mesa grocery stores, at almost any other grocery or convenience chain (you supply them with the number and pay, and they will immediately charge your phone with credit).

Note that Mexico's cellular phone service operates on a different system, called El Que Llama Paga (Whoever Calls, Pays). There are high surcharges for calling a cellular telephone, especially when you call a cellular phone in another city.

Email and Internet Access
Today, most hotels, coffee shops, and restaurants offer free wireless

Internet connections to patrons. If you bring your computer, tablet, or smartphone, you should have no problem connecting it while you are in Mexico City.

If you'd prefer to travel without your laptop, cybercafés are an excellent and inexpensive alternative. Scattered throughout the city, these public computer terminals charge by-hour or by-minute rates to use the Internet on shared computers. It rarely comes to more than a few dollars an hour, and most have printing and scanning services.

MEDIA
Newspapers
Among the national Spanish-language dailies, *Reforma* and *El Universal* are the two most popular mainstream papers. *La Jornada* is a highly political, leftist paper beloved by students and intellectuals, while *El Financiero* generally covers business and politics.

For local English-language news, Mexico City-based newspaper *The News* is a tabloid-format paper covering national and international news, with a strong focus on the United States. It publishes stories from the news wires, in addition to its own reporting. Once a subsidiary of a Mexican newspaper, *Novedades,* it is now an independent publication.

Magazines
In Spanish, *Proceso* (www.proceso.com.mx) is a political magazine known for its crack reporting. Its stories on Mexican politics are often excellent. Two glossy weekly magazines are *Milenio,* which also

has good international news stories, and *Cambio.*

For cultural events, nightlife, dining recommendations, fashion, and lifestyle-related stories, pick up a copy of the long-running magazine *Chilango,* sold at most newsstands. *Time Out México* also has excellent cultural listings; copies are free and distributed throughout the city. For more serious coverage of the arts in Mexico, including reviews and criticism, pick up a copy of *La Tempestad* or *Revista Código,* both in Spanish.

Revista de la Universidad de México is a must-read for the city's intellectuals, published by UNAM's cultural division.

International Publications
Newsstands in Mexico tend to be limited to national publications, though most airports and some bookshops will carry a wider range of imported titles like *Vanity Fair, Time, The Economist,* and other general interest magazines. The department-store chain Sanborns has a large newsstand, with dozens of national titles and many English-language titles as well.

Television
There are six broadcast networks in Mexico, four run by media conglomerate Televisa and two by TV Azteca. Channels run by Televisa and TV Azteca broadcast a mix of morning shows, news programs, sports, and American television series (usually dubbed into Spanish), as well as widely popular *telenovelas,* or soap operas.

There are two excellent public television channels in Mexico

City: the widely viewed Canal Once (Channel 11) and the Mexico City-based Canal 22 (Channel 22). These channels offer special programming on culture, politics, travel, and anthropology, in addition to airing high-quality movies and documentaries. There is also children's programming in the mornings.

Radio

Mexico City has a long history of excellent radio and boasts hundreds of AM and FM stations. Radio Universidad, 96.1 FM and 860 AM, is run by UNAM and has excellent educational and musical programming. Another good radio station with news 24 hours a day is Formato 21, 790 AM.

RESOURCES

Glossary

abarrotes: groceries

achiote: a seed used in traditional Yucatec cooking

adobado: a seasoned rub for meat

aduana: customs

aeropuerto: airport

agave: large Mexican succulent plant

agave azul: blue agave, used in tequila production

agua: water

aguas frescas or aguas de fruta: cold fruit drink

ahuehuete: a type of native Mexican cypress

alerta sísmica: seismic alert

almuerzo: meal eaten around midday

alquiler: rent

andador: pedestrian walkway

antigüedades: antiques

antojitos: snacks or appetizers

antro: nightclub

antropología: anthropology

arquitecto: architect

arrachera: Mexican skirt steak

arte: art

artesanía: traditional handicraft

atole: a sweet and hot beverage made with corn flour, often served with tamales

autobús: bus

autopista: highway

ayuntamiento: town council

azulejo: tile

bajo sexto: acoustic bass

banco: bank

baño: bathroom

barbacoa: pit-cooked lamb

barrio: neighborhood

biblioteca: library

billar: billiards, pool

birria: slow-roasted goat

boliche: bowling

bolillo: white roll

bomberos: firefighters

bosque: forest

botana: snack or appetizer, often served free with drinks at cantinas

buen provecho: an expression used to say "enjoy your meal"

café: coffee

café con leche: coffee with milk

café de chinos: traditional Chinese-run diner

café de olla: coffee prepared with unrefined sugar and cinnamon in a clay pot

cajero: cashier; automatic teller

caldo: broth

caldo de pollo: chicken broth

calle: street

callejón: alley

camion: bus, truck

canadiense: Canadian citizen

cantina: traditional bar or drinking establishment

capilla: chapel

capital: capital

capitaleño: capital resident (Mexico City resident)

carne: meat

carne asada: grilled meat

carnitas: braised pork

carretera: highway

casa: house

casa de cambio: currency exchange house

casita: small house

cempasúchil: marigold, a flower commonly used in Day of the Dead celebrations

centavo: cent

centro histórico: historic district

cerveza: beer

ceviche: lime-cured fish

chapulín: grasshopper

charreada: traditional Mexican show of horsemanship and ranch skills, similar to rodeo in the United States

charro: traditional Mexican cowboy

chilacayote: figleaf gourd, a type of small squash

chilango: Mexico City resident

chilaquiles: fried tortilla strips bathed in salsa, cream, and cheese

chiles en nogada: poblano pepper stuffed with meat, dried fruit, and nuts, covered in creamed walnut sauce, and sprinkled with pomegranate seeds

chile relleno: stuffed chile pepper

chinicuiles: a caterpillar that inhabits the maguey cactus

chipotle: a smoky dried chile pepper, derived from fresh jalapeño pepper

churro: a tube-shaped sweet bread, deep fried and dusted in sugar

clínica: medical clinic

cochinita pibil: Yucatec-style pulled pork

cocina: kitchen

colectivo: shared taxi service

colegio: school (private)

colonia: neighborhood

comal: griddle

comedor: informal eatery

comida: the large midday meal in Mexico, typically eaten around 2pm

comida corrida: an economical, set-price lunch served in restaurants

comida yucateca: Yucatec food

consulado: consulate

convento: convent

correos: postal service

corrida de toros: bullfight

corrido: popular ballad

costo: cost

criollo: a term used in New Spain to describe a Mexican-born person of Spanish descent

Cruz Roja: Red Cross

cuarto: room (hotel)

cuarto doble: double room

cuarto sencillo: single room

cuenta, la: the bill, or check, at a restaurant

cultura: culture

cumbia: a traditional musical style from Colombia

curado: drink made with pulque, sweetener, and fresh fruit or other natural flavors

delegación: borough

depósito: deposit

desayuno: breakfast

Día del Amor y la Amistad: Valentine's Day

Día de Muertos: Day of the Dead

distrito: district

Distrito Federal: Federal District; former official name for Mexico City

doctor, doctora: doctor

dulces: sweets

dulces típicos: traditional Mexican sweets

ejes vial: traffic axis, thoroughfare

ejido: communally owned land

elote: corn

embajada: embassy

entrada: appetizer

enviar: send (by mail)

escamoles: fire-ant eggs, a delicacy of pre-Columbian cooking

escuela: school

español: Spanish

esquites: corn on the cob, usually dressed with mayonnaise, grated cheese, and chile powder

estación: station

estacionamiento: parking

estadounidense: United States citizen

farmacia: pharmacy

feria: fair

ferrocarril: railroad

festival: festival

fideicomiso: bank trust

fiesta: party

fiesta brava: bullfighting

fiestas patrias: patriotic holidays

flan: egg custard dessert

flauta: deep fried and stuffed tortilla, topped with cream and salsa

flor de calabaza: squash flower

FMM: *forma migratoria multiple* (tourist card)

fonda: casual restaurant

fútbol: soccer

gachupín: Spanish person

galería: gallery

garnachas: snacks, street food

gordita: stuffed corn cake

gringa: a flour tortilla filled with melted cheese and meat

gringo: American

guayaba: guava

guayabera: a men's dress shirt from the Caribbean region

güero/a: light-colored; a fair-haired or fair-skinned person

guisado: stew or side dish

habitación: room (in hotel)

horchata: traditional drink made with ground rice, sugar, cinnamon, and water

huapango: a style of music typical to the Huasteca region

huarache: torpedo-shaped corn flatbread

huauzontle: a Mexican green vegetable

huésped: guest (as in a hotel)

huevo: egg

huevos a la mexicana: eggs scrambled with tomato, onion, and chile pepper

huevos rancheros: fried eggs in tomato-chili sauce

huipil: traditional women's tunic from southern Mexico

huitlacoche: corn fungus

iglesia: church

impuestos: taxes

indígena: indigenous person, or adj. indigenous

ingeniero: engineer

instituto: institute

IVA (impuesto al valor agregado): value-added tax

jamaica: hibiscus

jarana: large five-string guitar

jardín: garden

joyería: jewelry

lavandería: laundry

ley seca: dry law

libramiento: freeway

librería: bookstore

licuado: milk or fruit shake

limonada: limeade

llamada: call, phone call

llamada internacional: international phone call

llave: key

longaniza: a type of sausage

luchador: wrestler

lucha libre: wrestling

maciza: in *carnitas*, pork shoulder or leg

madre: mother

maestro: master; teacher

maguey: large succulent plant common in Mexico, used for making mezcal

majolica: tin-glazed pottery

mañana: tomorrow; morning

manta: lightweight cotton fabric frequently used in traditional Mexican clothing

manteca: lard

mariachi: a traditional Mexican music ensemble

masa: dough

mercado: market

mestizo: a person of mixed ethnic heritage

Metro: subway

Metrobús: high-speed bus service

mezcal: distilled spirit made from the maguey plant

mezcal de gusano: mezcal with the maguey worm inside the bottle

migración: immigration

mole: flavorful sauce made of ground nuts and spices

mole negro: ground sauce made of chocolate, nuts, and spices, originally from the state of Oaxaca

mole poblano: ground sauce made of chocolate, nuts, and spices, originally from the city of Puebla

mollete: a *bolillo* topped with beans, cheese, and salsa

municipio: municipality

museo: museum

navidad: Christmas

nevería: ice cream parlor

nieve: ice milk or ice cream

nopal: prickly pear cactus

noticias: news

padre: father

palacio: palace

pan: bread

pan árabe: pita

pan de dulce: sweet bread

papadzules: Yucatec tacos stuffed with hard-boiled egg

parada, parada de autobús: bus stop

parque: park

parroquia: parish

partido: political party

Partido Acción Nacional: National Action Party

Partido de la Revolución Democrática: Party of the Democratic Revolution

Partido Revolucionario Institucional: Institutional Revolutionary Party

pastor: taco preparation using chile pepper and spices

peatón: pedestrian

peninsular: colonial-era term for a person born in Spain

periodico: newspaper

pesera: small city bus

peso: Mexico's currency

picadillo: spiced ground beef

pico de gallo: salsa made of chopped tomatoes, onion, cilantro, and chile peppers

pipián: a sauce made of ground pumpkin seeds and spices

pirámide: pyramid

piso: floor

plata: silver

plaza: plaza or public square

plaza de toros: bullring

plazuela: small plaza

poblano: from the state or the city of Puebla

Porfiriato: historical period during the presidency of Porfirio Díaz

posada: inn

pozole: hominy soup

preparatoria: high school

presa: reservoir

presidente: president

priista: member of the PRI political party

primaria: primary school

propina: tip

Protección Civil: Civil Protection, or police

pueblo: small town

puesto: street stand or market stall

pulque: alcoholic drink made from fermented maguey

pulquería: traditional drinking establishment serving pulque

quelites: indigenous Mexican wild vegetables and greens

quesadilla: a warmed tortilla stuffed with cheese

queso: cheese

raicilla: a distilled spirit typical to the state of Jalisco

ranchera: musical style from northern Mexico

rebozo: shawl

receta: prescription

residente permanente: immigrant visa

residente temporal: nonimmigrant resident visa

restaurante: restaurant

retablo: devotional painting or altarpiece

revista: magazine

rosca de reyes: a traditional fruitcake served on Three Kings' Day

ruinas: ruins

salsa: sauce

salsa roja: condiment made with red tomatoes and chile peppers or just red chile peppers

salsa verde: condiment made with green tomatoes, chile peppers, and spices

sangrita: a tomato-based chaser for tequila

santa escuela: a Jesuit school in the colonial era

sección amarilla: yellow pages

secretaría: secretary, secretariat

segundaria: secondary school

Semana Santa: Holy Week

señor: mister; sir; man

señora: missus, madam; woman

señorita: miss; young woman

siesta: nap

sismo: earthquake

sitio: taxi stand

sombrero: hat

son: traditional musical styles

sopa: soup

sope: thick, round corn-based flatbread

sotol: a distilled spirit typical to northern Mexico

supermercado: supermarket

surtido: mixed

taco: seasoned meat or vegetables enclosed in a warm tortilla

tacos de guisado: tacos prepared with a variety of fillings

tacos dorados: deep-fried tacos

Talavera: hand-painted majolica-style pottery from Puebla

tamal: tamale, or steamed corn cake (plural: tamales)

tamal oaxaqueño: tamale prepared in a banana-tree leaf in the Oaxacan style

taquilla: ticket counter

tarifa: fare

teatro: theater

telera: a flat, white bread roll used for *tortas*

temblor: earthquake

templo: temple

tequila: a Mexican distilled spirit made from blue agave

terremoto: earthquake, usually bigger than a *temblor*

tianguis: open-air market

tinga: a preparation of seasoned shredded meat

tintorería: dry cleaning

tlacoyo: diamond-shaped stuffed corn flatbread, a common street snack

tlayuda: a large Oaxacan tortilla stuffed with beans, cheese, meat, and salsa

torta: hot or cold sandwich served on a white *telera* roll

tortería: shop selling *tortas,* or hot or cold Mexican-style sandwiches

transito: transit

tranvía: trolley

Tren Ligero: light-rail

tuna: prickly pear fruit

turismo: tourism

turista: tourist or traveler's diarrhea

universidad: university

vecindad: neighborhood

vendedor: seller

verano: summer

Viernes Santo: Good Friday

vino: wine

xoconostle: sour prickly pear fruit

zócalo: central square adjoined by a cathedral

zona arqueológica: archaeological zone

ABBREVIATIONS

Col.: *colonia* (neighborhood)

IMN: Instituto Nacional de Migración (National Institute of Immigration)

nte.: *norte* (north)

ote.: *oriente* (east)

PAN: Partido Acción Nacional (National Action Party)

PRD: Partido de la Revolución Democrática (Party of the Democratic Revolution)

PRI: Partido Revolucionario Institucional (Institutional Revolutionary Party)

prol.: *prolongación* (prolongation, usually of a city street)

pte.: *poniente* (west)

pp: *por persona* (per person)

s/n: *sin número* (without number, as in addresses)

Chilango Slang

The Spanish spoken in Mexico is lined with a rich vein of colloquialisms, slang expressions, and turns of phrase.

aguafiestas: a spoilsport, a party pooper

aguas: watch out!

a huevo: definitely, for sure

antro: nightspot, club

a toda madre: excellent

a todo dar: agreeable, wonderful

a todo mecate: similar to *a toda madre,* but softer, as *madre* has a slightly vulgar connotation when used in this sense

banda: people, as in *mucha banda,* meaning a lot of people

bicla: bicycle

cabrón: a jerk, a mean person

caer el viente: to realize

caer gordo: dislike

cámara: same as *simón;* cool

cantar oaxaca: to vomit

carnal: good friend, literally "of the flesh"

chafa: poor quality

chale: multipurpose exclamatory interjection (such as "really?" "wow!" "no way!" "right on!"); often used as *"chale, mano"*

chamaco, chamaca: little boy, little girl

chamba: work

changarro: small business

chavo, chava: young man, young woman

chela: beer

chesco: soft drink

chido: cool, right on

chilango: someone from Mexico City

chingar: to "screw" somebody, in both meanings of the word

chingo: a whole lot

chingón: really excellent

choncho: big

chupar: to drink

colonia: neighborhood, in Mexico City (*barrio* is more common elsewhere in Latin America)

cotorrear: chat

cuaderno: friend (literally, notebook)

cuate: buddy, good friend

cuero: handsome, good-looking

dar el gatazo: looks right

de pelos: excellent

desmadre: a big mess, really screwed up

donas: two

dos tres: more or less

duques: two

en un ratón: in a while, a twist on *"en un rato"*

escuincle: child

está cañón: a tough situation, a twist on *está cabrón,* which means the same but is more vulgar

está del nabo: it sucks

está grueso: literally "it's fat," meaning "wow, heavy, that's serious"

fajar: to make out, to kiss

fresa: literally "strawberry," meaning a snob

gabacho: American

gachupín, gachupina: someone from Spain

guácala: gross

guacarear: to vomit

guarro, guarura: bodyguard

güero: fair-haired or fair-skinned

güey: dude, guy; common throughout Mexico, but used every other word by young *chilangos,* and even *chilangas*

hueva: a drag, something boring or tedious

jefe, jefa: father, mother

jetón: asleep

la chota: police

lana: literally "wool"; i.e., money

la neta: the best; also the truth, the real deal

la pura neta: even better

la puritita neta: better still

madral: many

mamón: stuck-up, arrogant person

mango: attractive

mano: short for *hermano* (brother) and the Mexican equivalent of "bro"

melón: 1,000,000 pesos

móchate: pass it along already, give me one, or give me some (often *móchate, güey* or *móchate, cabrón*)

naco: someone with bad taste

nave: literally boat, but slang for car

neta: the truth

ni madres: no way, not a chance

no canta mal las rancheras: isn't so bad himself/herself

no mames: vulgar, meaning "no way, get out"; invariably said as *no mames, güey*

no manches: means the same as *mames,* but twisted at the end to make it sound less crude

ojete: a strong, vulgar insult

órale: exclamation; "right on," "wow"

pachanga: big party

pachangear: to go partying

pacheco: stoned (i.e., smoking marijuana)

pedo: literally "fart," but meaning either "drunk" (*está bien pedo*) or a problem; i.e., *¿que pedo?* ("what's the problem?") or *no hay pedo* ("no problem")

pendejo: vulgar, insulting adjective, i.e., "idiot"

perro: as an adjective, something very difficult

perro: as a noun, a guy who sleeps around a lot

pinche: a vulgar adjective; e.g., *"¡Abre la pinche puerta!"* ("Open the @#! door!")

pitufos: literally "smurfs," meaning the blue-uniformed police

ponerse las pilas: literally "to insert batteries"; to motivate yourself

ponerse punk: to get mad, as in *no te pongas punk* ("don't get mad")

¿que hongo?: literally "what mushroom?," a play on *¿que onda?*

que mal viaje: what a drag, what a bad trip

¿que onda?: what's up?

que oso: literally "what a bear," but meaning "what a fool," as in, "what a ridiculous spectacle they're making of themselves"

¿que pasión?: twist on *¿que pasó?* ("what's happening?")

¿que pedo?: twist on *¿que pasó?* ("what's happening?")

que poca madre: "can you believe that?" but with an indignant tone

¿que te picó?: literally, "what bit you?"; meaning "what's the matter?" or "what's your problem?"

quiúbule: also "what's up?"; usually *"quiúbule, cabrón"* or *"quiúbule güey"*

rajar: a verb, meaning to back out of doing something, to bail

ratero: a thief (literally, "ratter")

rayarse: to be lucky

refinar: to eat
reventón: big party
rola: a tune, a song
se puso hasta atrás: he/she got thoroughly drunk
se puso hasta las chanclas: he/she got thoroughly drunk
simón: a play on the word *sí* (yes), but more hip and current; combination of "I agree" and "right on"
taco de ojo: someone attractive, nice to look at
tamarindos: the *tránsito* police, with brown uniforms
tirar la onda: try to hit on someone

tostón: 50 pesos
trancazo: a blow, a hard hit
tranzar: to deceive somebody
tripas: three
uñas: one
un milagro: 1,000 pesos
varos: pesos
vecindad: a grouping of apartments around a single courtyard, common in working-class Mexico City neighborhoods
vientos: "winds"; right on
vientos huracanados: "hurricane winds"; excellent

Spanish Phrasebook

Your Mexican adventure will be more fun if you use a little Spanish. Mexican folks, although they may smile at your funny accent, will appreciate your halting efforts to break the ice and transform yourself from a foreigner to a potential friend.

Spanish commonly uses 30 letters—the familiar English 26, plus four straightforward additional consonants: ch, ll, ñ, and rr.

PRONUNCIATION

Once you learn them, Spanish pronunciation rules—in contrast to English—don't change. Spanish vowels generally sound softer than in English. (*Note:* The capitalized syllables below receive stronger accents.)

VOWELS

a   like ah, as in "hah": *agua* AH-gooah (water), *pan* PAHN (bread), and *casa* CAH-sah (house)
e   like ay, as in "may": *mesa* MAY-sah (table), *tela* TAY-lah (cloth), and *de* DAY (of, from)
i   like ee, as in "need": *diez* dee-AYZ (ten), *comida* ko-MEE-dah (meal), and *fin* FEEN (end)
o   like oh, as in "go": *peso* PAY-soh (weight), *ocho* OH-choh (eight), and *poco* POH-koh (a bit)
u   like oo, as in "cool": *uno* OO-noh (one), *cuarto* KOOAHR-toh (room), and *usted* oos-TAYD (you); when it follows a "q" the u is silent; when it follows an "h" or has an umlaut, it's pronounced like "w"

CONSONANTS

b, d, f, k, l, m, n, p, q, s, t, v, w, x, y, z, and ch pronounced almost as in English; h occurs, but is silent—not pronounced at all
c   like k as in "keep": *cuarto* KOOAR-toh (room), Tepic tay-PEEK (capital of Nayarit state); when it precedes "e" or "i," pronounce c like s, as in "sit":

cerveza sayr-VAY-sah (beer), *encima* ayn-SEE-mah (atop)

g like g as in "gift" when it precedes "a," "o," "u," or a consonant: *gato* GAH-toh (cat), *hago* AH-goh (I do, make); otherwise, pronounce **g** like h as in "hat": *giro* HEE-roh (money order), *gente* HAYN-tay (people)

j like h, as in "has": *Jueves* HOOAY-vays (Thursday), *mejor* may-HOR (better)

ll like y, as in "yes": *toalla* toh-AH-yah (towel), *ellos* AY-yohs (they, them)

ñ like ny, as in "canyon": *año* AH-nyo (year), *señor* SAY-nyor (Mr., sir)

r is lightly trilled, with the tongue at the roof of your mouth like a very light English d, as in "ready": *pero* PAY-doh (but), *tres* TDAYS (three), *cuatro* KOOAH-tdoh (four)

rr like a Spanish r, but with much more emphasis and trill. Let your tongue flap. Practice with *burro* (donkey), *carretera* (highway), and Carrillo (proper name), then really let go with *ferrocarril* (railroad).

Note: The single small but common exception to all of the above is the pronunciation of Spanish **y** when it's being used as the Spanish word for "and," as in "Ron y Kathy." In such case, pronounce it like the English ee, as in "keep": Ron "ee" Kathy (Ron and Kathy).

ACCENT

The rule for accent, the relative stress given to syllables within a given word, is straightforward. If a word ends in a vowel, an n, or an s, accent the next-to-last syllable; if not, accent the last syllable.

Pronounce *gracias* GRAH-seeahs (thank you), *orden* OHR-dayn (order), and *carretera* kah-ray-TAY-rah (highway) with stress on the next-to-last syllable.

Otherwise, accent the last syllable: *venir* vay-NEER (to come), *ferrocarril* fay-roh-cah-REEL (railroad), and *edad* ay-DAHD (age).

Exceptions to the accent rule are always marked with an accent sign: (á, é, í, ó, or ú), such as *teléfono* tay-LAY-foh-noh (telephone), *jabón* hah-BON (soap), and *rápido* RAH-pee-doh (rapid).

BASIC AND COURTEOUS EXPRESSIONS

Most Spanish-speaking people consider formalities important. Whenever approaching anyone for information or some other reason, do not forget the appropriate salutation—good morning, good evening, etc. Standing alone, the greeting *hola* (hello) can sound brusque.

Hello. *Hola.*

Good morning. *Buenos días.*

Good afternoon. *Buenas tardes.*

Good evening. *Buenas noches.*

How are you? *¿Cómo está usted?*

Very well, thank you. *Muy bien, gracias.*

Okay; good. *Bien.*

Not okay; bad. *Mal or feo.*

So-so. *Más o menos.*

And you? *¿Y usted?*

Thank you. *Gracias.*

Thank you very much. *Muchas gracias.*

You're very kind. *Muy amable.*

You're welcome. *De nada.*

Goodbye. *Adios.*

See you later. *Hasta luego.*

please *por favor*

yes *sí*

no *no*

I don't know. *No sé.*

Just a moment, please. *Momentito, por favor.*

Excuse me, please (when you're trying to get attention). *Disculpe* or *Con permiso.*

Excuse me (when you've made a boo-boo). *Lo siento.*

Pleased to meet you. *Mucho gusto.*

What is your name? *¿Cómo se llama usted?*

Do you speak English? *¿Habla usted inglés?*

Is English spoken here? (Does anyone here speak English?) *¿Se habla inglés?*

I don't speak Spanish well. *No hablo bien el español.*

I don't understand. *No entiendo.*

How do you say . . . in Spanish? *¿Cómo se dice . . . en español?*

My name is . . . *Me llamo . . .*

Would you like . . . *¿Quisiera usted . . .*

Let's go to . . . *Vamos a . . .*

Where is the bathroom? *¿Dónde está el baño?*

TERMS OF ADDRESS

When in doubt, use the formal *usted* (you) as a form of address.

I *yo*

you (formal) *usted*

you (familiar) *tu*

he/him *él*

she/her *ella*

we/us *nosotros*

you (plural) *ustedes*

they/them *ellos* (all males or mixed gender); *ellas* (all females)

Mr., sir *Sr., señor*

Mrs., madam *Sra., señora*

miss, young lady *Srta., señorita*

wife *esposa*

husband *esposo*

friend *amigo* (male); *amiga* (female)

sweetheart *novio* (male); *novia* (female)

son; daughter *hijo; hija*

brother; sister *hermano; hermana*

father; mother *padre; madre*

grandfather; grandmother *abuelo; abuela*

TRANSPORTATION

Where is . . . ? *¿Dónde está . . . ?*

How far is it to . . . ? *¿A cuánto está . . . ?*

from . . . to . . . *de . . . a . . .*

How many blocks? *¿Cuántas cuadras?*

Where (Which) is the way to . . . ? *¿Dónde está el camino a . . . ?*

the bus station *la terminal de autobuses*

the bus stop *la parada de autobuses*

Where is this bus going? *¿Adónde va este autobús?*

the taxi stand *la parada de taxis*

the train station *la estación de ferrocarril*

the boat *el barco*

the launch *lancha; tiburonera*

the dock *el muelle*

the airport *el aeropuerto*

I'd like a ticket to . . . *Quisiera un boleto a . . .*

first (second) class *primera (segunda) clase*

round-trip *ida y vuelta*

reservation *reservación*

baggage *equipaje*

Stop here, please. *Pare aquí, por favor.*

the entrance *la entrada*

the exit *la salida*

the ticket office *la oficina de boletos*

(very) near; far *(muy) cerca; lejos*

to; toward *a*

by; through *por*

from *de*

the right *la derecha*

the left *la izquierda*

straight ahead *derecho; directo*

in front *en frente*

beside *al lado*

behind *atrás*

the corner *la esquina*

the stoplight *la semáforo*

a turn *una vuelta*

right here *aquí*

somewhere around here *por acá*

right there *allí*

somewhere around there *por allá*

road *el camino*

street; boulevard calle; bulevar

block la cuadra

highway carretera

kilometer kilómetro

bridge; toll puente; cuota

address dirección

north; south norte; sur

east; west oriente (este); poniente (oeste)

ACCOMMODATIONS

hotel hotel

Is there a room? ¿Hay cuarto?

May I (may we) see it? ¿Puedo (podemos) verlo?

What is the rate? ¿Cuál es el precio?

Is that your best rate? ¿Es su mejor precio?

Is there something cheaper? ¿Hay algo más económico?

a single room un cuarto sencillo

a double room un cuarto doble

double bed cama matrimonial

twin beds camas gemelas

with private bath con baño

hot water agua caliente

shower ducha

towels toallas

soap jabón

toilet paper papel higiénico

blanket frazada; manta

sheets sábanas

air-conditioned aire acondicionado

fan abanico; ventilador

key llave

manager gerente

FOOD

I'm hungry. Tengo hambre.

I'm thirsty. Tengo sed.

menu carta; menú

order orden

glass vaso

fork tenedor

knife cuchillo

spoon cuchara

napkin servilleta

soft drink refresco

coffee café

tea té

drinking water agua pura; agua potable

bottled carbonated water agua mineral

bottled uncarbonated water agua sin gas

beer cerveza

wine vino

milk leche

juice jugo

cream crema

sugar azúcar

cheese queso

snack antojo; botana

breakfast desayuno

lunch almuerzo

daily lunch special comida corrida (or el menú del día depending on region)

dinner comida (often eaten in late afternoon); cena (a late-night snack)

the check la cuenta

eggs huevos

bread pan

salad ensalada

fruit fruta

mango mango

watermelon sandía

papaya papaya

banana plátano

apple manzana

orange naranja

lime limón

fish pescado

shellfish mariscos

shrimp camarones

meat (without) (sin) carne

chicken pollo

pork puerco

beef; steak res; bistec

bacon; ham tocino; jamón

fried frito

roasted asada

barbecue; barbecued barbacoa; al carbón

SHOPPING

money *dinero*

money-exchange bureau *casa de cambio*

I would like to exchange traveler's checks. *Quisiera cambiar cheques de viajero.*

What is the exchange rate? *¿Cuál es el tipo de cambio?*

How much is the commission? *¿Cuánto cuesta la comisión?*

Do you accept credit cards? *¿Aceptan tarjetas de crédito?*

money order *giro*

How much does it cost? *¿Cuánto cuesta?*

What is your final price? *¿Cuál es su último precio?*

expensive *caro*

cheap *barato; económico*

more *más*

less *menos*

a little *un poco*

too much *demasiado*

HEALTH

Help me please. *Ayúdeme por favor.*

I am ill. *Estoy enfermo.*

Call a doctor. *Llame un doctor.*

Take me to ... *Lléveme a ...*

hospital *hospital; sanatorio*

drugstore *farmacia*

pain *dolor*

fever *fiebre*

headache *dolor de cabeza*

stomachache *dolor de estómago*

burn *quemadura*

cramp *calambre*

nausea *náusea*

vomiting *vomitar*

medicine *medicina*

antibiotic *antibiótico*

pill; tablet *pastilla*

aspirin *aspirina*

ointment; cream *pomada; crema*

bandage *venda*

cotton *algodón*

sanitary napkins use brand name, e.g., Kotex

birth control pills *pastillas anticonceptivas*

contraceptive foam *espuma anticonceptiva*

condoms *preservativos; condones*

toothbrush *cepilla dental*

dental floss *hilo dental*

toothpaste *crema dental*

dentist *dentista*

toothache *dolor de muelas*

POST OFFICE AND COMMUNICATIONS

long-distance telephone *teléfono larga distancia*

I would like to call ... *Quisiera llamar a ...*

collect *por cobrar*

station to station *a quien contesta*

person to person *persona a persona*

credit card *tarjeta de crédito*

post office *correo*

general delivery *lista de correo*

letter *carta*

stamp *estampilla, timbre*

postcard *tarjeta*

aerogram *aerograma*

airmail *correo aereo*

registered *registrado*

money order *giro*

package; box *paquete; caja*

string; tape *cuerda; cinta*

AT THE BORDER

border *frontera*

customs *aduana*

immigration *migración*

tourist card *tarjeta de turista*

inspection *inspección; revisión*

passport *pasaporte*

profession *profesión*

marital status *estado civil*

single *soltero*

married; divorced *casado; divorciado*

widowed *viudado*

insurance *seguros*

title *título*

driver's license *licencia de manejar*

AT THE GAS STATION

gas station *gasolinera*

gasoline *gasolina*

unleaded *sin plomo*

full, please *lleno, por favor*

tire *llanta*

tire repair shop *vulcanizadora*

air *aire*

water *agua*

oil (change) *aceite (cambio)*

grease *grasa*

My ... doesn't work. *Mi ... no sirve.*

battery *batería*

radiator *radiador*

alternator *alternador*

generator *generador*

tow truck *grúa*

repair shop *taller mecánico*

tune-up *afinación*

auto parts store *refaccionería*

VERBS

Verbs are the key to getting along in Spanish. They employ mostly predictable forms and come in three classes, which end in *ar, er,* and *ir,* respectively:

to buy *comprar*

I buy, you (he, she, it) buys *compro, compra*

we buy, you (they) buy *compramos, compran*

to eat *comer*

I eat, you (he, she, it) eats *como, come*

we eat, you (they) eat *comemos, comen*

to climb *subir*

I climb, you (he, she, it) climbs *subo, sube*

we climb, you (they) climb *subimos, suben*

Here are more (with irregularities indicated):

to do or make *hacer* (regular except for *hago,* I do or make)

to go *ir* (very irregular: *voy, va, vamos, van*)

to go (walk) *andar*

to love *amar*

to work *trabajar*

to want *desear, querer*

to need *necesitar*

to read *leer*

to write *escribir*

to repair *reparar*

to stop *parar*

to get off (the bus) *bajar*

to arrive *llegar*

to stay (remain) *quedar*

to stay (lodge) *hospedar*

to leave *salir* (regular except for *salgo,* I leave)

to look at *mirar*

to look for *buscar*

to give *dar* (regular except for *doy,* I give)

to carry *llevar*

to have *tener* (irregular but important: *tengo, tiene, tenemos, tienen*)

to come *venir* (similarly irregular: *vengo, viene, venimos, vienen*)

Spanish has two forms of "to be":

to be *estar* (regular except for *estoy,* I am)

to be *ser* (very irregular: *soy, es, somos, son*)

Use *estar* when speaking of location or a temporary state of being: "I am at home." *"Estoy en casa."* "I'm sick." *"Estoy enfermo."* Use *ser* for a permanent state of being: "I am a doctor." *"Soy doctora."*

NUMBERS

zero *cero*
one *uno*
two *dos*
three *tres*
four *cuatro*
five *cinco*
six *seis*
seven *siete*
eight *ocho*
nine *nueve*
10 *diez*
11 *once*
12 *doce*
13 *trece*
14 *catorce*
15 *quince*
16 *dieciseis*
17 *diecisiete*
18 *dieciocho*
19 *diecinueve*
20 *veinte*
21 *veinte y uno* or *veintiuno*
30 *treinta*
40 *cuarenta*
50 *cincuenta*
60 *sesenta*
70 *setenta*
80 *ochenta*
90 *noventa*
100 *ciento*
101 *ciento y uno* or *cientiuno*
200 *doscientos*
500 *quinientos*
1,000 *mil*
10,000 *diez mil*
100,000 *cien mil*
1,000,000 *millón*
one-half *medio*
one-third *un tercio*
one-fourth *un cuarto*

TIME

What time is it? *¿Qué hora es?*
It's one o'clock. *Es la una.*
It's three in the afternoon. *Son las tres de la tarde.*
It's 4am. *Son las cuatro de la mañana.*
six-thirty *seis y media*
a quarter till eleven *un cuarto para las once*
a quarter past five *las cinco y cuarto*
an hour *una hora*

DAYS AND MONTHS

Monday *lunes*
Tuesday *martes*
Wednesday *miércoles*
Thursday *jueves*
Friday *viernes*
Saturday *sábado*
Sunday *domingo*
today *hoy*
tomorrow *mañana*
yesterday *ayer*
January *enero*
February *febrero*
March *marzo*
April *abril*
May *mayo*
June *junio*
July *julio*
August *agosto*
September *septiembre*
October *octubre*
November *noviembre*
December *diciembre*
a week *una semana*
a month *un mes*
after *después*
before *antes*

(Courtesy of Bruce Whipperman, author of *Moon Pacific Mexico*.)

Suggested Reading

JOURNALISM AND TRAVEL

Goldman, Francisco. *The Interior Circuit: A Mexico City Chronicle (Mexico City Chronicles)*. New York: Grove/Atlantic, 2011. Novelist Francisco Goldman's memoir about life in Mexico City is part personal story and part chronicle of Mexico City, addressing politics and crime, as well as anecdotes from daily life.

Hernandez, Daniel. *Down and Delirious in Mexico City*. New York: Scribner, 2011. An L.A.-based journalist chronicles his often-rowdy explorations into the underworld and counterculture of contemporary Mexico City.

Lewis, Oscar. *The Children of Sanchez: Autobiography of a Mexican Family*. New York: Random House, 1979. A gritty anthropological account of the city, based on the lives of a family whose patriarch works as a waiter at the restaurant Café de Tacuba.

Lida, David. *First Stop in the New World: Mexico City, the Capital of the 21st Century*. New York: Riverhead, 2008. Lida, who is also a fiction writer and has worked as a journalist in Mexico City for years, put together a great selection of essays and reportages about all sorts of unique subcultures in the megalopolis in this volume.

Martinez, Ruben. *The Other Side: Notes from the New L.A., Mexico City, and Beyond*. New York: Vintage Books, 1993. A stimulating account of the growing pan-Latino culture extending from Los Angeles to El Salvador, with plenty of pop culture information on Mexico City.

Novo, Salvador. *Los Paseos de la Ciudad de México*. Mexico City: Fondo de Cultura Económica, 2005. This slim volume presents a mix of history, anecdotes, memories, and meditations on six iconic places in the capital, including the Alameda Central and the street Bucareli. Spanish-language only.

Preston, Julia, and Sam Dillon. *Opening Mexico*. New York: Farrar, Straus, and Giroux, 2004. Preston and Dillon, former *New York Times* correspondents in Mexico, create an engrossing successor of sorts to Alan Riding's *Distant Neighbors*, starting in the mid-1980s but focusing principally on the *sexenio* of Ernesto Zedillo and the transition in 2000 with the victory of opposition candidate Vicente Fox.

Riding, Alan. *Distant Neighbors: A Portrait of the Mexicans*. New York: Vintage Books, 1986. Riding was the *New York Times* correspondent in Mexico City for six years, and when he finished, he wrote this excellent exposition of Mexican culture and history.

FICTION

Bolaño, Roberto. *The Savage Detectives*. New York: Picador, 2008. The celebrated Chilean-born author lived for many years in Mexico, and this entertaining, thought-provoking novel is largely set in the capital city, capturing the metropolis's unique youth culture with surprising acuity.

Burroughs, William. *Queer*. New York: Penguin Books, 1987. Set mainly in Mexico City during the Beat era, this autobiographical novel fictionalizes Burroughs's flight to Mexico to avoid drug charges in the United States.

Fuentes, Carlos. *The Old Gringo*. New York: Farrar, Straus, Giroux, 1985. The most famous novel by celebrated writer Carlos Fuentes takes place during the Mexican Revolution.

Fuentes, Carlos. *Where the Air Is Clear*. Champaign, IL: Dalkey Archive Press, 2014. This novel, Fuentes's first, is as much known for being a portrait of 1950s Mexico City as for its main character, Federico Robles.

Kerouac, Jack. *Mexico City Blues: 242 Choruses*. New York: Grove Press, 1990. Beat novelist and poet Kerouac lived intermittently in Mexico City during the 1950s, and he wrote parts of this seminal poem, as well as his novella *Tristessa*, in the capital.

Lida, David. *Travel Advisory*. New York: William Morrow & Company, 2000. A collection of 10 gritty short stories set in Mexico (several in Mexico City) from an American writer living in Mexico City.

Lowry, Malcolm. *Under the Volcano*. New York: Reynal & Hitchcock, 1990. Although it only sold two copies in two years when originally published in Canada in 1947, Lowry's tale of the alcoholic demise of a British consul in Cuernavaca has become a modern classic.

Poniatowska, Elena. *Tinisima*. Albuquerque: University of New Mexico Press, 2006. Using extensive historical research, Mexican essayist and intellectual Poniatowska reimagines the life of Italian-born film star, photographer, Edward Weston muse, and socialist revolutionary Tina Modotti in post-revolutionary Mexico in this moving book.

HISTORY

Coe, Michael D. *From the Olmecs to the Aztecs*. London: Thames and Hudson, 2008. Yale anthropologist Michael D. Coe has written extensively about Mesoamerican civilizations. In this volume, he introduces the great cultures of pre-Columbian Mexico.

De las Casas, Bartolomé. *Short Account of the Destruction of the Indies*. London: Penguin Books, 1992. A Dominican friar and humanitarian, de las Casas recounts his firsthand observations about the Spanish colonization of the Americas.

Johns, Michael. *The City of Mexico in the Age of Díaz*. Austin: University of Texas Press, 1997. A well-written, well-researched, and ultimately fascinating chronicle of the capital during the rule of dictatorial president Porfirio Díaz.

Krauze, Enrique. *Biography of Power: A History of Modern Mexico, 1810-1996*. New York: HarperCollins

Publishers, 1997. One of Mexico's most respected historians traces the course of Mexican history, principally through the actions of its leaders.

Paz, Octavio. *The Labyrinth of Solitude: Life and Thought in Mexico*. New York: Grove Press, 1961. Paz has no peer when it comes to expositions of the Mexican psyche, and this is his best prose work.

Reed, John. *Insurgent Mexico*. New York: International Publishers, 1994. Famed American journalist Reed, of *Ten Days That Shook the World* fame, wrote this breathless, entertaining, and unabashedly biased firsthand account of time spent with Villa's troops in northern Mexico during the Mexican Revolution.

Thomas, Hugh. *Conquest: Montezuma, Cortés, and the Fall of Old Mexico*. New York: Simon & Schuster, 1995. An exhaustively researched and beautifully written account of one of the greatest events in history: the meeting of two civilizations in Mexico in 1519.

Womack, John. *Zapata and the Mexican Revolution*. New York: Knopf, 1970. This is considered the classic account of the legendary *caudillo del sur*, Zapata, and his role in the Mexican Revolution. A must for anyone interested in understanding Zapata's mythic status in the Mexican pantheon of heroes.

Internet Resources

GENERAL INFORMATION

CDMX
www.cdmx.gob.mx

Mexico City's official government website, with links to information in Spanish on public transportation, driving restrictions, weather, and safety.

Visit Mexico
www.visitmexico.com/en

Mexico's tourism board maintains this website for travelers to Mexico, including an overview of sights, hotels, and other points of interest in Mexico City.

MEDIA

Chilango
www.chilango.com

The online version of the popular lifestyle magazine *Chilango* has restaurant reviews, event and nightlife listings, and other recommendations for what to do around the city.

Local
http://local.mx

This Mexico City-based Spanish-language magazine covers fashion, music, dining, and culture in Mexico City.

EVENTS

Cultura UNAM
www.cultura.unam.mx

Complete cultural listings for the multitude of museums, cinemas, concert halls, and galleries operated by the national university in Mexico City.

TRANSPORTATION

Metro System
www.metro.cdmx.gob.mx

Information (in Spanish) and maps of the Metro in Mexico City.

BLOGS

Mexico City Streets
http://mexicocitystreets.com/

A fun expat-penned blog covering food, markets, neighborhoods, and oddities around Mexico City.

Good Food Mexico
www.goodfoodmexico.com

Reviews of local restaurants as well as travel stories by a Mexico City-based food writer.

INDEX

Restaurants Index

417

Nightlife Index

Shops Index

Hotels Index

Photo Credits

Stunning Sights Around the World

Guides fo

MAP SYMBOLS

══ Major Hwy	Pedestrian Friendly	---- Trail	···· Ferry
── Road/Hwy	Tunnel	····· Stairs	----- Railroad

■ Sights	✪ City/Town		▲ Mountain
■ Restaurants	◉ State Capital		✦ Unique Feature
■ Nightlife	○ National Capital		🖜 Waterfall
■ Arts and Culture	◉ Highlight		▲ Park
■ Recreation	★ Point of Interest		⬓ Archaeological Site
■ Shops	● Accommodation		TH Trailhead
■ Hotels	▼ Restaurant/Bar		P Parking Area
	■ Other Location		m Metro

CONVERSION TABLES

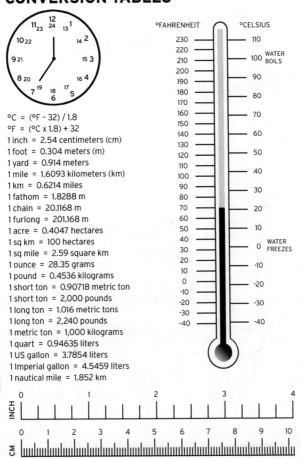

$°C = (°F - 32) / 1.8$
$°F = (°C \times 1.8) + 32$
1 inch = 2.54 centimeters (cm)
1 foot = 0.304 meters (m)
1 yard = 0.914 meters
1 mile = 1.6093 kilometers (km)
1 km = 0.6214 miles
1 fathom = 1.8288 m
1 chain = 20.1168 m
1 furlong = 201.168 m
1 acre = 0.4047 hectares
1 sq km = 100 hectares
1 sq mile = 2.59 square km
1 ounce = 28.35 grams
1 pound = 0.4536 kilograms
1 short ton = 0.90718 metric ton
1 short ton = 2,000 pounds
1 long ton = 1.016 metric tons
1 long ton = 2,240 pounds
1 metric ton = 1,000 kilograms
1 quart = 0.94635 liters
1 US gallon = 3.7854 liters
1 Imperial gallon = 4.5459 liters
1 nautical mile = 1.852 km

MOON MEXICO CITY
Avalon Travel
Hachette Book Group
1700 Fourth Street
Berkeley, CA 94710, USA
www.moon.com

Editor: Kimberly Ehart
Acquiring Editor: Nikki Ioakimedes
Series Manager: Leah Gordon
Copy Editor: Ashley Benning
Graphics and Production Coordinator: Lucie Ericksen
Cover Design: Toni Tajima
Map Editor: Karin Dahl
Cartographers: Karin Dahl, Brian Shotwell, and Kat Bennett
Foldout Map: Karin Dahl, Brian Shotwell
Indexer: Greg Jewett

ISBN-13: 978-1-64049-973-7

Printing History
1st Edition — 2000
8th Edition — August 2023
5 4 3 2 1

AUG 1 2 2023

Front cover photo: Fuente de los Coyotes by Gabriel Ponzanelli, Parque Centenaric
Coyoacan © Brian Overcast / Alamy Stock Photo

Back cover photo: view from Chapultepec Castle © Chon Kit Leong | Dreamstime.com

Printed in Malaysia for Imago